H. P. Lovecraft and Lovecraft Criticism
An Annotated Bibliography

H. P. Lovecraft and Lovecraft Criticism

An Annotated Bibliography

S. T. Joshi

The Kent State University Press

7279592

The Serif Series: Number 38
Bibliographies and Checklists

Dean H. Keller, General Editor
Kent State University

Library of Congress Cataloging in Publication Data

Joshi, S. T., 1958-
  H. P. Lovecraft and Lovecraft criticism.

  (The Serif series: bibliographies and check-
lists; no. 38)
  Bibliography: p.
  Includes index.
  1. Lovecraft, H. P. (Howard Phillips), 1890-1937—
Bibliography. I. Title. II. Series: Serif
series: bibliographies and checklists; no. 38.
Z8520.9.J67 1981 [PS3523.0833] 016.813'52 80-84662
ISBN 0-87338-248-X   AACR2

To
George T. Wetzel

Contents

Contents

Contents

Introduction

The difficulties involved in Lovecraft bibliography may perhaps be as formidable as those for any writer of this century, and they stem not only from the oddities of his publication history but from the ambivalent nature of his critical acceptance. Certain problems are now insuperable, and it is not likely that future generations will ever be successful in unearthing the whole of his published work, although the most important of his hitherto published writings have probably been located.

Had Howard Phillips Lovecraft (1890-1937) chosen to write in any other genre but fantasy, it is likely that the bibliography of his work would not remain so equivocal; for the somewhat provincial prejudice that America and England (but not, it is to be noted, France or Germany) have had toward weird fiction, ever since the Gothic novels of the late eighteenth century, has ensured the literary obscurity of virtually all fantasists save Edgar Allan Poe, who himself is but uneasily placed in the framework of American literature. It is a common assumption that fantasy fiction, because it does not concern itself directly with that stratum of observable daily life with which "mainstream" fiction deals, can make few significant statements on the human condition—an assumption which the greatest macabre writers have refuted both in theory and in practice. Had Lovecraft not taken to fantasy, and made it

xi

(unlike Poe, Ambrose Bierce, Nathaniel Hawthorne, or even Algernon Blackwood and Arthur Machen) the sole avenue of his fictional output, then he would perhaps have been less ignored by critics, his early work (poetry, essays, letters) not allowed to dwell for decades in oblivion; and it would not have been necessary to begin this bibliography anew. But many now know Lovecraft's celebrated dictum—"There is no field other than the weird in which I have any aptitude or inclination for fictional composition." Or perhaps we can unearth a less well-known remark: "I could not write about 'ordinary people' because I am not in the least interested in them. Without interest there can be no art." And readers know equally well the results of this aesthetic integrity: Lovecraft's descent into the "underworld" of the pulp magazines of the interwar years, then the only professional outlets for the weird; the fitful attention given him by established critics (Edmund Wilson, Peter Penzoldt, T. O. Mabbott, Colin Wilson, W. T. Scott); and the interpretation and preservation of his work entrusted to the valiant but oftentimes feeble hands of "fans" and his own associates. We are thus today faced with a writer who on the one hand has been translated in prestigious editions around the world, and whose undoubted merits— a writing style as polished, erudite, and correct as Addison's or Johnson's, an imaginative power rivaled only by Poe or Lord Dunsany, a cosmic viewpoint unique in its scope and manifestations, and a knowledge of aesthetics and metaphysics that might place him high in modern philosophy—have caused him to be hailed abroad as among the world's greatest writers. On the other hand, however, Lovecraft has in this country a scant critical reputation, his minor work still buried, his fiction still misprinted, misedited, and misunderstood. A new generation of scholars, however, is finally beginning to brush away some of the cobwebs enshrouding his *oeuvre*; but that a long road must still be traveled, all realize.

The location and identification of Lovecraft's complete published work is made difficult not merely by the prejudice held against the subject matter of his fiction: the whole of Lovecraft's published writing before his death is engulfed in obscurity, and the few occasions when his work received anything approaching wide dissemination were merely the fitful vanguards of a posthumous success. Lovecraft's earliest appearances in print were not horror tales but scientific writing contributed to newspapers published in or near his native Providence, Rhode Island. The extent of these contributions is still not wholly known, for the editor of this bibliography only a short while ago stumbled, purely by accident, upon a published letter by Lovecraft dating from August 1906—only a few months after his earliest published appearance, in *The Providence Sunday Journal* of 3 June 1906. That other articles may lurk uncovered is not improbable; indeed, there is a suspicion that we may have lost a whole series of articles from Lovecraft's pen published in a rural paper for which copies no longer seem to survive (see I-E-ii-1).

Aside from local appearances, future Lovecraft bibliographers must give more attention to the work which he published during his involvement with amateur journalism, beginning in 1914 and continuing spasmodically for the rest of his brief life. These amateur journals, some perhaps printed in less than fifty copies, typify the major problem for bibliographers: the scarcity of surviving copies of his published work. Lovecraft did not publish in any well-known journals of his time, nor did a major publisher ever issue a volume of his writings before his death; thus we are faced with the situation that many of his publications (for most of which manuscripts do not exist) now survive in a handful of copies, the majority carefully guarded in private hands. To be sure, his major fiction has now reached a universal audience, from Argentina to Japan; but it is symptomatic that his first pamphlet, *The Crime of Crimes* (1915?), published by an amateur associate in Wales, survives (to current knowledge) only in the hands of a single private collector. That pseudonymous and unsigned (need we recall Defoe?) articles from the amateur journals have not stopped being discovered to the present day—in such obscure periodicals as *The Bonnet*, *The Lake Breeze*, *The New Member*, and the like—makes us wonder whether the bewildering fecundity and energy which Lovecraft poured into the amateur press, and which has now made him a legend in that small field, will ever be definitively mapped.

When we enter into Lovecraft's publications in the pulps—*Weird Tales*, *Amazing Stories*, *Tales of Magic and Mystery*—we are on safer ground; for these serials, published in the thousands of copies, have now become not merely jewels for collectors but an authentic element of American popular culture, and thus find preservation in a number of institutions. But even here there are difficulties: not many know of Lovecraft's letter to *Dragnet*, and his letters to *The Argosy* and the *All-Story Weekly* are among his most famous but least available works. It may be that letters to the editor and other miscellany are not crucial in our understanding of Lovecraft; but, aside from academic considerations of bibliographic completeness, can it be doubted that even the smallest fragments from his pen—from juvenilia to death diaries—may help us in some way to grasp an author whom even Colin Wilson declared "one of the most interesting men of his generation"?

The several occasions where Lovecraft had a chance to find hard-cover publication of his work seem like the pathetic account of a man attempting the insuperable with two strikes already against him; and in Lovecraft's case the first strike was the subject matter (not the merit or lack thereof) of his work, and the other his artistic sincerity, which prevented him, as it did not prevent a number of his colleagues, from writing cheap formula-ridden hackwork designed to meet the needs of a reading public who, in choosing its best sellers, only rarely and accidentally hits upon literary worth, vaunting instead those works which —sometimes calculatingly—are designed to cater to its tastes. Some of Lovecraft's associates could not even understand why he refused to prostitute himself as they were doing, failing to realize that writing was to Lovecraft not a business but an art whose aim, far from inducing an ignorant rabble toward "smirking optimism," is self-satisfaction at capturing, however imperfectly, an image or idea or attitude which clamors for expression within the artist's mind. Aside from the handicap of his subject matter, Lovecraft was caught in the inevitable dilemma of the obscure author: who would publish a book by an unknown name, but how to achieve a name save by book publication? It was a dilemma that Lovecraft in his life never resolved, and which such firms as Knopf, Putnam's, Vanguard, and others did not help him resolve. The book publications (if any really deserve the name) predating his death all stemmed from amateur associates—W. Paul Cook, Walter J. Coates, William L. Crawford—and copies of them are now as scarce as appearances of his work in the amateur journals.

Considering the nature of his work and the milieu in which he wrote, it is not surprising that his fame was posthumous; indeed, it is in some ways surprising that he came to have any fame at all. It would surely have shocked the gentleman of Providence—writing less and less with the passing of the years, plagued at the last by ever-worsening cancer, famous only in the tiny worlds of amateur journalism and fantasy fandom, and perhaps envisioning in his mind's eye the ultimate oblivion that would overtake even his highly regarded fiction, to say nothing of his poetry, essays, and voluminous letters—to have found his work being published a few decades after his early death in 1937 by the World Publishing Company, Victor Gollancz of London, Denoël of Paris, Heyne of Munich, and—perhaps most astonishing of all—Sodosha of Tokyo. But even this worldwide dissemination could not have come about without the aid of friends. That August Derleth and Donald Wandrei (and before them R. H. Barlow) could be so convinced of Lovecraft's merit as to expend the time and money necessary for preserving his work between the covers of books bespeaks not only their foresight but the strong ties of friendship that Lovecraft could make even through the medium of correspondence. It is remarkable that Derleth and Wandrei, when founding Arkham House and publishing the epochal *The Outsider and Others* in 1939, were even then thinking of publishing Lovecraft's letters, clearly his most important (and in many ways his greatest) work. That dream, however, was not fulfilled for forty years, for only in 1976 did the last of the five large volumes of *Selected Letters* emerge under the Arkham House imprint. But while Wandrei was spending decades editing the letters (of which Lovecraft surely wrote more than anyone in the history of literature), Derleth was using his own fame as a writer and editor in giving the fiction wider publicity— first with the World Publishing Company and the Editions for the Armed Services (a now little-known but vastly popular organization, through which an astonishing number became acquainted with Lovecraft), then in England with Gollancz. The chain was now started and continued to be forged, link by link: the English appearances triggered the French translations of the 1950s; Spanish followed, and Italian and German were not far behind. The most remarkable occurrence, however, was the Japanese response, for there is evidence (as yet scanty) that Lovecraft was discovered there as early as the late 1940s, and his work was certainly appearing regularly in Japanese serials and anthologies in the 1950s. Back in Europe the tide of Lovecraft publications did not stop, and has yet to do so; Holland and Scandinavia are the latest to seize his work in earnest, though even here the earliest appearances date back several decades. That the foreign acclaim is so voluminous need not surprise us; for Europe seems not only to have a generally higher level of literary taste amongst its masses, but it lacks almost wholly the curious prejudice which the majority of Americans (the English are somewhere between the extremes) attach to fantasy fiction. There is no need to smile at the opinion held throughout France that Lovecraft matches, and perhaps even exceeds, Poe as America's greatest writer.

But, as noted, the tide is turning in America, too, whether because it is losing its provinciality (not, indeed, very likely), because its own literature is being increasingly laced with the fantastic and gruesome—Nathanael West, Ken Kesey, Thomas Pynchon, Kurt Vonnegut, Richard Brautigan—or because the other branch of imaginative fiction, science fiction, is coming under scholarly attention, despite (at present) its far greater limitations for aesthetic expression. Lovecraft still remains a popular figure among fans, and has still far to go to reach true critical acceptance; but the increasing number of academicians who refuse to follow an Edmund Wilson or a Colin Wilson in peremptorily dismissing Lovecraft is a healthy sign that the gentleman of Providence will ultimately come into his own, not merely in distant lands he never saw but in the very country that bore him.

We can date the commencement of Lovecraft criticism as early as 1914, when he and other readers conducted their debates in *The Argosy* about the type of material then appearing in that early pulp magazine—the incident that led directly to his entry into amateur journalism. But it is to the amateur journals themselves that we must look for the first real assessments of Lovecraft as a writer and thinker; for though here, too, he engaged in heated debates on political and associational matters, he was also given due credit for his fictional and poetic contributions. When he later began to publish his fiction professionally, the letter columns of the pulps—particularly *Weird Tales*—were flooded with praises of his work and even with haphazard attempts by readers to probe the sources of his horrific technique and imagination. But Lovecraft, having by necessity entered the literary underworld, rarely received attention from important critics, much less any systematic exploration of his work. Lovecraftians know well the few critics outside of the pulps—B. K. Hart, William Bolitho, J. Randle Luten—who deigned to write about Lovecraft before his demise, though even these mentions are so rare that some have yet to be located.

After Lovecraft's death the literary world remained slow to take notice of him, and even before Edmund Wilson's "blitz" (as L. Sprague de Camp aptly termed it) Lovecraft's reception was ambivalent: T. O. Mabbott and Will Cuppy stood up for him in brief book reviews, but he was presented as a psychotic by Marjorie Farber, a hack by Wilson, and an oddity whose life centered around spirits and bogies by magazine staff critics. What critical attention he received came, inevitably, from the science fiction fan magazines and from his erstwhile associates and correspondents. August Derleth was the spearhead, though to many it appeared that his "obsession" with Lovecraft was a rather pe-

Introduction xix

culiar blot upon the escutcheon of a writer whose "main-stream" work was so highly regarded. Still less regarded were the admittedly crude though sometimes useful magazines which centered around Lovecraft himself—*The Acolyte, The Lovecraft Collector*, for example—the "cult" that Edmund Wilson attempted to blast. Lovecraft began to appear as a cheap sensationalist—an inventor of outlandish names, gods, and places, a chronicler of improbable events, a writer whose style was unpleasantly archaic and ornate—whose popularity among fans only established their own puerility.

But the foreign response shows, as early as the 1950s, a firm attempt to take Lovecraft seriously and to analyze his literary and philosophic merit: the French in particular, always responsive to fine excursions into the *fantastique*, hailed Lovecraft as they had Poe in the previous century. Serious critics all around Europe—including such figures as Jean Cocteau, Jacques Bergier, Maurice Lévy, Hubert Lampo, Jacques van Herp, and many others—praised Lovecraft not merely as one who could successfully send a shiver or two up the reader's spine, but as a consummate prose stylist, one who through fantasy could say much about mankind and its relations to the cosmos. It is not insignificant that the first two doctoral dissertations on Lovecraft were written in Italy and France.

In the English-speaking world, the 1950s saw some key breakthroughs, both in the critical analysis and in the recognition of Lovecraft. In the fan world such great early scholars as Fritz Leiber, Matthew H. Onderdonk, and particularly George T. Wetzel were making significant additions to Lovecraft criticism—indeed, were laying the groundwork for later interpretation—while memoirs by associates were adding their weight to biographical study. Through the efforts of August Derleth—whose *H. P. L.: A*

Memoir (1945), for all its failings as a biography, did much to interest the literary world in one whom Vincent Starrett would have termed a "buried Caesar"—an increasing number of critics began having second thoughts about the ephemerality of Lovecraft; most notable was Peter Penzoldt, who in *The Supernatural in Fiction* (1952) devoted considerable space to the Providence scribe, and even used various aesthetic concepts expressed in Lovecraft's "Supernatural Horror in Literature" as the bases for his own analyses. In 1958 the University of Detroit's literary magazine, *Fresco*, devoted an entire issue to works by and about Lovecraft.

Fresco subsequently published an abridgement of the first academic paper on Lovecraft—James Warren Thomas' powerful if opinionated biographical study, "H. P. Lovecraft: A Self-Portrait" (1950). That Thomas' paper was written at Brown University is no accident, since the bulk of Lovecraft's private papers and publications were given to the John Hay Library of Brown by R. H. Barlow shortly after Lovecraft's death. Due to its rich holdings in unpublished letters by Lovecraft, Brown has produced several theses, including the valuable St. Armand and Klein papers. Columbia University can take pride in Arthur Koki's lengthy biographical account, which, along with Kenneth W. Faig's *Lovecraftian Voyages*, may still rank as the finest full-length biography of Lovecraft. Both papers, regrettably, are unpublished.

The late 1960s and 1970s have, perhaps because of the many new sides of Lovecraft suddenly revealed by the publication of his letters, seen the true emergence of scholarly Lovecraft research; for though such precocious individuals as Wetzel and Onderdonk were writing as early as the 1940s, they stand as independent figures in a fan world whose general run of criticism was almost painfully naïve

and irrelevant. And yet, despite the attention given Lovecraft by such established critics as Colin Wilson, Jorge Luis
Borges, Rafael Llopis, and others, the present scholarship
is still being conducted by fairly unknown researchers
who, though some sport Ph.D.'s, are still connected with
fandom. Such amateur magazines as *Nyctalops* and *Whispers*,
and such amateur press associations as the Esoteric Order
of Dagon and the Necronomicon, are the descendants of
the Lovecraft-oriented magazines of the 1940s. Though
much of the criticism in these journals hardly deserves the
name, it is nonetheless true that such major figures in
Lovecraft criticism as Dirk W. Mosig, Kenneth W. Faig, R.
Alain Everts, R. Boerem, Donald Burleson, David E.
Schultz, and others use such magazines as their major—
and in some cases only—outlets of criticsm. These scholars
are pursuing their subject of study with a subtlety, logic,
and accuracy hitherto unknown in the field, using all of
Lovecraft's works—obscure essays which are slowly being
reprinted, letters published and unpublished—in their
penetrating analyses of Lovecraft's life and thought, and
his place in literary and intellectual history. Whole new
sides of Lovecraft are being revealed: whereas the past saw
only Lovecraft the fiction-writer, poet, and amateur journalist, the present assesses him also as political thinker, literary critic, metaphysician, economic theorist, controver-
sialist, satirist, aesthetician, epistolarian, and antiquarian.
This scholarship, which from the closed world of fandom is
slowly seeping into the academic world through publication of articles in scholarly journals and books by university presses, will clearly establish Lovecraft as a significant
voice in American literature, while the continuing foreign
acclaim attests to the mark that he has made and will make
upon world thought.

   Not only has Lovecraft refused, as August Derleth said,

to "fade away"; he has, through the help of his posthumous champions, made a more significant impress upon our time than he ever did upon his own. That he will continue to ascend in stature is evident; that he deserves to do so is equally clear. The dissemination and explication of H. P. Lovecraft's work is a duty which the present and future must not shirk.

S. T. Joshi

Brown University
Providence, Rhode Island
1980

Explanatory Notes

As this bibliography has been compiled in rather a different manner from previous bibliographies of Lovecraft, and as its arrangement is somewhat complicated because of the amount of data that has been included, some words of explanation are necessary as to the arrangement of information.

To begin with, it is important to emphasize that the indexes are absolutely essential in locating any given item. It is not claimed that any single entry includes all the publications of the work, whether it be by or about Lovecraft, for often different publications will fit into different categories. Particular pains have, however, been taken to make the indexes complete, as cross-references are not numerous.

All titles of works by Lovecraft are given either according to the autograph manuscripts (where they exist), or the first appearance, or the titles which Lovecraft himself intended for the works (e.g., as revealed in his letters). Many of these titles may be unfamiliar to the user of this bibliography, since proper or original titles of many works have never been restored. The index of titles by Lovecraft, however, lists all title variants (save those of the most trivial nature) and will direct the user to the title under which information has here been recorded. All untitled works, whether by Lovecraft or by others, are placed at the end of their respective sections.

Books by Lovecraft (I-A and II-A) have been listed in chronological order. In certain cases the order of the volumes is not wholly certain (this applies particularly to more recent volumes, which have emerged in such unprecedented numbers, and to foreign volumes), so that the order is sometimes only approximate or hypothetical. The chronology of the very earliest and very latest volumes is, however, relatively secure.

Letters by Lovecraft that have been published as essays are listed in Chapter I-B-ii (Nonfiction), not I-B-v (Letters). The distinction is sometimes a fine one, and the index should be consulted when in doubt.

Lovecraft's dozen poems to Jonathan E. Hoag are listed chronologically at the end of Section I-B-iii.

No distinction has been made among Lovecraft's revisions, ghost-writings, and collaborations, since in all cases the process of composition was essentially similar. Some of the revisions probably contain much less original work by Lovecraft (e.g., the tales of Sonia H. Davis and Adolphe de Castro), and in some cases may not even belong in the Lovecraft corpus; but all have been listed uniformly. We are probably ignorant of the overwhelming bulk of Lovecraft's revisory work, which ranged from textbooks to verse to novels. Those works which he revised are usually listed here under the name of the author to whom the original publication was credited.

In works by Lovecraft in translation, many bibliographic details (place and dates of publication, subtitles, etc.) have been printed in English for the sake of convenience. The index of periodicals lists the language of a journal if it is not in English and (save for American, Canadian, and British periodicals) its place of origin; the index of foreign languages lists all works in a given language, including both works by and about Lovecraft.

Although duplication of material has been avoided where possible, it sometimes occurs. Important introductions and critical material included in books by Lovecraft are listed in Chapter III. Books or pamphlets about Lovecraft that have appeared in periodicals are listed in both section C and D of Chapter III. Book reviews in which more than one book is simultaneously reviewed are listed under each title reviewed. Books that contain more than one critical work are listed under the author or editor of the book, not under the individual authors.

Only a relatively small number of works about Lovecraft have received annotation, since the bulk of these works are ephemeral or their titles are self-explanatory. In general only important critical works have been annotated. Conversely, many obscure or unfamiliar works by Lovecraft himself have been annotated in order to give a brief idea of their content.

Very selective lists of critical works from the two Lovecraft-related amateur press associations (Esoteric Order of Dagon and Necronomicon) have been made because the overwhelming majority of material therein is inconsequential and because copies are extremely difficult to obtain (partial files can, however, be found in the John Hay Library). Nevertheless, some of the most important work in Lovecraft studies is being conducted in these pages; hence a partial listing is justified.

It is to be noted that Winifred Virginia Jordan and Winifred Virginia Jackson are the same person; so too Sonia H. Greene and Sonia H. Davis, Zealia B. Reed and Zealia Bishop, and Marion Zimmer and Marion Zimmer Bradley. Entries for these authors are usually filed under the latter of their names.

Works not included in this bibliography are:

(1) the so-called "Lovecraft-Derleth posthumous collab-

orations," because they are essentially the work of August
Derleth (see I-E-i);

(2) tales of the "Cthulhu Mythos" by other writers;

(3) poems about Lovecraft or parodies of his work;

(4) the various editions of the *Necronomicon* that have recently been issued;

(5) manuscripts and other unpublished work by Lovecraft;

(6) radio, television, cinema, or comic book adaptations
of Lovecraft's work, phonograph recordings of his stories,
or the opera based on *The Case of Charles Dexter Ward.*

Although this volume is rather more sizeable than any
other bibliography of Lovecraft, it nonetheless contains la-
cunae: the listing of foreign Lovecraftiana is somewhat incomplete (e.g., rumors of Russian translations of Lovecraft
have circulated for decades), as are Sections D, E, and F of
Chapter III. Nevertheless, every effort has been made to
examine each item personally rather than to borrow data
from previous bibliographies, and this volume contains
several thousand works by and about Lovecraft never before listed.

A word about locations. Due to Lovecraft's obscurity and
fitful recognition, many of the rarest works by and about
him cannot be found in institutions, but even now rest in
private hands. Nevertheless, several institutions house
important bodies of Lovecraft's work. Foremost is the John
Hay Library of Brown University, which has the most
comprehensive collection of Lovecraftiana in the world,
and is the place to turn for almost any item noted in this
volume. Its holdings of books by Lovecraft—both in English and in translation—is particularly outstanding. For
amateur journals of the 1910s to 1930s containing Lovecraft's work, consult also the New York Public Library
(C. W. Smith Collection), the Fales Library of New York

University (Fossil Collection), and the American Antiquarian Society. The Library of Congress has some rare books by Lovecraft plus other rare magazine and newspaper publications. For pulp magazines, consult the John Hay Library (complete file of *Weird Tales*), the University of California Library at Riverside, the Library of Texas A & M University, and the Massachusetts Institute of Technology Science Fiction Society. Lovecraft criticism is, aside from what is in the John Hay Library, very difficult to acquire, and private collectors and scholars may have to be contacted.

Although I have done much of the compilation of this bibliography myself, I have received valuable information and corroboration from many individuals. On the organization and arrangement of the bibliography I have received much advice from Tom Collins, Kenneth W. Faig, Jr., Dirk W. Mosig, and David E. Schultz. For Chapter I, Section A, I owe much to L. W. Currey, Frank Halpern, Dirk W. Mosig, Kennett Neily, and Roy A. Squires. For Chapter I, Section B, I have received aid from Scott Connors, R. Alain Everts, Marc A. Michaud, David E. Schultz, and George T. Wetzel. Chapter I, Section C has largely been compiled by Dirk W. Mosig, David E. Schultz, and myself. Many suggestions for Chapter I, Section E have come from Kenneth W. Faig, Jr. I have relied on Dirk W. Mosig for most of Chapter II. For information about Japanese publications of Lovecraft I am vastly indebted to Masaki Abe; for Italian, to Gianfranco de Turris and Sebastiano Fusco; for German, to Kalju Kirde, Heinz W. Kloos, and Franz Rottensteiner. For Chapter III I have received valuable aid from R. Boerem, Dirk W. Mosig, and Kennett Neily.

Many institutions have permitted me to use their materials. Above all I must single out the John Hay Library of Brown University, and in particular the curator of its Lovecraft collection, John H. Stanley, who has shared with me his formidable bibliographic knowledge over the past four years. I have also done much work at the American Antiquarian Society (Worcester, Mass.), the Fossil Collection of Amateur Journalism in the Fales Library of New York University (New York City), the New York Public Library (New York City), the Providence Public Library (Providence, R.I.), the Firestone Library of Princeton University (Princeton, N.J.), the Library of the Rhode Island Historical Society (Providence, R.I.), the John D. Rockefeller Library of Brown University (Providence, R.I.), the Bracken Library of Ball State University (Muncie, Indiana), the Muncie Public Libraries (Muncie, Indiana), and the Massachusetts Institute of Technology Science Fiction Society (Cambridge, Mass.).

Among the individuals, aside from those already named (most of whom have contributed much information aside from that outlined already), who have provided information for this bibliography are: Eddy C. Bertin; Anthony Bliss of the Northern Illinois University Library (DeKalb, Ill.); Hyman Bradofsky; Paul Buhle; Donald R. Burleson; T. G. L. Cockcroft; L. Sprague de Camp; Virginia Doris; Drake Douglas; Ray English of the Alderman Library of the University of Virginia; Meade Frierson III; William Fulwiler; William E. Hart; T. E. D. Klein; Edward S. Lauterbach; Don Chang Lee; Maurice Lévy; Robert A. W. Lowndes; Ronald F. Marshall; Paul R. Michaud; Harry O. Morris, Jr.; Vrest Orton; Barton L. St. Armand; J. Vernon Shea; John D. Squires; David A. Sutton; Macmillan & Co. (Andrea Thoms); Arkham House Publishers, Inc. (James Turner); James Wade; Robert Weinberg; and Edward Wood. Only I, however, can be held responsible for any inaccuracies that may exist in this bibliography.

I must thank Frank Halpern, Dirk W. Mosig, Kennett Neily, and David E. Schultz for proofreading the final draft

of this bibliography and making many valuable suggestions.

Perhaps most importantly, I must extend my profound
thanks to Dean H. Keller, General Editor of the Serif Series, and to his Editorial Advisory Board for their unstint-
ing aid in the four years during which this bibliography was
being compiled. Without their patient guidance this work
would never have reached its finished state.

S. T. J.

Abbreviations

General:

A.L.	autograph letter
A.Ms.	autograph manuscript
N.A.P.A.	National Amateur Press Association
T.L.	typewritten letter
T.Ms.	typewritten manuscript
tr.	translated by
U.A.P.A.	United Amateur Press Association

Works by Lovecraft (including revisions):

A	The Alchemist
ATMOM	At the Mountains of Madness
Az	Azathoth (fragment)
B	The Book
BC	The Beast in the Cave
BWS	Beyond the Wall of Sleep
C	Celephaïs
CA	Cool Air
CB	The Challenge from Beyond
CC	The Call of Cthulhu
CDW	The Case of Charles Dexter Ward
CrC	The Crawling Chaos (with Winifred V. Jackson)
CS	The Colour out of Space

Abbreviations

CU	The Cats of Ulthar
CY	The Curse of Yig (with Zealia Bishop)
D	Dagon
DAT	The Diary of Alonzo Typer (with William Lumley)
DDB	Deaf, Dumb and Blind (with C. M. Eddy, Jr.)
De	The Descendant
DH	The Dunwich Horror
DQ	The Dream-Quest of Unknown Kadath
DS	The Doom That Came to Sarnath
DWH	The Dreams in the Witch House
EC	The Evil Clergyman
EE	The Electric Executioner (with Adolphe de Castro)
EO	Ex Oblivione
F	The Festival
FAJ	Facts concerning the Late Arthur Jermyn and His Family
FB	From Beyond
FO	Four O'Clock (with Sonia H. Davis)
GE	The Ghost-Eater (with C. M. Eddy, Jr.)
GM	The Green Meadow (with Winifred V. Jackson)
H	The Hound
HB	The Horror in the Burying Ground (with Hazel Heald)
HD	The Haunter of the Dark
He	He
HM	The Horror in the Museum (with Hazel Heald)
HMB	The Horror at Martin's Beach (with Sonia H. Davis)
HRH	The Horror at Red Hook
HWR	Herbert West—Reanimator

Hy	Hypnos
IV	In the Vault
IWE	In the Walls of Eryx (with Kenneth Sterling)
LD	The Loved Dead (with C. M. Eddy, Jr.)
LF	The Lurking Fear
LT	The Last Test (with Adolphe de Castro)
M	Memory
MB	The Moon-Bog
MC	Medusa's Coil (with Zealia Bishop)
MEZ	The Music of Erich Zann
Mo	The Mound (with Zealia Bishop)
MS	The Man of Stone (with Hazel Heald)
N	Nyarlathotep (prose poem)
NC	The Nameless City
NO	The Night Ocean (with R. H. Barlow)
O	The Outsider
OE	Out of the Eons (with Hazel Heald)
OG	The Other Gods
P	Polaris
PG	Poetry and the Gods (with Anna Helen Crofts)
PH	The Picture in the House
PM	Pickman's Model
QI	The Quest of Iranon
RW	The Rats in the Walls
S	The Street
SH	The Shunned House
SHH	The Strange High House in the Mist
SHiL	Supernatural Horror in Literature
SK	The Silver Key
SOI	The Shadow over Innsmouth
SOOT	The Shadow out of Time
SRC	The Statement of Randolph Carter
T	The Tomb

Abbreviations

TAS	"Till A' the Seas" (with R. H. Barlow)
TBB	Two Black Bottles (with W. B. Talman)
TD	The Thing on the Doorstep
Te	The Temple
TGSK	Through the Gates of the Silver Key (with E. Hoffmann Price)
TJR	The Transition of Juan Romero
TM	The Thing in the Moonlight
TOM	The Terrible Old Man
Tr	The Tree
U	The Unnamable
UP	Under the Pyramids (with Harry Houdini)
WD	The Whisperer in Darkness
WiD	Winged Death
WMB	What the Moon Brings
WS	The White Ship

Institutions:

JHL	John Hay Library, Brown University
WHS	State Historical Society of Wisconsin, Madison

I. Works by Lovecraft in English

A. Books by Lovecraft

1. *The Crime of Crimes* (1915?)
   THE / CRIME OF CRIMES. / By H. P.
   LOVECRAFT.

   > [1]² [1-4]
   > [1]: title; [2-4]: "The Crime of Crimes: Lusitania, 1915"; [4]:
   > colophon.
   > Pamphlet; 16.7 × 10.5 cm.; no covers.
   > *Notes.* Published by "A. Harris, Selwyn House, Clifton Road,
   > Llandudno, Wales, England" (see colophon). Apparently Love-
   > craft's first pamphlet: it probably dates to 1915 (although no
   > date is printed in the pamphlet), presumably dating after the
   > poem's appearance in *Interesting Items* for July 1915 (I-B-iii-26).
   > There is no indication as to how many copies were printed.

2. *United Amateur Press Association: Exponent of Amateur Journalism* (1916?)
   United Amateur / Press Association / [rule] / EX-
   PONENT OF / AMATEUR JOURNALISM / [rec-
   tangular border around all the above] / [text
   commences]

   > [1]⁶ [1-12]
   > [1]: title; [1-12]: text.
   > Pamphlet; 14.9 × 8.6 cm.; no covers.
   > *Notes.* Pamphlet written by Lovecraft (then vice-president of
   > the U.A.P.A.) to encourage new members to join. His name ap-
   > pears on the last page of the text. Probably issued in early 1916
   > (Lovecraft's term ran from September 1915 to August 1916);
   > possibly printed by E. E. Ericson (Elroy, Wis.), then official prin-
   > ter for the U.A.P.A. There is no indication as to how many co-
   > pies were printed.

3. *Looking Backward* (1920)
   a. [There is no title page; cover reads as follows:]

LOOKING BACKWARD. / [rule] / BY H. P.
LOVECRAFT / [rule] / [illustration] / [orna-
ment] / C. W. Smith,   Haverhill, Mass.

[1-9]² [1] 2-6 [7] 8-14 [15] 16-22 [23] 24-30 [31] 32-37 36

[1]-36[i.e., 38]: "Looking Backward"; [1]-6: Part I; [7]-14:
Part II; [15]-22: Part III; [23]-30: Part IV; [31]-36[i.e., 38]:
Part V.

Pamphlet: 16 × 11.8 cm.; off-white paper covers.

Notes. The usual date given for publication of this pamphlet is 1935, but because the pamphlet was made from the
plates of the serialization in *The Tryout* of 1920 (I-B-ii-170), a
dating of 1920 itself seems more likely. Moreover, in an introductory note to Lovecraft's "Dr. Jekyll and Mr. Hyde" (I-
B-ii-125), Edwin Hadley Smith, associate both of Lovecraft
and C. W. Smith, states: "In 1916 C. W. Smith published a
36-page booklet called *Looking Backward*" (p. 7). The 1935
date was apparently arrived at by a pencilled note written
by Lovecraft on the inside back cover of a copy of the book
(JHL), dated 23 July 1935. But this was simply the date
when Lovecraft presented this copy to R. H. Barlow. In this
note Lovecraft states that "very few" copies were printed,
while E. H. Smith in the aforementioned article gives the
print run as 40. One copy seen contains two pp. 5-6, and in
all copies seen the last page (38) is misnumbered as 36.

b. *Second Edition.* West Warwick, R.I.: Necronomicon Press, July
1980. Facsimile of the serialization from *The Aonian* (I-B-ii-
170). Cover art by Jason Eckhardt.

4. *The Materialist Today* (1926)

No copy of this pamphlet has ever been located. Previous bibliographers have obtained data for it only from a "Check List of
Publications of *Driftwind Press*" by Walter J. Coates, appearing in
Driftwind, 6, No. 3 (November 1931), 17 ff. On p. 17 is this entry: "THE MATERIALIST TODAY. Howard P. Lovecraft. n.d.,
n.p. [May 1926]. *Not for sale.* 12mo, pa, 8 pp. Only 15 copies
printed." The pamphlet is an exact reprint (perhaps a sort of
offprint) of the essay of the title appearing in *Driftwind* for October 1926 (I-B-ii-174). The reference to "12mo" apparently indicates only size, not gathering, and the pamphlet ("pa" mean-

ing paper covers) was evidently 19 × 12.7 cm. The fact that the
pamphlet was "not for sale" implies that Coates (editor of
Driftwind Press) printed the pamphlet for private distribution,
presumably among Lovecraft's associates. No copy was recorded even in the listing (admittedly incomplete) of Lovecraft's
own personal library made by Mary Spink (ms., JHL), although
W. Paul Cook (letter to W. T. Scott, 26 April 1944; ms., JHL)
spoke of owning a copy. Lovecraft does not refer to the pamphlet in any correspondence seen. It is likely that none of the
15 copies of the pamphlet survives.

5. *The Shunned House* (1928)

   THE SHUNNED HOUSE / BY / H. P. LOVE-
   CRAFT / With a Preface by Frank Belknap Long,
   Jr. / [ornament] / ATHOL, MASS. / Published by
   W. Paul Cook / The Recluse Press [black-
   letter] / 1928 [copyright page:] COPYRIGHT
   1928 / BY W. PAUL COOK

   [1-7]⁴ [8]² [1-8] 9-15 [16] 17-25 [26] 27-37 [38] 39-49 [50] 51-
   58 [59-60]

   [1]: title; [2]: copyright page; [3]: dedication: "TO / W. PAUL
   COOK / TO WHOM / THE EXISTENCE OF THIS STO-
   RY / IS DUE"; [4]: blank; [5-6]: "Preface," by Frank Belknap
   Long, Jr.; [7]: half-title; [8]: blank; 9-[59]: SH; 9-15: Chapter i;
   [16]: blank; 17-25: Chapter ii; [26]: blank; 27-37: Chapter iii;
   [38]: blank; 39-49: Chapter iv; [50]: blank; 51-[59]: Chapter v;
   [60]: blank.

   Unbound sheets; 21.6 × 14.1 cm.

   Notes. The legendary stillborn first "book" by Lovecraft. Cook
   had wanted to publish SH in the first issue of *The Recluse* (see
   Lovecraft to August Derleth, 7 November 1926; ms., WHS),
   but, perhaps because of space limitations, did not do so, and
   thus decided to print the story as a small book. Long insisted on
   writing a preface. Cook printed approximately 300 copies in
   mid-1928 (see Will Ransom, *Private Presses and Their Books* [New
   York: R. R. Bowker, 1929], p. 394), but bound none. On all copies of this state the top edges of the first seven signatures are
   uncut. Paper bears the watermark "Canterbury Laid."

Copies Bound or Distributed by R. H. Barlow. In 1934 Barlow received about 225 copies of the unbound sheets. It is rumored that he bound only eight copies: one was bound in natural leather and was given to Lovecraft in 1935. The other seven were bound in boards; apparently, all differ from one another in the precise details of their binding. Binding measures 23.8 × 15.8 cm. Copies are variously stamped on spine and covers. These seven copies bear either a printed label (*"Copyright 1935 / R. H. Barlow"*) pasted over the copyright notice (p. [2]), or the original copyright notice crossed out by hand to read: "Copyright 1936 / R. H. Barlow." The copy given to Lovecraft bears no alteration of the copyright notice. Three copies of the state bound in boards were sold to Arkham House after Barlow's death, and one copy seen bears the printed Arkham House label pasted over the copyright notice. It is believed that Barlow distributed some copies in wrappers and other copies in an unbound state, both bearing his printed copyright notice, but none has been seen by the compiler. Of the 225 copies, Barlow apparently distributed only about 50, having found some unusable.

Copies Bound or Distributed by Arkham House. Aside from the three Barlow-bound copies noted above, Arkham House (Sauk City, Wis.), when obtaining the remainder of the unbound sheets, bound or distributed 150 as follows: 50 unbound copies bear a printed label pasted over the original copyright notice; 100 are bound in black cloth bearing the printed copyright notice. Spine stamped in gold. The former were distributed ca. 1959; the latter ca. 1961. The Arkham House copyright label is in two states: the one for the unbound sheets prints book and magazine titles in boldface, that for the bound sheets prints these titles in italics. Several bound copies bear the label intended for the unbound copies; apparently the labels printed for the unbound sheets were not sufficient for all the bound copies, so a new label was printed. One unbound copy seen bears both the Arkham House and Barlow printed copyright labels; one bound copy lacks any printed label. Arkham House trimmed the edges somewhat in the bound copies.

The Forgery. Around 1965 a forgery was issued (perhaps in England), consisting of an offset of the text bound in red half

leather, spine stamped in gold. Watermark on the paper reads
"Chantry," and the Arkham House copyright label is pasted on
the copyright page, not over Cook's original copyright, but over
a blank area.

6. *Further Criticism of Poetry* (1932)

   a. *Further | Criticism of Poetry | By H. P. Lovecraft |* [or-
      nament] / BUREAU OF CRITICS / [rectangular
      rule around all the above]

      [1]⁸ [1-2] 3-13 [14-16]

      [1]: title; [2]: blank; 3-13: text; [14]: colophon; [15-16]:
      blank.

      Pamphlet; 22.8 × 15.2 cm.; no covers.

      Notes. Printed on the Press of George G. Fetter Co.,
      Louisville, Ky., in 1932 (see colophon). The essay (original
      title: "Notes on Verse Technique") is dated 18 April 1932;
      this is the date of writing, not of printing (see A.Ms., JHL).

   b. *Sub-Edition.* Duluth, Minn.: Eric Carlson, November 1976;
      facsimile reproduction of the above. One hundred and fifty
      copies printed, some distributed through the Necronomicon
      amateur press association. Carlson's colophon appears on p.
      [15].

7. *The Battle That Ended the Century* (1934)

   THE BATTLE THAT ENDED THE CENTU-
   RY / (Ms. Found in a Time Machine)
   / *   *   * / [text commences]

   This title consists only of two separate unnumbered leaves,
   35.7 × 21.7 cm., each mimeographed only on the recto. All writing, including the title, is reproduced from typewritten copy.
   This collaboration between Lovecraft and Barlow (here unsigned) was written in the summer of 1934, when Lovecraft
   was visiting Barlow in Florida. Barlow mimeographed the tale
   in June 1934 at his home in De Land, Fla. (see Lovecraft to Barlow, 29 June 1934; ms., JHL) and circulated it among Lovecraft's associates; probably not more than 50 copies were produced. In all copies seen the text contains pencil corrections by
   Barlow. Lovecraft never directly acknowledged the collabora-

tion, but Barlow's typescript of the tale (JHL) contains extensive revisions and additions in pen by Lovecraft; Lovecraft, moreover, discussed the tale openly in his correspondence to Barlow. A list in Lovecraft's hand of associates to whom the farce was to be sent also survives.

8. *The Cats of Ulthar* (1935)

a.1. THE / Cats of Ulthar [in red] / H. P. LOVE-CRAFT / [ornament] / CHRISTMAS / 1935 [copyright page:] "Forty copies of this booklet have been printed at The Dragon-Fly Press, Cassia, Florida"

[1]⁸ [i-ii] 1-10 [11-14]

[i]: title; [ii]: copyright page; 1-10: CU; [11-14]: blank.

Pamphlet; 17.2 × 12.6 cm.; dark green paper covers, no print.

Notes. This is the legendary pamphlet issued by Barlow as a Christmas present for Lovecraft. The forty printed copies of this state are not numbered or marked in any other way. The text was handset by Barlow; the pamphlet was probably not sold but given to Lovecraft's associates. The ornament on the title page is a printed drawing in red of a cat's head. In all copies examined, the cat's whiskers have been added with a red pen, apparently by Barlow, and other portions of the head which may not have reproduced properly have been touched up in pen.

a.1(a). *Variant.* Lovecraft's own copy of the book (JHL) contains slight differences. [1]² [2]⁸; [i-vi] 1-10 [11-14]. [i-iv]: blank; [v]: title; [vi]: blank. Both pp. [i] and [14] are glued to the paper covers, which are of a dark grey. An inscription by Barlow on p. [iii] reads: "Dear HP— / Here is the booklet / I so long ago promised! / There were forty copies / on ordinary paper, and only / two on Red Lion Text. This / is one of the latter. / RHB." In the regular edition the covers were somewhat larger than the page size; here the difference is minimized, and dimensions are 16.2 × 12.4 cm. This copy bears the name "ULTHAR" in pen on the front cover, presumably written by Barlow.

b. *Second Edition*. West Warwick, R.I.: Necronomicon Press, 1977. Facsimile reproduction of the regular state of the above. Divergences: gathered [1]⁸ [i-iv] 1-10 [11-12]: [i]: colophon for reprint; [ii]: blank; [iii]: title; [iv]: original copyright page; 1-10: CU; [11-12]: blank. Pp. [iii]-10 each bear a double rectangular rule in red around the text. Blue paper covers; 550 numbered copies.

9. *Charleston* (1936)

a. [There is no title page; cover reads as follows:] CHARLESTON / by H. P. Lovecraft

[1] 2-20 [21-25] leaves

[1]-20: letter from Lovecraft to H. C. Koenig, 12 January 1936, giving guide and description of Charleston, S.C.; [21]: "List of Principal Sites in Preceding Itinerary"; [22]: "Charleston Itinerary (Pedestrian)"; [23-25]: photostatic reproductions of handwritten maps and illustrations of Charleston by Lovecraft.

Paper covers; 29.2 × 22 cm.; stapled at left margin.

Notes. In early January 1936, H. C. Koenig was planning to make a trip to Charleston and asked Lovecraft to write him a description of the highlights of the city. Lovecraft complied by writing the above letter, which Koenig, when returning to his home in New York after the trip (late January?), mimeographed. The above is the result. Pages are printed only on rectos. Entire text reproduced from typewritten copy. Probably fewer than 25 copies.

b. *Second Edition*. Some time after Koenig printed the first edition, he asked Lovecraft to rewrite the letter into an essay (February? 1936). This Lovecraft did. The changes in the text are minor: the first three paragraphs are altered, and the last two paragraphs and the closing are omitted. Koenig apparently retyped and remimeographed nearly the entire text, correcting printing and stenographic errors. The first page of the text now bears the title: "CHARLESTON [rule under title] / By H. P. Lovecraft." Koenig stated (letter to Ray H. Zorn, 6 December 1948) that 30-50 copies were printed.

Some copies of this edition contain two pages of errata, photostatic reproductions of a handwritten errata list prepared by Lovecraft (original in JHL). Koenig noted in the above letter to Zorn that these errata sheets were added some time after the edition had been issued.

Variant states of both editions exist: either they lack the binder and are in loose sheets or lack the illustrations on pp. [23-25] or both.

c. *Third Edition*. Madison, Wis.: The Strange Company, 1975. Facsimile reproduction of the second edition of the above, with introduction by R. Alain Everts. All pages tinted yellow. Unbound sheets; 27.9 × 21.5 cm.; enclosed in heavy buff paper folder. One hundred fifty copies signed and numbered by the editor.

10. *Some Current Motives and Practices* (1936)
[There is no title page; first page of text simply headed by title, "SOME CURRENT MOTIVES AND PRACTICES."]

1-2 [3-4]
1-[4]: "Some Current Motives and Practices."
Unbound sheets; 35.5 × 21.7 cm.

Notes. The title consists only of two loose sheets mimeographed on both sides of the leaf. The entire text (including title) is reproduced from typewritten copy. The essay is dated "June 4, 1936": this is date of writing (see A.Ms., JHL), not date of publication of the broadside; the latter must have been issued shortly afterward, perhaps by the end of June. It has long been believed that Lovecraft himself may have printed the broadside, but it appears more likely that he had R. H. Barlow print it for him from the latter's home in De Land, Fla. Possible proofs for this assertion are as follows: 1) Lovecraft was never greatly involved in printing even during his heyday in amateur journalism and even in so elementary a process as mimeograph; 2) the face of the typewriter used in typing the text is not Lovecraft's but Barlow's (identical to the face used to type *The Battle That Ended the Century* [I-A-7], which undoubtedly was prepared by Barlow); 3) Lovecraft's A.Ms. of the essay is written in an unusually legible hand, as if he were writing it so that someone else could prepare it from his copy. The broadside, of which perhaps 50 to 100 copies were printed, was probably sent privately to members of the National Amateur Press Association.

11. *The Shadow over Innsmouth* (1936)

THE SHADOW / OVER / INNSMOUTH / BY / H. P. LOVECRAFT / Illustrated By / FRANK A. UT-PATEL / VISIONARY PUBLISHING CO. / EVE-RETT, PENNSYLVANIA / 1936

[1]8 [2]20 [3]16 [4-6]12 [7-8]8 [i-xvi] [1-12] 13-72 [73] 74-125 [126] 127-42 [143] 144-58 [159-76]

[i-ii]: front flyleaf; [iii-xvi]: blank; [1]: half-title; [2]: blank; [3]: title; [4-5]: blank; [6]: copyright page; [7]: blank; [8]: frontispiece; [9]: list of illustrations; [10]: blank; [11]: part-title; [12]: blank; 13-72, 74-125, 127-42, 144-58: SOI; [73, 126, 143]: illustrations; [159-74]: blank; [175-76]: back flyleaf.

Bound in black cloth; spine and front cover stamped in white; 18.3 × 13 cm.; white dust jacket (illustration tinted green).

Notes. Copyright page declares that the book was published in April 1936, but it was not actually distributed until the end of the year; Lovecraft received his copy only in November. First and last leaves of the book have been glued to the front and back cover. Interior illustrations are black-and-white.

William L. Crawford, publisher of the volume, has declared ("Lovecraft's First Book," in III-D-409) that 400 copies were printed; 200 of these were bound, the others later being destroyed. The book was originally distributed without the dust jacket, the latter being printed later and sent to most who had purchased the book without it. Also after initial publication an errata slip (one leaf printed only on recto) was prepared and circulated. Several copies examined contain Lovecraft's own pencilled corrections of the numerous printing errors.

Some time before distribution, publisher's dummies were issued so that the book could be examined. According to Wilson H. Shepherd, about 8 or 10 such copies were printed and bound. Gathered [1]18 [2]16 [3-5]12 [6-7]8. Pagination divergences: [i-xvi], [1-4] eliminated; [5-6]: pasted down to inside front cover; [7-8]: pasted upon [5-6]. Title on front cover stamped on all-capitals (only initial letters capitalized in regular state).

12. *HPL* (1937)

[There is no title page; cover reads: H / P / L arranged diagonally from left to right in black-letter.]

[1]¹² [1-24]

[1]: illustration of Lovecraft as an eighteenth-century gentleman by Virgil Finlay; [2]: blank; [3]: "Foreword," by [Corwin F. Stickney]; [4]: blank; [5]: "The Wood"; [6]: blank; [7]: "Homecoming"; [8]: blank; [9]: "Nostalgia"; [10]: blank; [11]: "Night Gaunts" [sic]; [12]: blank; [13]: "The Dweller"; [14]: blank; [15]: "Harbour Whistles"; [16]: blank; [17]: Explanatory note to following poem, by [Corwin F. Stickney]; [18]: blank; [19]: "In a Sequestered Churchyard Where Once Poe Walked"; [20]: blank; [21, 23]: "Astrophobos"; [22, 24]: blank.

Pamphlet; 15.2 × 9.8 cm.; off-white paper covers (in imitation leatherette).

Notes. Published by Corwin F. Stickney (Bellville, N.J.) in 1937, although no printing information appears anywhere in the book. Twenty-five copies printed and given free to whoever paid a year's subscription of $.25 to Stickney's *Amateur Correspondent*.

13. *A History of the Necronomicon* (1938)

a. A HISTORY / of / THE NECRONOMI-CON / Being a short, but complete outline of the history of this / book, its author, its various translations and editions from / the time of the writing (A. D. 730) of the Necronomicon to / the present day. / —BY— / H. P. LOVECRAFT / Limited Memorial Edition / WILSON H. SHEPHERD / THE REBEL PRESS / OAKMAN, ALABAMA

[1]² [1-4]

[1]: title; [2-4]: History of the Necronomicon: (AN OUTLINE)"; [4]: "Chronology" and advertisement by Shepherd for Lovecraft's "The Nameless City" as published in *Fanciful Tales* (I-B-i-37).

Pamphlet; 16.5 × 12 cm.; no covers.

Notes. Those bibliographers who do not inexplicably date this pamphlet to 1936 (how can there be, one might ask, a Memorial Edition predating death?) usually date it to 1938, based on the testimony of Shepherd's colleague William H. Evans. Shepherd has recently stated that 80 copies were printed.

b.1. *Second Edition.* West Warwick, R.I.: Necronomicon Press, 1977. Facsimile reproduction of above. [1]⁴ [i–ii] [1–6]: [i]: colophon for new edition; [ii]: blank; [1–4]: as above; [5–6]: blank. Blue paper covers; 500 numbered copies.

b.2. *Second Printing.* West Warwick, R.I.: Necronomicon Press, 1977 (actually April 1978). Green paper covers; 500 numbered copies.

c. *Third Edition.* West Warwick, R.I.: Necronomicon Press, July 1980. Added to an enlarged facsimile of the pamphlet is an "Afterword" by S. T. Joshi. 21.3 × 17.4 cm. Cover art by Jason Eckhardt. About 500 copies.

14. *The Notes and Commonplace Book* (1938)

a. [rule] / *The Notes &* / COMMONPLACE BOOK / *employed by the late* / H. P. LOVECRAFT / including his Suggestions for Story-Writing / Analyses of the Weird Story, / *and a List of* / CERTAIN BASIC UNDERLYING HORRORS, / *&c., &c.,* / DESIGNED TO STIMULATE THE IMAGINATION / [rule] / LAKEPORT, CALIFORNIA / THE FUTILE PRESS / MDCCCCXXXVIII / [rule]

[1–16]² [i–xiv] 1–14 [14a] [15] 16–45 [46–49]

[i–viii]: blank; [ix]: half-title; [x]: blank; [xi]: title; [xii]: colophon; [xiii]: contents list for Part One; [xiv]: blank; 1–6: "I. Suggestions for Writing Story (the *idea* and plot being tentatively decided on)"; 7: "II. Elements of a Weird Story & Types of Weird Story"; 8–12: "III. A List of Certain Basic Underlying Horrors Effectively Used in Weird Fiction"; 13–14: "IV. List of Primary Ideas Motivating Possible Weird Tales"; [14a]: half-title to Part Two: "Commonplace Book";

[15]: note to the *Commonplace Book* by Lovecraft (7 May
1934); 16-[46]: *Commonplace Book*; [47]: blank; [48]: "Errata";
[49]: blank.

    Notes. Seventy-five numbered copies were printed in May
and June 1938. Of these about half were bound in boards
(not seen), the others remaining as unbound sheets. 16 ×
10.3 cm. The "Suggestions for Writing Story" is an early
version of "Notes on Writing Weird Fiction."

b. *Second Edition.* West Warwick, R.I.: Necronomicon Press, October 1978. Divergences: [i-viii]: eliminated; [xii] (i.e., [iv]):
new colophon. Wraparound cover art by Steven Mendelson.
About 500 copies.

15. *The Outsider and Others* (1939)
[rule] / The Outsider and Others / [rule] / *By* / H.
P. Lovecraft / *Collected by* / August Derleth and Donald Wandrei / [rule] / Arkham House · Sauk City,
Wisconsin / 1939

    [1-18]¹⁶ [i-vi] vii [viii-ix] xi-xiv [1-2] 3-506 [507-08] 509-53
[554-58]

    [i]: half-title; [ii]: blank; [iii]: title; [iv]: copyright page; [v]:
dedication: "For Annie E. Phillips Gamwell"; [vi]: blank; vii: contents list; [viii]: blank; [ix]: half-title to introduction; [x]: blank;
xi-xiv: "H. P. Lovecraft: Outsider," by August Derleth and Donald Wandrei; [1]: part-title; [2]: blank; 3-6: D; 7-9: P; 10-13: C;
14-18: Hy; 19-21: CU; 22-27: SHH; 28-31: SRC; 32-39: SK; 40-
62: TGSK; 63-66: O; 67-72: MEZ; 73-85: RW; 86-91: CA; 92-
98: He; 99-112: HRH; 113-20: Te; 121-26: FAJ (as "Arthur Jermyn"); 127-31: PH; 132-37: F; 138-39: TOM; 140-46: T; 147-63:
SH; 164-69: IV; 170-78: PM; 179-93: HD; 194-216: DWH; 217-
33: TD; 234-41: NC; 242-54: LF; 255-73: CC; 274-91: CS; 292-
318: DH; 319-58: WD; 359-99: SOI; 400-41: SOOT; 442-506:
ATMOM; [507]: half-title to SHiL; [508]: blank; 509-53: SHiL;
[554]: blank; [555]: colophon; [556-58]: blank.

    Bound in black cloth; spine stamped in gold; 24 × 16 cm.; dust
jacket illustration by Virgil Finlay.

    Notes. First major collection of Lovecraft's tales, published
posthumously by the firm founded by Derleth and Wandrei;
1,268 copies.

16. *Fungi from Yuggoth* (1943)

FUNGI FROM YUGGOTH [rule under title] / by / HOWARD PHILLIPS LOVECRAFT / FAPA / June   1943 / Bill Evans

Perfect-bound: [1-14]

[1]: title; [2]: blank; [3-13]: *Fungi from Yuggoth* i-xxxiii; [14]: blank.

No covers; 27.4 × 21.5 cm.; stapled at left margin.

Notes. Place of publication is possibly Washington, D.C., where Evans produced his rare edition of *The Challenge from Beyond* (I-A-30), although Salem, Oreg. has also been suggested. Entire text reproduced (mimeograph) from typewritten copy. The book was not sold but sent through the Fantasy Amateur Press Association (F.A.P.A.). Probably fewer than 100 copies were issued. The last three sonnets of the *Fungi* are excluded.

17. *Beyond the Wall of Sleep* (1943)

[rule] / BEYOND THE / WALL OF SLEEP / [rule] / *By* / H. P. Lovecraft / *Collected by* / August Derleth and Donald Wandrei / [rule] / Arkham House · Sauk City, Wisconsin / 1943

[1-15]¹⁶ [i-iv] v-vii [viii] ix-xxix [xxx] [1-2] 3-353 [354-56] 357-411 [412-14] 415-58 [459-62]

[i]: half-title; [ii]: blank; [iii]: title; [iv]: copyright page; v-vii: contents list; [viii]: blank; ix-x: "By Way of Introduction," by Derleth and Wandrei; xi-xiv: "Autobiography: Some Notes on a Nonentity"; xv-xxvii: *The Commonplace Book*; xxviii-xxix: "History and Chronology of the *Necronomicon*" (i.e., "History of the *Necronomicon*"); [xxx]: blank; [1]: part-title; [2]: blank; 3: M; 4-5: WMB; 6-7: N; 8-9: EO; 10-12: Tr; 13-15: OG; 16-19: QI; 20-23: DS; 24-27: WS; 28-32: FB; 33-39: BWS; 40-44: U; 45-49: H; 50-54: MB; 55-57: EC; 58-75: HWR; 76-134: DQ; 135-209: CDW; 210-14: CrC; 215-18: GM; 219-29: CY; 230-46: HM; 247-62: OE; 263-305: Mo; 306-18: DAT; 319-28: CB; 329-45: IWE; 346-48: "Ibid"; 349-53: "Sweet Ermengarde"; [354]: blank; [355]: half-title to poetry section; [356]: blank; 357-58: "Providence"; 358-59: "On a Grecian Colonnade in a Park"; 359-65: "Old Christmas"; 365-69: "New England Fallen"; 369-70: "On a New

England Village Seen by Moonlight"; 370-71: "Astrophobos"; 371: "Sunset"; 371-72: "A Year Off"; 372-73: "A Summer Sunset and Evening"; 373: "To Mistress Sophia Simple, Queen of the Cinema"; 374-75: "The Ancient Track"; 375-77: "The Eidolon"; 377-78: "The Nightmare Lake"; 378-79: "The Outpost"; 379-80: "The Rutted Road"; 380-81: "The Wood"; 381-83: "Hallowe'en in a Suburb"; 383-84: "October" [2]; 384-85: "To a Dreamer"; 385-86: "Despair"; 386-87: "Nemesis"; 388-94: "Psychopompos"; 395-407: *Fungi from Yuggoth*; 408: "Yule Horror"; 408: "To Mr. Finlay . . ."; 409: "To Clark Ashton Smith, Esq., . . ."; 409: "Where Once Poe Walked" (i.e., "In a Sequestered Churchyard Where Once Poe Walked"); 409: "Christmas Greeting to Mrs. Phillips Gamwell—1925"; 409-11: "Brick Row" (i.e., "The East India Brick Row"); 411: "The Messenger"; [412]: blank; [413]: half-title: "Addenda"; [414]: blank; 415-23: "The Cthulhu Mythology: A Glossary" (revised), by Francis T. Laney; 424-58: "An Appreciation of H. P. Lovecraft," by W. Paul Cook; [459]: colophon; [460-62]: blank.

Bound in black cloth; spine stamped in gold; 24 × 16 cm.; dust jacket—a photograph of sculptures by Clark Ashton Smith—by Burt Trimpey.

Notes. The second major omnibus of Lovecraft's work; 1,217 copies.

18. *The Weird Shadow over Innsmouth* (1944)
[rule] / The / Weird Shadow / Over Innsmouth / And Other Stories / of the / Supernatural / By H. P. Lovecraft / [publisher's device] / *Published by* / BARTHOLOMEW HOUSE, INC. / 205 EAST 42ND STREET, NEW YORK 17, N. Y. / [rule] [copyright page:] 1944

Perfect-bound: [1-4] 5-190 [191-92]

[1]: title; [2]: copyright page; [3]: contents list; [4]: blank; 5-82: SOI (as "The Weird Shadow over Innsmouth"); 83-93: F; 94-106: He; 107-14: O; 115-90: WD; [191]: blurb: "OUR BOYS need and deserve books. . . . Give them books—give them this book"; [192]: blank.

Bound in paper; 16.3 × 11.4 cm.

Notes. Bart House Novel [sic] No. 4 (see cover).

19. *Marginalia* (1944)

MARGINALIA / [rule] / *By* / H. P. LOVECRAFT / *Collected by* / AUGUST DERLETH *and* DONALD WANDREI / [publisher's device] / [rule] / ARKHAM HOUSE · SAUK CITY, WISCONSIN / 1944

[1-12]¹⁶ [i-v] vi-vii [viii-ix] x [1-3] 4-36 [37] 38-84 [85] 86-115 [116] 117-34 [135] 136-39 [140] 141-47 [148] 149-60 [161] 162-73 [174] 175-83 [184] 185-98 [199] 200-37 [238] 239-67 [268] 269-75 [276] 277-84 [285] 286-302 [303] 304-06 [307-09] 310-31 [332] 333-37 [338] 339-41 [342] 343-50 [351] 352-54 [355] 356-61 [362] 363-77 [378]

[i]: half-title; [ii]: blank; [iii]: title; [iv]: copyright page; [v]-vii: "Foreword," by Derleth and Wandrei; [viii]: blank; [ix]-x: contents and illustrations lists; [1]: part-title; [2]: blank; [3]-36: UP; [37]-84: MC; [85]-115: WiD; [116]-34: MS; [135]-39: "Notes on Writing Weird Fiction"; [140]-47: "Some Notes on Interplanetary Fiction"; [148]-60: "Lord Dunsany and His Work"; [161]-73: "Heritage or Modernism"; [174]-83: "Some Backgrounds of Fairyland"; [184]-98: "Some Causes of Self-Immolation"; [199]-237: "A Guide to Charleston, South Carolina" (i.e., "Charleston"); [238]-67: "Observations on Several Parts of America"; [268]-75: BC; [276]-84: TJR; [285]-86: Az; 286-89: B; 290-94: De; 294-302: "The Very Old Folk"; [303]-05: TM; 305-06: "Two Comments"; [307]: half-title: "In Appreciation: Howard Phillips Lovecraft"; [308]: blank; [309]-31: "His Own Most Fantastic Creation," by Winfield Townley Scott; [332]-37: "Some Random Memories of H. P. L.," by Frank Belknap Long; [338]-41: "H. P. Lovecraft: An Appreciation," by T. O. Mabbott; [342]-50: "The Wind That Is in the Grass: A Memoir of H. P. Lovecraft in Florida," by R. H. Barlow; [351]-54: "Lovecraft and Science," by Kenneth Sterling; [355]-61: "Lovecraft as a Formative Influence," by August Derleth; [362]-69: "The Dweller in Darkness: Lovecraft, 1927," by Donald Wandrei; 370-71: "To Howard Phillips Lovecraft" [poem], by Clark Ashton Smith; 371-72: "H. P. L." [poem], by Henry Kuttner; 372: "Lost Dream" [poem], by Emil Petaja; 373: "To Howard Phillips Lovecraft" [poem], by Francis Flagg (i.e., Henry George Weiss); 373-74: "H. P. Lovecraft" [poem], by Frank Belknap Long; 374-75: "Elegy: In Providence the Spring . . ." [poem], by August Der-

leth; 375-76: "For the Outsider: H. P. Lovecraft" [poem], by Charles E. White; 376-77: "In Memoriam: H. P. Lovecraft" [poem], by Richard Ely Morse; [378]: colophon.

Bound in black cloth; spine stamped in gold; 19.3 × 13.2 cm.; dust jacket illustration by Virgil Finlay (reproduction of his illustration for SH in *Weird Tales*, October 1937).

Notes. Interior illustrations include photographs of Lovecraft's correspondents, of Lovecraft's home, illustrations by Lovecraft, facsimiles of letters and mss. in his hand, and Alfred Galpin's composition for piano solo, *Lament for H. P. L.*; 2,035 copies.

20. *The Dunwich Horror and Other Weird Tales* (1945?)
[Title page is divided vertically into two portions, with a double rule around the entire page and a single rule dividing left and right portions.] [right portion]: THE / Dunwich Horror / AND / Other Weird Tales / By H. P. LOVECRAFT / *Editions for the Armed Services, Inc.* / A NON-PROFIT ORGANIZATION ESTABLISHED BY / THE COUNCIL ON BOOKS IN WARTIME, NEW YORK / [left portion]: PUBLISHED BY ARRANGEMENT WITH / ARKHAM HOUSE, SAUK CITY. / [publisher's device] / *Manufactured in the United States of America* / [left corner, outside of double rule]: 730

[1-16]¹² [1-4] 5-383 [384]

[1]: title; [2]: copyright page; [3]: contents list; [4]: blank; 5-6: "Introduction," by August Derleth; 7-59: DH; 59-69: IV; 70-93: RW; 94-109: PM; 110-19: MEZ; 120-54: CS; 155-62: O; 163-200: CC; 201-82: WD; 283-363: SOI; 364-74: MB; 375-[84]: H.

Bound in paper; 11 × 16.4 cm.

Notes. Published ca. 1945. Armed Services Editions 730. The text of the book (longer horizontally than vertically) is printed in two columns on each page.

21. *Supernatural Horror in Literature* (1945)

  a.1. *Supernatural Horror* / [ornament] *in Literature* / By
      HOWARD PHILLIPS LOVECRAFT / WITH
      AN INTRODUCTION BY AUGUST DER-
      LETH / [rule] / BEN ABRAMSON *Publisher*
      New York   1945

      [1-7]⁸ [1-8] 9-106 [107-12]
      [1]: half-title; [2]: blank (printed black); [3]: title; [4]: co-
      pyright page; [5]: contents list; [6]: blank; [7]: part-title;
      [8]: blank; 9-11: "Foreword" by Derleth; 12-106: SHiL;
      [107-11]: index; [112]: blank.
      Bound in black cloth; spine stamped in silver; 20.9 ×
      14.2 cm.; no dust jacket.
      Notes. The text contains unsigned footnotes by Derleth;
      the index is also, apparently, by Derleth (or the publish-
      er). On some copies seen there are a few blank pages
      where the type failed to print. There are numerous typo-
      graphical errors.

  a.2. *Second Printing.* New York: Ben Abramson, 1945. According
      to a review copy, this printing (nowhere listed as a second
      printing) was issued on 1 October 1945. Bound in red
      cloth; spine stamped in gold; dust jacket. Typographical
      errors have been corrected.

  b.1. *Second Edition.* New York: Dover Publications, 1973, follow-
      ing the second Abramson printing in facsimile. Gathered
      [1-4]¹⁶: [a-d] [i-ii] iii-ix [10-11] 12-106 [107-26] as follows:
      [a-b]: blank; [c]: half-title; [d]: blank; [i]: title; [ii]: copy-
      right page; iii-viii: "Introduction to the Dover Edition," by
      E. F. Bleiler; ix: contents list; [10]: blank; [11]: part-title;
      12-[111] as above; [112]: blank; [113-26]: advertisements.
      Cover design by Theodore Menten. Some of Derleth's
      footnotes have been omitted, some by Bleiler (signed "E.
      F. B.") added.

  b.2. *Second Printing.* Not listed as such. The only apparent dif-
      ference between this and the first printing seems to be
      the addition of a publisher's symbol to the very bottom of
      the spine. No date can be assigned to this printing.
      The Dover edition was distributed in England by John

Constable, London, but these copies seem to be unaltered. Some copies were bound in red cloth (spine stamped in black) by Peter Smith (Gloucester, Mass.). These copies do not bear the paper covers.

22. *Best Supernatural Stories of H. P. Lovecraft* (1945)

a.1. BEST SUPERNATURAL / STORIES / OF H. P. LOVECRAFT / EDITED, WITH AN IN-TRODUCTION, BY / August Derleth / [publisher's device] / Cleveland and New York / THE WORLD PUBLISHING COM-PANY [copyright page:] *First printing April 1945*

[1-8]¹⁶ [9]¹² [10]¹⁶ [1-6] 7-307 [308-12]

[1]: half-title; [2]: blank; [3]: title; [4]: copyright page; [5]: contents list; [6]: blank; 7-9: "Something about How-ard Phillips Lovecraft," by Derleth; 10-18: IV; 19-32: PM; 33-52: RW; 53-59: O: 60-88: CS; 89-97: MEZ; 98-120: HD; 121-29: PH; 130-59: CC; 160-202: DH; 203-11: CA; 212-77: WD; 278-80: TOM; 281-307: TD; [308-12]: blank.

Bound in black cloth; spine stamped in violet; 20.5 × 13.8 cm.; dust jacket design by Leo Manso.

Notes. A Tower Mystery T-338 (see copyright page). Arkham House reprinted this text in its *Dunwich Horror and Others* (I-A-34), adding two novelettes and a new introduction.

a.2. *Second Printing.* Cleveland and New York: World Publishing Co., September 1945.

a.3. *Third Printing.* Cleveland and New York: World Publishing Co., June 1946. Gathered [1-10]¹⁶; pp. [313-20] blank. Spine dark blue; stamped in orange.

a.4. *Fourth Printing.* Cleveland and New York: World Publishing Co., September 1950 (copyright page: "WP9-50" = World Publishing Co., Sept. 1950). Gathered [1-5]¹⁶ [6]¹² [7-10]¹⁶. Bound in black paper; spine stamped in violet. Front cover contains illustration replacing "A TOWER MYS-TERY" on previous printings. Dust jacket not seen.

23. *The Dunwich Horror* (1945)

[rule] / THE / DUNWICH / HORROR / —by— / H. P. LOVECRAFT / [ornament] / [publisher's device] / *Published by* / BARTHOLOMEW HOUSE, Inc. / 205 East 42nd St., New York 17, N. Y. / [rule] [copyright page:] 1945

Perfect-bound: [1-8] 9-186 [187-92]

[1-2]: blank; [3]: half-title; [4]: blank; [5-6]: blurb; [7]: title; [8]: copyright page; 9-65: DH; 66-151: SOOT; 152-86: TD; [187]: blurb: "OUR BOYS need and deserve books. . . . Give them books—give them this book"; [188-90]: advertisements; [191-92]: blank.

Bound in paper; 16.2 × 10.7 cm.

Notes. Bart House Mystery No. 12 (see cover).

24. *The Lurking Fear and Other Stories* (1947)

a. THE / LURKING FEAR / AND OTHER STO-RIES / By / H. P. LOVECRAFT / [pub-lisher's device] / AVON BOOK COMPANY / JOS. MEYERS   E. B. WILLIAMS / 119 West 57th Street, New York 19, N. Y. / [rule] / *Published by special arrangement with* / *ARKHAM HOUSE* / [rectangular border around all the above] [copyright page:] 1947

Perfect-bound: [3-6] 7-223 [224-26]

[3]: title; [4]: copyright page; [5]: contents list; [6]: half-title; 7-32: LF; 33-68: CS; 69-83: NC; 84-100: PM; 101-12: FAJ (as "Arthur Jermyn"); 113-22: U; 123-59: CC; 160-69: MB; 170-80: CA; 181-90: H; 191-223: SH; [224-26]: advertisements.

Bound in paper; 16.2 × 10.7 cm.

Notes. No. 136 of the New Avon Library (see inside covers).

b. *Second Edition.* New York: Avon Book Company, [1958?] [as *Cry Horror! (Original Title: The Lurking Fear and Other Stories)*]. 191[+1] pp. New cover art.

c.   *Canadian Printing.* [Toronto]: Avon Book Company, [1958?].

d.1.   *Third Edition.* London: World Distributors, Ltd., 1959 (as *Cry, Horror!*). Not seen.

d.2.   *Second Printing.* London: World Distributors, Ltd., January 1960. Follows second Avon edition.

25. *Something about Cats and Other Pieces* (1949)

a. H. P. LOVECRAFT / [rule] / SOMETHING ABOUT CATS / AND OTHER PIECES / *Collected by* / AUGUST DERLETH / [publisher's device] / [rule] / 1949 / ARKHAM HOUSE / SAUK CITY, WISCONSIN

[1-10]^{16} [i-v] vi [vii] viii-ix [x] [1-3] 4-18 [19] 20-25 [26] 27-30 [31] 32-45 [46] 47-95 [96] 97-116 [117] 118-47 [148] 149-52 [153] 154-55 [156] 157-59 [160] 161-64 [165] 166-69 [170] 171-74 [175] 176-89 [190-91] 192-217 [218] 219-28 [229] 230-33 [234] 235-46 [247] 248-77 [278] 279-89 [290] 291-303 [304] 305 [306-10]

[i]: half-title; [ii]: blank; [iii]: title; [iv]: copyright page; [v]-vi: contents list; [vii]-ix: "A Prefatory Note" by Derleth; [x]: blank; [1]: part-title; [2]: blank; [3]-18: "Something about Cats" (i.e., "Cats and Dogs"); [19]-25: HMB (as "The Invisible Monster"); [26]-30: FO; [31]-45: HB; [46]-95: LT; [96]-116: EE; [117]-47: "Satan's Servants," by Robert Bloch; [148]-49: "The Despised Pastoral"; 149-50: "Time and Space"; 151-52: "Merlinus Redivivus"; [153]-55: "At the Root"; [156]-59: "The Materialist Today"; [160]-64: "Vermont: A First Impression"; [165]-69: "The Battle That Ended the Century" [with R. H. Barlow]: [170]-[75]: "Notes for *The Shadow over Innsmouth*"; 176-84: "Discarded Draught of 'The Shadow over Innsmouth' "; 184-89: "Notes for *At the Mountains of Madness*"; [190]: "Notes for *The Shadow out of Time*"; [191]: "Phaeton"; [191]-92: "August"; 192-93: "Death" [by Jonathan E. Hoag; see I-E-i-3]; 193: "To the American Flag"; 194-95: "To a Youth"; 195-96: "My Favourite Character"; 197: "To Templeton and Mount Monadnock"; 198-99: "The House"; 199-201: "The City"; 201-11: "The Poe-et's Nightmare"; 211-12: "Sir Thomas Tryout";

213-14: "Lament for the Vanished Spider"; 215-17: "Regnar Lodbrug's Epicedium"; [218]-28: "A Memoir of Lovecraft," by Rheinhart Kleiner; [229]-33: "Howard Phillips Lovecraft," by Samuel Loveman; [234]-46: "Lovecraft as I knew Him" (i.e., "Howard Phillips Lovecraft as His Wife Remembers Him"), by Sonia H. Davis; [247]-77: "Addenda to 'H. P. L.: A Memoir,' " by August Derleth; [278]-89: "The Man Who Was Lovecraft," by E. Hoffmann Price; [290]-303: "A Literary Copernicus," by Fritz Leiber, Jr.; [304]-05: "Providence: Two Gentlemen Meet at Midnight" [poem], by August Derleth; [306]: "HPL" [poem], by Vincent Starrett; [307]: colophon; [308-10]: blank.

Bound in black cloth; spine stamped in gold; 19.4 × 13.4 cm.; dust jacket art by Ronald Clyne.

Notes. Illustrations include photographs of Lovecraft, Sonia Davis, Adolphe de Castro, and facsimiles of illustrations and notes in Lovecraft's hand; 2,995 copies.

b.1. *Second Edition.* Freeport, N.Y.: Books for Libraries Press, 1971. Facsimile reprint of the above with the exclusion of pp. [307-10]. Bound in blue cloth, spine stamped in gold within a red rectangle. No dust jacket.

b.1(a). *Variants.* One copy seen contains a radically different cloth binding, of a grey blue with spine stamped in gold. Place of publication on title page is "Plainview, New York." Other copies with different colored bindings have been reported.

26. *The Haunter of the Dark and Other Tales of Horror* (1951)
  a.1. THE HAUNTER OF / THE DARK / *And Other Tales of Horror* / by / H. P. LOVECRAFT / Edited, and with an Introduction / by / AUGUST DERLETH / LONDON / VICTOR GOLLANCZ LTD / 1951

[A]16 B-H16 I8 K16 [1-4] 5-9 [10] 11-17 [18] 19-87 [88] 89-135 [136] 137-207 [208] 209-39 [240] 241-303 [304]
[1]: half-title; [2]: blank; [3]: title; [4]: copyright page; 5-8: "An Introduction to H. P. Lovecraft," by Derleth; 9: contents list; [10]: blank; 11-17: O; [18]: blank; 19-40: RW; 41-54: PM; 55-87: CC; [88]: blank; 89-135: DH; [136]: blank;

137-207: WD; [208]: blank; 209-39: CS; [240]: blank; 241-66: HD; 267-94: TD; 295-303: MEZ; [304]: blank.

Bound in orange cloth; spine stamped in black; 18.9 × 12.6 cm.; dust jacket not seen.

a.2. *Second Printing.* London: Victor Gollancz, 1966. Bound in maroon cloth, spine stamped in gold. Dust jacket is the usual yellow Gollancz jacket.

a.3. *Third Printing.* Not seen. Dated 1969.

a.4. *Fourth Printing.* Not seen. Dated May 1971.

a.5. *Fifth Printing.* London: Victor Gollancz, 1977. Gathered [A]8 B-E16 F12 G-K16. Bound in black cloth; spine stamped in gold. Dust jacket is black with white and yellow lettering.

b.1. *Second Edition.* St. Albans: Panther Books, February 1963. 255[+1] pp. Bound in paper.

b.2. *Second Printing.* St. Albans: Panther Books, 1965. Cover art changed.

b.3. *Third Printing.* St. Albans: Panther Books, 1970. Cover art changed.

b.4. *Fourth Printing.* St. Albans: Panther Books, 1972. New wraparound cover art.

b.5. *Fifth Printing.* St. Albans: Panther Books, 1974.

27. *The Case of Charles Dexter Ward* (1951)

a. THE CASE OF / CHARLES DEXTER WARD / *A Novel* / by / H. P. LOVECRAFT / LONDON / VICTOR GOLLANCZ LTD / 1951

[A]16 B-E16 [1-4] 5 [6] 7-160

[1]: half-title; [2]: quotations from reviews of I-A-26; [3]: title; [4]: copyright page; 5: contents list; [6]: quotation from Borrellus; 7-160: CDW.

Bound in red cloth; spine stamped in black; 19 × 13 cm.; dust jacket yellow with red and black lettering.

b.1. *Second Edition.* St. Albans: Panther Books, May 1963. 126[+2] pp. Bound in paper; cover art by R. Reynolds.

b.2. *Second Printing* (?). Not identified as such: copyright page lists only date of 1963. Text identical to above, but cover

art somewhat different. Third printing (below) lists a
second printing dating to 1969; either this is the second
printing or a variant of the first.

b.3. *Third Printing.* St. Albans: Panther Books, 1970. New cover
art.

b.4. *Fourth Printing.* St. Albans: Panther Books, 1973. New
cover art.

c.1. *Third Edition.* New York: Belmont Books, February 1965.
141[+3] pp. Bound in paper.

c.2. *Second Printing.* New York: Belmont Books, 1969. New
cover art.

d.1. *Fourth Edition.* New York: Beagle Books, August 1971.
127[+1] pp. Bound in paper. Volume 9 of the Arkham
Edition of H. P. Lovecraft (see cover).

d.2. *Second Printing.* New York: Ballantine Books, August 1976.
New cover art (by Murray Tinkelman); inside front and
back covers contain black-and-white illustrations by
Tinkelman. Bears the imprint of Ballantine Books; when
Random House (controlling both Beagle and Ballantine)
dissolved Beagle Books, it was declared that the first
Beagle printing was the first Ballantine printing.

28. *The Lovecraft Collectors Library* (1952-55)

a. All volumes were mimeographed in an edition of 75
numbered copies. The texts are reproduced from typewritten
copy with both margins justified. All volumes are with paper
covers, 28 × 21.6 cm.

Volume I:
SELECTED ESSAYS / HOWARD PHILLIPS
LOVECRAFT / VOLUME ONE / THE
LOVECRAFT COLLECTORS LIBRARY / EDITED
BY GEORGE WETZEL / [publisher's device] 1952 /
SSR PUBLICATIONS / North Tonawanda   New
York

Perfect-bound: [a-b] [i] ii-iii [4] 5-26 [27-28]
[a]: half-title and copy number; [b]: blank; [i]: title; ii:
acknowledgments and colophon; iii: contents list; [4]: blank; 5-

10: PG; 11-18: "Idealism and Materialism—A Reflection"; 19-22: "A Confession of Unfaith"; 23-26: "Nietscheism [sic] and Realism"; [27-28]: blank.

Notes. Enclosed was a flyer advertising the other volumes in the series.

Volume II:

SELECTED ESSAYS / HOWARD PHILLIPS LOVECRAFT / VOLUME TWO / THE LOVECRAFT COLLECTORS LIBRARY / EDITED BY GEORGE WETZEL / [publisher's device] 1953 / SSR PUBLICATIONS / North Tonawanda   New York

Perfect-bound: [a-b] [i] ii-iii [4] 5-23 [24-28]

[a]: half-title and copy number; [b]: blank; [i]: title; ii: acknowledgments and colophon; iii: contents list; [4]: blank; 4-8: S; 9-10: "A Descent to Avernus"; 11-12: "The Brief Autobiography of an Inconsequential Scribbler"; 13: "Anglo-Saxondom"; 15-16: "Revolutionary Mythology"; 17-18: "The Trip of Theobald"; 19-[25]: A; [26-28]: blank.

Volume III:

SELECTED POETRY / HOWARD PHILLIPS LOVECRAFT / VOLUME THREE / THE LOVECRAFT COLLECTORS LIBRARY / EDITED BY GEORGE WETZEL / [publisher's device] 1953 / SSR PUBLICATIONS / North Tonawanda   New York

Perfect-bound: [a-d] [i] ii-iii [4] 5-28 [29-30]

[a]: letter by W. Paul Ganley, 30 January 1954; [b]: blank; [c]: half-title and copy number; [d]: blank; [i]: title; ii: acknowledgments and colophon; iii: contents list; [4]: blank; 5-6: "Bells"; 7-8: "The Voice"; 9-10: "On the Death of a Rhyming Critic"; 11: "Monos: An Ode"; 12: "Inspiration"; 13-17: "Hylas and Myrrha, a Tale"; 17: "Ambition"; 18-20: "The Bookstall"; 20: "On Receiving a Picture of Swans"; 21-22: "To Edward John Moreton Drax Plunkett, Eighteenth Baron Dunsany"; 23: "To Mr. Lockhart, on His Poetry"; 24-25: "Autumn"; 26: "Iterum Conjunctae"; 26-27: [Editor's note on Lovecraft's "Archibald

Maynwaring" pseudonym]; 27: "To the Eighth of November";
28: "The Pensive Swain"; [29-30]: blank.

Volume IV:

SELECTED POETRY / HOWARD PHILLIPS
LOVECRAFT / VOLUME IV / THE LOVECRAFT
COLLECTORS LIBRARY / EDITED BY GEORGE
WETZEL / [rule] / SSR [acknowledgments page:]
March, 1955

Perfect-bound: [a-b] [i] ii [iii] [4] 5-32 [33-34]

[a]: half-title and copy number; [b]: blank; [i]: title; ii:
acknowledgments; [iii]: contents list; [4]: blank; 5-6: "A Cycle of
Verse" (includes "Oceanus," p. 5; "Clouds," p. 5; "Mother
Earth," p. 6); 7-9: "Ver Rusticum"; 10: "Earth and Sky"; 11:
"Prologue" [to "Fragments from an Hour of Inspiration" by
Jonathan E. Hoag]; 11-12: "Solstice"; 12: "The Garden" (i.e., "A
Garden"); 13-15: "Nathicana"; 15: "The Poet of Passion"; 15-17:
"Lines for Poet's Night at the Scribblers' Club"; 18: "Cindy:
Scrub Lady in a State Street Skyscraper"; 18-19: "The Dead
Bookworm"; 20-21: "Ave atque Vale"; 22-23: "The Dream"; 24-
25: "Ye Ballade of Patrick von Flynn"; 26: "Pacifist War Song—
1917"; 27: "The Nymph's Reply to the Modern Business Man";
27-28: "Grace" (with introductory paragraph entitled "Ward
Phillips Replies"); 28-30: "To Greece, 1917"; 30-32: "Lines on
the 25th Anniversary of the Providence Evening News, 1892-
1917"; 32: "Fact and Fancy"; [33-34]: blank.

Volume V:

THE AMATEUR JOURNALIST / HOWARD
PHILLIPS LOVECRAFT / VOLUME FIVE / THE
LOVECRAFT COLLECTORS LIBRARY / EDITED
BY GEORGE WETZEL / [rule] / SSR / 1955

Perfect-bound: [a-b] [i] ii-iii [4] 5-17 [18] 19-21 [22] 23-33
[34-36]

[a]: half-title and copy number; [b]: blank; [i]: title; ii:
acknowledgments; iii: contents list; [4]: blank; 5-6: "The Simple
Spelling Mania"; 7-10: "President's Message" (from *The National
Amateur*, July 1923); 11-12: "Amateur Criticism"; 13-14: "The
Symphonic Ideal"; 15-17: "The Professional Incubus"; [18]:
blank; 19-20: "A Reply to *The Lingerer*"; 21: "Concerning

'Persia—in Europe' "; [22]: blank; 23-24: "*Les Mouches
Fantastiques*"; 25-33: "Looking Backward" (abridged); [34-36]:
blank.

b. *Second Edition.* All seven volumes reprinted in facsimile (in
one volume) by The Strange Co., Madison, Wis., in 1979.
Additional material by R. Alain Everts and Robert E.
Briney. One hundred fifty numbered copies.

For Volumes VI and VII, see III-B-35, C-27.

29. *The Curse of Yig* (1953)

ZEALIA B. BISHOP / [rule] / THE CURSE / OF /
YIG / [publisher's device] / ARKHAM HOUSE
SAUK CITY · WISCONSIN / 1953

[1-16]¹⁶ [i-vi] [1-2] 3-136 [137-38] 139-51 [152] 153-75
[176-78]

[i]: half-title; [ii]: blank; [iii]: title; [iv]: copyright page; [v]:
contents list; [vi]: blank; [1]: part-title; [2]: blank; 3-20: CY; 21-
60: MC; 61-136: Mo; [137]: half-title: "Two Profiles"; [138]:
blank; 139-51: "H. P. Lovecraft: A Pupil's View"; [152]: blank;
153-75: "A Wisconsin Balzac: A Profile of August Derleth";
[176]: blank; [177]: colophon; [178]: blank.

Bound in black cloth; spine stamped in gold; 19.4 × 13.6 cm.;
dust jacket art by Ronald Clyne.

Notes. The three fiction tales were all revised (or ghost-
written) by Lovecraft; the two profiles were of course by
Bishop, although perhaps touched up by Derleth. Illustrations
include photographs of Lovecraft and Derleth and a
reproduction of Virgil Finlay's portrait of Lovecraft; 1,217
copies.

30. *The Challenge from Beyond* (1954)

a. THE / CHALLENGE FROM / BEYOND / by /
C. L. Moore, A. Merritt, H. P. Lovecraft, Robert
E. Howard, / and Frank Belknap Long, Jr. /
FAPA [copyright page:] February 1954

Perfect-bound: [i-ii] [1] 2-11 leaves

[i]: title; [ii]: copyright page; [1]-11: CB; [1]-2: Moore's
portion; 2-4: Merritt's portion; 4-8: Lovecraft's portion; 8-

10: Howard's portion; 10-11: Long's portion and key to each author's portions.

28 × 21.6 cm.; no covers; stapled at left margin.

Notes. Printed only on rectos (13 leaves total). Published by William H. Evans under the imprint of the Pennsylvania Dutch Cheese Press [Washington, D.C.] for the Fantasy Amateur Press Association (F.A.P.A.); "A Weltschmerz Publication" (see copyright page).

b. *Second Edition.* West Warwick, R.I.: Necronomicon Press, 1978 (with title: *The Illustrated Challenge from Beyond*). [28] pp. Illustrations by David Ireland. Green paper covers.

31. *The Dream Quest of Unknown Kadath* (1955)
THE DREAM QUEST OF UNKNOWN KADATH [vertically from bottom to top at left margin] / *by* / *HOWARD PHILLIPS LOVECRAFT* / INTRODUCTION [vertically from top to bottom at right margin] / *by* / *GEORGE T. WETZEL* / 1955 / SHROUD, publishers / Buffalo [copyright page:] FIRST EDITION / First printing, November 1955

Perfect-bound: [1-9] 10-107 [108-12]

[1-2]: blank; [3]: title; [4]: copyright page; [5-6]: "Introduction" by Wetzel; [7]: part-title; [8]: blank; [9]-107: DQ; [108]: blank; [109]: colophon; [110-12]: blank.

Bound in paper; 21 × 14 cm.

Notes. Fifteen hundred numbered copies. The text was reproduced from the pages of the *Arkham Sampler* serialization (I-B-i-16), hence retains the division of the novel into four parts. The paper covers are orange and bear the title plus a small illustration on the front; back is blank. The spine is backed with tape. This state has a dust jacket in white with an illustration in black and red on the front, a list of other books from Shroud on the back, a blurb on the inside front flap, and a list of Lovecraft-related books on the inside back flap.

Of the 1,500 copies, 50 (or more) were bound in black cloth, spine stamped in gold; there seems to be no numerical sequence to these copies, as copy numbers range from 51 to 644. On the colophon page has been glued a notice announcing the special hard-cover state, signed in red ink by Kenneth J. Krueger, editor of Shroud. The dust jacket is entirely different from that of the paperbound state: it is tinted yellow, bears a pen-and-ink illustration on the front along with the blurb that was printed on the inside front flap of the paperbound dust jacket, while on the back is an advertisement (with pen-and-ink illustration) for *The Moon Maker* by Arthur Train and Robert W. Wood. The inside front flap announces the "Limited Collector's Edition"; the inside back flap contains more advertisements for books from Shroud.

Both states of the book seem to have innumerable variants. Some paperbound copies have yellow mimeographed paper covers with the advertisement for *The Moon Maker* on the back. The color of the tape backing of the paperbound state is either orange or black or brown, or is omitted altogether. Some dust jackets for the paperbound state bear a new address (the address listed on the hardcover dust jacket) added by a rubber stamp. Some paperbound copies bear the yellow hardcover dust jacket. Apparently many copies were lost or destroyed when Krueger moved his publishing firm to California.

In 1972 Gerry de la Ree (Saddle River, N.J.) bound 12 numbered copies of the paperbound state in black cloth stamped in gold, and added a label declaring his state on the colophon page.

32. *The Shuttered Room and Other Pieces* (1959)

THE SHUTTERED ROOM / AND OTHER PIECES / *by* / H. P. LOVECRAFT / *& Divers Hands* / *Compiled by* AUGUST DERLETH / [publisher's device] / [rule] / ARKHAM HOUSE: *Publishers*   *Sauk City, Wisconsin* / 1959

[1-10]¹⁶ [i-ix] x [xi-xiii] xiv [1-3] 4-38 [39] 40-43 [44] 45-53 [54] 55-75 [76] 77-84 [85] 86-96 [97] 98-123 [124] 125-40 [141] 142-70 [171] 172-77 [178] 179-90 [191] 192-201 [202] 203-05 [206] 207-11 [212] 213-49 [250] 251-67 [268] 269-77 [278] 279-86 [287] 288-90 [291] 292-96 [297] 298-306 [307] 308-13 [314]

[i]: half-title; [ii]: blank; [iii]: title; [iv]: copyright page; [v]: list of books by Lovecraft; [vi]: editor's acknowledgments; [vii]: dedication; [viii]: blank; [ix]-x: contents list; [xi]: list of

illustrations; [xii]: blank; [xiii]-xiv: "Foreword" by Derleth; [1]:
part-title; [2]: blank; [3]-28: "The Shuttered Room," by [August
Derleth] (see I-E-i-18); [39]-43: "The Fisherman of Falcon
Point," by [August Derleth]; [44]-53: "Juvenilia and Early Tales"
([44]: editor's note; 45-46: "The Little Glass Bottle"; 46-47:
"The Secret Cave: or John Lees Adventure"; 48-52: "The
Mystery of the Grave-Yard: or 'A Dead Man's Revenge': A
Detective Story"; 52-53: "The Mysterious Ship"); [54]-63: A;
63-70: PG; 70-75: S; [76]-84: "Old Bugs"; [85]-96: "Idealism and
Materialism—A Reflection"; [97]-123: *The Commonplace Book*
(annotated by August Derleth and Donald Wandrei); [124]-40:
"Lovecraft in Providence," by Donald Wandrei; [141]-70:
"Lovecraft as Mentor," by August Derleth; [171]-77: "Out of
the Ivory Tower," by Robert Bloch; [178]-90: "Three Hours
with H. P. Lovecraft," by Dorothy C. Walter; [191]-201:
"Memories of a Friendship," by Alfred Galpin; [202]-03:
"Homage to H. P. Lovecraft" [poem], by Felix Stefanile; 204:
"H. P. L." [poem], by Clark Ashton Smith; 204: "Lines to H. P.
Lovecraft" [poem], by Joseph Payne Brennan; 205: "Revenants:
for Howard Phillips Lovecraft" [poem], by August Derleth;
[206]-11: "The Barlow Tributes" [poems by R. H. Barlow];
[212]-49: "H. P. Lovecraft: The Books," by Lin Carter; [250]-67:
"H. P. Lovecraft: The Gods," by Lin Carter; [268]-77:
"Addendum: Some Observations on the Carter Glossary," by
T. G. L. Cockcroft; [278]-86: "Notes on the Cthulhu Mythos,"
by George T. Wetzel; [287]-90: "Lovecraft's First Book," by
William L. Crawford; [291]-96: D; [297]-306: SHH; [307]-13: O;
[314]: colophon.

Bound in black cloth; spine stamped in gold; 19.4 × 13.3 cm.;
dust jacket illustration by Richard Taylor.

Notes. Interior illustrations include photographs of Lovecraft
and his family, his homes, some sites in Providence that
inspired his tales, and reproductions of illustrations by Frank
Utpatel from I-A-11; 2,527 copies.

33. *Dreams and Fancies* (1962)
Dreams / and / Fancies / by / H. P. LOVECRAFT /
[publisher's device] / [rule] / Arkham House:
Publishers   1962   Sauk City, Wisconsin

[1-6]¹⁶ [i-vii] viii-x [1-3] 4-56 [57-59] 60 [61] 62-68 [69] 70-76 [77] 78-84 [85] 86-88 [89] 90-93 [94] 95-96 [97] 98-174 [175-78]

[i]: half-title; [ii]: list of books by Lovecraft; [iii]: title; [iv]: copyright page; [v]: contents list; [vi]: blank; [vii]-x: "Introduction," by August Derleth; [1]: part-title; [2]: blank; [3]-56: excerpts of letters by Lovecraft; 56: "Night-Gaunts"; [57]: half-title: "Stories"; [58]: blank; [59]-60: M; [61]-68: SRC; [69]-76: C; [77]-84: DS; [85]-88: N; [89]-93: EC; [94]-96: TM; [97]-174: SOOT; [175]: colophon; [176-78]: blank.

Bound in black cloth; spine stamped in gold; 19.5 × 13.5 cm.; dust jacket art by Richard Taylor.

Notes. Two thousand thirty copies.

34. *The Dunwich Horror and Others* (1963)

a.1. THE DUNWICH HORROR / AND OTHERS / THE BEST SUPERNATURAL / STORIES / OF H. P. LOVECRAFT / Selected and with an Introduction by August Derleth / [publisher's device] / ARKHAM HOUSE: Publishers / Sauk City, Wisconsin / 1963

[1-14]¹⁶ [i-iv] v [vi-viii] ix-xx [9] 10-431 [432-36]

[i]: half-title; [ii]: blank; [iii]: title; [iv]: copyright page; v: contents list; [vi]: blank; [vii]: part-title; [viii]: blank; ix-xx: "H. P. Lovecraft and His Work," by Derleth; [9]: blank; 10-18: IV; 19-32: PM; 33-52: RW; 53-59: O; 60-88: CS; 89-97: MEZ; 98-120: HD; 121-29: PH; 130-59: CC; 160-202: DH; 203-11: CA; 212-77: WD; 278-80: TOM; 281-307: TD; 308-69: SOI; 370-431: SOOT; [432]: colophon; [433-36]: blank.

Bound in black cloth; spine stamped in gold; 20.5 × 14.1 cm.; dust jacket art by Lee Brown Coye.

Notes. The volume has used the text of the World *Best Supernatural Stories* (I-A-22) for pp. 10-307, hence the odd pagination; 3,000 copies.

a.2. *Second Printing.* Sauk City, Wis.: Arkham House, [October 1966]; 3,000 copies.

a.3. *Third Printing.* Sauk City, Wis.: Arkham House, [August 1970]; 3,000 copies.

a.4. *Fourth Printing.* Sauk City, Wis.: Arkham House, December 1973; 5,000 copies.

35. *Collected Poems* (1963)

a. COLLECTED POEMS / H. P. LOVECRAFT / Illustrations by Frank Utpatel / [publisher's device] / ARKHAM HOUSE: Publishers   Sauk City, Wisconsin / 1963

[1-2]¹⁶ [3]⁵ [4-5]¹⁶ [i-x] [1-7] 8-57 [58-61] 62-83 [84] 85-92 [93-95] 96-100 [101] 102-03 [104] 105-06 [107-09] 110-11 [112] 113 [114] 115 [116] 117 [118] 119-22 [123] 124-27 [128] 129-30 [131] 132-34 [135-38]

[i]: half-title; [ii]: blank; [iii]: title; [iv]: copyright page; [v-vii]: contents list; [viii]: blank; [ix]: list of illustrations; [x]: frontispiece; [1]: part-title; [2]: blank; [3]: "Foreword," by August Derleth; [4]: blank; [5]: half-title: "Early Poems"; [6]: blank; [7]-8: "Providence" (three stanzas omitted); 8-10: "On a Grecian Colonnade in a Park"; 10-20: "Old Christmas"; 20-25: "New-England Fallen"; 26-27: "On a New-England Village Seen by Moonlight"; 27-28: "Astrophobos"; 28-29: "Sunset"; 29-30: "To Pan"; 30-31: "A Summer Sunset and Evening"; 31-32: "To Mistress Sophia Simple, Queen of the Cinema"; 32-34: "A Year Off"; 34-35: "Sir Thomas Tryout"; 36: "Phaeton"; 36-37: "August"; 37-38: "Death" [by Jonathan E. Hoag; see I-E-i-3]; 38: "To the American Flag"; 39-40: "To a Youth"; 40-41: "My Favourite Character"; 41-42: "To Templeton and Mount Monadnock; 42-51: "The Poe-et's Nightmare: A Fable"; 51-53: "Lament for the Vanished Spider"; 53-56: "Regnar Lodbrug's Epicedium"; 56: "Little Sam Perkins"; 56-57: "Drinking Song from The Tomb" [i.e., "Gaudeamus"]; [58]: blank; [59]: half-title: "The Ancient Track"; [60]: blank; [61]-62: "The Ancient Track"; 62-65: "The Eidolon"; 65-67: "The Nightmare Lake"; 68-70: "The Outpost"; 70-71: "The Rutted Road"; 71-72: "The Wood"; 72-73: "The House"; 74-75: "The City"; 75-76: "Hallowe'en in a Suburb"; 77-79: "Primavera"; 79-80: "October" [2]; 81-82: "To a Dreamer"; 82-83: "Despair"; 83, 85-86: "Nemesis"; [84]: illustration; 87: "Yule Horror"; 87-88: "To Mr. Finlay . . ."; 88: "Where

Once Poe Walked" (i.e., "In a Sequestered Churchyard Where Once Poe Walked"); 88: "Christmas Greeting to Mrs. Phillips Gamwell—1925"; 89-90: "Brick Row" (i.e., "The East India Brick Row"); 91: "The Messenger"; 92: "To Klarkash-Ton, Lord of Averoigne" (i.e., "To Clark Ashton Smith, Esq. . . ."); [93]: half-title to "Psychopompos"; [94]: blank; [95]-100, 102-03, 105-06: "Psychopompos"; [101, 104]: illustrations; [107]: half-title to *Fungi from Yuggoth*; [108]: blank; [109]-11, 113, 115, 117, 119-22, 124-27, 129-30, 132-34: *Fungi from Yuggoth*; [112, 114, 116, 118, 123, 128, 131]: illustrations; [135]: blank; [136]: colophon; [137-38]: blank.

Bound in black cloth; spine stamped in gold; 19.4 × 13.2 cm.; dust jacket art by Frank Utpatel.

Notes. Other illustrations appear on pp. 11, 24, 32, 66, 68, 81, and 91; 2,013 copies.

b. *Second Edition.* New York: Ballantine Books, February 1971; as *Fungi from Yuggoth and Other Poems (Formerly Titled* Collected Poems). xvi[+ii], 138[+4] pp. Text as above with the exclusion of "To the American Flag." Cover art by Gervasio Gallardo.

36. *Autobiography: Some Notes on a Nonentity* (1963)
AUTOBIOGRAPHY: / SOME NOTES ON A NONENTITY / by H. P. LOVECRAFT / *Annotated by August Derleth* / [publisher's device] / Printed for / Arkham House: Publishers——Sauk City, Wisconsin / 1963 / by Villiers Publications, Ltd., London, N.W.5, England

[1]¹⁰ [1-4] 5-17 [18-20]

[1]: title; [2]: copyright page; [3]: "Editor's Note" [by Derleth]; [4]: blank; 5-17: text; [18-20]: blank.

Pamphlet; 18.5 × 12.7 cm.; white paper covers.

Notes. About 500 copies. The annotations by Derleth are included in italics and within parentheses throughout the text.

37. *The Dunwich Horror and Others* (1963)

a. THE DUNWICH HORROR / AND
OTHERS / H. P. LOVECRAFT / LANCER
BOOKS· NEW YORK [copyright page:] 1963

Perfect-bound: [1-6] 7-158 [159-60]

[1]: blurb; [2]: publisher's note; [3]: title; [4]: copyright
page; [5]: contents list; [6]: blank; 7-18: "H. P. Lovecraft and
His Work," by August Derleth; 19-27: IV; 28-40: PM; 41-59:
RW; 60-68: MEZ; 69-91: HD; 92-133: DH; 134-58: TD;
[159-60]: advertisements.

Bound in paper; 18.1 × 10.5 cm.

Notes. The second edition (see I-37-b.1) states that the
book was issued in December 1963.

b.1. *Second Edition.* New York: Lancer Books, March 1969.
191[+1] pp. Reset. New cover art.

b.2. *Second Printing.* Not identified as such, but contains a
different cover from both the previous entries. No date
for this printing, but it probably dates to 1971.

c. *Third Edition.* New York: Jove Publications, Inc. (Harcourt
Brace Jovanovich), April 1978, under the imprint of
Jove/HBJ. Reset. Cover art by Rowena Morrell.

38. *The Colour out of Space* (1964)

a.1. THE COLOUR / OUT OF SPACE / and
others / H. P. LOVECRAFT / LANCER
BOOKS · NEW YORK [copyright page:] 1964

Perfect-bound: [1-6] 7-222 [223-24]

[1]: blurb; [2]: publisher's note; [3]: title; [4]: copyright
page; [5]: contents list; [6]: blank; 7-35: CS; 36-44: PH; 45-
75: CC; 76-84: CA; 85-151: WD; 152-55: TOM; 156-222:
SOOT; [223-24]: advertisements.

Bound in paper; 17.8 × 10.7 cm.

Notes. The third printing (see following) states that the
book was issued in June 1964.

a.2. *Second Printing.* New York: Lancer Books, 1967 (June 1967
according to third printing). New cover art.

a.3. *Third Printing*. New York: Lancer Books, March 1969. Cover lettering altered.

a.4. *Fourth Printing*. Not identified as such: copyright page bears only the date of 1969. Like I-37-b-2, this probably dates to 1971. New wraparound cover art.

b. *Second Edition*. New York: Zebra Books, October 1975.

c.1. *Third Edition*. New York: Jove Publications, Inc. (Harcourt Brace Jovanovich), May 1978, under the imprint of Jove/HBJ. Divergences: [1]: new blurb; [6]: blurb (quotation from SOOT); 156-219: SOOT; [220]: blank; [221-23]: advertisements; [224]: blank. Front and back cover by Rowena Morrell. Cover and title page announce new preface by Frank Belknap Long, but it does not appear in the book.

c.2. *Second Printing*. New York: Jove Publications, August 1978. Here the preface by Long has been inserted. Pagination is now rather confused: [1-4] as above; [5]: contents list; vi-x [sic]: preface; 7-[220] as above; [221-24] eliminated. Blurb on p. [6] now added to p. [2].

39. *At the Mountains of Madness and Other Novels* (1964)
   a. *American Edition*
   a.1 AT THE MOUNTAINS / OF MADNESS / AND OTHER NOVELS / by H. P. LOVECRAFT / Selected and with an Introduction by August Derleth / [publisher's device] / ARKHAM HOUSE: Publishers / Sauk City, Wisconsin / 1964

   [1-14]¹⁶ [i-viii] ix-xi [xii] 1-432 [433-36]
   [i]: half-title; [ii]: blank; [iii]: title; [iv]: copyright page; [v]: contents list; [vi]: blank; [vii]: part-title; [viii]: blank; ix-xi: "H. P. Lovecraft's Novels" by Derleth; [xii]: blank; 1-100: ATMOM; 101-221: CDW; 222-47: SH; 248-83: DWH; 284-89: SRC; 290-385: DQ: 386-97: SK; 398-432: TGSK; [433]: blank; [434]: colophon; [435-36]: blank.
   Bound in black cloth; spine stamped in gold; 20.6 × 13.9 cm.; green dust jacket (art by Lee Brown Coye).
   Notes. Three thousand copies.

a.2. *Second Printing*. Sauk City, Wis.: Arkham House, July 1968. Orange red dust jacket (identical art); 3,000 copies.

a.3. *Third Printing*. Sauk City, Wis.: Arkham House, June 1971. Orange red dust jacket (identical art); 3,000 copies.

a.4. *Fourth Printing*. Sauk City, Wis.: Arkham House, July 1975. Green dust jacket (identical art); 4,000 copies.

b. *British Sub-Edition*

b.1. London: Victor Gollancz, 1966. Bound in maroon cloth; spine stamped in gold. Dust jacket is usual yellow Gollancz jacket with black and violet lettering.

b.2. *Second Printing*. Not seen. Dated 1971.

40. *The Lurking Fear and Other Stories* (1964)

a.1. H. P. LOVECRAFT / THE LURKING / FEAR / AND OTHER STORIES / [publisher's device] / A PANTHER BOOK [copyright page:] St Albans . . . 1964

> Perfect-bound: [1-6] 7-208
> [1]: blurb; [2]: list of other books by Lovecraft; [3]: title; [4]: copyright page; [5]: contents list; [5]: copyright, acknowledgments; 7-23: LF; 23-45: SH; 45-51: IV; 51-59: FAJ (as "Arthur Jermyn"); 59-65: CA; 66-72: MB; 72-82: NC; 82-88: U; 88-94: PH; 94-97: TOM; 97-103: H; 103-55: SOI; 152-208: SOOT.
> Bound in paper; 17.6 × 11.1 cm.

a.2. *Second Printing*. St. Albans: Panther Books, 1970. New cover art by Michael McInnerney.

a.3. *Third Printing*. St. Albans: Panther Books, 1974. New cover art.

41. *Selected Letters I* (1965)

a.1. H. P. LOVECRAFT / SELECTED LETTERS / 1911-1924 / Edited by August Derleth and Donald Wandrei / [publisher's device] / ARKHAM HOUSE: Publishers / Sauk City, Wisconsin / 1965

[1-10]¹⁶ [11]⁶ [12-13]¹⁶ [i-iv] v-xviii [xix-xx] xxi-xxix
[xxx] [1-2] 3-362 [363-66]

[i]: half-title; [ii]: list of books by Lovecraft; [iii]: title;
[iv]: copyright page; v-xviii: contents list; [xix]: list of
illustrations; [xx]: blank; xxi-xxix: "Preface" by Derleth
and Wandrei; [xxx]: blank; [1]: part-title; [2]: blank; 3-362:
letters (Nos. 1-178); [363]: colophon; [364-66]: blank.

Bound in black cloth; spine stamped in gold; 20.7 × 14.1
cm.; dust jacket (uniform save in color for all five volumes
of the letters) by Ronald Rich, Virgil Finlay, and Gary
Gore; here tinted blue grey.

Notes. Illustrations include photographs of Lovecraft,
Alfred Galpin, Rheinhart Kleiner, Sonia H. Greene
(Davis), and facsimiles of Lovecraft A.Ls. Kleiner's first
name is throughout misspelled as "Reinhardt"; 2,504
copies.

a.2. *Second Printing.* Sauk City, Wis.: Arkham House, [1974?];
3,000 copies.

42. *Dagon and Other Macabre Tales* (1965)

a. *American Edition*

a.1. DAGON AND OTHER / MACABRE TALES /
by H. P. Lovecraft / Selected and with an
Introduction by August Derleth / [publisher's
device] / ARKHAM HOUSE: Publishers / Sauk
City, Wisconsin / 1965

[1-7]¹⁶ [8]⁵[9-14]¹⁶ [i-iv] v-ix [x] [1-2] 3-344 [345-46]
347-413 [414]

[i]: half-title; [ii]: blank; [iii]: title; [iv]: copyright page; v-
vi: contents list; vii-ix: "Introduction" by Derleth; [x]:
blank; [1]: part-title; [2]: blank; 3-8: D; 9-18: T; 19-22: P;
22-33: BWS; 34-40: DS; 41-46: WS; 47-55: FAJ (as
"Arthur Jermyn");56-59: CU; 60-65: C; 66-72: FB; 73-85:
Te; 86-90: Tr; 91-98: MB; 99-110: NC; 111-15: OG; 116-
22: QI; 123-51: HWR; 152-59: H; 160-66: Hy; 167-86: LF;
187-95: F; 196-203: U; 204-29: UP; 230-39: He; 240-59:
HRH; 260-68: SHH; 269-96: IWE; 297-301: EC; 302-08:
BC; 308-16: A; 316-22: PG; 322-27: S; 327-34: TJR; 335-
36: Az; 336-39: De; 340-42: B; 342-44: TM; [345]: half-

title to SHiL; [346]: blank; 347-413: SHiL; [414]: colophon.
Bound in black cloth; spine stamped in gold; 20.6 × 14.1
cm.; dust jacket art by Lee Brown Coye.
Notes. 3,500 copies.

a.2. *Second Printing*. Sauk City, Wis.: Arkham House, [1969];
3,000 copies.

a.3. *Third Printing*. Sauk City, Wis.: Arkham House, [1971].
Not seen.

a.4. *Fourth Printing*. Sauk City, Wis.: Arkham House, November
1975; 4,000 copies.

b. *British Sub-Edition*. London: Victor Gollancz, 1967. Bound
in violet cloth; spine stamped in gold; dust wrapper is the
usual yellow Gollancz jacket with violet and black lettering.

43. *The Dark Brotherhood and Other Pieces* (1966)
The Dark Brotherhood | *and Other Pieces* | *by* | H. P.
LOVECRAFT | & DIVERS HANDS | [publisher's
device] | ARKHAM HOUSE: Publishers   Sauk
City, Wisconsin | 1966

[1-2]^{16} [3]^{22} [4-10]^{16} [i-v] vi [vi-ix] x [1-3] 4-29 [30] 31-63 [64]
65-81 [82] 83-87 [88] 89-90 [91] 92-96 [97] 98-133 [134] 135-52
[153] 154-63 [164] 165-78 [179] 180-97 [198] 199-241 [242]
243-45 [246] 247-61 [262] 263-67 [268] 269-301 [302] 303-32
[322]

[i]: half-title; [ii]: blank; [iii]: title; [iv]: copyright page; [v]-vi:
contents list; [vii]: list of illustrations; [viii]: blank; [ix]-x:
"Introduction," by August Derleth; [1]: part-title; [2]: blank; [3]-
29: "The Dark Brotherhood," by [August Derleth] (see I-E-i-8);
[30]-63: "Suggestions for a Reading Guide"; [64]-81: "Alfredo:
A Tragedy"; [82]-87: "Amateur Journalism: Its Possible Needs
and Betterment"; [88]-90: "What Belongs in Verse"; [91]-96:
"Six Poems" ([91]-92: "Bells"; 92-93: "Oceanus"; 93-94:
"Clouds"; 94-95: "Mother Earth"; 95: "Cindy, Scrub Lady in a
State Street Skyscraper"; 96: "On a Battlefield in France"); [97]-
133: "Three Stories," by C. M. Eddy, Jr. ([97]-100: note by
August Derleth; 100-10: LD; 111-23: DDB; 123-33: GE); [134]-
52: "The Lovecraft 'Books,' " by William Scott Home; [153]-63:
"To Arkham and the Stars" [fiction], by Fritz Leiber; [164]-78:

"Through Hyperspace with Brown Jenkin," by Fritz Leiber;
[179]-97: "Lovecraft and the New England Megaliths," by
Andrew E. Rothovius; [198]-241: "Howard Phillips Lovecraft: A
Bibliography," by Jack Laurence Chalker; [242]-45: "Walks with
H. P. Lovecraft," by C. M. Eddy, Jr.; [246]-61: "The Cancer of
Superstitition" (unfinished, with C. M. Eddy, Jr.); [262]-67:
"The Making of a Hoax," by August Derleth; [268]-301:
"Lovecraft's Illustrators," by John E. Vetter; [302]-21: "Final
Notes," by August Derleth; [322]: colophon.

Bound in black cloth; spine stamped in gold; 19.3 × 13.5 cm.;
dust jacket art by Frank Utpatel.

Notes. Illustrations include photographs of C. M. Eddy, Jr., the
De Bry plate in Pigafetta's *Regnum Congo* (mentioned in PH),
some New England megaliths, and illustrations by Clark
Ashton Smith, Virgil Finlay, Utpatel, and others; 3,460 copies.

44. *3 Tales of Horror* (1967)

3 / TALES / OF / HORROR / by H. P. Lovecraft /
[publisher's device] / illustrated by LEE BROWN
COYE / ARKHAM HOUSE / [illustration to the
left of all the above] [copyright page:] Sauk City,
Wisconsin . . . 1967

[1]⁶ [2-3]¹⁶ [4]¹⁴ [5]⁸ [6]⁵ [a-b] [i-ii] iii [iv] v [vi] [1-2] 3-134
[a]: half-title; [b]: blank; [i]: title; [ii]: copyright page; iii:
contents list; [iv]: blank; v: list of illustrations; [vi]: blank; [1]:
part-title; [2]: blank; 3-41: CS; 42-99: DH; 100-34: TD.

Bound in black cloth; spine stamped in gold; 23.5 × 18.2 cm.;
dust jacket art by Lee Brown Coye.

Notes. Title page, copyright page, and all interior illustrations
printed on glossy paper. Other illustrations face pp. 4, 12, 24,
30, 40, 48, 68, 98, 100, 104, 108, 114, and 134; 1,522 copies.

45. *Selected Letters II* (1968)

a.1. H. P. LOVECRAFT / SELECTED LETTERS /
1925-1929 / Edited by August Derleth and
Donald Wandrei / [publisher's device] /
ARKHAM HOUSE: Publishers / Sauk City,
Wisconsin / 1968

[1-12]¹⁶ [i-iv] v-xxiv [1-2] 3-359 [360]

[i]: half-title; [ii]: list of books by Lovecraft; [iii]: title; [iv]: copyright page; v-xx: contents and illustrations lists; xxi-xxiv: "Preface" by Derleth and Wandrei; [1]: part-title; [2]: blank; 3-359: letters (Nos. 179-359); [360]: colophon.

Bound in black cloth; spine stamped in gold; 20.7 × 14.1 cm.; dust jacket (see I-A-41) tinted deep red.

Notes. Illustrations include photographs of Lovecraft, Sonia Greene (Davis), Frank Belknap Long, Rheinhart Kleiner, Clark Ashton Smith, August Derleth, Samuel Loveman, Donald Wandrei, and a drawing by Lovecraft. Kleiner's first name is throughout misspelled as "Reinhardt"; 2,482 copies.

a.2. *Second Printing.* Sauk City, Wis.: Arkham House, [1974?]; 3,000 copies.

46. *The Shadow out of Time and Other Tales of Horror* (1968)

a.1. THE SHADOW OUT OF TIME / AND OTHER TALES OF HORROR / by / H. P. LOVECRAFT / & AUGUST DERLETH / LONDON / VICTOR GOLLANCZ LTD / 1968

[1]¹⁶ 2-12¹⁶ [1-8] 9-185 [186-88] 189-384

[1]: half-title; [2]: list of books by Lovecraft; [3]: title; [4]: copyright page; [5]: contents list; [6]: blank; [7]: half-title: "Stories by H. P. Lovecraft"; [8]: blank; 9-18: IV; 19-27: PH; 28-37: CA; 38-41: TOM; 42-113: SOOT; 114-85: SOI; [186]: blank; [187]: half-title: "Stories by H. D. [sic] Lovecraft and August Derleth"; [188]: blank; 189-211: "The Survivor"; 212-23: "Wentworth's Day"; 224-47: "The Peabody Heritage"; 248-65: "The Gable Window"; 266-81: "The Ancestor"; 282-303: "The Shadow out of Space"; 304-14: "The Lamp of Alhazred"; 315-19: "The Fisherman of Falcon Point"; 320-47: "The Dark Brotherhood"; 348-84: "The Shuttered Room."

Bound in red cloth; spine stamped in gold; 20 × 13 cm.; dust jacket is usual yellow Gollancz jacket with red and black lettering.

a.2. *Second Printing*. London: Victor Gollancz, February 1973.

a.3. *Third Printing*. London: Victor Gollancz, November 1977. Dust jacket black with gold and white lettering.

47. *At the Mountains of Madness and Other Tales of Terror* (1968)

a.1. *H. P. Lovecraft* / At the Mountains of Madness / and other tales of terror / selected and with an introduction / by August Derleth / *A Panther Book* [copyright page:] St Albans . . . 1968

[A]^{16} B-D^{16} E-G^8 H-L^{16} [1-6] 7-9 [10] 11-300 [301-04]
[1]: blurb; [2]: list of books by Lovecraft; [3]: title; [4]: copyright page; [5]: contents list; [6]: blank; 7-9: "H. P. Lovecraft's Novels," by Derleth [10]: blank; 11-112: ATMOM; 113-48: DWH; 149-54: SRC; 155-252: DQ; 253-64: SK; 265-300: TGSK; [301-04]: advertisements.
Bound in paper; 17.6 × 11.1 cm.; cover art by John Dore and John Claridge.

a.2. *Second Printing*. St. Albans: Panther Books, 1970.

a.3. *Third Printing*. St. Albans: Panther Books, 1973.

a.4. *Fourth Printing*. Not seen. Dated 1974.

48. *Dagon and Other Macabre Tales* (1969)

a.1. H. P. Lovecraft / Dagon / and other macabre tales / *selected by August Derleth* / A Panther Book [copyright page:] St Albans . . . 1969

Perfect-bound: [1-6] 7-221 [222] 223 [224]
[1]: blurb; [2]: list of books by Lovecraft; [3]: title; [4]: copyright page; [5]: contents list; [6]: blank; 7-13: D; 14-18: P; 19-30: BWS; 31-38: DS; 39-45: WS; 46-49: CU; 50-56: C; 57-65: FB; 66-80: Te; 81-85: Tr; 86-91: OG; 92-98: QI; 99-132: HWR; 133-40: Hy; 141-221: SHiL; [222]-23: "Complete Chronology"; [224]: blank.
Bound in paper; 17.7 × 11 cm.

a.2. *Second Printing*. Not seen. Dated 1969.

a.3. *Third Printing*. St. Albans: Panther Books, 1973. New cover art.

49. *The Tomb and Other Tales* (1969)

a.1. H. P. Lovecraft / **The Tomb** / and other
tales / *selected* by **August Derleth** / *A Panther Book*
[copyright page:] St Albans . . . 1969

Perfect-bound: [1-7] 8-17 [18] 19-27 [28] 29-57 [58] 59-
69 [70] 71-93 [94] 95-103 [104] 104-34 [135] 136-39 [140]
141-56 [157] 168-77 [178] 179-83 [184] 185-86 [187] 188-
90 [191-92]

[1]: blurb; [2]: list of books by Lovecraft; [3]: title; [4]:
copyright page; [5]: contents list; [6]: blank; [7]-17: T;
[18]-27: F; [28]-57: UP; [58]-69: He; [70]-93: HRH; [94]-
103: SHH; [104]-34: IWE; [135]-39: EC; [140]-77: "Early
Tales" ([140]: introductory note [by August Derleth];
[140]-47: BC; 147-56: A; [157]-64: PG; 164-70: S; 170-77:
TJR); [178]-88: "Four Fragments" ([178]: introductory
note [by August Derleth]; [178]-79: Az; 179-83: De; [184]-
86: B; [187]-88: TM); 188-90: "Complete Chronology";
[191-92]: advertisements.

Bound in paper; 17.7 X 11.1 cm.; cover photograph by
Tony Marshall.

a.2. *Second Printing.* Not seen. Dated 1969.

a.3. *Third Printing.* St. Albans: Panther Books, 1974. New
wraparound cover art. Pp. [191-92] eliminated.

a.4. *Fourth Printing.* Not seen. Dated 1975.

b.1. *Second Edition.* New York: Beagle Books, December 1970.
Cover art follows that of the first Panther printing. Part
of the Arkham Edition of H. P. Lovecraft (see cover).

b.2. *Second Printing.* New York: Beagle Books, June 1971.
Volume 1 of the Arkham Edition.

b.3. *Third Printing.* New York: Ballantine Books, April 1973
(see I-A-27, *Notes*). New cover art by John Holmes.

b.4. *Fourth Printing.* New York: Ballantine Books, 1974.

b.5. *Fifth Printing.* New York: Ballantine Books, January 1975.
Cover lettering altered.

c.1. *Canadian Printing.* [Toronto:] Ballantine Books, April 1973.

50. *The Prose Poems of H. P. Lovecraft* (1969-70)

These four volumes were published by Roy A. Squires (Glendale, Calif.), although his name appears on none of them. There were 125 copies of each pamphlet printed, 99 numbered and 26 lettered (A-Z). Each pamphlet is 25.1 × 16.5 cm., enclosed in a white envelope with the title printed on it.

Volume I:
MEMORY [in red] / H. P. Lovecraft / [publisher's device] / The Prose Poems / Miskatonic Edition / 1969

[1]⁸ [1-16]
[1-2]: blank; [3]: title; [4-6]: blank; [7-10]: M; [11-13]: blank; [14]: colophon; [15-16]: blank.
Grey brown paper covers.
Notes. Published in October 1969 (see colophon).

Volume II:
The Prose Poems of / H. P. LOVECRAFT / Ex Oblivione [in green] / Miskatonic Edition / 1969

[1]⁸ [1-16]
[1-2]: blank; [3]: title; [4-5]: blank; [6-11]: EO; [12-13]: blank; [14]: colophon; [15-16]: blank.
Dark green paper covers.
Notes. Published in November 1969 (see colophon).

Volume III:
THE PROSE POEMS / H. P. LOVECRAFT / NYARLATHOTEP [in brown] / MISKATONIC EDITION / 1970

[1]¹⁰ [1-20]
[1-2]: blank; [3]: title; [4-5]: blank; [6-15]: N; [16-17]: blank; [18]: colophon; [19-20]: blank.
Brown paper covers.
Notes. Published in December 1969 (see colophon).

Volume IV:
H. P. LOVECRAFT / *The* / *Prose* / *Poems*   WHAT [in blue] / THE [in blue] / MOON [in blue] / BRINGS [in blue] / *Miskatonic Edition* / 1970

[1]¹⁰ [1-20]

[1-2]: blank; [3]: title; [4-6]: blank; [7-14]: WMB; [15-17]: blank; [18]: colophon; [19-20]: blank.

Light blue paper covers.

Notes. Published in January and February 1970 (see colophon).

51. *The Dream-Quest of Unknown Kadath* (1970)

a.1. THE / DREAM-QUEST / OF / UNKNOWN KADATH / H. P. LOVECRAFT / EDITED, AND WITH AN / INTRODUCTION BY LIN CARTER / BALLANTINE BOOKS · NEW YORK / An Intext Publisher [copyright page:] First Printing: May, 1970

Perfect-bound: [i-vi] vii-xi [xii] 1-242 [243-44]

[i]: blurb; [ii]: publisher's device; [iii]: title; [iv]: copyright page; [v]: contents list; [vi]: blank; vii-xi: "Through the Gates of Deeper Slumber," by Lin Carter; [xii]: blank; 1-141: DQ; 142-50: C; 151-67: SK; 168-219: TGSK; 220-28: WS; 229-41: SHH; 242: "Postscript about *The Dream Quest* [sic] *of Unknown Kadath* and H. P. Lovecraft" [poem], by Lin Carter; [243-44]: advertisements.

Bound in paper; 17.8 × 10.6 cm.; cover art by Gervasio Gallardo.

Notes. Part of the Adult Fantasy series (see cover).

a.2. *Second Printing.* New York: Ballantine Books, July 1971.

a.3. *Third Printing.* New York: Ballantine Books, September 1973.

a.4. *Fourth Printing.* New York: Ballantine Books, October 1974.

b. *Second Edition.* New York: Ballantine Books, November 1976. [viii], 241[+7] pp. Introduction by Carter eliminated. New cover art by Murray Tinkelman. No longer part of the Adult Fantasy series.

c.1. *First Canadian Printing.* [Toronto]: Ballantine Books, May 1970.

c.2. *Second Canadian Printing.* [Toronto]: Ballantine Books, July 1971.

52. *The Horror in the Museum and Other Revisions* (1970)

a.1. THE HORROR IN THE / MUSEUM AND
OTHER / REVISIONS / by H. P. Lovecraft /
[publisher's device] / Arkham House:
Publishers   Sauk City, Wisconsin / 1970

[1-7]¹⁶ [8]⁶ [9-12]¹⁶ [13]¹⁴ [i-iv] v [vi] vii-ix [x] [1-2] 3-
383 [384-86]

[i]: half-title; [ii]: blank; [iii]: title; [iv]: copyright page; v:
contents list; [vi]: blank; vii-ix: "Lovecraft's 'Revisions,' "
by August Derleth; [x]: blank; [1]: part-title; [2]: blank; 3-
9: CrC; 10-15: GM; 16-21: HMB (as "The Invisible
Monster"); 22-26: FO; 27-41: MS; 42-64: WiD; 65-74: LD;
75-85: DDB; 86-94: GE; 95-97, 99-103: TAS; 98: facsimile
of a page from the ms. of TAS showing Lovecraft's
revisions; 104-30: HM; 131-55: OE; 156-75: DAT; 176-
88: HB; 189-233: LT; 234-51: EE; 252-67: CY; 268-304:
MC; 305-72: Mo; 373-83: TBB; [384]: colophon; [385-86]:
blank.

Bound in black cloth; spine stamped in gold; 21 × 14
cm.; dust jacket art by Gahan Wilson.

Notes. Four thousand copies.

a.2. *Second Printing.* Sauk City, Wis.: Arkham House, April
1976. Gathered [1-2]¹⁶ [3]⁸ [4-13]¹⁶. Pagination
divergences: [384-89]: blank; [390]: colophon; 4,000
copies.

53. *At the Mountains of Madness and Other Tales of Terror*
(1971)

a.1. AT THE MOUNTAINS / OF MADNESS /
AND OTHER TALES / OF TERROR / H. P.
Lovecraft / BEAGLE BOOKS · NEW
YORK / An Intext Publisher [copyright page:]
First printing: January 1971

Perfect-bound: [i-viii] 1-184

[i]: blurb; [ii]: list of books by Lovecraft; [iii]: title; [iv]:
copyright page; [v]: contents list; [vi]: blank; [vii]: part-
title; [viii]: blank; 1-110: ATMOM; 111-38: SH; 139-77:
DWH; 178-84: SRC.

Bound in paper; 17.7 × 10.6; cover art by John Dore and John Claridge (following I-A-47).

a.2. *Second Printing.* New York: Beagle Books, June 1971. Volume 2 of the Arkham Edition of H. P. Lovecraft (see cover).

a.3. *Third Printing.* New York: Ballantine Books, April 1973 (see I-A-27, *Notes*). New cover art by John Holmes.

a.4. *Fourth Printing.* New York: Ballantine Books, February 1974.

a.5. *Fifth Printing.* New York: Ballantine Books, October 1974. Cover lettering altered.

a.6. *Sixth Printing.* New York: Ballantine Books, November 1975.

b. *Canadian Printing.* [Toronto]: Ballantine Books, April 1973.

54. *The Lurking Fear and Other Stories* (1971)

a.1. THE LURKING FEAR / AND OTHER STORIES / H. P. Lovecraft / BEAGLE BOOKS · NEW YORK / An Intext Publisher [copyright page:] First Printing: January 1971

Perfect-bound: [i-viii] 1-47 [48] 49-89 [90] 91-113 [114] 115-82 [183-84]

[i]: blurb (quotation from SOI); [ii]: list of other books by Lovecraft; [iii]: title; [iv]: copyright page; [v]: contents list; [vi]: blank; [vii]: part-title; [viii]: blank; 1-22: LF; 23-28: D; 29-40: BWS; 41-47: WS; [48]: blank; 49-58: FAJ (as "Arthur Jermyn"); 59-66: FB; 67-80: Te; 81-89: MB; [90]: blank; 91-98: H; 99-106: U; 107-13: O; [114]: blank; 115-82: SOI; [183-84]: advertisements.

Bound in paper; 18 × 10.7 cm.; cover art follows I-A-40-a-2.

Notes. Part of the Arkham Edition of H. P. Lovecraft (see cover).

a.2. *Second Printing.* New York: Beagle Books, June 1971. Volume 3 of the Arkham Edition (see cover).

a.3. *Third Printing.* New York: Ballantine Books, April 1973 (see I-A-27 *Notes*). New cover art by John Holmes.

a.4. *Fourth Printing.* New York: Ballantine Books, February 1974.

a.5. *Fifth Printing.* New York: Ballantine Books, January 1975. Cover lettering altered.

55. *The Doom That Came to Sarnath* (1971)

a.1. THE DOOM / THAT CAME / TO SARNATH / H. P. Lovecraft / EDITED, WITH AN INTRODUCTION / AND NOTES, BY / LIN CARTER / BALLANTINE BOOKS · NEW YORK / An Intext Publisher [copyright page:] First Printing: February, 1971

Perfect-bound: [i-viii] ix-xiv [xv-xvi] 1-63 [64] 65-69 [70] 71-79 [80] 81-119 [120] 121-29 [130] 131-208

[i]: blurb; [ii]: publisher's device and note; [iii]: title; [iv]: copyright page; [v]: dedication by Carter; [vi]: blank; [vii]: contents list; [viii]: blank; ix-xiv: "Farewell to the Dreamlands," by Carter; [xv]: part-title (with epigraph from "Phaeton"); [xvi]: blank; 1: editor's note; 2-7: OG; 8-12: Tr; 13-20: DS; 21: editor's note; 22-33: T; 34-38: P; 39-50: BWS; 51: editor's note; 52-53: M; 54-56: WMB; 57-60: N; 61-63: EO; [64]: blank; 65: editor's note; 66-69: CU; [70]: blank; 71: editor's note; 72-79: Hy; [80]: blank; 81: editor's note; 82-84: "Nathicana"; 85: editor's note; 86-94: FB; 95-104: F; 105: editor's note; 106-19: NC; [120]: blank; 121: editor's note; 122-29: QI; [130]: blank; 131: editor's note; 132-40: CC; 141: editor's note; 142-74: IWE; 175: editor's note; 176-205: UP; 206-08: "A Partial Chronology of Lovecraft's Early Work," by Carter.

Bound in paper; 17.8 × 10.6 cm.; cover art by Gervasio Gallardo.

Notes. Part of the Adult Fantasy series (see cover).

a.2. *Second Printing.* New York: Ballantine Books, September 1976. New cover art by Murray Tinkelman. Inside front and back covers contain black-and-white illustrations by Tinkelman. No longer part of the Adult Fantasy series.

56. *Hail, Klarkash-Ton!* (1971)

HAIL, KLARKASH-TON! / [ornament] / *being nine missives* / *inscribed upon postcards* / *by* / H. P. LOVECRAFT / *to* / *Clark Ashton Smith* / [rectangular border around all the above]

[1]¹⁸ [1-36]

[1-2]: blank; [3]: copy number; [4-6]: blank; [7]: title; [8]: copyright page; [9-10]: blank; [11, 14-15, 18-19, 22-23, 26-27]: postcards; [12-13, 16-17, 20-21, 24-25, 28-29]: blank; [30]: "Notes & Glossary" [by Roy A. Squires]; [31-33]: blank; [34]: colophon; [35-36]: blank.

Pamphlet; 24.2 × 15.2 cm.; brown paper covers (white dust jacket).

Notes. Eighty numbered and nine lettered (A, C, E, F, L, O, R, T, V) copies printed by Roy A. Squires (Glendale, Calif.) in 1971 (see colophon). The lettered copies (an "Autograph Edition") each contained one of the actual postcards. Each book is enclosed in a white envelope with the title printed upon it. The leaves are unopened at the top edge.

57. *Nine Stories from The Horror in the Museum* (1971)

a.1. H. P. LOVECRAFT / *Nine stories from* / THE HORROR / IN THE MUSEUM / and other revisions / BEAGLE BOOKS · NEW YORK / An Intext Publisher [copyright page:] First printing: October, 1971

Perfect-bound: [i-viii] 1-245 [246-48]

[i]: blurb; [ii]: list of books by Lovecraft; [iii]: title; [iv]: copyright page; [v]: contents list; [vi]: blank; [vii]: part-title; [viii]: blank; 1-9: CrC; 9-15: GM; 16-42: WiD; 43-73: HM; 74-97: DAT; 97-112: HB; 112-33: EE; 134-52: CY; 152-232: Mo; 233-45: TBB; [246-48]: advertisements.

Bound in paper; 17.8 × 10.7 cm.

Notes. The Arkham Edition of H. P. Lovecraft, Volume 11 (see cover).

a.2. *Second Printing.* New York: Ballantine Books, July 1976 (see I-A-27 *Notes*). New cover art by Murray Tinkelman. Inside front and back covers contain black-and-white illustrations by Tinkelman.

58. *The Shadow over Innsmouth and Other Stories of Horror* (1971)

The Shadow over Innsmouth / and Other Stories of Horror / [rule] / H. P. LOVECRAFT / SCHOLASTIC BOOK SERVICES / New York Toronto London Auckland Sydney [copyright page:] 1st printing . . . December 1971

Perfect-bound: [1-9] 10-255 [256]

[1]: title; [2]: copyright page; [3]: contents list; [4]: blank; [5-9]: "A Word to the Reader . . ." by Margaret Ronan; 10-50: CS; 51-60: O; 61-99: UP; 100-09: TJR; 110-50: IWE; 151-63: F; 164-255: SOI; [256]: blank.

Bound in paper; 17.7 × 10.4 cm.

Notes. Margaret Ronan was formerly Margaret Sylvester, correspondent of Lovecraft's. The volume was made available only through Scholastic Book Services and could not be purchased in bookstores.

59. *Selected Letters III* (1971)

H. P. LOVECRAFT / SELECTED LETTERS / 1929-1931 / Edited by August Derleth and Donald Wandrei / [publisher's device] / ARKHAM HOUSE: Publishers / Sauk City, Wisconsin / 1971

[1-13]16 [14]8 [15]16 [16]8 [a-b] [i-iv] v-xix [xx] xxi-xxiii [xxiv] [1-2] 3-451 [452-54]

[a-b]: blank; [i]: half-title; [ii]: list of books by Lovecraft; [iii]: title; [iv]: copyright page; v-xix: contents list; [xx]: blank; xxi-xxiii: "Preface" by Derleth and Wandrei; [xxiv]: blank; [1]: part-title; [2]: blank; 3-451: letters (Nos. 360-516); [452]: colophon; [453-54]: blank.

Bound in black cloth; spine stamped in gold; 20.7 × 14.1 cm.; dust jacket (cf. I-A-41) tinted green.

Notes. Interior illustrations include photographs of Lovecraft, Frank Belknap Long, James F. Morton, Farnsworth Wright, Robert Bloch, August Derleth, Lovecraft's homes in Providence, Donald Wandrei, a facsimile of a page from a Lovecraft A.L., and others; 2,500 copies.

60. *E'ch-Pi-El Speaks* (1972)

> *E'ch-Pi-El Speaks* / An Autobiographical Sketch by / H. P. LOVECRAFT / [illustration] *Illustrations by Virgil Finlay* [illustration] / *Published by Gerry de la Ree—1972* / *Design—Bob Lynn/Tony Raven, Waldwick, N. J.* / *Copyright 1972 by Gerry de la Ree, 7 Cedarwood Lane, Saddle River, N. J. 07458*

[1]⁶ [1-2] 3-4 [5] 6-7 [8] 9-12 leaves

[1]: title; [2]: "Preface" by de la Ree; 3-4, 6-7, 9-11: text (excerpt of a letter to [Unknown], July 1929); [5, 8], 12: illustrations.

Bound in paper; 27.2 × 21.2 cm.

Notes. Leaves printed only on rectos; paper tinted light green. The illustration on p. [8] tinted violet, that on p. 12 red. Back cover contains colophon. Another Finlay illustration is on p. 3. Five hundred numbered copies; one bound in black cloth, front cover stamped in gold; twenty-five bound in maroon cloth, front cover stamped in gold; 474 in paper.

61. *Supernatural Horror in Literature as Revised in 1936* (1974)

> [There is no title page; cover reads as follows:] SU-PERNATURAL [in red] / HORROR IN [in red] / LIT-ERATURE [in red] / AS REVISED IN 1936 [in green] / [green rule] / *By* H. P. LOVECRAFT [in red] / [green rectangular border and rule around all the above] [copyright page:] 1974

[1]⁶ [1-6] leaves

[1]: "Foreword," by [Willis Conover]; [2-5]: T.Ms. of SHiL as revised/abridged in 1936; [6]: colophon.

Pamphlet; 28.5 × 22 cm.; yellow paper covers.

Notes. The pages on which Lovecraft's text is printed are tinted yellow; others are white. Leaves printed only on rectos. The inside front cover is the copyright page. Two thousand numbered copies printed by Carrollton-Clark (Arlington, Va.). Many copies were sent gratis to prepublication subscribers to the *de luxe* edition of *Lovecraft at Last* (I-A-62).

62. *Lovecraft at Last* (1975)
Lovecraft [in red] / at Last [in red] / By H. P.
LOVECRAFT / and WILLIS
CONOVER / FOREWORD BY / HAROLD
TAYLOR / [publisher's device] / MISKATONIC
UNIVERSITY CLASSICS: VOLUME
I / CARROLTON· CLARK / ARLINGTON ·
VIRGINIA / [double rectangular rule, one red, the
other black, around all the above] [copyright page:]
1975

[1-18]⁸ [i-viii] ix [x] xi-xii [xiii-xiv] xv-xix [xx] xxi-xxii [1-4] 5-
7 [8] 9-13 [14] 15 [16] 17 [18-24] 25 [26-27] 28 [29] 30-34 [35-
38] 39-47 [48-50] 51-57 [58] 59 [60-63] 64-66 [67-70] 71 [72]
73-81 [82] 83 [84] 85-92 [93-96] 97-103 [104-05] 106-07 [108-
10] 111-15 [116] 117-19 [120-22] 123 [124] 125 [126] 127-37
[138-40] 141 [142] 143-45 [146] 147-53 [154-56] 157-59 [160-
62] 163 [164] 165 [166] 167 [168] 169 [170-72] 173-86 [187-90]
191-95 [196-98] 199-211 [212] 213 [214-20] 221 [222] 223 [224-
25] 226-30 [231-34] 235 [236] 237 [238] 239 [240] 241 [242] 243
[244] 245 [246] 247 [248-51] 252-53 [254-58] 259-63 [264] 265-
72 [273-74]

[i-ii]: blank; [iii]: half-title; [iv]: blank; [v]: title; [vi]: copyright
page; [vii]: dedication by Conover; [viii]: blank; ix: contents list;
[x]: blank; xi-xii: "Foreword," by Harold Taylor; [xiii]: note by
John Chancellor; [xiv]: blank; xv-xix: "Preface," by Willis
Conover; [xx]: blank; xxi-xxii: "Editorial Method" (explanatory
notes); [1]: epigraph from Laurence Sterne; [2]: blank; [3]-255
passim: text (excerpts of letters by Lovecraft and Conover);
[21]: A.Ms. of "Homecoming"; 52-54: "A Visit with H. P.
Lovecraft" (fictional reminiscence), by Robert Bloch; [60-63]:
facsimile of *Fantasy Magazine* appearance of "H. P. Lovecraft: A
Biographical Sketch," by F. Lee Baldwin; 103: text of Donald
A. Wollheim's "review" of *The Necronomicon*; [104-05]: facsimile
of A.Ms. of "History of the *Necronomicon*"; 106-07: printed text
of same; [146]: facsimile of portions of T.Ms. of SHiL as revised
in 1936; 147-53: printed text of same; 158-59: text of "H. P.
Lovecraft: Viewed by E. Hoffmann Price"; [198]: facsimile of
portions of T.L., Lovecraft to Edwin Baird, 3 February 1924;

200-11: text of same (includes "To Mr. Hoag, upon His 93rd Birthday," pp. 210-11); [218]: reproduction of Virgil Finlay's portrait of Lovecraft, with A.N. by Finlay; [224-25]: facsimile of A.Ms., "Tales of H. P. Lovecraft"; 259-60: "Acknowledgments"; 261-63: "Bibliography"; 263: "Calendar Location"; [264]: blank; 265-72: index; [273]: colophon; [274]: blank.

Bound in maroon cloth; spine stamped in gold within a black rectangle; 28.4 × 21 cm.; gold dust jacket (with Finlay's illustration of Lovecraft).

Notes. Although a beautifully produced book, a bizarre one from a bibliographical standpoint. It consists of portions of the correspondence between Lovecraft and Conover, arranged in a conversational format so that the location of exact portions of Lovecraft's letters in the text is somewhat difficult, despite the "Calendar Location" which purports to identify their appearances. One thousand numbered and 2,000 unnumbered copies printed on 15 May 1975 (see colophon); the 1,000 were boxed in a yellow slipcase.

63. *The Occult Lovecraft* (1975)

The OCCULT / LOVECRAFT / By H. P. Lovecraft / With additional material and interpretations / By Anthony Raven / Illustrated by Stephen E. Fabian / Published by Gerry de la Ree / Saddle River, N.J.— 1975 / Graphic design—Bob Lynn/Tony Raven, Waldwick, N.J.

[1-2]¹⁰ [1-2] 3-24 [25] 26-28 [29] 30-40
[1]: title; [2]: copyright page; 3-4: "Publisher's Note"; 5-6, 8-10, 12: "The Cosmos and Religion"; 13-16, 18: "The Horned God Lives On!" by Anthony Raven; 19-21: "H. P. L. in Red Hook," by Frank Belknap Long; 21-22: "Of Gold and Sawdust," by Samuel Loveman; 23-24, 26, 28, 30: "The Incantation from Red Hook"; 31-32, 34-40: "Lovecraft & Black Magic," by Anthony Raven; 7, 11, 17, [25], 27, [29], 33: illustrations.

Bound in paper; 21.5 × 14 cm.; beige paper covers.

Notes. Nine hundred ninety numbered copies. An additional 128 numbered copies bound in black cloth, spine and cover stamped in gold. This cover was bound directly over the paper covers. A frontispiece—a photograph of Lovecraft—has been inserted upon the inside flap of the front paper cover.

64. *The Horror in the Museum and Other Tales* (1975)

H. P. Lovecraft / and others / The Horror in the / Museum / and Other Tales / Panther [copyright page:] St Albans . . . 1975

[1]¹⁰ 2-4¹⁰ 5-6¹² 7-10¹⁰ [1-6] 7-9 [10] 11-206 [207-08]

[1]: blurb; [2]: list of books by Lovecraft; [3]: title; [4]: copyright page; [5]: contents list; [6]: blank; 7-9: "Lovecraft's 'Revisions,' " by August Derleth; [10]: blank; 11-38: HM; 39-46: CrC; 47-51: FO; 52-75: WiD; 76-85: LD; 86-95: GE; 96-116: DAT; 117-35: EE; 136-206: Mo; [207-08]: advertisements.

Bound in paper; 17.8 × 11 cm.; cover art by Bob Fowke.

65. *The Horror in the Burying Ground* (1975)

H. P. Lovecraft / and others / The Horror in the / Burying Ground / and Other Tales / Panther [copyright page:] St Albans . . . 1975

[1]¹² 2¹² 3-8¹⁰ 9-10¹² [1-6] 7-9 [10] 11-211 [212-16]

[1]: blurb; [2]: list of books by Lovecraft; [3]: title; [4]: copyright page; [5]: contents list; [6]: blank; 7-9: "Lovecraft's 'Revisions,' " by August Derleth; [10]: blank; 11-24: HB; 25-30: GM; 31-37: HMB (as "The Invisible Monster"); 38-52: MS; 53-64: DDB; 65-73: TAS; 74-99: OE; 100-44: LT; 145-61: CY; 162-99: MC; 200-11: TBB; [212]: blank; [213-15]: advertisements; [216]: blank.

Bound in paper; 17.9 × 11.1 cm.; cover art by Bob Fowke.

66. *Medusa: A Portrait* (1975)

H. P. LOVECRAFT / MEDUSA: / A PORTRAIT [copyright page:] 1975

[1]⁶ [1-12]

[1-2]: blank; [3]: title; [4]: copyright page; [5-7]: "Medusa: A Portrait"; [8-9]: "Afterword," by Tom Collins; [10]: colophon; [11-12]: blank.

Bound in paper; 24.5 × 16 cm.; grey paper covers.

Notes. Printed by Ronald Gordon at The Oliphant Press, New York (see colophon). Five hundred numbered and 26 lettered copies.

67. *First Writings: Pawtuxet Valley Gleaner: 1906* (1976)

H. P. LOVECRAFT / FIRST WRITINGS /
PAWTUXET VALLEY GLEANER / 1906 / EDITED
BY MARC A. MICHAUD / FOREWORD BY /
RAMSEY CAMPBELL / NECRONOMICON
PRESS 1976 / $2.95 [copyright page:] West
Warwick, R.I.

Perfect-bound: [i] [1] 2-47 [48] leaves

[i]: blank; [1]: title; 2: copyright page, acknowledgments; 3-4:
"Embryo Lovecraft" by Campbell; 5-6: "Introduction" by
Michaud; 7-47: astronomy articles for *Pawtuxet Valley Gleaner*;
[48]: blank.

Yellow paper covers; 27.9 × 21.5 cm.; stapled at left margin.

Notes. Leaves printed only on rectos. Entire text save cover
and title page reproduced from typewritten copy. Five hundred
numbered copies.

68. *Selected Letters IV* (1976)

H. P. LOVECRAFT / SELECTED LETTERS / 1932-
1934 / Edited by August Derleth and James
Turner / [publisher's device] / ARKHAM HOUSE
PUBLISHERS, Inc. / Sauk City, Wisconsin / 1976

[1-15]¹⁶ [i-iv] v-xxvi [xxvii-xxviii] xxix-xxxii [1-2] 3-424
[425-28]

[i]: half-title; [ii]: list of books by Lovecraft; [iii]: title; [iv]:
copyright page; v-xxvi: contents list; [xxvii]: list of illustrations;
[xxviii]: blank; xxix-xxxii: "Preface" by Turner; [1]: part-title;
[2]: blank; 3-424: letters (Nos. 517-710); [425]: colophon; [426-
28]: blank.

Bound in black cloth; spine stamped in gold; 20.5 × 13.7 cm.;
dust jacket (see I-A-41) tinted yellow.

Notes. Five thousand copies. Interior illustrations include
photographs of Lovecraft, Henry S. Whitehead, Robert Bloch,
Robert E. Howard, E. Hoffmann Price, Wilfred B. Talman,
Duane Rimel, F. Lee Baldwin, R. H. Barlow, and Helen V. Sully,
a reproduction of a drawing by Lovecraft, and others.

69. *Selected Letters V* (1976)

H. P. LOVECRAFT / SELECTED LETTERS / 1934-1937 / Edited by August Derleth and James Turner / [publisher's device] / ARKHAM HOUSE PUBLISHERS, Inc. / Sauk City, Wisconsin / 1976

[1-15]¹⁶ [i-iv] v-xxx [xxxi-xxxii] xxxiii-xxxvii [xxxviii] [1-2] 3-436 [437-38]

[i]: half-title; [ii]: list of books by Lovecraft; [iii]: title; [iv]: copyright page; v-xxx: contents list; [xxxi]: list of illustrations; [xxxii]: blank; xxxiii-xxxvii: "Preface" by Turner; [xxxviii]: blank; [1]: part-title; [2]: blank; 3-436: letters (Nos. 711-930); [437]: facsimile of portion of obituary from *The* [Providence] *Evening Bulletin* (III-A-29); [438]: colophon.

Bound in black cloth; spine stamped in gold; 20.5 × 13.7 cm.; dust jacket (see I-A-41) tinted violet.

Notes. Five thousand copies. Interior illustrations include photographs of Lovecraft, August Derleth, Henry Kuttner, Clark Ashton Smith, E. Hoffmann Price, Emil Petaja, Robert H. Barlow and his family, Kenneth Sterling, Willis Conover, Virgil Finlay, Fritz and Jonquil Leiber, Robert Bloch, Farnsworth Wright, a reproduction of a Frank Utpatel illustration, and a reproduction of a Lovecraft A.L.

70. *The Conservative: Complete 1915–1923* (1976)

a.1. H. P. LOVECRAFT / The Conservative / COMPLETE 1915–1923 / EDITED BY MARC A. MICHAUD / FOREWORD BY / FRANK BELKNAP LONG / NECRONOMICON PRESS 1976 [copyright page:] West Warwick, R.I.

Perfect-bound: [i] [1-2] 3-124 [125] leaves

[i]: blank; [1]: title; [2]: copyright, acknowledgments, colophon; 3-4: "Foreword" by Long; 5: "Introduction" by Michaud; 6-15: *The Conservative*, April 1915; 16-27: July 1915; 28-43: October 1915; 44-49: January 1916; 50-54: April 1916; 55-59: July 1916; 60-78: October 1916; 79-85: January 1917; 86-91: July 1917; 92-102: July 1918; 103-14:

July 1919; 115-17: March 1923; 117-24: July 1923; [125]:
blank.

Red paper covers; 27.9 × 21.5 cm.; stapled at left
margin.

Notes. Four hundred numbered copies signed by the
editor (see colophon; but see also next entry). Leaves
printed only on rectos. A strange compendium of reset
material (reproduced from typewritten copy) and
facsimiles of the original periodical; the last two issues are
wholly in facsimile. The contents of the first issue have
been printed in incorrect order (see I-D-ii-2).

a.1(a) *Variant ("Second Edition").* Surely one of the strangest
publications in the history of Lovecraft studies. Not a
second edition, as stated on colophon, but variant of the
first: there is new copyright and acknowledgments page
[2], and a darker shade of red has been used for the cover
(which bears the date 1977, although title page is
unaltered). Pages from the original state, with the new
cover and p. [2], have been used to make up this "edition."
Copyright page here states that the "first edition" was
limited to 50 copies (!), but probably more are still extant.
There cannot be 400 copies, as noted in the original state,
since some of these were used to form the "second
edition." Colophon for variant states that 2,500 signed
and numbered copies were printed, but there must be far
fewer; indeed, the bulk of the volume was printed only
once, hence there can be only 400 (if that many) total
copies of both states.

71. *Writings in The United Amateur: 1915–1925* (1976)
H. P. LOVECRAFT / WRITINGS IN / THE
UNITED AMATEUR / 1915–1925 / EDITED BY
MARC A. MICHAUD / FOREWORD BY / T. E. D.
KLEIN / NECRONOMICON PRESS 1976 [copy-
right page:] West Warwick, R. I.

Perfect-bound: [a] [i-iii] iv-xi [1] 2 [3] 4-136 [137] 138-46
[147] leaves

[a]: blank; [i]: title; [ii]: copyright page, acknowledgments, colophon; [iii]-xi: "Foreword" by Klein; [1]-2: "Introduction" by

Michaud; [3]: facsimile of cover of *The United Amateur*, September 1915 (with photograph of Lovecraft); 4-6: *United Amateur Press Association: Exponent of Amateur Journalism*; 7-10: "Department of Public Criticism" (hereafter abbreviated "DPC"), January 1915; 10-14: DPC, March 1915; 14-15: "March"; 15-20: DPC, May 1915; 21-31: DPC, September 1915; 31-33: "Little Journeys to the Homes of Prominent Amateurs," by Andrew Francis Lockhart; 33-34: "The Teuton's Battle-Song"; 35-41: DPC, April 1916; 42-48: DPC, June 1916; 49: "Content"; 50-54: DPC, August 1916; 54-60: DPC, September 1916; 61-65: A; 65-71: DPC, March 1917; 71-79: DPC, May 1917; 80: "Ode for July Fourth, 1917"; 81-83: DPC, July 1917; 84: "News Notes" (with "To M. W. M."); 84-87: "A Reminiscence of Dr. Samuel Johnson"; 87-90: DPC, November 1917 (not by Lovecraft); 90-91: "President's Message" (November 1917); 91: "President's Message" (January 1918); 92: "President's Message" (March 1918); 92: "Sunset"; 93-98: DPC, May 1918 (not by Lovecraft); 98-99: "President's Message" (May 1918); 99: "Astrophobos"; 100: "At the Root"; 101: "President's Message" (July 1918); 102-06: "The Literature of Rome"; 106: "To Alan Seeger"; 107: "Theodore Roosevelt"; 108: "A Note on Howard P. Lovecraft's Verse," by Rheinhart Kleiner; 109-12: DPC, March 1919; 113: "Helene Hoffman Cole—Litterateur"; 114-15: "Americanism"; 115-18: WS; 118: "To Mistress Sophia Simple, Queen of the Cinema"; 119-23: "Literary Composition"; 123: "For What Does the United Stand?"; 124-27: PG; 128-29: N; 129: "Editorial" (November 1920); 130: "Official Organ Fund" (November 1920 and January 1921); 130-34: "Winifred Virginia Jackson: A 'Different' Poetess"; 134: EO; 134: "Official Organ Fund" (March 1921); 135: Editor's Note in *The United Amateur*, September 1921; 136-[37]: "Editorial" (September 1921); 138: Editor's Note in *The United Amateur*, November 1921; 138: "Official Organ Fund" (November 1921); 139: "Editorial" (January 1922); 140: "Official Organ Fund" (March 1922 and May 1922); 140: "At the Home of Poe," by Frank Belknap Long (dedicated to Lovecraft); 141: "Bacchanale" [poem], by Samuel Loveman (dedicated to Lovecraft); 141-44: "The Work of Frank Belknap Long, Jr."; 145-46: "Editorial" (July 1925); [147]: blank.

Green paper covers; 27.9 × 21.5 cm.; stapled at left margin. *Notes.* Leaves printed only on rectos. Facsimile reproductions of the original magazine appearances; two articles (DPC, November 1917 and May 1918) are not by Lovecraft; 500 numbered copies.

72. *To Quebec and the Stars* (1976)

TO QUEBEC / AND / THE STARS / H. P. LOVE-CRAFT / EDITED BY / L. SPRAGUE de CAMP / DONALD M. GRANT, PUBLISHER / WEST KINGSTON, RHODE ISLAND / 1976 [copyright page:] "First Edition"

[1-10]¹⁶ [1-8] 9 [10-12] 13 [14] 15 [16] 17-27 [28] 29-33 [34] 35 [36-38] 39 [40] 41-49 [50] 51-65 [66] 67-69 [70-72] 73-75 [76] 77-79 [80] 81-92 [93-94] 95-97 [98] 99-101 [102] 103-09 [110-14] 115-252 [253] 254-56 [257] 258-80 [281] 283-83 [284] 285-318 [319-20]

[1]: half-title; [2]: blank; [3]: title; [4]: copyright page; [5]: contents list; [6]: blank; [7]: dedication by the editor; [8]: blank; 9: "Introduction" by de Camp; [10]: blank; [11]: half-title to section: "Science"; [12]: blank; 13: editor's introduction to section; [14]: blank; 15: "Trans-Neptunian Planets"; [16]: blank; 17-22: "November Skies" (1 November 1915); 23-27: "June Skies" (1 June 1916); [28]: blank; 29-33: "May Skies" (1 May 1917); [34]: blank; 35: "The Truth about Mars"; [36]: blank; [37]: half-title to section: "Literature and Esthetics"; [38]: blank; 39: editor's introduction to section; [40]: blank; 41-44: "Metrical Regularity"; 45-49: "The Allowable Rhyme"; [50]: blank; 51-56: "A Reminiscence of Dr. Samuel Johnson"; 57-65: "The Literature of Rome"; [66]: blank; 67-69: "What Belongs in Verse"; [70]: blank; [71]: half-title to section: "Philosophy"; [72]: blank; 73-75: editor's introduction to section; [76]: blank; 77-79: "The Crime of the Century"; [80]: blank; 81-86: "Nietzscheism and Realism"; 87-92: "A Confession of Unfaith"; [93]: half-title to section: "Travel, Description, and History"; [94]: blank; 95-97: editor's introduction to section; [98]: blank; 99-101: "A Descent to Avernus"; [102]: blank; 103-6: "Some Dutch Footprints in New England"; 107-09: "The Unknown City in the Ocean"; [110]: blank; [111]: facsimile of Lovecraft's handwritten title for *A Description of the Town of Quebeck . . .* ; [112]: blank; [113-14]: contents list for *A Description . . .* ; 115-252, 254-56, 258-80,

282-83, 285-309: *A Description of the Town of Quebeck, in New France, Lately Added to His* Britannick *Majesty's Dominions*; [253, 257, 281, 284]: facsimiles of hand-drawn maps by Lovecraft; 310-12: "Appendix: Place-names in Quebeck which differ substantially in form according to common French & English Usage"; 313-18: "Notes" [by L. Sprague de Camp and M.-Louis Paré]; [319-20]: blank.

Bound in blue cloth; spine stamped in gold; dust jacket art and design by Robert MacIntyre.

Notes. Other facsimiles of illustrations by Lovecraft appear on pp. 231, 235, 240, 241, 242, 243, 244, 245, 246, 248, 300, 301, and 305.

73. *The Statement of Randolph Carter* (1976)

THE STATEMENT OF RANDOLPH CARTER/ by / Howard Phillips Lovecraft / being: / Both the Original Holograph Version and its Transcription, / With an Introduction by R. Alain Everts. / [publisher's device in red] / *The Strange Company* [copyright page:] Madison, Wisconsin . . . 1976

Perfect-bound: [1-17] leaves

[1]: title; [2]: copyright page and colophon; [3]: photograph of Lovecraft and Rheinhart Kleiner; [4-5]: introduction by Everts; [6]: photograph of Samuel Loveman; [7-14]: A.Ms. of SRC; [15-17]: printed text of same.

Unbound sheets; 28 × 21.8 cm.; with white paper folder.

Notes. All leaves save pp. [1-2] printed only on rectos (=16 leaves). Thirty copies, signed and numbered by the editor, printed for members of the Necronomicon amateur press association; not for sale. An additional 150 copies printed; this trade edition, however, has not been seen.

74. *Antarktos* (1977)

Antarktos [black-letter] / [rule] / BY / H. P. Lovecraft [black-letter] / *Illustration by C. M. James* / [publisher's device] / Fantome Press / Warren, Ohio [copyright page:] 1977

[1]⁴ [1-8]

[1]: title; [2]: copyright page; [3]: blank; [4]: illustration (signed by artist): [5]: "Antarktos"; [6-7]: blank; [8]: colophon.

Pamphlet; 16 × 12 cm.; bound in paper.

Notes. One hundred fifty numbered copies printed in January 1977 (see colophon). Included is a separate printed flyer containing "Editor's Notes" by C. M. James.

75. *The Californian: 1934-1938* (1977)

H. P. LOVECRAFT / THE / CALIFORNIAN / 1934-1938 / EDITED BY MARC A. MICHAUD / FOREWORDS BY / HYMAN BRADOFSKY / DIRK W. MOSIG / NECRONOMICON PRESS 1977 / $3.95 [copyright page:] West Warwick, R.I.

Perfect-bound: [i] [1] 2-67 [68] leaves

[i]: blank; [1]: title; 2: copyright page, acknowledgments, colophon; 3-4: "Foreword" by Bradofsky; 5-9: "Perfectionist Emeritus" by Mosig; 10-12: "Homes and Shrines of Poe"; 13-18: "Heritage or Modernism"; 19-23: TAS; 24-27: "Some Notes on Interplanetary Fiction"; 28-34: "Literary Review"; 35: dedication page of Summer 1937 issue of *The Californian* (with dedication to and photograph of Lovecraft); 36-37: "Amateur Affairs," by Hyman Bradofsky; 38-41: "Howard Phillips Lovecraft," by Rheinhart Kleiner; 42: "Yet Still We Mourn" [poem], by Frank Earle Schermerhorn; 43-56: "By Post from Providence"; 57: "Sunset," "Phaeton," "August," "Death" [by Jonathan E. Hoag; see I-E-i-3]; 58: "Providence," "To the American Flag"; 59-67: "Mrs. Miniter—Estimates and Recollections"; [68]: blank.

Orange paper covers; 27.9 × 21.5 cm.; stapled at left margin.

Notes. Facsimile reproductions of the original magazine appearances. Printed only on rectos; 1,000 numbered copies signed by the editor.

76. *Herbert West Reanimator* (1977)

H. P. LOVECRAFT / HERBERT WEST / REANIMATOR / EDITED BY MARC A. MICHAUD / A SHORT NOVEL / IN FACSIMILE / NECRONOMICON PRESS 1977 / $3.95 [copyright page:] West Warwick, R.I.

Perfect-bound: [1] 2-32 [33] 34-45 [46] leaves

[1]: title; 2: acknowledgments, copyright page, colophon; 3, 11, 18, 25, 32, 39: facsimiles of covers of *Home Brew*, February-July 1922; 4-10, 12-17, 19-24, 26-31, [33]-38, 40-45: HWR; [46]: blank.

Brown paper covers; 27.9 × 21.5 cm.; stapled at left margin.

Notes. Facsimile reproduction of the story as serialized in *Home Brew*. Leaves printed only on rectos; 1,000 numbered copies.

77. *Writings in* The Tryout (1977)

H. P. LOVECRAFT / WRITINGS IN / *THE TRYOUT* / including / A WINTER WISH, BELLS / THE RUTTED ROAD, OLD CHRIST-MAS / THE WOOD, THE TREE / EDITED BY MARC A. MICHAUD / FOREWORD BY / S. T. JOSHI / NECRONOMICON PRESS 1977 / $3.95

Perfect-bound: [i] [1] 2-59 [60] leaves

[i]: blank; [1]: title; 2: copyright page, acknowledgments, colophon; 3-4: "Foreword" by Joshi; 4: "Editor's Note"; 5: "Concerning 'Persia—in Europe' "; 6: "The Rutted Road," "The Nymph's Reply to the Modern Business Man"; 7: "Fact and Fancy"; 7-8: "Lines on Graduation from the R. I. Hospital's School of Nurses"; 9: "Iterum Conjunctae"; 9-10: "The Peace Advocate"; 11-12: "A Reply to *The Lingerer*"; 13: "The Poet of Passion"; 13-14: "Lines on the 25th. Anniversary of the Providence *Evening News*"; 14: "Sunset"; 15-16: "A Winter Wish"; 16-17: "Laeta; a Lament"; 17-18: "April"; 19: "A June Afternoon," "Lovecraft—an Appreciation," by Arthur Goodenough; 20: "August"; 20-22: "Damon and Delia, a Pastoral"; 22-23: "To Arthur Goodenough, Esq."; 23-24: "To Delia, Avoiding Damon"; 25-26: "The Eidolon"; 27-29: "Germania—1918"; 29-34: "Old Christmas"; 35: "Spring," "Pan" (i.e., "To Pan"); 36: "The Last Pagan Speaks" (i.e., "To the Old Pagan Religion"), "To Selene" (i.e., "Ode to Selene or Diana"); 37-39: "Hylas and Myrrha"; 40: "Monody on the Late King Alcohol"; 41: "The Pensive Swain"; 41-42: "Bells"; 42: "To Phillis"; 42-43: "Tryout's Lament for the Vanished Spider"; 44: "Ad Scribam"; 45: "On Religion"; 45-46: "On a Grecian Colonnade in a Park"; 46-47: "The Dream"; 47: "October" [1]; 48-50: TOM; 50-52: "The Haverhill Conven-

tion"; 53-57: Tr; 57-58: "To Rheinhart Kleiner, upon His Town Elegies and Fables"; 58-59: "Around the Circle," by [C. W. Smith]; 59: "The Wood"; [60]: blank.

Blue paper covers; 27.9 × 21.5 cm.; stapled at left margin.

Notes. Facsimile reproductions of the original magazine appearances. "The Tree" contains handwritten corrections by Lovecraft (reproduced from a copy of the journal in JHL). Leaves printed only on rectos; 1,000 numbered copies.

78. *The Lurking Fear* (1977)

[There is no title page; cover reads as follows:] H. P. LOVECRAFT / THE LURKING FEAR / with illustrations by / CLARK ASHTON SMITH / NECRONOMICON PRESS 1977 / $3.95 [copyright page:] West Warwick, R.I.

[1]²⁰ [1-40]

[1]: copyright page, colophon (includes advertisement for LF from *Home Brew*, Dec. 1922); [2]: blank; [3, 11, 18, 28]: reproduction of covers from *Home Brew*, January–April 1923; [4-10, 12-17, 19-27, 29-36]: LF; [37-39]: blank; [40]: advertisements.

Bound in paper; 27.9 × 21.5 cm.

Notes. Facsimile reproduction of the story as serialized in *Home Brew*. The Smith illustrations appear on pp. [5, 6, 7, 15, 17, 20-21, 23, 30-31, 33]; 550 numbered copies.

79. *Collapsing Cosmoses* (1977)

[photograph of Lovecraft] H. P. LOVECRAFT / C O L L A P S I N G   C O S M O S E S   [rule under title] / R. H. BARLOW [photograph of Barlow]

[1]⁴ [1-8]

[1]: title; [2]: blank; [3]: editor's note [by Marc A. Michaud]; [3-8]: "Collapsing Cosmoses"; [8]: colophon.

Pamphlet; 17.9 × 10.9 cm.; blue paper covers.

Notes. West Warwick, R.I.: Necronomicon Press, [1977]. F & SF Fragments 1 (see cover). Title page and text reproduced from typewritten copy; 500 numbered copies.

80. *Memoirs of an Inconsequential Scribbler* (1977)
[There is no title page; cover reads as follows:] F &
SF SELF-PORTRAITS 3 / H. P. LOVECRAFT /
Memoirs of an / Inconsequential Scribbler / NE-
CRONOMICON PRESS / $1 [copyright page:]
West Warwick, R.I.

[1]⁴ [1-8]
[1]: photograph of Lovecraft; [1-5]: "The Brief Autobiography
of an Inconsequential Scribbler"; [6-8]: "Autobiography of
Howard Phillips Lovecraft"; [8]: colophon.
Pamphlet; 18.1 × 10.9 cm.; grey paper covers.
Notes. Published in 1977, although no date is indicated in the
book. Text reproduced from typewritten copy; 500 copies.

81. *The Fungi from Yuggoth* (1977)
H. P. LOVECRAFT / THE FUNGI / FROM
/ YUGGOTH / Necronomicon Press [copyright
page:] West Warwick, R.I. . . . 1977

[1]¹² [1-24]
[1-2]: blank; [3]: title; [4]: copyright, colophon page; [5-22]:
Fungi from Yuggoth; [23-24]: blank.
Pamphlet; 21.4 × 17.5 cm.; grey paper covers.
Notes. All pages save title page are reproduced from typewritten copy; each page containing text ([5-22]) has rectangular
black border around the two poems on the page; 475 numbered
copies.

82. *A Winter Wish* (1977)
A WINTER WISH / by H. P. LOVECRAFT / Edited
by Tom Collins / [publisher's device: "Whispers
Press"] / 1977

[1-4]¹⁶ [5]²⁰ [6]¹⁶ [i-iv] v-ix [x] 1-11 [12-14] 15-24 [25-26] 27-
153 [154] 155-80 [181-84] 185-90
[i]: title; [ii]: copyright and colophon page; [iii]: dedication;
[iv]: blank; v-ix: contents list; [x]: blank; 1-11: "Introduction" by
Collins; [12]: blank; [13]: half-title: "Essays"; [14]: blank; 15: "A
Note on Howard P. Lovecraft's Verse," by Rheinhart Kleiner;
16-17: "The Despised Pastoral"; 18-20: "Metrical Regularity";

21-24: "The Allowable Rhyme"; [25]: half-title: "Poetry"; [26]:
blank; 27-28: "The Voice"; 29-30: "Chloris and Damon"; 30-32:
"To Delia, Avoiding Damon"; 32-36: "Damon and Delia, a Pas-
toral"; 36-37: "Myrrha and Strephon"; 38-40: "The Smile"; 41-
43: "Quinsnicket Park"; 44: "The Rose of England"; 44-46: "An
American to Mother England"; 46: "Pacifist War Song—1917";
47-49: "The Peace Advocate"; 49-51: "Lines on Gen. Robert
Edward Lee"; 51: "Ode for July Fourth, 1917"; 52-54: "Ad
Britannos—1918"; 54-58: "Germania—1918"; 58: "On a Battlefield in France" (i.e., "On a Battlefield in Picardy"); 59: "To Alan
Seeger"; 60-61: "To Maj.-Gen. Omar Bundy, U.S.A."; 61-62:
"North and South Britons"; 62-63: "Temperance Song"; 64:
"January"; 64-65: "March"; 65-66: "April"; 67: "April Dawn";
67-68: "A June Afternoon"; 68-69: "A Rural Summer Eve"; 70-
71: "A Mississippi Autumn"; 71-72: "A Winter Wish"; 73:
"Brumalia"; 73-74: "Solstice"; 74-75: "Greetings"; 75: "Ye Mer-
ry Christmas" (i.e., Untitled: "As Saturnalian days draw
near . . ."); 75-76: "A Christmas Greeting to Tryout" (i.e., Un-
titled: "May Nymphs and Graces ever bless . . ."); 77-78: "To
Members of the United Amateur Press Ass'n from the Provi-
dence Amateur Press Club"; 78-80: "The Simple Speller's Tale";
80-81: "To Arthur Goodenough"; 81-82: "To Mr. Lockhart, on
His Poetry"; 82-83: "To Samuel Loveman, Esquire, on His Poe-
try and Drama . . ."; 83-84: "To the Members of the Pin-
Feathers . . ."; 84: "The Bay-Stater's Policy"; 84-85: "On a
Modern Lothario"; 85-86: "George Willard Kirk"; 86-87: "R.
Kleiner, Laureatus, in Heliconem"; 87: "To M. W. M."; 87-88:
"On the Return of Maurice Winter Moe, Esq. . . ."; 88-89:
"The Return of Mr. Smith" (i.e., "The Return"); 89-91: "The
Prophecy of Capys Secundus"; 92: "Oct. 17, 1919"; 92: "To S. S.
L.—Oct. 17, 1920"; 92-93: "To the Eighth of November"; 93:
"Birthday Lines to Margfred Galbraham"; 93-95: "To Mr. Gal-
pin, upon His 20th Birthday . . ."; 95-96: "To Endymion"; 97-
98: "An Elegy on Franklin Chase Clark, M.D."; 98-99: "An
Elegy on Phillips Gamwell, Esq."; 100: "The Absent Leader";
101: "In Memoriam: J. E. T. D."; 101-02: "Edith Miniter"; 102-
03: "To the Late John H. Fowler, Esq."; 103: "Percival Lowell";
104-05: "Theodore Roosevelt"; 106: "Fact and Fancy"; 107: "On
Reading Lord Dunsany's *Book of Wonder*"; 107-08: "To Edward
John Moreton Drax Plunkett . . ."; 109-11: "Nathicana"; 111-

13: "The Bride of the Sea"; 113-14: "Laeta; a Lament"; 114-15: "The Garden" (i.e., "A Garden"); 115-16: "Revelation"; 116-17: "The Cats"; 117-18: "The Conscript"; 119-20: "Only a Volunteer," by Sgt. Hayes P. Miller; 120-21: "The Volunteer"; 122: "The Modern Business Man to His Love," by Olive G. Owen; 123: "The Nymph's Reply to the Modern Business Man"; 123-24: "John Oldham," by Rheinhart Kleiner; 124: "John Oldham—a Defence"; 124-25: "To Mary of the Movies," by Rheinhart Kleiner; 125-26: "To Charlie of the Comics"; 126-27: "To a Movie Star," by Rheinhart Kleiner; 127: "To Mistress Sophia Simple, Queen of the Cinema"; 128: "Ruth," by Rheinhart Kleiner; 128: "Grace"; 129: "To Miriam," by Rheinhart Kleiner; 129: "To Phillis"; 130-31: "The Dead Bookworm"; 131: "Gems from 'In a Minor Key' "; 132: "Epigram" (i.e., Untitled: "Slang is the life of speech, the critics say, . . ."); 132: "Futurist Art"; 132: "The Magazine Poet"; 133: "The Poet of Passion"; 133-35: "The State of Poetry"; 135: "Fragment on Whitman"; 136: "Tosh Bosh"; 137: "Life's Mystery," by "L. Phillips Howard"; 137: "On Mr. L. Phillips Howard's Profound Poem Entitled 'Life's Mystery' "; 138-41: "Waste Paper"; 142: "Sonnet on Myself"; 142: "Alone in Space" (i.e., poem included in "May Skies" [I-B-ii-86]); 143: "On the Vanity of Human Ambition"; 144: "The Last Pagan Speaks" (i.e., "To the Old Pagan Religion"); 144-45: "On Religion"; 145: "To Selene" (i.e., "Ode to Selene or Diana"); 146-47: "Lines on Graduation from the R. I. Hospital's School of Nurses"; 147-49: "Lines on the 25th. Anniversary of the Providence *Evening News*"; 149: "On Receiving a Picture of Swans," "On Receiving a Picture of the Marshes at Ipswich"; 150: "On the Ruin of Rome"; 150-51: "Sonnet Study"; 151: "On the Cowboys of the West"; 152: "Inspiration"; 152-53: "Monos: An Ode"; 153: "Respite"; [154]: blank; 155-80: "Notes" [by Collins]; [181]: half-title (?); [182]: blank; [183]: half-title to index; [184]: blank; 185-90: "Index of Titles and First Lines."

Bound in white cloth; spine stamped in gold; 23.5 × 15.8 cm.; dust jacket art by Steve Fabian.

Notes. Two thousand copies printed by Whispers Press (Chapel Hill, North Carolina). A special boxed edition, signed by the editor, cover artist, a publisher (Stuart D. Schiff), was offered to prepublication subscribers. The texts of the poems have not always been faithfully printed.

83. *Uncollected Prose and Poetry* (1978)
    H. P. LOVECRAFT / UNCOLLECTED / PROSE
    AND POETRY / EDITED BY S. T. JOSHI / &
    MARC A. MICHAUD / NECRONOMICON
    PRESS 1978 [copyright page:] West Warwick,
    R.I. . . . First Printing—August 1978

> [1]⁴⁶ [a-b] [i-v] vi-vii [viii] [1] 2-77 [78] 79-80 [81-82]
>
> [a-b]: blank; [i]: title; [ii]: explanatory note, copyright page;
> [iii]: contents list; [iv]: blank; [v]-vii: "Introduction" by Joshi;
> [viii]: blank; [1]-3: "Letters to the Editor of *The Providence Sunday
> Journal*" (27 May 1906 and 6 August 1906); 3-5: "Providence in
> 2000 A. D."; 5-7: "Two Letters to the Editor of *The Argosy*"
> (issues of January and March 1914); 8: "New England"; 8-9:
> "Prologue" to "Fragments from an Hour of Inspiration" by Jon-
> athan E. Hoag; 9-11: "The Simple Spelling Mania"; 12-15: "The
> Case for Classicism"; 15-16: "Helene Hoffman Cole" [poem];
> 17-18: "Trimmings"; 19-21: "Editorial Notes in *The United Ama-
> teur*" (issues of November 1920, September 1921, November
> 1921); 27-30: "Lucubrations Lovecraftian"; 31-33: "East and
> West Harvard Conservatism"; 33-34: "Letter to the Editor of
> *Weird Tales*" (issue of September 1923); 35: Review of *Ebony and
> Crystal* by Clark Ashton Smith; 36-37: "The Omnipresent Phil-
> istine"; 38-43: "The Very Old Folk"; 44: "Biographical Notice";
> 44-45: "Sleepy Hollow To-day"; 45: "Letter to the Editor of
> *Driftwind*" (issue of July 1932); 45-47: "The Sorcery of Aphlar"
> (with Duane W. Rimel); 47-48: "The Odes of Horace: III, ix";
> 48-66: NO; 67-77: "Commentary" [by Joshi]; [78]: blank; 79-80:
> "Bibliography"; [81]: "Errata"; [82]: blank.
>
> Pamphlet; 21.3 × 17.3 cm.; cover art by Jason Eckhardt.
> *Notes*. About 500 copies.

Addendum:

84. *At the Mountains of Madness and Other Tales of Terror*
    (1974)

> An edition in Braille of I-A-53 in three volumes.

    Volume I:
    AT THE MOUNTAINS / OF MADNESS / and

Other Tales of Terror / By H. P. Lovecraft / Em-
bossed in Three Volumes / Volume I / Copyright ©
1939, 1943 by August Derleth and Donald Wandrei
/ Copyright © 1964 by August Derleth / All rights
reserved. / Printed for the Library of Congress /
Washington, D.C. / By Permission of the Copyright
Holder / August Derleth / American Printing
House for the Blind / Louisville, Kentucky / 1974

Perfect-bound: [i-ii] iii [iv] v [vi] vii [viii] 1-123 [123a-c]

[i]: title; [ii]: blank; iii, v: title page in Braille; [iv, vi]: blank; vii:
contents list; [viii]: blank; 1-123: beginning of ATMOM; [123a-
c]: blank.

Volume II:

[Title page is identical to above save that the volume number
has been changed accordingly.]

Perfect-bound: [i-ii] iii [iv] v [vi] 124-236

[i]: title; [ii]: blank; iii: copyright page; [iv]: blank; v: contents
list; [vi]: blank; 124-216: conclusion of ATMOM; 217-36: beginning of SH.

Volume III:

[Title page is identical to above save that the volume number
has been changed accordingly.]

Perfect-bound: [i-ii] iii [iv] v [vi] 237-359 [360]

[i]: title; [ii]: blank; iii: copyright page; [iv]: blank; v: contents
list; [vi]: blank; 237-72: conclusion of SH; 273-346: DWH; 347-
59: SRC; [360]: blank.

Notes. All volumes bound in red spiral cloth binders; spine
stamped in gold; 28.2 × 28 cm. All page numbers are in Braille.
Each volume is provided with a built-in page marker.

B. Contributions to Periodicals

i. Fiction

1. "The Alchemist." *The United Amateur*, 16, No. 4 (November 1916), 53-57.

    Juvenilia; written in 1908.

2. *At the Mountains of Madness. Astounding Stories*, 16, No. 6 (February 1936), 8-32; 17, No. 1 (March 1936), 125-55; 17, No. 2 (April 1936), 132-50.

    This text differs from the manuscript and from the book appearances, primarily in paragraphing changes and deletions (about 1,000 words) made by the editor of the magazine, F. Orlin Tremaine. These errors are only partially corrected in the book versions.

3. "Azathoth." *Leaves*, 2 (1938), 107.

    Fragment.

4. "The Beast in the Cave." *The Vagrant*, No. 7 (June 1918), pp. 113-20. *The Acolyte*, 2, No. 1 (Fall 1943), 23-26.

    Juvenilia; written on 21 April 1905.

5. "Beyond the Wall of Sleep." *Pine Cones*, 1, No. 6 (October 1919), 2-10. *The Fantasy Fan*, 2, No. 2 (October 1934), 25-32. *Weird Tales*, 31, No. 3 (March 1938), 331-38.

6. "The Book." *Leaves*, 2 (1938), 110-12.

    Fragment. The title is not Lovecraft's.

7. "The Call of Cthulhu." *Weird Tales*, 11, No. 2 (February 1928), 159-78, 287.

    Includes the subtitle, "(Found among the Papers of the Late Francis Wayland Thurston, of Boston)," as a footnote. The appearance in I-C-99 also includes it.

8. *The Case of Charles Dexter Ward. Weird Tales*, 35, No. 9
   (May 1941), 8-40; 35, No. 10 (July 1941), 84-121.

   Later printings of the novel restored the deletions in the text
   made here by the editor of the magazine, Dorothy McIlwraith.

9. "The Cats of Ulthar." *The Tryout*, 6, No. 11 (November
   1920), [3-9]. *Weird Tales*, 7, No. 2 (February 1926),
   252-54. *Weird Tales*, 21, No. 2 (February 1933), 259-
   61. *The Aonian*, 1, No. 4 (Winter 1943), 73-75. *Fantastic Novels Magazine*, 4, No. 5 (January 1951), 114-16.

10. "Celephaïs." *The Rainbow*, No. 2 (May 1922), pp. 10-
    12. *Marvel Tales*, 1, No. 1 (May 1934), 26, 28-32.
    Weird Tales, 34, No. 1 (June-July 1939), 129-32.

    No published versions include the diaeresis over the *i* in the
    title.

11. "The Colour out of Space." *Amazing Stories*, Vol. 2,
    No. 6 (September 1927), 557-67. *Famous Fantastic
    Mysteries*, 3, No. 4 (October 1941), 98-115.

12. "Cool Air." *Tales of Magic and Mystery*, 1, No. 4 (March
    1928), 29-34. *Weird Tales*, 34, No. 3 (September
    1939), 95-101. *Weird Tales* (British) (1944). *Strange
    Tales*, 2 [1946], 50-56.

    British *Weird Tales* appearance not seen.

13. "Dagon." *The Vagrant*, No. 11 (November 1919), pp.
    23-29. *Weird Tales*, 2, No. 3 (October 1923), 23-25.
    Weird Tales, 27, No. 1 (January 1936), 118-23. *Weird
    Tales*, 44, No. 1 (November 1951), 32-35.

14. "The Descendant." *Leaves*, 2 (1938), 107-10.
    Fragment. The title is not Lovecraft's.

15. "The Doom That Came to Sarnath." *The Scot*, No. 44
    (June 1920), pp. 90-98. *Marvel Tales of Science and Fan-
    tasy*, 1, No. 4 (March-April 1935), 157-63. *Weird*

Tales, 31, No. 6 (June 1938), 742-46. *Kaleidoscope*, 1, No. 2 (1960), 6-10. *Bizarre Fantasy Tales*, 1, No. 1 (Fall 1970), 81-88.

16. *The Dream-Quest of Unknown Kadath. The Arkham Sampler*, 1, No. 1 (Winter 1948), 49-74; 1, No. 2 (Spring 1948), 62-83; 1, No. 3 (Summer 1948), 61-87; 1, No. 4 (Autumn 1948), 52-75.

17. "The Dreams in the Witch House." *Weird Tales*, 22, No. 1 (July 1933), 86-111. *Magazine of Horror*, 1, No. 4 (May 1964), 88-123.

    All appearances include a hyphen between the last two words of the title; but the hyphen does not appear in Lovecraft's A.Ms.

18. "The Dunwich Horror." *Weird Tales*, 13, No. 4 (April 1929), 481-508.

19. "The Evil Clergyman." *Weird Tales*, 33, No. 4 (April 1939), 135-37. *Fantasmith*, No. 1 (May 1953), pp. 3-5.

    Extract of a letter to Bernard Austin Dwyer. Both as "The Wicked Clergyman" (a title given by Dwyer).

20. "Ex Oblivione." *The United Amateur*, 20, No. 4 (March 1921), 59-60 (as by "Ward Phillips"). *The Phantagraph*, 6, No. 3 (July 1937), 2-4. *Magazine of Horror*, 4, No. 6 (November 1968), 46-48.

    Prose poem.

21. "Facts concerning the Late Arthur Jermyn and His Family." *The Wolverine*, No. 9 (March 1921), pp. 3-11; No. 10 (June 1921), pp. 6-11. *Weird Tales*, 3, No. 4 (April 1924), 15-18 (as "The White Ape"). *Weird Tales*, 25, No. 5 (May 1935), 642-48 (as "Arthur Jermyn").

    All anthological appearances and book publications (save where noted) print the title as "Arthur Jermyn."

22. "The Festival." *Weird Tales*, 5, No. 1 (January 1925), 169-74. *Weird Tales*, 22, No. 4 (October 1933), 519-20, 522-28. *Edgar Wallace Mystery Magazine*, No. 1 (March 1966).

   Last appearance not seen.

23. "From Beyond." *The Fantasy Fan*, 1, No. 10 (June 1934), 147-51, 160. *Weird Tales*, 31, No. 2 (February 1938), 227-31. *Mayfair Magazine* (December 1969).

   Last appearance not seen.

24. "The Haunter of the Dark." *Weird Tales*, 28, No. 5 (December 1936), 538-53.

25. "He." *Weird Tales*, 8, No. 3 (September 1926), 373-80. *Weird Terror Tales*, 1, No. 1 (Winter 1969-70), 56-65.

26. "Herbert West—Reanimator." Published as a six-part serial in *Home Brew* (as "Grewsome Tales") and in *Weird Tales* as follows:

   I. "From the Dark." *Home Brew*, 1, No. 1 (February 1922), 19-25. *Weird Tales*, 36, No. 4 (March 1942), 84-88; II. "The Plague Demon." *Home Brew*, 1, No. 2 (March 1922), 45-50. *Weird Tales*, 36, No. 6 (July 1942), 86-90; III. "Six Shots by Moonlight." *Home Brew*, 1, No. 3 (April 1922), 21-26. *Weird Tales*, 36, No. 7 (September 1942), 75-78; IV. "The Scream of the Dead." *Home Brew*, 1, No. 4 (May 1922), 53-58. *Weird Tales*, 36, No. 8 (November 1942), 96-99; V. "The Horror from the Shadows." *Home Brew*, No. 5 (June 1922), 45-50. *Weird Tales*, 37, No. 1 (September 1943), 88-91; VI. "The Tomb-Legions." *Home Brew*, 1, No. 6 (July 1922), 57-62. *Weird Tales*, 37, No. 2 (November 1943), 101-07.

27. "History of the *Necronomicon*." *The Arkham Sampler*, 1, No. 1 (Winter 1948), 15-19. *Mirage*, 1, No. 6 (Winter 1963-64), 34-36.

   A tongue-in-cheek account of the origins of the mythical book invented by Lovecraft. The first publication contains remarks by August Derleth which he later rewrote into the essay, "The Making of a Hoax" (III-D-396). Both as "History and Chronology of the *Necronomicon*."

28. "The Horror at Red Hook." *Weird Tales*, 9, No. 1 (January 1927), 59-73. *Weird Tales*, 44, No. 3 (March 1952), 56-68. *Bizarre Mystery Magazine*, 1, No. 1 (October 1965), 112-35.

29. "The Hound." *Weird Tales*, 3, No. 2 (February 1924), 50-52, 78. *Weird Tales*, 14, No. 3 (September 1929), 421-25, 432.

30. "Hypnos." *The National Amateur*, 45, No. 5 (May 1923), 1-3. *Weird Tales*, 4, No. 2 (May-June-July 1924), 33-35. *Weird Tales*, 30, No. 5 (November 1937), 626-31.

31. "Ibid." *The O-Wash-Ta-Nong*, 3, No. 1 (January 1938), 11-13. *The Phantagraph*, 8, No. 2 (June 1940), 2-7.

    Mock biography of "Ibid," originally taken from a letter to Maurice W. Moe (ca. 1928).

32. "In the Vault." *The Tryout*, 10, No. 6 (November 1925), [3-17]. *Weird Tales*, 19, No. 4 (April 1932), 459-65.

    The first appearance contains a dedication: "Dedicated to C. W. Smith, from whose suggestion the central situation is taken."

33. "The Lurking Fear." *Home Brew*, 2, No. 6 (January 1923), 4-10 (with subtitle: "The Shadow on the Chimney"); 3, No. 1 (February 1923), 18-23 (with subtitle: "A Passer in the Storm"); 3, No. 2 (March 1923), 31-37, 44, 48 (with subtitle: "What the Red Glare Meant"); 3, No. 3 (April 1923), 35-42 (with subtitle: "The Horror in the Eyes"). *Weird Tales*, 11, No. 6 (June 1928), 791-804. *Startling Mystery Stories*, 1, No. 1 (Summer 1966), 51-71.

    Each installment of the *Home Brew* serialization contained illustrations by Clark Ashton Smith.

34. "Memory." *The United Co-operative*, 1, No. 2 (June 1919), 8. *Gargoyle*, 1, No. 1 (1950), 9. *Magazine of Horror*, 4, No. 6 (November 1968), 41-42.

     Prose poem.

35. "The Moon-Bog." *Weird Tales*, 7, No. 6 (June 1926), 805-10.

36. "The Music of Erich Zann." *The National Amateur*, 44, No. 4 (March 1922), 38-40. *Weird Tales*, 5, No. 5 (May 1925), 219-24. *The Evening Standard* (London), No. 33,754 (24 October 1932) pp. 20-21. *Weird Tales*, 24, No. 5 (November 1934), 644-48, 655-56. *Famous Fantastic Mysteries*, 12, No. 3 (March 1951), 90-94. *Fresco*, 8, No. 3 (Spring 1958), 61-68.

37. "The Nameless City." *The Wolverine*, No. 11 (November 1921), pp. 3-15. *Fanciful Tales*, 1, No. 1 (Fall 1936), 5-18. *Weird Tales*, 32, No. 5 (November 1938), 617-26. *Young Americans*, 2, No. 10 (October 1959), 36-42.

     Prior bibliographies have listed a "Transatlantic Circular [sic]" appearance of 1921. The Transatlantic Circulator was, however, a group of English and American *littérateurs* who exchanged works in manuscript and criticized them. Lovecraft sent nearly a dozen poems and stories through the Circulator.

38. "Nyarlathotep." *The United Amateur*, 20, No. 2 (November 1920), 19-21. *The National Amateur*, 43, No. 6 (July 1926), 53-54. *Supramundane Stories*, 1, No. 2 (Spring 1938), 1-2, 4. *Magazine of Horror*, 4, No. 6 (November 1968), 44-46. *The Arkham Collector*, No. 6 (Winter 1970), pp. 163-66.

     Prose poem.

39. "The Other Gods." *The Fantasy Fan*, 1, No. 3 (November 1933), 35-38. *True Supernatural Stories* (October 1934). *Weird Tales*, 32, No. 4 (October 1938), 489-92.

      Second appearance not seen.

40. "The Outsider." *Weird Tales*, 7, No. 4 (April 1926), 449-53. *Weird Tales*, 17, No. 4 (June-July 1931), 566-71. *Famous Fantastic Mysteries*, 11, No. 5 (June 1950), 114-18. *Startling Mystery Stories*, 3, No. 2 (Winter 1969), 47-53.

41. "Pickman's Model." *Weird Tales*, 10, No. 4 (October 1927), 505-14. *Weird Tales*, 28, No. 4 (November 1936), 495-505. *Famous Fantastic Mysteries*, 13, No. 1 (December 1951), 88-94.

42. "The Picture in the House." *The National Amateur*, 41, No. 6 (July 1919), 246-49. *Weird Tales*, 3, No. 1 (January 1924), 40-42. *Weird Tales*, 29, No. 3 (March 1937), 370-73.

      This tale was written in December 1920; for the explanation of its appearance in the "July 1919" issue of *The National Amateur*, see W. Paul Cook's book on Lovecraft (III-C-4).

43. "Polaris." *The Philosopher*, 1, No. 1 (December 1920), 3-5. *The National Amateur*, 48, No. 5 (May 1926), 48-49. *The Fantasy Fan*, 1, No. 6 (February 1934), 83-85. *Weird Tales*, 30, No. 6 (December 1937), 749-51, 759.

44. "The Quest of Iranon." *The Galleon*, 1, No. 5 (July-August 1935), 12-20. *Weird Tales*, 33, No. 3 (March 1939), 125-29. *Mirage*, 1, No. 5 (Summer 1962), 16-20.

45. "The Rats in the Walls." *Weird Tales*, 3, No. 3 (March 1924), 25-31. *Weird Tales*, 15, No. 6 (June 1930), 841-

    53. *Rex Stout Mystery Magazine*, No. 3 (February 1946), pp. 68-84.

46. "A Reminiscence of Dr. Samuel Johnson." *The United Amateur*, 17, No. 2 (November 1917), 21-24 (as by "Humphry Littlewit, Esq.").

47. "The Shadow out of Time." *Astounding Stories*, 17, No. 4 (June 1936), 110-54.

48. "The Shadow over Innsmouth." *Weird Tales*, 36, No. 3 (January 1942), 6-33. *Weird Tales* (Canadian), 36, No. 3 (May 1942), 16-45.

    Both *Weird Tales* appearances are abridged.

49. "Discarded Draught: The Shadow over Innsmouth." *The Acolyte*, 2, No. 2 (Spring 1944), 3-7.

    Collection of the surviving fragments of Lovecraft's first draft of the story.

50. "The Shunned House." *Weird Tales*, 30, No. 4 (October 1937), 418-36.

51. "The Silver Key." *Weird Tales*, 13, No. 1 (January 1929), 41-49, 144.

52. "The Statement of Randolph Carter." *The Vagrant*, No. 13 (May 1920), pp. 41-48. *Weird Tales*, 5, No. 2 (February 1925), 149-53. *Weird Tales*, 30, No. 2 (August 1937), 242-46.

53. "The Strange High House in the Mist." *Weird Tales*, 18, No. 3 (October 1931), 394-400.

54. "The Street." *The Wolverine*, No. 8 (December 1920), pp. 2-12. *The National Amateur*, 44, No. 3 (January 1922), 25-27.

    Often listed as juvenilia, this tale was probably written in 1919 or 1920.

55. "Sweet Ermengarde; or, the Heart of a Country Girl." *Mirage*, 2, No. 1 (1965), 15-20 (without subtitle).

> A parody on stories of the Horatio Alger type.

56. "The Temple." *Weird Tales*, 6, No. 3 (September 1925), 329-36, 429-31. *Weird Tales*, 27, No. 2 (February 1936), 239-44, 246-49.

57. "The Terrible Old Man." *The Tryout*, 7, No. 4 (July 1921), [10-14]. *Weird Tales*, 8, No. 2 (August 1926), 191-92.

58. "The Thing in the Moonlight." *Bizarre*, 4, No. 1 (January 1941), 5, 20. *The Arkham Collector*, No. 4 (Winter 1969), pp. 107-10.

> Fragment. The title is probably not Lovecraft's; indeed, whether the entire text is Lovecraft's is now under question.

59. "The Thing on the Doorstep." *Weird Tales*, 29, No. 1 (January 1937), 52-70.

60. "The Tomb." *The Vagrant*, No. 14 (March 1922), pp. 50-64. *Weird Tales*, 7, No. 1 (January 1926), 117-23.

61. "The Tree." *The Tryout*, 7, No. 7 (October 1921), [3-10]. *Weird Tales*, 32, No. 2 (August 1938), 234-36.

62. "The Unnamable." *Weird Tales*, 6, No. 1 (July 1925), 78-82.

> Some have believed that this tale first appeared in some issue of *The Vagrant*; this is not the case.

63. "What the Moon Brings." *The National Amateur*, 45, No. 5 (May 1923), 9. *Cosmic Tales*, No. 15 (April-May-June 1941). *Magazine of Horror*, 4, No. 6 (November 1968), 42-44.

> Prose poem. Second appearance not seen.

64. "The Whisperer in Darkness." *Weird Tales*, 18, No. 1 (August 1931), 32-73.

65. "The White Ship." *The United Amateur*, 19, No. 2 (November 1919), 30-33. *Weird Tales*, 9, No. 3 (March 1927), 386-89. *Whispers*, 1, No. 4 (July 1974), [32-40] (facsimile of the A.Ms.).

ii. Nonfiction

1. "The Allowable Rhyme." *The Conservative*, 1, No. 3 (October 1915), 3-6.

    A brief history of rhyming tendencies in English verse from "Chevy-Chase" to Thomas Moore.

2. "Amateur Notes." *The Conservative*, 1, No. 2 (July 1915), 11 (unsigned).

    Remarks on the "peculiar appearance of [the] preceding issue" of *The Conservative*.

3. "The Amateur Press." *The Lake Breeze*, No. 19 (April 1915), pp. 136-37.

    Review of *Ole Miss*, March 1915. Lovecraft wrote only part of the article: other journals were reviewed by other critics.

4. "Amateurdom." *The Conservative*, 5, No. 1 (July 1919), 12 (unsigned).

    Remarks on current amateur papers.

5. "Americanism." *The United Amateur*, 18, No. 6 (July 1919), 118-20.

    A diatribe on the "melting pot" notion in American racial policies.

6. "Among the Amateurs." *The Conservative*, 2, No. 3 (October 1916), [11] (unsigned).

    Notes on John Russell, amateur versification, amateur factions, Maurice W. Moe, W. Paul Cook, Jonathan E. Hoag, and the 1916-17 Yearbook of the U.A.P.A.

7. "Among the New-Comers." *The United Amateur*, 15,
   No. 10 (May 1916), 134-36 (as by "El Imparcial").

8. "Astrology and the Future." *The* [Providence] *Evening
   News*, 45, No. 123 (13 October 1914), 8 (as
   "Astrlogh and the Future"; as by "Isaac Bickerstaffe,
   Jr.").

   Reply to J. F. Hartmann against astrology.

Astronomical articles for The Pawtuxet Valley Gleaner (Phenix, R.I.), 1906.

9. "The Heavens for August: Celestial Phenomena to
   Happen Next Month." 31, No. 30 (27 July 1906), 1.

10. "The Skies of September: Planetary and Stellar
    Motions Described." 31, No. 35 (31 August 1906),
    1.

11. "Is Mars an Inhabited World? Startling Theories of
    Prof. Lowell on the Subject." 31, No. 36 (7
    September 1906), 1.

12. "Is There Life on the Moon? Strange Revelations of
    Modern Science." 31, No. 37 (14 September 1906),
    1.

13. "An Interesting Phenomenon: Occultation of a Star
    on the 25th of This Month." 31, No. 38 (21
    September 1906), 1.

14. "October Heavens: Celestial Scenery for the Coming
    Month." 31, No. 39 (28 September 1906), 1.

15. "Are There Undiscovered Planets? Boundaries of
    Our System Still Shrouded in Obscurity." 31, No.
    40 (5 October 1906), 3.

16. "Can the Moon Be Reached by Man? Showing That
    the Trip to Our Satellite, Heretofore Attempted

Only in Fiction, May Be a Scientific Possibility." 31, No. 41 (12 October 1906), 2.

17. "The Moon: A Brief Description of Our Satellite." 31, No. 42 (19 October 1906), 7.

18. [Untitled.] 31, No. 43 (26 October 1906), 8.

19. "The Sun: Centre of the Planetary System." 31, No. 44 (2 November 1906), 5.

20. "The Leonids: Directions How to Observe the Coming Shower." 31, No. 45 (9 November 1906), 5.

21. "Comets: The Wanderers of Our System." 31, No. 46 (16 November 1906), 1.

22. "December Skies: Celestial Events for the Christmas Month." 31, No. 48 (30 November 1906), 5.

23. "The Fixed Stars: An Account of the Sidereal Heavens." 31, No. 49 (7 December 1906), 4.

24. "Clusters-Nebulae: Strange Bodies of Interstella [sic] Space." 31, No. 51 (21 December 1906), 5.

25. "January Heavens." 31, No. 52 (28 December 1906), 5.

    See also I-E-ii-1.

Astronomical articles for The [Providence] Morning Tribune, The [Providence] Evening Tribune, and The [Providence] Sunday Tribune, 1906-08.

    Note. Abbreviations: *MT* (*Morning Tribune*); *ET* (*Evening Tribune*); *ST* (*Sunday Tribune*). All articles, save where indicated, are illustrated by H. P. Lovecraft (maps of the prominent constellations for the month).

26. "In the August Sky." *MT*, 1, No. 25 (1 August 1906), 6. *ET*, 1, No. 121 (1 August 1906), 6.

The latter paper was then called *The* [Providence] *Evening Tribune and Telegram.* This article had no illustration.

27. "The September Heavens: Celestial Motions for the Coming Month." *MT*, 1, No. 52 (1 September 1906), 6. *ET*, 1, No. 148 (1 September 1906), 6.

    No illustration.

28. "Astronomy in October: Autumn Views of the Celestial Bodies during Present Month." *MT*, 1, No. 77 (1 October 1906), 10. *ET*, 1, No. 172 (1 October 1906), 9.

29. "The Skies of November: Planets, Stars and Meteors Conspicuous This Month." *MT*, 1, No. 104 (1 November 1906), 5. *ET*, 1, No. 199 (1 November 1906), 4.

30. "The Heavens for December: Unusually Brilliant Skies during the Closing Month of 1906." *MT*, 1, No. 130 (1 December 1906), 10. *ET*, 1, No. 224 (1 December 1906), 11 (unsigned).

31. "The Heavens in January: Astronomical Events of the Opening Months of 1907." *MT*, 1, No. 156 (1 January 1907), 8. *ET*, 2, No. 1 (1 January 1907), 9.

32. "The Heavens in February: Celestial Phenomena during the Shortest Month of the Year." *MT*, 2, No. 28 (1 February 1907), 9.

33. "The Heavens in March: Astronomy for the Opening Month of Spring." *MT*, 2, No. 53 (2 March 1907), 12. *ET*, 2, No. 53 (2 March 1907), 3.

34. "April Skies: The Heavens for the Coming Month." *ET*, 2, No. 78 (1 April 1907), 15.

35. "The Heavens in May: Celestial Motions for the

Coming Month." *MT*, 2, No. 104 (1 May 1907), 5. *ET*, 2, No. 104 (1 May 1907), 6.

36. "The Heavens in June: Planetary and Stellar Configurations for the Opening Month of Summer." *MT*, 2, No. 131 (1 June 1907), 8.

      No illustration.

37. "Astronomy in August: The Heavens for This Month.—Mars the Ruling Planet." *MT*, 2, No. 183 (1 August 1907), 8. *ET*, 2, No. 181 (1 August 1907), 12.

38. "The Heavens for September: Astronomy during the First Month of Autumn." *ST*, 2, No. 35 (1 September 1907), 8.

39. "The Skies of October: Celestial Events for the Coming Month." *MT*, 2, No. 235 (1 October 1907), 2. *ET*, 2, No. 232 (1 October 1907), 13.

40. "The Heavens in November: Transit of Mars Forms Chief Event of the Coming Month." *MT*, 2, No. 262 (1 November 1907), 5. *ET*, 2, No. 259 (1 November 1907), 17.

      Unsigned in both appearances.

41. "Heavens for December: Planetary and Stellar Motions for the Closing Month of 1907." *ST*, 2, No. 47 (1 December 1907), 15.

42. "The Heavens in January: Astronomical Phenomena for the Coming Month." *ET*, 3, No. 1 (1 January 1908), 4. *MT*, 3, No. 2 (2 January 1908), 10.

43. "February Skies: Celestial Events for the Coming Month." *ET*, 3, No. 28 (1 February 1908), 5.

44. "The Heavens in the Month of March: Jupiter and
    Venus Principal Objects: Neptune Is the Least
    Prominent of All the Planets in the Evening Sky,
    Being Invisible to the Naked Eye.—The Moon's
    Phases." *MT*, 3, No. 53 (2 March 1908), 4. *ET*, 3,
    No. 54 (3 March 1908), 6.

    In the latter, only the illustration, titled, "The Evening Sky in
    March," appeared.

45. "Solar Eclipse Feature of June Heavens: Supposed
    Discovery of an Eighth Satellite Attending Jupiter Is
    Attracting Much Attention to That Planet.—The
    Evening Sky Offers Field for Study." *MT*, 3, No.
    131 (1 June 1908), 4. *ET*, 3, No. 130 (1 June 1908),
    Sec. 2, p. 2.

    No illustration.

Astronomical Articles for The [Providence] Evening News, 1914-18.

46. "The January Sky." 44, No. 38 (1 January 1914), 6.

47. "The February Sky." 44, No. 63 (31 January 1914), 6.

48. "The March Sky." 44, No. 88 (2 March 1914), 8.

49. "The April Sky." 44, No. 113 (31 March 1914), 8.

50. "May Sky." 44, No. 141 (1 May 1914), 12.

51. "The June Sky." 45, No. 11 (29 May 1914), 12, 5.

52. "The July Sky." 45, No. 37 (30 June 1914), 6.

53. "The August Sky." 45, No. 64 (1 August 1914), 8.

54. "The September Sky." 45, No. 89 (1 September
    1914), 8.

55. "The October Sky." 45, No. 113 (30 September 1914), 6.

56. "The November Sky." 45, No. 139 (31 October 1914), 10.

57. "The December Sky." 46, No. 10 (30 November 1914), 8.

58. "The January Sky." 46, No. 35 (31 December 1914), 8.

59. "The February Sky." 46, No. 61 (30 January 1915), 8.

60. "The March Sky." 46, No. 85 (27 February 1915), 10.

61. "April Skies." 46, No. 113 (1 April 1915), 7.

62. "The May Sky." 46, No. 138 (30 April 1915), 8.

63. "The June Skies." 47, No. 1 (1 June 1915), 8.

64. "The July Skies." 47, No. 27 (30 June 1915), 6.

65. "The August Skies." 47, No. 53 (31 July 1915), 8.

66. "September Skies." 47, No. 79 (1 September 1915), 8.

67. "October Skies." 47, No. 104 (1 October 1915), 8.

68. "November Skies." 47, No. 129 (1 November 1915), 8.

69. "December Skies." 47, No. 153 (30 November 1915), 8.

70. "January Skies." 48, No. 25 (31 December 1915), 8.

71. "The February Skies." 48, No. 52 (1 February 1916), 8.

72. "March Skies." 48, No. 76 (1 March 1916), 6.

73. "April Skies." 48, No. 103 (1 April 1916), 8.

74. "May Skies." 48, No. 130 (3 May 1916), 8.

75. "June Skies." 49, No. 1 (1 June 1916), 6.

76. "July Skies." 49, No. 27 (1 July 1916), 8.

77. "August Skies." 49, No. 52 (1 August 1916), 6.

78. "September Skies." 49, No. 79 (1 September 1916), 6.

79. "October Skies." 49, No. 104 (2 October 1916), 6.

80. "November Skies." 49, No. 129 (31 October 1916), 2.

81. "December Skies." 50, No. 3 (1 December 1916), 8.

82. "January Skies." 50, No. 26 (2 January 1917), 8.

83. "February Skies." 50, No. 52 (1 February 1917), 6.

84. "March Skies." 50, No. 73 (28 February 1917), 6.

85. "April Skies." 50, No. 102 (2 April 1917), 6.

86. "May Skies." 50, No. 127 (1 May 1917), 5.

87. "June Skies." 50, No. 153 (1 June 1917), 3.

88. "July Skies." 51, No. 25 (2 July 1917), 4.

89. "August Skies." 51, No. 49 (31 July 1917), 3.

90. "September Skies." 51, No. 76 (31 August 1917), 3.

91. "October Skies." 51, No. 96 (2 October 1917), 4.

92. "November Skies." 51, No. 125 (5 November 1917), 3.

93. "December Skies." 51, No. 147 (1 December 1917), 3.

94. "January Skies." 52, No. 19 (2 January 1918), 3.

95. "February Skies." 52, No. 45 (1 February 1918), 7.

96. "March Skies." 52, No. 66 (1 March 1918), 7.

97. "April Skies." 52, No. 92 (1 April 1918), 4.

98. "May Skies." 52, No. 119 (2 May 1918), 9.

---

99. "At the Root." *The United Amateur*, 17, No. 6 (July 1918), 111-12.

    On the innate militant instincts of man.

100. "Autobiography of Howard Phillips Lovecraft." *The Boys' Herald*, 71, No. 1 (October 1941), 7.

    Very brief autobiographical sketch largely concerned with his amateur activities.

101. "Bolshevism." *The Conservative*, 5, No. 1 (July 1919), 10-11 (unsigned).

    Comments on the "almost sub-human Russian rabble."

102. "The Brief Autobiography of an Inconsequential Scribbler." *The Silver Clarion*, 3, No. 1 (April 1919), 8-9.

103. "Brumalia." *The Tryout*, 3, No. 1 (December 1916), [22].

    A note on the poem of the same name; see I-B-iii-19.

104. "Bureau of Critics." *The National Amateur*, 45, No. 4 (March 1923), 1-3 (unsigned); 56, No. 4 (June 1934), 7-8 (verse section); 58, No. 2 (December 1935), 14-15 (section titled "Some Current Amateur Verse").

    A regular review section of amateur journals. Part of the first article was probably written by Lovecraft (the section labelled "Contributed"); Samuel Loveman and Edward H. Cole also wrote sections of it.

105. "Bureau of Critics Comment on Verse, Typography, Prose." *The National Amateur*, 56, No. 2 (December 1933), 1-2.

106. "The Case for Classicism: A Reply to Prof. Philip B. McDonald." *The United Co-operative*, 1, No. 2 (June 1919), 3-5.

    A defense of the study of the classics for literary and intellectual edification.

107. "Cats and Dogs." *Leaves*, 1 (Summer 1937), 25-34 (as by "Lewis Theobald, Jun.").

    Witty essay on the aesthetic supremacy of cats over dogs.

108. "Chairman of the Bureau of Critics Reports on Poetry: Lovecraft Finds Much Good Verse; Commends Improvement Campaign." *The National Amateur*, 57, No. 1 (5 September 1934), Sec. 2, p. 3.

109. "Comment." *The Silver Clarion*, 2, No. 3 (June 1918), 6-8.

110. "Concerning 'Persia—in Europe.' " *The Tryout*, 3, No. 2 (January 1917), [7-8].

    Remark on a curious factual error made in James F. Morton's " 'Conservatism' Run Mad" (III-D-460).

111. "A Confession of Unfaith." *The Liberal*, 1, No. 2 (February 1922), 17-23.

    Significant autobiographical essay devoted largely to Lovecraft's religious and philosophical beliefs. Lovecraft copied verbatim much of this essay in his autobiographical letter to Edwin Baird of 3 February 1924.

112. "The Conservative and His Critics." *The Conservative*, 1, No. 2 (July 1915), 5-6 (unsigned).

    Remarks on criticisms of the first issue of *The Conservative* by other amateurs.

113. "The Conservative and His Critics." *The Conservative*, 1, No. 3 (October 1915), 7-8 (unsigned).

    On Charles D. Isaacson.

114. "Consolidation's Autopsy." *The Lake Breeze*, No. 19
(April 1915), p. 133 (as by "El Imparcial").

    A plea to unite the United and National Amateur Press
    Associations.

115. "The Convention." *The Tryout*, 13, No. 8 (July 1930),
[3-11] (as by "Theobald").

116. "The Crime of the Century." *The Conservative*, 1, No.
1 (April 1915), [4-5]. *The Trail*, 1, No. 2 (January
1916), 22.

    On the shameful tactics of the British and the Germans, who
    are "blood brothers" but who are battling each other in "the
    present European war."

117. "Critics Submit First Report: H. P. Lovecraft and
Helm C. Spink Turn in Criticisms." *The National
Amateur*, 55, No. 2 (December 1932), 1-2 (section
titled "Verse Section").

118. "Defining the 'Ideal' Paper: A Discussion of
Amateur Papers, by Babcock, Lovecraft, and
Edkins." *The National Amateur*, 62, No. 3 (June 1940),
8-12.

    The Lovecraft portion appears, with no separate heading, on
    pp. 10-12.

119. "Delavan's Comet and Astrology." *The* [Providence]
Evening News, 45, No. 134 (26 October 1914), 8 (as by
"Isaac Bickerstaffe, Jr.").

    Essay against astrology satirizing J. F. Hartmann.

120. "Department of Public Criticism." *The United
Amateur*, 14, No. 2 (November 1914), 21-25; 14, No.
3 (January 1915), 35-38; 14, No. 4 (March 1915), 61-
65; 14, No. 5 (May 1915), 87-92; 15, No. 2
(September 1915), 17-27; 15, No. 5 (December

1915), 63-69; 15, No. 9 (April 1916), 111-17; 15, No.
11 (June 1916), 143-49; 16, No. 1 (August 1916), 6-
10 (with subtitle: "First Annual Report 1915-1916");
16, No. 2 (September 1916), 25-31; 16, No. 7
(March 1917), 85-91; 16, No. 8 (May 1917), 106-14;
16, No. 9 (July 1917), 122-24; 18, No. 1 (September
1918), 3-8 (unsigned); 18, No. 2 (November 1918),
29-32 (unsigned); 18, No. 3 (January 1919), 53-59
(unsigned); 18, No. 4 (March 1919), 79-82; 18, No. 5
(May 1919), 99-103.

> Criticisms of amateur journals. Only a part of the article for
> September 1918 appears to be Lovecraft's.

121. "A Descent to Avernus." *Bacon's Essays*, 2, No. 2
(Summer 1929), 8.

> On visiting the Endless Caverns in Virginia.

122. "The Despised Pastoral." *The Conservative*, 4, No. 1
(July 1918), 2.

> A defense of pastoral poetry.

123. "The Dignity of Journalism." *Dowdell's Bearcat*, 4, No.
4 (July 1915), [6-9].

> On the regrettable prevalence of slang in amateurdom.

124. "Dr. Eugene B. Kunz [sic]." *Hodge Podge*, 5, No. 6
(September 1935), [1].

> A plug for *Thoughts and Pictures* (see I-D-i-3).

125. "Dr. Jekyll and Mr. Hyde." *The Boys' Herald*, 63, No. 1
(1 January 1934), 7-8.

> Excerpt from "Looking Backward" (see I-B-ii-170) with a
> three-paragraph introduction by Edwin Hadley Smith.

126. "East and West Harvard Conservatism." *Mind Power
Plus*, [1922], pp. 55-56.

> On the success of Dr. David Van Bush's new psychological

theories in a conservative and sophisticated New England. Only a clipping of this essay, not the periodical containing it, has been seen.

127. "Editorial." *The Conservative*, 1, No. 1 (April 1915), [5-6]; 1, No. 2 (July 1915), 4-5; 1, No. 3 (October 1915), 6-7.

All are unsigned.

128. "Editorial." *The Providence Amateur*, 1, No. 2 (February 1916), 9-13.

129. "Editorial." *The United Amateur*, 20, No. 2 (November 1920), 29; 21, No. 1 (September 1921), 7-8 (unsigned); 21, No. 3 (January 1922), 36 (unsigned); 23, No. 1 (May 1924), 10-11; 24, No. 1 (July 1925), 8-9.

130. "Editorial Excerpt from *The United Amateur*." *Interesting Items* (July 1950).

Not seen.

131. "Editorially." *The United Amateur*, 16, No. 9 (July 1917), 130-31 (unsigned).

132. "Editor's Note" to "The Genesis of the Revolutionary War" by Henry Clapham McGavack. *The Conservative*, 3, No. 1 (July 1917), [1].

133. "Editor's Note" to "The Irish and the Fairies" by Peter J. MacManus. *The Providence Amateur*, 1, No. 2 (February 1916), 2-3.

134. "Editor's Note" to "A Scene for Macbeth" by Samuel Loveman. *The United Amateur*, 20, No. 2 (November 1920), 17.

135. "The Fall of Astrology." *The* [Providence] *Evening News*, 46, No. 25 (17 December 1914), 8.

Attack on J. F. Hartmann and astrology.

136. "The Falsity of Astrology." *The* [Providence] *Evening News*, 45, No. 122 (10 October 1914), 8.

Another attack on astrology.

137. "Finale." *The Badger*, No. 2 (June 1915), pp. 17-16 [sic].

The pagination is incorrect; the article appeared on pp. 17, 18, 19, and 16 [i.e., 20]. It was divided into three parts: "Campbell's Plan" (pp. 17-18), "Amateur Journalism and Education" (pp. 18-16), and "Encouraging Recruits" (p. 16).

138. "For Official Editor—Anne Tillery Renshaw." *The Conservative*, 5, No. 1 (July 1919), 11-12 (unsigned).

139. "For President—Leo Fritter." *The Conservative*, 1, No. 1 (April 1915), [3] (unsigned).

140. "For What Does the United Stand?" *The United Amateur*, 19, No. 5 (May 1920), 101.

"The United . . . stands for education in the eternal truths of literary art, and for personal aid in the realisation of its members' literary potentialities."

141. " '408 Groveland Street.' " *The Boys' Herald*, 72, No. 1 (January 1943), 4-5.

Includes the essay, "The Haverhill Convention," and a letter to Rheinhart Kleiner (17 July 1917) originally published in "By Post from Providence" (see I-B-v-a-1).

142. "The Haverhill Convention." *The Tryout*, 7, No. 4 (July 1921), [21-25].

On visiting C. W. Smith's home in Haverhill, Mass.

143. "Helene Hoffman Cole—Litterateur." *The United Amateur*, 18, No. 5 (May 1919), 92-93. *The Phoenix*, 5, No. 4 (March 1946), 348-49.

Memorial to a deceased amateur associate.

144. "Heritage or Modernism: Common Sense in Art Forms." *The Californian*, 3, No. 1 (Summer 1935), 23-28.

   Opposes the abandonment of tradition in modern art and architecture.

145. "Homes and Shrines of Poe." *The Californian*, 2, No. 3 (Winter 1934), 8-10. *The Acolyte*, 2, No. 1 (Fall 1943), 5-7.

   On important existing Poe sites, including the Poe cottage at Fordham, N.Y.

146. "Idealism and Materialism—a Reflection." *The National Amateur*, 41, No. 6 (July 1919), 278-81. *Inside and Science Fiction Advertiser*, No. 14 (March 1956), pp. 2-10.

   Powerful philosophical essay championing mechanistic materialism over idealism or religiosity.

147. "An Impartial Spectator." *The Conservative*, 1, No. 3 (October 1915), 12 (unsigned).

   Paragraphs prefacing and following John Russell's poem, "Metrical Regularity; or, Broken Metre."

148. "In a Major Key." *The Conservative*, 1, No. 2 (July 1915), 9-11 (unsigned).

   Remarks on Charles D. Isaacson's journal, *In a Minor Key*.

149. "In Defense of Dagon." *Leaves*, 2 (1938), 117-19.

   An excerpt from the two otherwise unpublished essays, "The Defence Reopens!" and "The Defence Remains Open!", made by R. H. Barlow.

150. "In Memoriam: Henry St. Clair Whitehead." *Weird Tales*, 21, No. 3 (March 1933), 391 (unsigned).

   Tribute to a deceased weird fiction writer and correspondent of Lovecraft's.

151. "In Memoriam: Robert Ervin Howard." *Fantasy Magazine*, No. 38 (September 1936), pp. 29-31.

152. "In the Editor's Study." *The Conservative*, 2, No. 3 (October 1916), [7-11] (unsigned).

    Includes the sections, "The Proposed Author's Union" pp. [7-9], "Revolutionary Mythology" pp. [9-10], and "The Symphonic Ideal" pp. [10-11].

153. "In the Editor's Study." *The Conservative*, 2, No. 4 (January 1917), [2-4] (unsigned).

    Includes the sections, "The Vers Libre Epidemic" (pp. [2-3]) and "Amateur Standards" (pp. [3-4]).

154. "In the Editor's Study." *The Conservative*, 4, No. 1 (July 1918), 5-7 (unsigned).

    Includes the sections, "Anglo-Saxondom" (p. 5), "Amateur Criticism" (pp. 5-6), "The United 1917-1918" (p. 6), "The Amateur Press Club" (pp. 6-7), and "Grace" [poem; prefaced by introductory paragraph entitled "Ward Phillips Replies"] (p. 7).

155. "In the Editor's Study." *The Conservative*, No. 12 (March 1923), pp. 5-8 (unsigned).

    Includes the sections, "Rursus Adsumus" (pp. 5-6) and "Rudis Indigestaque Moles" (pp. 6-8).

156. "In the Editor's Study." *The Conservative*, No. 13 (July 1923), pp. 21-24 (unsigned).

157. "In the Editor's Study: The League." *The Conservative*, 5, No. 1 (July 1919), 9-10 (unsigned).

    On the League of Nations.

158. "In the Editor's Study: A Remarkable Document." *The Conservative*, 3, No. 1 (July 1917), [4] (unsigned).

    On a temperance article by Booth Tarkington.

159. "In the Editor's Study." *The National Amateur*, 46, No. 2 (November 1923), 13-14.

    Reprint of I-B-ii-156 plus I-B-ii-253.

160. "Introducing Mr. Chester Pierce Munroe." *The Conservative*, 1, No. 1 (April 1915), [2] (unsigned).

161. "Introducing Mr. James Pyke." *The Conservative*, 1, No. 4 (January 1916), 1-2 (unsigned).

162. "Introducing Mr. John Russell." *The Conservative*, 1, No. 2 (July 1915), 8-9 (unsigned).

163. "Japanese Hokku." *The O-Wash-Ta-Nong*, 3, No. 1 (January 1938), 13.
      Taken from a letter (to M. W. Moe) from 1936.

164. "Life for Humanity's Sake." *The American Amateur*, 2, No. 1 (September 1920), 93-94.

165. "Liquor and Its Friends." *The Conservative*, 1, No. 3 (October 1915), 10-11 (unsigned).
      On temperance.

166. "Literary Composition." *The United Amateur*, 19, No. 3 (January 1920), 56-60.
      A guide of basic grammatical rules to follow in writing; designed to increase the literary standards of the U.A.P.A.

167. "Literary Review." *The Californian*, 4, No. 3 (Winter 1936), 27-33.
      Lovecraft discusses the contributions of several amateur journals, including *The Californian, Causerie, Ahoy!, Pine Needles*, and others.

168. "The Literature of Rome." *The United Amateur*, 18, No. 2 (November 1918), 17-21, 35-38.
      Brief history of Latin literature. The latter half of this essay (pp. 35-38, unsigned) has never been reprinted.

169. "Little Journeys to the Homes of Prominent Amateurs." *The United Amateur*, 15, No. 3 (October 1915), 39-41; 16, No. 9 (July 1917), 125-28.
      Second and fifth (last), respectively, in a series of articles, the

former concerning Andrew F. Lockhart, the latter Eleanor J. Barnhart. The first article in the series was written by Lockhart himself (see III-D-387). Both articles cited signed "El Imparcial."

170. "Looking Backward." *The Tryout*, 6, No. 2 (February 1920), [3-8]; 6, No. 3 (March 1920), [1-8]; 6, No. 4 (April 1920), [3-10]; 6, No. 5 (May 1920), [3-10]; 6, No. 6 (June 1920), [3-10]. *The Aonian*, 2, No. 3 (Autumn 1944), 146-51; 2, No. 4 (Winter 1944), 177-86.

> A history of amateur journalism from 1882 to 1889.

171. "Lord Dunsany and His Work." *Eldritch Dream-Quest*, No. 3 (1963).

> Not seen.

172. "Lovecraft Offers Verse Criticism." *The National Amateur*, 57, No. 4 (June 1935), 5-6.

173. "Lucubrations Lovecraftian." *The United Co-operative*, 1, No. 3 (April 1921), 8-15.

> Includes the sections, "The Loyal Coalition" (pp. 8-11), "Criticism Again!" (pp. 11-15), "Lest We Forget" (p. 15), and "A Conjecture" (p. 15). These discuss the Irish question and certain remarks directed toward Lovecraft by other amateur writers.

174. "The Materialist Today." *The Drift-Wind*, 1, No. 7 (October 1926), [6-9].

> Brief exposition of materialist thought.

175. "A Matter of Uniteds." *Bacon's Essays*, 1, No. 1 (Summer 1927), 1-3.

> On the split in the U.A.P.A. which occurred in 1912 and which was still causing controversy.

176. "Merlinus Redivivus." *The Conservative*, 4, No. 1 (July 1918), 4-5.

> On the baleful rise of spiritualism in a "war-torn world."

177. "Metrical Regularity." *The Conservative*, 1, No. 2 (July 1915), 2-4.

> On the "ill effects of metrical laxity on the younger generation of poets."

178. "Mrs. Miniter—Estimates and Recollections." *The Californian*, 5, No. 4 (Spring 1938), 47-55.

> Lengthy memoir recounting Lovecraft's visits to Mrs. Miniter's home in Wilbraham, Mass., where he received inspiration for some of his tales from the local folklore.

179. "More 'Chain Lightning.' " *The United Official Quarterly*, 2, No. 1 (October 1915), [1-4].

> On Andrew F. Lockhart's journal, *Chain Lightning*.

180. "The Morris Faction." *The Conservative*, 1, No. 1 (April 1915), [3] (unsigned).

> On a faction within the U.A.P.A.

181. "*Les Mouches Fantastiques.*" *The Conservative*, 4, No. 1 (July 1918), 7-8 (unsigned).

> On the "extreme literary radicalism" of an amateur journal of the title.

"Mysteries of the Heavens Revealed by Astronomy." The Asheville [N.C.] Gazette-News, 1915.

182. "I. The Sky and Its Contents." 20, No. 4 (16 February 1915), 4.

183. [II.] "The Solar System." 20, No. 8 (20 February 1915), 4.

184. "III. The Sun." 20, No. 10 (23 February 1915), 4.

185. "IV. The Inferior Planets." 20, No. 14 (27 February 1915), 4.

186. "V. Eclipses." 20, No. 16 (2 March 1915), 8.

187. "VI. The Earth and Its Moon." 20, No. 20 (6 March 1915), 3.

188. "VII. Mars and the Asteroids." 20, No. 22 (9 March 1915), 5.

189. "VIII. The Outer Planets." 20, No. 26 (13 March 1915), 3.

190. "IX. Comets and Meteors." 20, No. 28 (16 March 1915), 3.

191. "X. The Stars." 20, No. 32 (20 March 1915), 10.

192. ["The Stars," Part II]. 20, No. 34 (23 March 1915), 4.

193. "The Rings of Saturn" ["The Outer Planets," Part II]. 20, No. 38 (27 March 1915), 9.

194. "Comets and Meteors" [Part II]. 20, No. 40 (30 March 1915), 8.

195. "XI. Clusters and Nebulae." 20, No. 44 (13 April 1915), 5.

196. ["Clusters and Nebulae," Part II]. 20, No. 46 (6 April 1915).

197. "XII. The Constellations." 20, No. 64 (27 April 1915), 4.

198. "The Summer Stars" ["The Constellations," Part II]. 20, No. 68 (1 May 1915), 4.

199. "XIII. Telescopes and Observatories." 20, No. 76 (11 May 1915), 8.

200. "Magnifying Power" ["Telescopes and Observatories," Part II]. 20, No. 81 (17 May 1915), 2.

　　The series was originally announced as in fourteen parts, but no further installments have been located.

201. "New Department Proposed: Instruction for the Recruit." *The Lake Breeze*, No. 20 (June 1915), pp. 143-44 (as by "El Imparcial").

>A plan to create a "Department of Instruction" to educate amateurs in literacy.

202. "News Notes." *The United Amateur*, 16, No. 9 (July 1917), 128, 131, 134, 137; 20, No. 1 (September 1920), 16; 20, No. 2 (November 1920), 30-32; 20, No. 3 (January 1921), 43-44; 20, No. 4 (March 1921), 60; 20, No. 5 (May 1921), 66-67; 20, No. 6 (July 1921), 73-74; 21, No. 1 (September 1921), 8, 12; 21, No. 2 (November 1921), 21-23; 21, No. 3 (January 1922), 31-33; 21, No. 4 (March 1922), 43-45; 21, No. 5 (May 1922), 55-56; 23, No. 1 (May 1924), 7-8; 24, No. 1 (July 1925), 7, 11-12.

>All articles are unsigned, but are undoubtedly by Lovecraft, who was editor of *The United Amateur* for the issues in which these articles appeared.

203. "Nietscheism [sic] and Realism." *The Rainbow*, No. 1 (October 1921), pp. 9-11.

>Compendium of letter excerpts from Lovecraft to Sonia Davis, touching upon random philosophical and political matters.

204. "Notes for The Round Tower: (An Unwritten Story)." *Golden Atom*, 1, No. 10 (Winter 1943), 30.

>Notes incorporated by August Derleth into the "collaboration," *The Lurker at the Threshold* (see I-E-i, I-E-i-14).

205. "Notes on Verse Technique." *The National Amateur*, 67, No. 2 (December 1944), 53-65.

>All publications use the title "Further Criticism of Poetry."

206. "Notes on Writing Weird Fiction." *Amateur Correspondent*, 2, No. 1 (May-June 1937), 7-10.

Supramundane Stories, 1, No. 2 (Spring 1938), 11-13 (as "Notes on Weird Fiction-Writing—The 'Why' and 'How' "). *The Arkham Collector*, No. 2 (Winter 1968), pp. 26-28 (as "Notes on the Writing of Weird Fiction").

An explanation of the aesthetic motives behind Lovecraft's fictional technique and a guide to constructing an outline of a weird tale.

207. "Old England and the 'Hyphen.' " *The Conservative*, 2, No. 3 (October 1916), [1-2].

On the need for America to maintain political, racial, and cultural ties with Great Britain.

208. "The Omnipresent Philistine." *The Oracle*, 4, No. 3 (May 1924), 14-17.

A reply to some naïve literary comments by Paul Livingston Keil.

209. "Other Notes." *Golden Atom*, 1, No. 10 (Winter 1943), 30, 33.

Notes for fiction tales which August Derleth later wrote into the unfinished "collaboration," "The Watchers out of Time" (see I-E-i, I-E-i-20).

210. "Poesy." *The Tryout*, 4, No. 7 (July 1918), [13-14].

Reply to Pearl K. Merritt defending poetry.

211. "Poetry and the Artistic Ideal." *The Acolyte*, 1, No. 3 (Spring 1943), 3-6.

From a letter to Elizabeth Toldridge, 3 September 1929.

212. "The Poetry of John Ravenor Bullen." *The United Amateur*, 25, No. 1 (September 1925), 1-3, 6.

Later revised into the preface to I-C-6.

213. "The President's Annual Report." *The National Amateur*, 46, No. 1 (September 1923), 1-3.

214. "President's Message." *The National Amateur*, 45, Nos. 2-3 (November [1922]-January 1923), 1-3; 45, No. 4 (March 1923), 4-5; 45, No. 5 (May 1923), 5-6; 45, No. 6 (July 1923), 4-6.

215. "President's Message." *The United Amateur*, 17, No. 1 (September 1917), 12-13; 17, No. 2 (November 1917), 29-30; 17, No. 3 (January 1918), 48-49; 17, No. 4 (March 1918), 70; 17, No. 5 (May 1918), 96-97; 17, No. 6 (July 1918), 127-28.

216. "The Professional Incubus." *The National Amateur*, 46, No. 4 (March 1924), 35-36.

    The lack of good fiction in amateurdom is due to the pernicious influence of professional fiction.

217. "The Question of the Day." *The Conservative*, 1, No. 1 (April 1915), [6] (unsigned).

    The folly of prohibiting amateur journals from discussing matters outside of amateurdom.

218. "The Renaissance of Manhood." *The Conservative*, 1, No. 3 (October 1915), 8-10 (unsigned).

    On the folly of pacifism.

219. "A Reply to *The Lingerer*." *The Tryout*, 3, No. 7 (June 1917), [9-12].

    Rebuttal to Graeme Davis' criticism of *The Conservative* in his journal, *The Lingerer*.

220. "Report of Bureau of Critics." *The National Amateur*, 55, No. 3 (March 1933), 3 (section titled "Verse Criticism"); 55, No. 4 (June 1933), 8 (section titled "Verse Criticism"); 57, No. 2 (December 1934), 1 (section titled "Verse Department"); 57, No. 3 (March 1935), 1 (section titled "Verse Department").

221. "Report of First Vice-President." *The United Amateur*, 15, No. 4 (November 1915), 56; 15, No. 6 (January 1916), 72.

222. "Report of the Executive Judges." *The National Amateur*, 58, No. 4 (June 1936), 2-3.

    With Vincent B. Haggerty and Jennie K. Plaisier.

223. "A Request." *The Conservative*, 2, No. 4 (January 1917), 4 (unsigned).

    Request for assistance in compiling the 1916-17 U.A.P.A. Yearbook, which, however, never appeared.

224. Review of *Ebony and Crystal* by Clark Ashton Smith. *L'Alouette*, 1, No. 1 (January 1924), 20-21. *Golden Atom*, 1, No. 10 (Winter 1943), 22.

225. "Robert Ervin Howard: 1906-1936." *The Phantagraph*, 4, No. 5 (August 1936), 4-5 (unsigned).

    Memoriam to a deceased colleague. Later expanded and altered as "In Memoriam: Robert Ervin Howard" (see I-B-ii-151).

226. "Science versus Charlatanry." *The* [Providence] *Evening News*, 45, No. 95 (9 September 1914), 8.

    Rebuttal to J. F. Hartmann's remarks on astrology.

227. "The Simple Spelling Mania." *The United Co-operative*, 1, No. 1 (December 1918), 1-3.

    A history of the use of simplified spelling, from Elizabethan times to the present.

228. "Some Backgrounds of Fairyland." *Mirage*, No. 8 (June 1966), pp. 34-39.

    Taken from a letter to Wilfred B. Talman.

229. "Some Dutch Footprints in New England." *De Halve Maen*, 9, No. 1 (18 October 1933), 2, 4.

230. "Some Notes on Interplanetary Fiction." *The Californian*, 3, No. 3 (Winter 1935), 39-42. *The Acolyte*, 1, No. 4 (Summer 1943), 15-18 (as "Notes on Interplanetary Fiction").

> Other bibliographies have noted that this essay was published in *The Recluse*, No. 1 (1927); this is incorrect. The essay, suggesting means for improving the aesthetic quality of the then-poor interplanetary (or "scientifiction") tale, was written specifically for *The Californian*.

231. "Some Political Phases." *The Conservative*, 1, No. 2 (July 1915), 6-8 (unsigned).

> Remarks on candidates and amendments for the U.A.P.A. in the upcoming election.

232. "Supernatural Horror in Literature." *The Recluse*, No. 1 (1927), pp. 23-59. *The Fantasy Fan*, 1, No. 2 (October 1933), 25-26 (first section of Part I: Introduction); 1, No. 3 (November 1933), 34 (second section of Part I); 1, No. 4 (December 1933), 58, 61 (third section of Part I); 1, No. 5 (January 1934), 74, 80 (first section of Part II: The Dawn of the Horror Tale); 1, No. 6 (February 1934), 94, 96 (second section of Part II); 1, No. 7 (March 1934), 105, 112 (third section of Part II); 1, No. 8 (April 1934), 125-27 (first section of Part III: The Early Gothic Novel); 1, No. 9 (May 1934), 135-36 (second section of Part III); 1, No. 10 (June 1934), 154-55, 159 (first section of Part IV: The Apex of Gothic Romance); 1, No. 11 (July 1934), 169, 171, 176 (second section of Part IV); 1, No. 12 (August 1934), 185-87 (first section of Part V: The Aftermath of Gothic Fiction); 2, No. 1 (September 1934), 3-5, 12 (second section of Part V); 2, No. 2 (October 1934), 20-22 (first section of Part VI: Spectral Literature on the Continent); 2, No. 3 (November 1934), 38-39 (second section of

Part VI); 2, No. 4 (December 1934), 51-55 (Part VII: Edgar Allan Poe); 2, No. 5 (January 1935), 68-69 (first section of Part VIII: The Weird Tradition in America); 2, No. 6 (February 1935), 82-84 (second [not last] section of Part VIII). *Weird Tales*, 47, No. 2 (Fall 1973), 53-56.

The incomplete *Fantasy Fan* serialization represents a revision of the original version. The *Weird Tales* appearance is the 1936 abridgement (see I-A-61). The essay, "The Weird Work of William Hope Hodgson" (1936), was intended as an addition to Chapter IX, and has been so inserted in book publications.

233. "Symphony and Stress." *The Conservative*, 1, No. 3 (October 1915), 12-14 (unsigned).

Rebuttal to remarks included in an amateur journal, *The Symphony*.

234. "Systematic Instruction in the United." *Ole Miss*, No. 2 (December 1915), pp. 4-5.

The use of the Department of Instruction to educate amateur journalists in proper English.

235. "A Task for Amateur Journalists." *The New Member*, No. 7 (July 1914), p. [3].

Amateur journalists must help to keep the language pure and free from "pernicious" corruptions.

236. "Time and Space." *The Conservative*, 4, No. 1 (July 1918), 3-4.

On man's "utter insignificance" in the realms of time and space.

237. "Trimmings." *The Bonnet*, 1, No. 1 (June 1919), 10-12 (unsigned).

Includes the sections, "Our Bow to the Public" (p. 10) and "Our Candidate—Anne T. Renshaw" (pp. 10-12).

238. "The Trip of Theobald." *The Tryout*, 11, No. 8

(September 1927), [27-30] (as by "Theobald").

> On a trip through New England.

239. "The Truth about Mars." *The Phoenician*, 1, No. 3 (Autumn 1917), 8.

> The possibility of life on Mars.

240. "The United's Problem." *The Conservative*, 3, No. 1 (July 1917), [4] (unsigned).

> On dwindling enthusiasm in the U.A.P.A.

241. "The Unknown City in the Ocean." *The Perspective Review*, Winter 1934 (Fourth Anniversary Number), pp. 7-8.

> Description of Nantucket Island.

242. "Vermont: A First Impression." *Driftwind*, 2, No. 5 (March 1928), [5-9].

243. "The Vivisector." *The Wolverine*, No. 10 (June 1921), pp. 11-14; No. 12 (March 1922), pp. 10-13; No. 14 (Spring 1923), pp. [11-13].

> All as by "Zoilus." Two other issues of *The Wolverine*—Nos. 9 (March 1921) and 11 (November 1921)—contained the column, but from internal evidence these do not seem to be by Lovecraft; they may be by James F. Morton. The column for November 1921 discusses Lovecraft's work at length.

244. "The Weird Work of William Hope Hodgson." *The Phantagraph*, 5, No. 5 (February 1937), 5-7. *The Reader and Collector*, 3, No. 1 (June 1944), 5-6.

> Later incorporated into "Supernatural Horror in Literature" (see I-B-ii-232).

245. "What Amateur Journalism and I Have Done for Each Other." *The Boys' Herald*, 46, No. 1 (August 1937), 6-7 (as by "Harold P. Lovecraft").

> Speech, dated 21 February 1921, given to the Boston Conference of Amateur Journalists.

246. "What Belongs in Verse." *The Perspective Review*, Spring 1935, pp. 10-11.

247. "What Is Amateur Journalism?" *The Lake Breeze*, No. 18 (March 1915), pp. 127-28 (as by "El Imparcial").

On the role of amateur journalism in developing "finished writers."

248. "Winifred Virginia Jackson: A 'Different' Poetess." *The United Amateur*, 20, No. 4 (March 1921), 48-52.

249. "The Work of Frank Belknap Long, Jr." *The United Amateur*, 23, No. 1 (May 1924), 1-4 (unsigned).

250. "The Youth of Today." *The Conservative*, 1, No. 3 (October 1915), 11-12 (unsigned).

On a promising young member of the U.A.P.A., David H. Whittier.

251. [Untitled.] *The Conservative*, 1, No. 1 (April 1915), [2, 7-8] (unsigned).

Short paragraphs on amateur journalistic interests; discussing Ira A. Cole, Rheinhart Kleiner, Leo Fritter, Paul J. Campbell, versification, Edward H. Cole, Ernest A. Dench, and other subjects.

252. [Untitled.] *The Conservative*, 1, No. 3 (October 1915), 14-16 (unsigned).

Short paragraphs on amateur journalism, concerning William J. Dowdell, *The Coyote*, C. W. Smith, Victor L. Basinet, John T. Dunn, "metrical precision," and other matters.

253. [Untitled.] *The Conservative*, No. 13 (July 1923), pp. 24-28 (unsigned).

Paragraphs on amateur journalism, discussing Charles A. A. Parker, H. A. Joslen, Jonathan E. Hoag, Edward H. Cole, Jennie E. T. Dowe, Alfred Galpin, the "current Philistine-Grecian controversy," and other matters.

254. [Untitled.] *The Tryout*, 6, No. 7 (July 1920), [8].

On the permanence of amateur journalism. Sometimes listed in bibliographies as "Comment."

255. [Untitled.] *The United Amateur*, 20, No. 1 (September 1920), 4; 20, No. 3 (January 1921), 39, 42; 21, No. 1 (September 1921), 3, 6; 21, No. 2 (November 1921), 24.

> Notes on amateur journalism matters. All are unsigned.

256. [Untitled.] *The United Amateur*, 20, No. 2 (November 1920), 32 (unsigned).

> Excerpt from his pamphlet, *United Amateur Press Association: Exponent of Amateur Journalism.*

iii. Poetry

1. "Ad Britannos, 1918." *The Tryout*, 4, No. 4 (April 1918), [3-6].*National Enquirer*, 4, No. 4 (25 April 1918), 10.

2. "Ambition." *The United Co-operative*, 1, No. 1 (December 1918), 5 (as by "Ward Phillips").

3. "An American to Mother England." *Poesy*, 1, No. 7 (January 1916), 62. *Dowdell's Bearcat*, No. 16 (November 1916), pp. [12-14].

4. "An American to the British Flag." *The Little Budget of Knowledge and Nonsense* (December 1917).

> Not seen.

5. "Amissa Minerva." *Toledo Amateur*, May 1919, pp. 11-14.

6. "The Ancient Track." *Weird Tales*, 15, No. 3 (March 1930), 300.

7. "April." *The* [Providence] *Evening News*, 50, No. 121 (24 April 1917), 6. *The Tryout*, 4, No. 3 (March 1918), [3-5]. *The Tryout*, 4, No. 4 (April 1918), [16] (abridged).

> In the last appearance only eight lines are printed.

8. "April Dawn." *The Silver Clarion*, 4, No. 1 (April 1920), 1.

9. "Astrophobos." *The United Amateur*, 17, No. 3 (January 1918), 38 (as by "Ward Phillips"). *Phantasmagoria* (March 1937). *Golden Atom* (March 1940).

   Last two appearances not seen.

10. "August." *The Tryout*, 4, No. 8 (August 1918), [3]. *National Enquirer*, 6, No. 21 (22 August 1918), 10. *The Californian*, 5, No. 1 (Summer 1937), 25. *Weird Tales*, 47, No. 4 (Spring 1974), 8.

11. "Autumn." *The Tryout*, 3, No. 12 (November 1917), [3-5]. *The* [Providence] *Evening News*, 51, No. 125 (5 November 1917), 3.

12. "Ye Ballade of Patrick von Flynn: Or, the Hibernio-German-American England-Hater." *The Conservative*, 2, No. 1 (April 1916), 3-4 (as by "Lewis Theobald, Jun.").

13. "The Bay-Stater's Policy." *The Bay-Stater*, 4, No. 3 (June 1915), [3].

14. "The Beauties of Peace." *The* [Providence] *Evening News*, 49, No. 123 (27 June 1916), 6.

15. "Bells." *The Tryout*, 5, No. 12 (December 1919), [9-10] (as by "Ward Phillips"). *L'Herne*, No. 12 (1969), pp. 245-46 (as "The Bells"; as by "H. Paget Lowe"; in English).

16. "The Bookstall." *The United Official Quarterly*, 2, No. 2 (January 1916), [9-11].

17. "Britannia Victura." *The Inspiration*, Tribute number (April 1917), pp. 3-4. *The Little Budget of Knowledge and Nonsense*, 1, No. 2 (May 1917), 27-28. *National Enquirer*, 6, No. 8 (23 May 1918), 10.

18. "Brotherhood." *The Tryout*, 3, No. 1 (December 1916), [7] (as by "Lewis Theobald, Jun."). *The National Magazine*, 45, No. 3 (December 1916), 415.

19. "Brumalia." *The Tryout*, 3, No. 1 (December 1916), [1]. *The* [Providence] *Evening News*, 51, No. 152 (7 December 1917), Sec. 2, p. 2.

20. "Chloris and Damon." *The Tryout*, 8, No. 8 (June 1923), [12-13] (as by "Edward Softly").

21. "Christmas." *The Tryout*, 6, No. 11 (November 1920), [16] (as by "Edward Softly").

22. "Cindy: Scrub-Lady in a State Street Skyscraper." *The Tryout*, 6, No. 6 (June 1920), [19-20] (as by "L. Theobald, Jun.").

23. "The City." *The Vagrant*, No. 10 (October 1919), pp. 6-7 (as by "Ward Phillips"). *Weird Tales*, 42, No. 5 (July 1950), 48-49. *L'Herne*, No. 12 (1969), pp. 243-44 (in English).

24. "Clouds." *Spaceways*, 1, No. 3 (February 1939). *Stars* (June 1940). *Fantasy Commentator*, 2, No. 6 (Spring 1948), 190.

> First two appearances not seen. See also "A Cycle of Verse" (I-B-iii-27).

25. "Content." *The United Amateur*, 15, No. 11 (June 1916), 150.

26. "The Crime of Crimes: Lusitania, 1915." *Interesting Items*, No. 459 (July 1915), pp. 8-10.

27. "A Cycle of Verse." *The Tryout*, 5, No. 7 (July 1919), [19-22] (as by "Ward Phillips").

> Includes "Oceanus," pp. [19-20]; "Clouds," p. [20]; and "Mother Earth," pp. [20-22].

28. "Damon—a Monody." *The United Amateur*, 18, No. 5

(May 1919), 106 (as by "Theobaldus Senectissimus, Esq.").

29. "Damon and Delia, a Pastoral." *The Tryout*, 4, No. 8 (August 1918), [23-26] (as by "Edward Softly").

30. "The Dead Bookworm." *The United Amateur*, 19, No. 1 (September 1919), 1 (as by "John J. Jones").

31. "Despair." *Pine Cones*, 1, No. 4 (June 1919), 13.

32. "The Dream." *The Tryout*, 6, No. 9 (September 1920), [15-16] (as by "Edward Softly").

33. "Earth and Sky." *The Little Budget of Knowledge and Nonsense* (July 1917). *Pine Cones*, 1, No. 1 (December 1918), 1.

     First appearance not seen.

34. "The East India Brick Row." *The Providence Journal*, 102, No. 7 (8 January 1930), 13.

     All book publications print the title as "Brick Row."

35. "Edith Miniter: Born on Wilbraham Mountain, Massachusetts, May 5, 1869. Died at North Wilbraham, Massachusetts, June 8, 1934." *The Tryout*, 16, No. 8 (August 1934), [5-6]. *The Arkham Collector*, No. 3 (Summer 1968), pp. 68-69.

     The issue of *The Tryout* was a special memorial issue to Edith Miniter.

36. "The Eidolon." *The Tryout*, 4, No. 10 (October 1918), [3-6] (as by "Ward Phillips").

37. "An Elegy on Franklin Chase Clark, M.D.: (Died April 26, 1915)." *The* [Providence] *Evening News*, 46, No. 137 (29 April 1915), 6.

38. "An Elegy on Phillips Gamwell, Esq.: April 23, 1898- December 31, 1916." *The* [Providence] *Evening News*, 50, No. 29 (5 January 1917), 8.

39. "Ex-Poet's Reply." *Epgephi*, September 1920, p. 14 (as by "L. Theobald, Jr.").

40. "Fact and Fancy." *The Tryout*, 3, No. 3 (February 1917), [7]. *The National Magazine*, 46, No. 11 (August 1917), 718.

41. "The Feast: (Hub Journalist Club, March 10, 1923)." *The Hub Club Quill*, 15, No. 2 (May 1923), [13-15].

   Prefaced by a letter by Lovecraft to "Wisecrack [i.e., Albert A.] Sandusky," March 1923, explaining the poem.

Fungi from Yuggoth [The entire sonnet series has never appeared in one periodical. Individual publications follow.]

42. I. "The Book." *The Fantasy Fan*, 2, No. 2 (October 1934), 24. *Driftwind*, 11, No. 9 (April 1937), 342.

43. II. "Pursuit." *The Fantasy Fan*, 2, No. 2 (October 1934), 24.

44. III. "The Key." *The Fantasy Fan*, 2, No. 5 (January 1935), 72.

45. IV. "Recognition." *Driftwind*, 11, No. 5 (December 1936), 180.

46. V. "Homecoming." *The Fantasy Fan*, 2, No. 5 (January 1935), 72. *Science-Fantasy Correspondent*, 1, No. 1 (November-December 1936), 24. *Weird Tales*, 37, No. 5 (May 1944), 52-53.

47. VI. "The Lamp." *Driftwind*, 5, No. 5 (March 1931), 16. *Weird Tales*, 33, No. 2 (February 1939), 151.

48. VII. "Zaman's Hill." *Driftwind*, 9, No. 4 (October 1934), 125. *Weird Tales*, 33, No. 2 (February 1939), 151.

49. VIII. "The Port." *Driftwind*, 5, No. 3 (November 1930), 36. *Weird Tales*, 39, No. 7 (September 1946), 65. *L'Herne*, No. 12 (1969), p. 246 (in English).

50. IX. "The Courtyard." *Weird Tales*, 16, No. 3 (September 1930), 322.

51. X. "The Pigeon-Flyers." *Weird Tales*, 39, No. 9 (January 1947), 96.

52. XI. "The Well." *The Providence Journal*, 102, No. 116 (14 May 1930), 15. *The Phantagraph*, 6, No. 3 (July 1937), 1. *Weird Tales*, 37, No. 5 (May 1944), 53.

53. XII. "The Howler." *Driftwind*, 7, No. 3 (November 1932), 100. *Weird Tales*, 34, No. 1 (June-July 1939), 66.

54. XIII. "Hesperia." *Weird Tales*, 16, No. 4 (October 1930), 464.

55. XIV. "Star-Winds." *Weird Tales*, 16, No. 3 (September 1930), 322.

56. XV. "Antarktos." *Weird Tales*, 16, No. 5 (November 1930), 692.

57. XVI. "The Window." *Driftwind*, 5 (April 1931 [Special issue]), 15. *Weird Tales*, 37, No. 5 (May 1944), 53. *Weird Tales* (Canadian), 38, No. 3 (September 1945), 75.

58. XVII. "A Memory." *Weird Tales*, 39, No. 10 (March 1947), 69.

59. XVIII. "The Gardens of Yin." *Driftwind*, 6, No. 5 (March 1932), 34. *Weird Tales*, 34, No. 2 (August 1939), 151.

60. XIX. "The Bells." *Weird Tales*, 16, No. 6 (December 1930), 798.

61.   XX. "Night-Gaunts." *The Providence Journal*, 102, No. 73 (26 March 1930), 15. *The Phantagraph*, 4, No. 3 ([June] 1936), 8. *Weird Tales*, 34, No. 6 (December 1939), 59. *Drab*, 1, No. 2 (n.d.), [2] (in English).

62.   XXI. "Nyarlathotep." *Weird Tales*, 17, No. 1 (January 1931), 12.

63.   XXII. "Azathoth." *Weird Tales*, 17, No. 1 (January 1931), 12.

64.   XXIII. "Mirage." *Weird Tales*, 17, No. 2 (February-March 1931), 175. *Mirage*, 1, No. 5 (Summer 1962), 3.

65.   XXIV. "The Canal." *Driftwind*, 6, No. 5 (March 1932), 34. *Weird Tales*, 31, No. 1 (January 1938), 20. *Weird Tales*, 47, No. 1 (Summer 1973), 96.

66.   XXV. "St. Toad's." *Weird Tales*, 37, No. 5 (May 1944), 52. *Weird Tales* (Canadian), 38, No. 3 (September 1945), 105 (as by "J. H. Brownlow").

67.   XXVI. "The Familiars." *Driftwind*, 5, No. 1 (July 1930), 35. *Weird Tales*, 39, No. 9 (January 1947), 96.

68.   XXVII. "The Elder Pharos." *Weird Tales*, 17, No. 2 (February-March 1931), 175.

69.   XXVIII. "Expectancy." [Never periodically published.]

70.   XXIX. "Nostalgia." *The Providence Journal*, 102, No. 61 (12 March 1930), 15. *The Phantagraph*, 4, No. 4 (July 1936), 1. *Stars*, Dec. [1940]-Jan. 1941, p. 2.

71.   XXX. "Background." *The Providence Journal*, 102, No. 91 (16 April 1930), 13. *The Galleon*, 1, No. 4 (May-June 1935), 8. *The Lovecrafter*, 47, No. 1 (20 August 1936), [1] (as "A Sonnet").

72. XXXI. "The Dweller." *The Providence Journal*, 102, No. 110 (7 May 1930), 15. *The Phantagraph*, 4, No. 2 (November-December 1935), [3]. *Weird Tales*, 35, No. 2 (March 1940), 20. *Weird Fiction Times*, No. 44 (February 1976), p. 29 (in English).

73. XXXII. "Alienation." *Weird Tales*, 17, No. 3 (April-May 1931), 374.

74. XXXIII. "Harbour Whistles." *The Silver Fern*, 1, No. 5 (May 1930), [1]. *L'Alouette*, 3, No. 6 (September-October 1930), 161. *The Phantagraph*, 5, No. 2 (November 1936), 1. *Weird Tales*, 33, No. 5 (May 1939), 134.

75. XXXIV. "Recapture." *Weird Tales*, 15, No. 5 (May 1930), 693. *Weird Tales*, 39, No. 3 (January 1946), 37. *Weird Tales* (Canadian), 38, No. 4 (March 1946), 78.

76. XXXV. "Evening Star." *Weird Tales*, 37, No. 5 (May 1944), 52. *Weird Tales* (Canadian), 38, No. 3 (July 1945), 100.

77. XXXVI. "Continuity." *Causerie*, February 1936, p. 1. *The Phantagraph*, 9, No. 1 (May-June 1941), 7. *The Acolyte*, 1, No. 4 (Summer 1943), 6. *Weird Tales*, 39, No. 10 (March 1947), 69. *L'Herne*, No. 12 (1969), p. 247 (in English).

---

78. "Futurist Art." *The Conservative*, 2, No. 4 (January 1917), [2].

79. "A Garden." *The Vagrant*, [Spring 1927], p. 60.

80. "Gems from 'In a Minor Key': (With Remarks by THE CONSERVATIVE)." *The Conservative*, 1, No. 3 (October 1915), 8 (unsigned).

Contains three replies (in verse) to opinions quoted from Charles D. Isaacson's magazine, *In a Minor Key*.

81. "George Willard Kirk." *The National Amateur*, 49, No. 5 (May 1927), 5.

82. "Germania—1918." *The Tryout*, 4, No. 11 (November 1918), [3-7].

83. "Greetings." *The Silver Clarion*, 2, No. 10 (January 1919), 3.

    Contains greetings to "Arthur Goodenough, Esq.," "W. Paul Cook, Esq.," "E. Sherman Cole: (Born February 1918)," and "The Silver Clarion."

84. "Hallowe'en in a Suburb." *The National Amateur*, 48, No. 4 (March 1926), 33 (as "In a Suburb"). *The Phantagraph*, 6, No. 2 (June 1937), 3-4. *Weird Tales*, 44, No. 6 (September 1952), 9.

85. "Helene Hoffman Cole: 1893-1919: The Club's Tribute." *The Bonnet*, 1, No. 1 (June 1919), 8-9 (unsigned).

86. "Hellas." *The United Amateur*, 18, No. 1 (September 1918), 3.

87. "The House." *The Philosopher*, 1, No. 1 (December 1920), 6 (as by "Ward Phillips"). *Weird Tales*, 40, No. 3 (March 1948), 27. *Weird Tales*, 42, No. 3 (Winter 1973), 25.

88. "Hylas and Myrrha: A Tale." *The Tryout*, 5, No. 5 (May 1919), [6-11] (as by "Lawrence Appleton").

89. "In a Sequestered Churchyard Where Once Poe Walked." *Science-Fantasy Correspondent*, 1, No. 3 (March-April 1937), 16-17. *Weird Tales*, 31, No. 5 (May 1938) 578 (as "Where Poe Once Walked: An Acrostic Sonnet"). *Brown Alumni Monthly*, 72, No. 5 (February 1972), 25. *Il Re in Giallo*, 1, No. 2 [1976], 105 (in English).

    In the fall of 1936 Maurice W. Moe duplicated this sonnet,

along with others by R. H. Barlow, Adolphe de Castro, and Moe himself, as "Four Acrostic Sonnets on Poe" and distributed them to the high school classes that he taught in Appleton, Wisconsin. The title on Lovecraft's A.Ms. is "In a Sequester'd Providence Churchyard Where Once Poe Walk'd."

90. "In Memoriam: J. E. T. D." *The Tryout*, 5, No. 3 (March 1919), [6] (as by "Ward Phillips").

91. "Inspiration." *The Conservative*, 2, No. 3 (October 1916), [12] (as by "Lewis Theobald, Jun."). *The National Magazine*, 45 (November 1916), 287.

92. "Iterum Conjunctae." *The Tryout*, 3, No. 6 (May 1917), [3]. *The* [Providence] *Evening News*, 51, No. 8 (12 June 1917), 6. *The Little Budget of Knowledge and Nonsense* (September 1917). *National Enquirer*, 6, No. 5 (2 May 1918), 10 (with subtitle: "America and England, 1918"). *The Tryout*, 19, No. 3 (May 1938), [16] (as "Intrum Donjunctae").

   Third appearance not seen.

93. "January." *The Silver Clarion*, 3, No. 10 (January 1920), 1 (as by "H. Paget Lowe").

94. "John Oldham: A Defence." *The United Co-operative*, 1, No. 2 (June 1919), 7.

95. "A June Afternoon." *The Tryout*, 4, No. 6 (June 1918), [1]. *National Enquirer*, 6, No. 12 (20 June 1918), 10. *Vanity Fair*, No. 13 (September 1919), p. 8.

96. "Laeta; a Lament." *The Tryout*, 4, No. 2 (February 1918), [15-16] (as by "Ames Dorrance Rowley").

97. "Lines for Poets' Night at the Scribblers' Club." *The National Amateur*, 46, No. 3 (January 1924), 25. *Pegasus*, No. [2] (February 1924), pp. 31-33.

98. "Lines on Gen. Robert Edward Lee: Born Jan. 19, 1807." *The Coyote*, 3, No. 1 (January 1917),

99. "Lines on Graduation from the R. I. Hospital's School of Nurses." *The Tryout*, 3, No. 3 (February 1917), [15-17].

> Attributed to John T. Dunn.

100. "Lines on the 25th. Anniversary of the Providence Evening News, 1892-1917." *The Tryout*, 4, No. 1 (December 1917), [3-5]. *The* [Providence] *Evening News*, 51, No. 154 (10 December 1917), 7 (as "Our 25th Anniversary, 1892-1917").

101. "The Link." *The Tryout*, 4, No. 7 (July 1918), [7]. *National Enquirer*, 6, No. 21 (22 August 1918), 10.

102. "The Magazine Poet." *The United Amateur*, 15, No. 3 (October 1915), 51.

103. "March." *The United Amateur*, 14, No. 4 (March 1915), 68. *The* [Providence] *Evening News*, 52, No. 66 (1 March 1918), 7.

104. "Medusa: A Portrait." *The Tryout*, 7, No. 9 (December 1921), [32-34] (as by "Jeremy Bishop").

> Lacks a prefatory letter to Ida C. Haughton found on the T.Ms.

105. "The Messenger." *Weird Tales*, 32, No. 1 (July 1938), 52.

106. "A Mississippi Autumn: Being the Much Appreciated Prose-Poetical Conclusion of Mrs. Renshaw's Letter of October the 1st, Done into Regular Heroic Couplets." *Ole Miss*, No. 2 (December 1915), pp. 5-6 (as by "Howard Phillips Lovecraft, Metrical Mechanic").

107. "Monody on the Late King Alcohol." *The Tryout*, 5, No. 8 (August 1919), [15-16] (as by "Lewis Theobald, Jun.").

108. "Monos: An Ode." *The Silver Clarion*, 2, No. 7 (October 1918), 3-4.

109. "Mother Earth." *L'Herne*, No. 12 (1969), pp. 242-43 (in English).

> See also "A Cycle of Verse" above.

110. "My Favourite Character." *The Brooklynite*, 16, No. 1 (January 1926), 1.

> All appearances of the poem print the title as "My Favorite Character."

111. "Myrrha and Strephon." *The Tryout*, 5, No. 7 (July 1919), [9-10] (as by "Lawrence Appleton").

112. "Nathicana." *The Vagrant*, [Spring 1927], pp. 61-64 (as by "Albert Frederick Willie").

113. "Nemesis." *The Vagrant*, No. 7 (June 1918), pp. 41-43. *Weird Tales*, 3, No. 4 (April 1924), 78.

114. "New England." *The* [Providence] *Evening News*, 46, No. 26 (18 December 1914), 11.

115. "The Nightmare Lake." *The Vagrant*, No. 12 (December 1919), pp. 13-14. *Scienti-Snaps*, 3, No. 3 (Summer 1940), 13-14.

116. "1914." *Interesting Items*, No. 457 (March 1915), pp. 3-5.

117. "North and South Britons." *The Tryout*, 5, No. 5 (May 1919), [13] (as by "Alexander Ferguson Blair").

118. "The Nymph's Reply to the Modern Business Man." *The Tryout*, 3, No. 3 (February 1917), [2] (as by "Lewis Theobald, Jr.").

119. "Oceanus." *Cataclysm* (November 1952). *L'Herne*, No. 12 (1969), p. 243 (in English).

> First appearance not seen. See also "A Cycle of Verse" (I-B-iii-27).

120. "October." [1] *The Tryout*, 6, No. 10 (October 1920), [17] (as by "Henry Paget-Lowe").

121. "October." [2] *The Tryout*, 10, No. 7 (January 1926), [3-5].

     The above two poems are entirely different, and share only their titles.

122. "Ode for July Fourth, 1917." *The United Amateur*, 16, No. 9 (July 1917), 121. *The National Magazine*, 46, No. 10 (July 1917), 616 (as "Ode to July 4th: 1917"). *The* [Providence] *Evening News*, 51, No. 26 (3 July 1917), 3.

123. "Ode to Selene or Diana." *The Tryout*, 5, No. 4 (April 1919), [18] (as by "Edward Softly"; as "To Selene").

     Juvenilia; ca. 1902.

124. "The Odes of Horace, Book III, ix: A Dialogue betwixt Horace and Lydia [Translated by a Gentleman of New-England]." *Sappho*, 1, No. 4 [1940s], 11 (as "Horace: Book III Ode IX: Theobald's Translation").

     The published title was taken from an unrevised ms.; the present one is taken from the final draft.

125. "Old Christmas." *The Tryout*, 4, No. 12 (December 1918), [1-11].

126. "On a Battlefield in Picardy." *National Enquirer*, 6, No. 9 (30 May 1918), 10. *The Voice from the Mountains*, July 1918, p. 11 (as "On a Battlefield in France").

127. "On a Grecian Colonnade in a Park." *The Tryout*, 6, No. 9 (September 1920), [11-12] (as by "Henry Paget-Lowe").

128. "On a Modern Lothario." *The Blarney Stone*, 2, No. 4 (July-August 1914), 7-8.

129. "On a New-England Village Seen by Moonlight."
     The Trail, No. 2 (Summer 1915), pp. 8-9.

130. "On Reading Lord Dunsany's Book of Wonder." *The
     Silver Clarion*, 3, No. 12 (March 1920), 4.

     The poem also appeared in *Kadath*, No. 1 (1973), ed. Lin
     Carter, but as less than a dozen copies of the journal were
     circulated, it hardly qualifies as a publication.

131. "On Receiving a Picture of Swans." *The Conservative*,
     1, No. 4 (January 1916), 2-3. *The National Magazine*,
     46, No. 7 (April 1917), 25.

132. "On Receiving a Picture of the Marshes at Ipswich."
     The National Magazine, 45 (January 1917), 588. *Merry
     Minutes*, 3, No. 12 (March 1917), 3.

133. "On Receiving a Picture of ye Towne of Templeton,
     in the Colonie of Massachusetts-Bay, with Mount
     Monadnock, in New-Hampshire, shewn in the
     Distance." *The Vagrant*, No. 5 (June 1917), 5. *Arkham
     House Catalogue*, 1949, p. 18[c].

     In all publications except the *Arkham House Catalogue* (a
     facsimile of the A.Ms.), the poem is titled "To Templeton and
     Mount Monadnock."

134. "On Religion." *The Tryout*, 6, No. 8 (August 1920),
     [18] (as by "Henry Paget-Lowe").

135. "On the Cowboys of the West: In Whom Is
     Embodied the Nature-Worshipping Spirit of
     Classical Antiquity." *The Plainsman*, 1, No. 4
     (December 1915), 1-2.

136. "On the Death of a Rhyming Critic." *Toledo Amateur*,
     July 1917, pp. 11-12.

137. "On the Return of Maurice Winter Moe, Esq., to
     the Pedagogical Profession." *The Wolverine*, No. 10
     (June 1921), pp. 15-16 (as by "Lewis Theobald,
     Jun.").

138. "The Outpost." *Bacon's Essays*, 3, No. 1 (Spring 1930),
7. *Fantasy Magazine*, 3, No. 3 (May 1934), 24-25. *The
O-Wash-Ta-Nong*, 3, No. 1 (January 1938), 1.
Spaceways (December 1940).

    Last appearance not seen.

139. "Pacifist War Song—1917." *The Tryout*, 3, No. 4
(March 1917), [10] (as by "Lewis Theobald, Jun.").

140. "The Peace Advocate." *The Tryout*, 3, No. 6 (May
1917), [12-14] (attributed to "Elizabeth Berkeley"
[i.e., W. V. Jackson]).

    See also "Perverted Poesie . . ." (I-B-iii-143).

141. "The Pensive Swain." *The Tryout*, 5, No. 10 (October
1919), [20] (as by "Archibald Maynwaring").

142. "Percival Lowell: 1855-1916." *Excelsior*, 1, No. 1
(March 1917), 3.

143. "Perverted Poesie or Modern Metre." *The O-Wash-
Ta-Nong*, 2, No. 3 (December 1937), [10-12].

    Includes "The Introduction" (p. [10]), "Unda, or, the Bride of
    the Sea" (as "The Bride of the Sea") (pp. [10-11]), "The Peace
    Advocate" (pp. [11-12]), "A Summer Sunset and Evening: In the
    Metre (though Perchance not the Manner) of the 'Poly-Olbion'
    of MIKE DRAYTON, ESQ." (p. [12]). As by "Humphry
    Littlewit, Esq., of Grubstreet Manor." An "Epilogue" has here
    been added to "Unda, or, the Bride of the Sea," and appears on
    all subsequent publications of the poem.

144. "Phaeton." *The Silver Clarion*, 2, No. 5 (August 1918),
3. *The Californian*, 5, No. 1 (Summer 1937), 24. *Golden
Atom*, 1, No. 10 (Winter 1943), 22-23.

145. "The Poe-et's Nightmare." *The Vagrant*, No. 8 (July
1918), pp. [13-23]. *Weird Tales*, 44, No. 5 (July 1952),
43-46 (central portion only; titled "Aletheia
Phrikodes").

146. "The Poet of Passion." *The Tryout*, 3, No. 7 (June 1917), [25] (as by "Louis [sic] Theobald, Jun.").

147. "The Poet's Rash Excuse." *The Tryout*, 6, No. 7 (July 1920), [13] (as by "L. Theobald, Jun.").

148. "The Power of Wine: A Satire." *The* [Providence] *Evening News*, 46, No. 46 (13 January 1915), 8. *The Tryout*, 2, No. 5 (April 1916), [5-7]. *National Enquirer*, 5, No. 26 (28 March 1918), 3. *Fantasy Sampler*, No. 4 (June 1956), 22-23 (as "The Pow'r of Wine").

149. "Primavera." *The Brooklynite*, 15, No. 2 (April 1925), 1. *Interesting Items* (April 1950).

    Second appearance not seen.

150. "Prologue" to "Fragments from an Hour of Inspiration" by Jonathan E. Hoag. *The Tryout*, 3, No. 8 (July 1917), [17].

151. "Providence." *The Brooklynite*, 14, No. 4 (November 1924), 2-3. *The Brooklynite*, 17, No. 2 (May 1927), 1. *The Californian*, 5, No. 1 (Summer 1937), 26-27.

    This poem also appeared in a Providence newspaper, but this publication has not been found.

152. "Providence in 2000 A. D." *The* [Providence] *Evening Bulletin*, 50, No. 55 (4 March 1912), Sec. 2, p. 6.

    Lovecraft's first published poem; prefaced by the note, "(It is announced in the Providence Journal that the Italians desire to alter the name of Atwell's Avenue to 'Columbus Avenue')."

153. "Psychopompos: A Tale in Rhyme." *The Vagrant*, No. 10 (October 1919), pp. 13-22. *Weird Tales*, 30, No. 3 (September 1937), 341-48 (without subtitle).

    Book publications omit the subtitle.

154. "Quinsnicket Park." *The Badger*, No. 2 (June 1915), pp. 7-10.

    Prefaced by a two-paragraph description of Quinsnicket Park.

This poem appeared in *The* [Providence] *Evening News,* but the publication has not been found.

155. "R. Kleiner, Laureatus, in Heliconem." *The Conservative,* 2, No. 1 (April 1916), 2.

156. "Regnar Lodbrug's Epicedium: (An 8th Century Funeral Song . . . , Translated from Olaus Wormius)." *The Acolyte,* 2, No. 3 (Summer 1944), 14-15.

157. "Respite." *The Conservative,* 2, No. 3 (October 1916), [6-7]. *The National Magazine,* 45, 6 (March 1917), 826.

158. "The Return." *The Tryout,* 11, No. 1 (December 1926), [7-8].

159. "Revelation." *The Tryout,* 5, No. 3 (March 1919), [3-4].

160. "The Rose of England." *The Scot,* No. 14 (October 1916), p. 7.

161. "A Rural Summer Eve." *The Trail,* 1, No. 2 (January 1916), 12-13.

162. "The Rutted Road." *The Tryout,* 3, No. 2 (January 1917), [17] (as by "Lewis Theobald, Jun."). *The Tryout,* 10, No. 8 (March 1926), [17].

163. "The Simple Speller's Tale: (Translated into English.)" *The Conservative,* 1, No. 1 (April 1915), [1].

164. "Sir Thomas Tryout: Died November 15, 1921." *The Tryout,* 7, No. 9 (December 1921), [31-32] (as by "Ward Phillips"). *The Tryout,* 21, No. 1 (March 1941), [3-4].

165. "The Smile." *The Symphony,* No. 12 (July 1916), pp. [3-4]. *The Little Budget of Knowledge and Nonsense,* 1, No. 5-6 (August-September 1917), 68.

166. "Solstice." *The Tryout*, 9, No. 11 (January 1925), [8].

167. "Sonnet on Myself." *The Tryout*, 4, No. 7 (July 1918), [2] (as by "Lewis Theobald, Jun.").

168. "The Spirit of Summer." *The Conservative*, 4, No. 1 (July 1918), 1. *National Enquirer*, 6, No. 13 (27 June 1918), 10.

169. "Spring: Paraphrased from the Prose of Clifford Raymond, Esq., in the *Chicago Tribune*." *The Tryout*, 5, No. 4 (April 1919), [15-16].

170. "The State of Poetry." *The Conservative*, 1, No. 3 (October 1915), 1-3.

171. "Sunset." *The Tryout*, 4, No. 1 (December 1917), [8]. *The United Amateur*, 17, No. 5 (May 1918), 90. *The Californian*, 5, No. 1 (Summer 1937), 24. *The Tryout*, 19, No. 3 (May 1938), [15].

172. "Temperance Song: [Tune: 'The Bonnie Blue Flag.']." *The Dixie Booster*, 4, No. 4 (Spring 1916), 9.

173. "The Teuton's Battle Song." *The United Amateur*, 15, No. 7 (February 1916), 85.

    Appended to the poem is an "Author's Note" (pp. 85-86).

174. "Theodore Roosevelt: 1858-1919." *The United Amateur*, 18, No. 3 (January 1919), 52.

175. "To a Dreamer." *The Coyote*, No. 16 (January 1921), p. 4. *Weird Tales*, 4, No. 3 (November 1924), 54.

176. "To a Youth." *The Tryout*, 7, No. 1 (February 1921), [18] (as by "Richard Raleigh").

177. "To Alan Seeger: Author of a 'Message to America,' Who Fell in the Cause of Civilisation at Belloy-en-Santerre, July, 1916." *The Tryout*, 4, No. 7

(July 1918), [1-2]. *National Enquirer*, 6, No. 20 (15 August 1918), 10. *The United Amateur*, 18, No. 2 (November 1918), 24.

178. "To Alfred Galpin, Esq.: President of the United Amateur Press Association, on His Nineteenth Birthday, November 8, 1920." *The Tryout*, 6, No. 12 (December 1920), [7-8] (as by "L. Theobald").

179. "To an Infant." *The Brooklynite*, 15, No. 4 (October 1925), 2. *The Arkham Collector*, No. 4 (Winter 1969), pp. 113-16.

180. "To Arthur Goodenough, Esq." *The Tryout*, 4, No. 9 (September 1918), [1-2].

181. "To Charlie of the Comics: (With Profuse Apologies to Rheinhart Kleiner, Esq., Poet-Laureate and Author of 'To Mary of the Movies.')." *The Providence Amateur*, 1, No. 2 (February 1916), 13-14 (unsigned).

182. "To Clark Ashton Smith, Esq., upon His Fantastic Tales, Verses, Pictures, and Sculptures." *Weird Tales*, 31, No. 4 (April 1938), 392 (as "To Clark Ashton Smith"). *Asmodeus*, No. 2 (Fall 1951), p. 30 (as "To Clark Ashton Smith, Esq.").

183. "To Damon: (Alfred Galpin, Jun., upon His Coming of Age, Nov. 8, 1922)." *The Tryout*, 8, No. 9 (August 1923), [7-9] (as by "L. Theobald").

184. "To Delia, Avoiding Damon." *The Tryout*, 4, No. 9 (September 1918), [5-7] (as by "Edward Softly").

185. "To Edward John Moreton Drax Plunkett, Eighteenth Baron Dunsany." *The Tryout*, 5, No. 11 (November 1919), [11-12].

186. "To Endymion: (Frank Belknap Long, Jr.): Upon His Coming of Age, April 27, 1923." *The Tryout*, 8, No. 10 (September 1923), [15-16] (as by "L. Theobald, Jun.").

187. "To General Villa." *The Blarney Stone*, 2, No. 6 (November-December 1914), 8.

188. "To Greece, 1917." *The Vagrant*, No. 6 (November 1917), pp. 15-17.

189. "To Maj.-Gen. Omar Bundy, U.S.A." *The Tryout*, 5, No. 1 (January 1919), [3-5] (as by "Ames Dorrance Rowley"). *The Tryout*, 20, No. 6 (March 1940), [19].

    Prefaced by a paragraph about Bundy. In the second appearance only three stanzas are printed.

190. "To Miss Beryl Hoyt: Upon Her First Birthday— February 21, 1927." *Justice*, February 1927, p. 3.

191. "To Mr. Finlay, upon His Drawing for Mr. Bloch's Tale, 'The Faceless God.' " *The Phantagraph* (May 1937) (as "To Mr. Finlay"). *Weird Tales*, 30, No. 1 (July 1937), 17.

    First appearance not seen.

192. "To Mr. Galpin, upon His 20th Birthday, Nov. 8, 1921." *The Tryout*, 7, No. 9 (December 1921), [16-17] (as by "L. Theobald, Jun.").

193. "To Mr. Lockhart, on His Poetry." *The Tryout*, 3, No. 4 (March 1917), [7-8]. *The Little Budget of Knowledge and Nonsense*, 1, No. 3 (June 1917), 35-36 (as "To Mr. Lockhart of Milbank, South Dakota, U.S.A., on His Poetry").

    Also appeared in a South Dakota newspaper, but this publication has not been found.

194. "To Mistress Sophia Simple, Queen of the Cinema: (With Humblest Apologies to Randolph St. John, Gent.)." *The United Amateur*, 19, No. 2 (November 1919), 34 (as by "L. Theobald, Jun.").

195. "To Pan." *The Tryout*, 5, No. 4 (April 1919), [16] (as by "Michael Ormonde O'Reilly"; as "Pan"). *The Tryout*, 13, No. 2 (September 1929), [15] (as by "M. O. O."; as "Pan").

    Juvenilia; ca. 1902.

196. "To Phillis: (With Humblest Apologies to Randolph St. John, Gent.")." *The Tryout*, 6, No. 1 (January 1920), [10] (as by "L. Theobald, Jun.").

197. "To Rheinhart Kleiner, Esq., upon His Town Fables and Elegies." *The Tryout*, 8, No. 7 (April 1923), [11-14] (as by "Lewis Theobald, Jun.").

198. "To Samuel Loveman, Esquire, on His Poetry and Drama, Writ in the Elizabethan Style." *Dowdell's Bearcat*, 4, No. 5 (December 1915), [7].

199. "To the American Flag." *The Californian*, 5, No. 1 (Summer 1937), 27. *The Rochester-American Patriot* (Summer 1942).

    Second appearance not seen. [It has just been discovered that this poem is not by Lovecraft but by Jonathan E. Hoag.]

200. "To the Eighth of November." *The Tryout*, 5, No. 11 (November 1919), [13] (as by "Archibald Maynwaring").

201. "To the Late John H. Fowler, Esq.: Author of Poems of the Supernatural." *The Scot*, No. 7 (March 1916), pp. 25-26.

202. "To the Members of the Pin-Feathers on the Merits of Their Organisation, and of Their New

Publication, *The Pinfeather*." *The Pinfeather*, 1, No. 1 (November 1914), 3-4.

203. "To the Members of the United Amateur Press Ass'n from the Providence Amateur Press Club." *The Providence Amateur*, 1, No. 1 (June 1915), [1-3].

204. "To the Old Pagan Religion." *The Tryout*, 5, No. 4 (April 1919), [17] (as by "Ames Dorrance Rowley"; as "The Last Pagan Speaks").

> Juvenilia; ca. 1902.

205. "To the Rev. James Pyke." *The United Official Quarterly*, 1, No. 1 (November 1914), 1.

206. "Tryout's Lament for the Vanished Spider." *The Tryout*, 6, No. 1 (January 1920), [18-19] (as by "Edward Softly").

207. "Unda, or, the Bride of the Sea: A Dull, Dark, Drear, Dactylic Delirium in Sixteen Silly, Senseless, Sickly Stanzas." *The Providence Amateur*, 1, No. 2 (February 1916), 14-16 (as "The Bride of the Sea"; as by "Lewis Theobald, Jr."). *The Phantagraph*, 9, No. 2 (August 1941), 1-3 (as "The Bride of the Sea: A Dull, Dark, Dactylic Delirium in Sixteen Silly Stanzas").

> The last appearance contains the epilogue; see "Perverted Poesie . . . " (I-B-iii-143).

208. "Ver Rusticum." *The* [Providence] *Evening News*, 52, No. 92 (1 April 1918), 4. *National Enquirer*, 6, No. 7 (16 May 1918), 2. *The Voice from the Mountains*, July 1918, pp. 27-29.

209. "The Voice." *The Linnet*, August 1920, pp. [1-2].

210. "The Volunteer: (A Reply to the Lines of Sergt. Miller in the National Enquirer)." *The* [Providence] *Evening News*, 52, No. 45 (1 February 1918), 7. *National Enquirer*, 5, No. 19 (7 February 1918), 6. *The Tryout*, 4, No. 4 (April 1918), [11-13] (as by "Ames Dorrance Rowley").

   Also appeared in *The Appleton* [Wis.] *Post, The St. Petersburg* [Fla.] *Evening Independent*, and *Trench and Camp* (military paper at San Antonio, Tex.).

211. "Waste Paper: A Poem of Profound Insignificance." *Books at Brown*, 26 (1978), 48-52.

   Parody of T. S. Eliot's *The Waste Land*.

212. "A Winter Wish: (A Pseudo-Poetical Disaster Occasioned by the Recent Spell of Cold Weather)." *The* [Providence] *Evening News*, 52, No. 19 (2 January 1918), 3 (without subtitle). *The Tryout*, 4, No. 2 (February 1918), [3-5].

213. "Wisdom." *The Silver Clarion*, 3, No. 8 (November 1919), 1-2 (as by "Archibald Maynwaring").

   Contains an introductory note: "The 28th or 'Gold-Miner's' Chapter of Job, paraphrased from a literal Translation of the original Hebrew text, supplied by Dr. S. Hall Young."

214. "The Wood." *The Tryout*, 11, No. 2 (January 1929), [16] (as by "L. Theobald, Jun."). *Weird Tales*, 32, No. 3 (September 1938), 324.

   This poem was also scheduled to appear in *The Planeteer*, 2, No. 1 (September 1936), 5-6 (ed. Jim Blish), but the issue was neither completed nor published; pages containing "The Wood," however, were printed.

215. "Yule Horror." *Weird Tales*, 8, No. 6 (December 1926), 846.

216. [Untitled: "As Saturnalian days draw near . . ."]

The Tryout, 7, No. 9 (December 1921), [35].

Poems written to Jonathan E. Hoag. Arranged chronologically.

217. "To Jonathan E. Hoag, Esq., on His 87th Birthday: February 10, 1918." *Eurus*, 1, No. 1 (February 1918), 5-6.

218. "To Jonathan E. Hoag, Esq., on His 88th Birthday, February 10, 1919." *Pine Cones*, 1, No. 2 (February 1919), 2-3.

219. "Ad Scribam: (Jonathan E. Hoag): Aetat LXXXIX: February 10, 1920." *The Tryout*, 6, No. 2 (February 1920), [9-10].

220. "To Mr. Hoag, on His Ninetieth Birthday, Feb. 10, 1921." *The Tryout*, 7, No. 1 (February 1921), [15] (as by "Ward Phillips"). *The Troy* [N.Y.] *Times*, 10 February 1921 [as "On His Ninetieth Birthday: February 10, 1921: (To Jonathan Hoag of Greenwich)"].

221. "On a Poet's Ninety-first Birthday: (To Jonathan Hoag, Esq., Feb. 10, 1922)." *The Troy* [N.Y.] *Times*, 10 February 1921. *The Tryout*, 7, No. 11 (March 1922), [15-16] (as by "Lewis Theobald, Jun.").

222. "To J. E. Hoag, Esq.: On His Ninetyecond [sic] Birthday, Feb. 10, 1293 [sic]." *The Tryout*, 8, No. 11 (November 1923), [13-14] (as by "L. Theobald, Jun.").

223. "To Mr. Hoag upon His 93rd Birthday, February 10, 1924." *The Troy* [N.Y.] *Times*, 9 February 1924 (as "His Ninety-third Birthday: To Jonathan Hoag of Greenwich—a Poem to the Poet—February 10th Anniversary"). *Pegasus*, No. [3] (July 1924), 33.

224. "To Mr. Hoag on His Ninety-fourth Birthday, February 10, 1925." *The Troy* [N.Y.] *Times*, 10 February 1925 (as "To Jonathan Hoag of Greenwich: Upon His Ninety-fourth Birthday, February 10, 1925"). *The Tryout*, 9, No. 12 (March 1925), [3-4].

225. "To Jonathan Hoag: (Upon His 95th Birthday)." *The Troy* [N.Y.] *Times*, 10 February 1926. *The Brooklynite*, 16, No. 1 (May 1926), 1.

226. "To Jonathan E. Hoag, Esq., upon His Ninety-Sixth Birthday, February 10, 1927." *The National Amateur*, 49, No. 5 (May 1927), 10.

227. "Ave Atque Vale: To Jonathan E. Hoag, Esq.: February 10, 1831-October 17th, 1927." *The Tryout*, 11, No. 10 (December 1927), [3-4].

iv. Revisions and Collaborations

a. *Fiction*

1. [With Barlow, R. H.] "The Battle That Ended the Century (MS. Found in a Time Machine)." *The Acolyte*, 2, No. 4 (Fall 1944), 9-12.

   Also contains letters of comment on the farce by August Derleth, Clark Ashton Smith, and H. P. Lovecraft.

2. [With Barlow, R. H.] "Collapsing Cosmoses." *Leaves*, 2 (1938), 100-01 (unsigned).

   This collaboration was never completed.

3. Barlow, R. H. "A Fragment." *The Californian*, 3, No. 2 (Winter 1935), 73.

   An excerpt of the last paragraphs of "The Night Ocean" (see next entry).

4. Barlow, R. H. "The Night Ocean." *The Californian*, 4, No. 3 (Winter 1936), 41-56.

5. Barlow, R. H. " 'Till A' the Seas.' " *The Californian*, 3, No. 1 (Summer 1935), 3-7. *The Arkham Collector*, No. 4 (Winter 1969), pp. 90-101 (as " 'Till All the Seas' ").

   All subsequent publications use the latter title.

6. Bishop, Zealia Brown Reed. "The Curse of Yig." *Weird Tales*, 14, No. 5 (November 1929), 625-36. *Weird Tales*, 33, No. 4 (April 1939), 140-51.

7. Bishop, Zealia Brown Reed. "Medusa's Coil." *Weird Tales*, 33, No. 1 (January 193[9]), 26-53.

   The issue of *Weird Tales* was misdated as January 1938.

8. Bishop, Zealia Brown Reed. "The Mound." *Weird Tales*, 35, No. 6 (November 1940), 98-120 (abridged).

9. Bloch, Robert. "Satan's Servants." *Magazine of Horror*, 5, No. 6 (December 1969), 9-35.

10. With Crofts, Anna Helen. "Poetry and the Gods." *The United Amateur*, 20, No. 1 (September 1920), 1-4 (as by "Anna Helen Crofts and Henry Paget-Lowe").

11. Davis, Sonia H. "The Horror at Martin's Beach." *Weird Tales*, 2, No. 4 (November 1923), 75-76, 83 (as by "Sonia H. Greene"; as "The Invisible Monster").

12. de Castro, Adolphe. "The Electric Executioner." *Weird Tales*, 16, No. 2 (August 1930), 223-36.

13. de Castro, Adolphe. "The Last Test." *Weird Tales*, 12, No. 5 (November 1928), 625-56.

14. Eddy, C. M., Jr. "Ashes." *Weird Tales*, 3, No. 3 (March 1924), 22-24.

15. Eddy, C. M., Jr. "Deaf, Dumb and Blind." *Weird Tales*, 5, No. 4 (April 1925), 25-30, 177-79.

16. Eddy, C. M., Jr. "The Ghost-Eater." *Weird Tales*, 3, No. 4 (April 1924), 72-75.

17. Eddy, C. M., Jr. "The Loved Dead." *Weird Tales*, 4, No. 2 (May-June-July 1924), 54-57. *The Arkham Sampler*, 1, No. 3 (Summer 1948), 21-31.

18. With Farley, Ralph Milne, David H. Keller, Clark Ashton Smith, Harl Vincent, E. E. Smith, Otis Adelbert Kline, and Stanton A. Coblentz. "Cigarette Characterizations." *Fantasy Magazine*, 3, No. 4 (June 1934), 15-16, 32.

    A contest in which readers were invited to deduce the authors of eight brief prose selections which had been written by these eight authors in a way that parodied their own characteristic writing styles.

19. Heald, Hazel. "The Horror in the Burying Ground." *Weird Tales*, 29, No. 5 (May 1937), 596-606.

20. Heald, Hazel. "The Horror in the Museum." *Weird Tales*, 22, No. 1 (July 1933), 49-68.

21. Heald, Hazel. "The Man of Stone." *Wonder Stories*, 4, No. 5 (October 1932), 440-45, 470.

22. Heald, Hazel. "Out of the Eons." *Weird Tales*, 25, No. 4 (April 1935), 478-96.

23. Heald, Hazel. "Winged Death." *Weird Tales*, 23, No. 3 (March 1934), 299-315.

24. Houdini, Harry. "Under the Pyramids." *Weird Tales*, 4, No. 2 (May-June-July 1924), 3-12. *Weird Tales*, 34, No. 1 (June-July 1939), 133-50.

    Both as "Imprisoned with the Pharaohs" (used in all subsequent publications) and as by "Houdini." The proper title has been deduced from an advertisement placed by Lovecraft in *The Providence Journal* (3 March 1924) declaring the loss of the T.Ms.

25. With Jackson, Winifred V. "The Crawling Chaos." *The United Co-operative*, 1, No. 3 (April 1921), 1-6 (as by "Elizabeth Berkeley and Lewis Theobald, Jun."). *Tesseract*, 2, No. 4 (April 1937), 7-8; 2, No. 5 (May 1937), 7-8. *Tesseract Annual*, No. 1 (1939), pp. 5-8.

    Bibliographies have listed the story as appearing in *The United Amateur*, 1920; this is incorrect. Confusion has been made with the prose poem, "Nyarlathotep" (I-B-i-38), which opens with the words, "The crawling chaos. . . ."

26. With Jackson, Winifred V. "The Green Meadow." *The Vagrant*, [Spring 1927], pp. 188-95 (as by "Elizabeth Neville Berkeley and Lewis Theobald, Jr.").

27. Lumley, William. "The Diary of Alonzo Typer." *Weird Tales*, 31, No. 2 (February 1938), 152-66.

28. With Moore, C. L.; Merritt, A.; Howard, Robert E.; and Long, Frank Belknap, Jr. "The Challenge from Beyond." *Fantasy Magazine*, 5, No. 4 (September 1935), 221-29 (Lovecraft portion on pp. 223-27). *Fantastic*, 9, No. 5 (May 1960), 51-59 (Lovecraft portion only).

    A round robin tale arranged by Julius Schwartz, editor of *Fantasy Magazine*. Lovecraft's is the third and longest segment of the tale.

29. With Price, E. Hoffmann. "Through the Gates of the Silver Key." *Weird Tales*, 24, No. 1 (July 1934), 60-85.

30. Rimel, Duane W. "The Sorcery of Aphlar." *The Fantasy Fan*, 2, No. 4 (December 1934), 57-58. *Tri-State* [N.Y.] *Times*, 1, No. 1 (Spring 1937), 3-4 (as "The Sourcery of Alphar").

31. Rimel, Duane W. "The Tree on the Hill." *Polaris,* September 1940, pp. 4-11.

32. With Sterling, Kenneth. "In the Walls of Eryx." *Weird Tales,* 34, No. 4 (October 1939), 50-68.

33. Talman, Wilfred Blanch. "Two Black Bottles." *Weird Tales,* 10, No. 2 (August 1927), 251-58.

34. Whitehead, Henry S. "Bothon." *Amazing Stories,* 20, No. 5 (August 1946), 122-42.

   > In his letters Lovecraft refers to this story as "The Bruise"; it is not certain who made the title change.

35. Whitehead, Henry S. "The Trap." *Strange Tales of Mystery and Terror,* 2, No. 1 (March 1932), 73-88. *Weird Terror Tales,* 1, No. 3 (Fall 1970), 48-71.

b. *Poetry*

1. Davis, Sonia H. "Mors Omnibus Communis: (Written in a Hospital)." *The Rainbow,* No. 1 (October 1921), p. 8.

2. Hoag, Jonathan E. "Alone." *The Tryout,* 10, No. 7 (January 1926), [7].

3. Shepherd, Wilson. "Wanderer's Return." *The Literary Quarterly,* 1, No. 1 (Winter 1937), 5-6 (as "Wander's Return").

v. Letters

a. *Multiple Publications*

1. "By Post from Providence." *The Californian,* 5, No. 1 (Summer 1937), 10-23.

Contains letters to Rheinhart Kleiner:

28 March 1915, pp. 10-11 (as "Early Enthusiasms"); 27 December 1916, p. 11 (as "Some Landmarks of Amateur Letters"); 31 January 1917, p. 11 (continuation of "Some Landmarks"); 17 July [1917], pp. 11-12 (as "C. W. Smith—The First Weird Tales"); 27 August [1917], p. 12 (continuation of "C. W. Smith"); 24 September [1917], pp. 12-13 (as "Remarks on Poetry—and Poets" and "First Meeting with W. Paul Cook"); 8 November [1917], pp. 13-14 (as "He Joins the National"); 4 April [1918], pp. 14-15 (as "Hard Times in the United"); 5 May [1918], pp. 15-16 (as "The Humors of Recruiting," "Some Possible Laureate Judges," and " 'The Vagrant'—the Fossils"); 5 June [1918], p. 16 (as "His Room at 598 Angell St."); 4 December [1918], pp. 16-18 (as "A Passing Mood" and "Literary Chit-Chat"); 16 July 1919, p. 18 (as "Battles Long Ago"); 30 July [1919], p. 18 (continuation of "Battles Long Ago"); 27 September [i.e., 3 December] [1919], pp. 18-19 (as "Lord Dunsany"); 25 June 1920, p. 19 (as "Edward F. Daas—Cosmic Futility"); 12 August [1920], pp. 19-20 (as "The Hub Club Picnic"); 10 September [1920], pp. 20-21 (as "The Hub Club Conference"); 13 September [1920], pp. 21-22 (continuation of "Hub Club Conference"); 11 January 1923, pp. 22-23 (as "As National President," "In Boston with Edward H. Cole," and "An Added Visit to Marblehead").

2. "Excerpts from the Letters of H. P. Lovecraft." *The Acolyte*, 1, No. 1 (Fall 1942), 4-5, 15.

Contains letters to Duane Rimel:

19 November 1934, p. 4; 10 March 1935, pp. 4-5; 16 April 1935, p. 5; 12 November 1935, pp. 5, 15.

3. "Four Letters to Clark Ashton Smith." *Witchcraft and Sorcery*, 1, No. 5 (January-February 1971), 27-28.

Contains letters to Clark Ashton Smith:

16 February 1932, p. 27; 2 March 1932, pp. 27-28; 4 April 1932, p. 28; 18 February 1933, p. 28.

4. "A Group of Letters." *The Arkham Sampler*, 1, No. 2 (Spring 1948), 13-19.

Contains letters:

To Mrs. F. C. Clark, 29-30 September 1924, pp. 13-14; to
Frank Belknap Long, 2 August 1925, p. 14; to Frank Belknap
Long, 10 August 1925, pp. 14-15; to Frank Belknap Long, 23
April 1926, p. 15; to Clark Ashton Smith, 28 January 1932, pp.
15-16; to Clark Ashton Smith, 8 February 1932, p. 16; to
Clark Ashton Smith, 18 February 1932, pp. 16-17; to Clark
Ashton Smith, October 1932, pp. 17-18; to Richard Ely Morse,
15 January 1934, p. 18; to Richard Ely Morse, 28 January 1937,
pp. 18-19.

5. "Letters to Virgil Finlay." *Fantasy Collector's Annual*,
   1974, pp. 9-13.

   Contains letters to Virgil Finlay:

   9 September 1936, pp. 9-11; 25 September 1936, p. 11; 10
   October 1936, p. 11; 24 October 1936, pp. 11-12; 30 November
   1936, pp. 12-13 (includes facsimile of part of the A.L.); [ca. 1
   January 1937], p. 13 (postcard).

   With running commentary on the letters by Gerry de la Ree.

6. [Six letters.] *Phantastique/The Science Fiction Critic*, No. 13
   (March 1938), pp. 3-10.

   Contains letters:

   To Jim Blish and William Miller, Jr., 13 May 1936, p. 3; to Jim
   Blish and William Miller, Jr., 19 May 1936, p. 3; to Jim Blish
   and William Miller, Jr., 3 June 1936, pp. 3-4; to Nils H. Frome,
   19 December 1937 [i.e., 1936], p. 4; to Nils H. Frome, 20
   January 1937, pp. 4-6; to Nils H. Frome, 28 (?) February 1939
   [i.e., 1937], pp. 6-10.

b. *Individual Publications*

1. To the Editor of the Sunday Journal, 27 May 1906.
   The Providence Sunday Journal, 21, No. 49 (3 June 1906),
   Sec. 2, p. 5 (as "No Transit of Mars"). *Nyctalops*, 2,
   No. 2 (July 1974), 44.

Lovecraft's first appearance in print, noting a scientific error by an astrologer whose letter had appeared in the *Journal* for 27 May.

2. To the Editor of the *Scientific American*, 16 July 1906. *Scientific American*, 95, No. 8 (25 August 1906), 135 (as "Trans-Neptunian Planets").

3. To the Editor of the Sunday Journal, 6 August 1906. *The Providence Sunday Journal*, 22, No. 7 (12 August 1906), Sec. 2, p. 5 (as "The Earth not Hollow").

   Ridicules the hollow earth theory as expressed in a letter to the *Journal* of August 5.

4. To the Editor of *The All-Story Cavalier*, [January 1913?]. *The All-Story Cavalier*, 8 February 1913, p. 361.

   On Irvin S. Cobb's "Fishhead."

5. To the Editor of *The Argosy*, [August 1913?]. *The Argosy*, September 1913.

6. To the Editor of *The Argosy*, [December 1913?]. *The Argosy*, 74, No. 2 (January 1914), 479-80 (as "Lovecraft Comes Back: Ad Criticos"). *Golden Atom*, No. 9 (December 1940), p. 12.

   In verse.

7. To the Editor of *The Argosy*, [January 1914?]. *The Argosy*, 74, No. 3 (February 1914) (as "Ad Criticos: Liber Secundus").

   In verse.

8. To the Editor of *The Argosy*, [January 1914?]. *The Argosy*, [74], No. 4 (March 1914), 956 (as "Correction for Lovecraft").

   Notes printing errors in the text of I-B-v-b-6.

9. To the Editor of *The All-Story Weekly*, [February 1914?]. *The All-Story Weekly*, 7 March 1914.

10. To the Editor of *The Argosy*, [March 1914?]. *The Argosy*, April 1914 (as "Ruat Caelum").
    In verse.

11. To the Editor of *The All-Story Cavalier*, [July 1914?]. *The All-Story Cavalier*, 15 August 1914. *Golden Atom*, No. 9 (December 1940), p. 13.

12. To the Editor of *The Argosy*, [September 1914?]. *The Argosy*, October 1914.

13. To the Editor of *The Evening News*, [19? December 1915]. *The* [Providence] *Evening News*, 46, No. 28 (21 December 1914), 3 (as by "Isaac Bickerstaffe, Jr.").

14. To [Gavin T. McColl], [early 1916]. *The Scot*, No. 7 (March 1916), p. 36 (in section titled "Appreciations").

15. To the Honorable Bureau of Critics, National Amateur Press Ass'n, [late 1918?]. *The National Amateur*, 41, No. 3 (January 1919), 93 (as by "Ned Softly" and "Ward Phillips"; in section titled "The Members' Forum").

16. To the Editor of *The Argosy*, [November? 1919]. *The Argosy*, 15 November 1919. *Golden Atom*, No. 9 (December 1940), pp. 13-14.

    Both as by "Augustus T. Swift."

17. To the Editor of *The Argosy*, [April? 1920]. *The Argosy*, 121, No. 2 (22 May 1920), 288 (as "Not Out for Blood"). *Golden Atom*, No. 9 (December 1940), p. 14.
    Both as by "Augustus T. Swift."

18. To [John Milton Heins], [March? 1921]. *The American Amateur*, 2, No. 5 (April 1921), 153.

19. To John Milton Heins, 4 November 1921. *The National Amateur*, 44, No. 3 (January 1922), 27.

20. To Sonia Greene, ca. 1922. *The Arkham Collector*, No. 8 (Winter 1971), pp. 242-46 (as "Lovecraft on Love").

21. To the Board of Executive Judges, National Amateur Press Association, Mrs. E. D. Houtain, Chairman, 30 November 1922. *The National Amateur*, 45, Nos. 2/3 (November [1922]-January 1923), 6.

22. To Edwin Baird, [early May 1923]. *Weird Tales*, 2, No. 2 (September 1923), 81-82.

23. To the Ohio Amateur Journalists' Club, 29 May 1923. *The Buckeye*, 3, No. 1 (June 1923), 3 (as "Lovecraft's Greeting").

24. To Edwin Baird, [September? 1923]. *Weird Tales*, 2, No. 3 (October 1923), 82.

25. To Edwin Baird, [December 1923?]. *Weird Tales*, 3, No. 1 (January 1924), 86, 88.

26. To Edwin Baird, [February 1924?]. *Weird Tales*, 3, No. 3 (March 1924), 89-92.

27. To Farnsworth Wright, [January 1926?]. *Weird Tales*, 7, No. 2 (February 1926), 273.

28. To the Editor of *The Sunday Journal*, 5 October 1926. *The Providence Sunday Journal*, 42, No. 15 (10 October 1926), Sec. A, p. 5 (as "Asks Preservation of Old Buildings").

29. To Farnsworth Wright, 5 July 1927. *Weird Tales*, 11, No. 2 (February 1928), 282.

    Also included in I-A-19 as the second of "Two Comments" (pp. 305-06).

30. To Clark Ashton Smith, 30 August 1927. *Xenophile*, 2, No. 6 (October 1975), 14.

    Postcard.

31. To Donald Wandrei, 2 November 1927. *Scienti-Snaps*, 3, No. 3 (Summer 1940), 4-8 (as "The Very Old Folk").

32. To Frank Belknap Long, [November 1927]. *Weird Tales*, 17, No. 2 (February-March 1931), 251-56.

    Basically the same text as I-B-v-b-31: this is Lovecraft's great "Roman dream" which, with Lovecraft's permission, Long incorporated directly into his novel, *The Horror from the Hills* (published in *Weird Tales* as above). Another account of the dream is in a letter to B. A. Dwyer (see I-A-33).

33. To Farnsworth Wright, [December 1927?]. *Weird Tales*, 11, No. 1 (January 1928), 136.

34. To Walter J. Coates, February [1928]. *Carry Back Books Catalogue*, No. 8 (Fall 1975), pp. 52-53.

35. To Farnsworth Wright, [February 1928?]. *Weird Tales*, 11, No. 3 (March 1928), 427.

36. To the Editor of *Dragnet*, [early 1929]. *Dragnet*, 2, No. 3 (April 1929), 372. *The Phantagraph*, 12, No. 3 (November 1944), 3-4.

37. To the Editor of *The Sunday Journal*, 20 March 1929. *The Providence Sunday Journal*, 44, No. 39 (24 March 1929), Sec. A, p. 5 (as "Retain Historic 'Old Brick Row' ").

38. To Clark Ashton Smith, [ca. 1929]. *Tolometh*, 1, No. 1 [January 1976], 2.

    Postcard.

39. To Forrest J. Ackerman, [1930s]. *Imagination!*, 1, No. 4 (January 1938), 9-10.

40. To [Walter J. Coates], [June? 1932]. *Driftwind*, 7, No. 1 (July 1932), 13.

41. To E. Hoffmann Price, 15 February 1933. *The Arkham Sampler*, 3 (Summer 1948), 36-40 (as "A Letter to E. Hoffmann Price").

42. To Edwin Hadley Smith, 10 March 1933. *The Boys' Herald*, 71, No. 1 (October 1941), 7-8 (as "Lovecraft on Poetry Writing").

43. To [Charles D. Hornig], [September? 1933]. *The Fantasy Fan*, 1, No. 2 (October 1933), 14, 27-28 (the latter as part of the column, "The Boiling Point").

44. To [Charles D. Hornig], [October? 1933]. *The Fantasy Fan*, 1, No. 3 (November 1933), 33.

45. To [Charles D. Hornig], [November? 1933]. *The Fantasy Fan*, 1, No. 4 (December 1933), 50.

46. To [Charles D. Hornig], [December? 1933]. *The Fantasy Fan*, 1, No. 5 (January 1934), 68 (as part of the column, "The Boiling Point").

47. To Farnsworth Wright, [December 1933?]. *Weird Tales*, 23, No. 1 (January 1934), 132.

48. To [Charles D. Hornig], [February? 1934]. *The Fantasy Fan*, 1, No. 7 (March 1934), 97.

49. To [Charles D. Hornig], [February? 1934]. *The Fantasy Fan*, 1, No. 7 (March 1934), 105 (part of the column, "Your Views"). *Leaves*, 2 (1938), 99 (as "From a Letter").

    Also included in I-A-19 as the first of "Two Comments" (p. 305).

50. To [Charles D. Hornig], [March? 1934]. *The Fantasy Fan*, 1, No. 8 (April 1934), 113.

51. To [Charles D. Hornig], [April? 1934]. *The Fantasy Fan*, 1, No. 9 (May 1934), 127.

52. To [Charles D. Hornig], [June? 1934]. *The Fantasy Fan*, 1, No. 11 (July 1934), 162.

53. To [Charles D. Hornig], [September? 1934]. *The Fantasy Fan*, 2, No. 2 (October 1934), 17.

54. To James F. Morton, 24 September 1924. *The Olympian*, No. 35 (Autumn 1940), pp. 35-36.

55. To [Charles D. Hornig], [November? 1934]. *The Fantasy Fan*, 2, No. 4 (December 1934), 49.

56. To F. Lee Baldwin, ca. 1934. *The Acolyte*, 1, No. 4 (Summer 1943), 21, 23 (as "Lovecraft as an Illustrator").

57. To [Vincent B. Haggerty], [mid-1935?]. *Amateur Affairs*, 1, No. 9 (October 1935), [4] (in section titled "Fragments").

58. To [Duane Rimel], [28 September 1935]. *The Phantagraph*, 5, No. 5 (February 1937), 4-8 (as "What's the Trouble with Weird Fiction?"; unsigned).

59. To Alvin Earl Perry, 4 October 1935. *Whispers*, 2, Nos. 2/3 (June 1975), 80-84 (as "Story-Writing: A Letter from HPL").

60. To [Donald A. Wollheim], [October? 1935]. *The Phantagraph*, 4, No. 2 (November-December 1935), [1].

61. To Farnsworth Wright, [January 1936?]. *Weird Tales*, 27, No. 2 (February 1936), 250.

62. To Farnsworth Wright, [June 1936?]. *Weird Tales*, 28, No. 3 (October 1936), 378.

    On the death of Robert E. Howard.

63. To the Convention of the N. A. P. A., Grand Rapids, Michigan, 22 June 1936. *Lest We Forget*, October 1936, p. 28.

64. To E. Hoffmann Price, 5 July 1936. *The Howard Collector*, 3, No. 1 (Autumn 1970), 14-20.

    On the death of Robert E. Howard.

65. To Willis Conover, [24 August 1936]. *Science-Fantasy Correspondent*, 1, No. 1 (November-December 1936), 28.

66. To Willis Conover, [23 September 1936]. *Science-Fantasy Correspondent*, 1, No. 2 (January-February 1937), 28.

67. To Clark Ashton Smith, 5 February 1937. *Science-Fantasy Correspondent*, No. 1 (1975), pp. 32-35 (as "Last Autumn, Last Winter: Three Episodes").

68. To James F. Morton, March [?] 1937. *The Arkham Collector*, No. 4 (Winter 1969), pp. 102-06 (as "Lovecraft's Last Letter").

C. Material Included in Books by Others

1. Asbury, Herbert, ed. *Not at Night!* New York: Macy-
   Macius (The Vanguard Press), Nov. 1928. 386 pp.
   Contains: "The Horror at Red Hook," pp. 27-52.

2. Bacon, Jonathan, and Steve Troyanovich, eds.
   *Omniumgathum: An Anthology of Verse by Top Authors in
   the Field of Fantasy.* Lamoni, Iowa: Stygian Isle Press,
   1976. 64 pp.
   Contains: "Bells," pp. 13-14; "To the Old Pagan Religion" (as
   "The Last Pagan Speaks"), p. 25; "Hellas," p. 29; "Laeta; a
   Lament," p. 35; "Unda, or, the Bride of the Sea" (as "The Bride
   of the Sea"), pp. 36-39; "Inspiration," p. 48; "The Simple
   Speller's Tale: (Translated into English)," p. 55; "The Dead
   Bookworm," p. 55; "The Power of Wine" (as "The Pow'r of
   Wine"), p. 58.

3. Beck, Robert E., ed. *Literature of the Supernatural.*
   Evanston, Ill.: McDougal, Littell & Co., 1974, 1978.
   191 pp.
   Contains: "In the Vault," pp. 35-42.

4. Blaisdell, Elinore, ed. *Tales of the Undead: Vampires and
   Visitants.* New York: Thomas Y. Crowell Co., 1947.
   ix, 372 pp.
   Contains: "The Tomb," pp. 185-95.

5. Boyer, Robert H., and Kenneth J. Zahorski, eds. *Dark
   Imaginings: A Collection of Gothic Fantasy.* New York:
   Dell Publishing Co. (Delta Books), Apr. 1978. 348
   pp.
   Contains: "The Haunter of the Dark," pp. 275-95.

6. Bullen, John Ravenor. *White Fire.* Athol, Mass.: The
   Recluse Press, 1927. 86 pp.
   Contains: "Preface," pp. 7-13.

7. Carter, Lin, ed. *New Worlds for Old*. New York:
   Ballantine Books, Sept. 1971. xvii, 326 pp.

   Contains: "The Green Meadow," by H. P. Lovecraft and
   "Elizabeth Berkeley" (i.e., W. V. Jackson), pp. 145-51.

8. Carter, Lin, ed. *Realms of Wizardry*. Garden City, N.Y.:
   Doubleday & Co., 1976. xv, 269 pp.

   Contains: "The Doom That Came to Sarnath," pp. 7-13.

9. Carter, Lin, ed. *The Spawn of Cthulhu*. New York:
   Ballantine Books, Oct. 1971. [x], 274 pp.

   Contains: "The Whisperer in Darkness," pp. 8-90; "The
   Curse of Yig," by Zealia Bishop, pp. 235-56.

10. Carter, Lin, ed. *The Young Magicians*. New York:
    Ballantine Books, Oct. 1969 (first British printing:
    March 1971). [vii], 280 pp.

    Contains: "The Quest of Iranon," pp. 88-95; "The Cats of
    Ulthar," pp. 96-100.

11. Chalker, Jack L., ed. *Mirage on Lovecraft: A Literary View*.
    Baltimore: Jack L. Chalker and Mark Owings (The
    Anthem Series), 1965. ix, 46 pp.

    Contains: "Autobiography: Some Notes on a Nonentity"
    (annotated by August Derleth), pp. 3-10; "Notes on the Writing
    of Weird Fiction" (i.e., "Notes on Writing Weird Fiction"), pp.
    13-15; "Some Notes on Interplanetary Fiction," pp. 19-23.

12. Coates, Walter John, ed. *Harvest: A Sheaf of Poems from
    Driftwind*. North Montpelier, Vt.: The Driftwind
    Press, May 1933. 57 pp.

    Contains: "The Canal," p. 33.

13. Coblentz, Stanton A., ed. *Unseen Wings: The Living
    Poetry of Man's Immortality*. New York: The Beechurst
    Press, 1949. 282 pp.

    Contains: "Continuity," p. 229; "A Memory," p. 229.

14. Collins, Charles M., ed. *Fright*. New York: Avon, 1963. 141 pp. New York: Avon, August 1975 (as *Harvest of Fear: Formerly titled* Fright). 172 pp.

   Contains: "The Horror at Red Hook," pp. 120-41 (1963 ed.); pp. 147-72 (1975 ed.).

15. Conklin, Groff, ed. *The Graveyard Reader: Twelve Terrifying Tales*. New York: Ballantine Books, 1958. 156 pp.

   Contains: "The Outsider," pp. 134-41.

16. Conklin, Groff, ed. *In the Grip of Terror*. New York: Perma Books, 1951. xii, 354 pp.

   Contains: "In the Vault," pp. 89-99.

17. Conklin, Groff, ed. *Omnibus of Science Fiction*. New York: Crown, 1952. xi, 562 pp. New York: Crown, 1952 (Book Club Edition). xiii, 560 pp.

   Contains: "The Colour out of Space," pp. 146-67 (both editions).

18. Conklin, Groff, ed. *Science Fiction Omnibus*. New York: Berkley, Aug. 1956. 187 pp. New York: Berkley Medallion, Nov. 1963. 190 pp.

   Contains: "The Colour out of Space," pp. 22-51 (1956 ed.); pp. 24-53 (1963 ed.). Abridged edition of the above.

19. Conklin, Groff, ed. *Strange Travels in Science Fiction*. London: Grayson & Grayson, 1954. 256 pp.

   Contains: "The Colour out of Space," pp. 34-64. Abridged edition of I-C-17 but with different contents from I-C-18.

20. Conklin, Groff, ed. *Twisted*. New York: Belmont Books, May 1962; London: New English Library, Nov. 1965. 189 pp.

   Contains: "The Shunned House," pp. 148-71.

21. Crawford, Nelson Antrim, comp. *Cats in Prose and Verse*. New York: Coward-McCann, 1947. xxvii, 387 pp.

> Contains: "Little Sam Perkins," p. 76.

22. Cross, John Keir, ed. *Best Horror Stories 2*. London: Faber & Faber, 1965. 270 pp.

> Contains: "The Thing on the Doorstep," pp. 81-112.

23. Daniels, Les, ed. *Dying of Fright: Masterpieces of the Macabre*. New York: Charles Scribner's Sons, 1976. x, 271 pp.

> Contains: "The Call of Cthulhu," pp. 160-78.

24. Daniels, Les. *Living in Fear: A History of Horror in the Mass Media*. New York: Charles Scribner's Sons, 1975; London: Paladin, 1977. 248 pp.

> Contains: "The Outsider," pp. 125-29.

25. Daniels, Les, and Diane Thompson, eds. *Thirteen Tales of Terror*. New York: Charles Scribner's Sons, 1977. xviii, 260 pp.

> Contains: "The Music of Erich Zann," pp. 152-62.

26. Davenport, Basil, ed. *Famous Monster Tales*. Princeton, N.J.: D. Van Nostrand Co., 1967. 201 pp.

> Contains: "The Outsider," pp. 79-85.

27. Davis, Sonia H., ed. *The Rainbow: Vol. I, No. 1: October, 1921*. [West Warwick, R.I.: Necronomicon Press,] 1977. 14 pp.

> Contains: "Mors Omnibus Communis," by Sonia H. Greene, p. 8; "Nietscheism [sic] and Realism," pp. 9-11. Facsimile reproduction of the periodical.

28. de Camp, L. Sprague, ed. *The Fantastic Swordsmen*. New York: Pyramid, May 1967. 204 pp.

> Contains: "The Other Gods," pp. 149-54.

29. de Camp, L. Sprague, ed. *Swords and Sorcery.* New York: Pyramid, Dec. 1963. 186 pp.

> Contains: "The Doom That Came to Sarnath," pp. 123-29.

30. de Camp, L. Sprague, and Catherine Crook de Camp, eds. *3000 Years of Fantasy and Science Fiction.* New York: Lothrop, Lee, and Shepard, 1972. 256 pp.

> Contains: "The Cats of Ulthar," pp. 95-99.

31. Derleth, August, ed. *Dark of the Moon: Poems of Fantasy and the Macabre.* Sauk City, Wis.: Arkham House, 1947; Freeport, N.Y.: Books for Libraries Press, 1969. xvi, 418 pp.

> Contains: "Psychopompos," pp. 289-98; *Fungi from Yuggoth*, pp. 299-316 ("I. The Book," "II. Pursuit," p. 299; "III. The Key," "IV. Recognition," p. 300; "V. Homecoming," "VI. The Lamp," p. 301; "VII. Zaman's Hill," "VIII. The Port," p. 302; "IX. The Courtyard," "X. The Pigeon-Flyers," p. 303; "XI. The Well," "XII. The Howler," p. 304; "XIII. Hesperia," "XIV. Star-Winds," p. 305; "XV. Antarktos," "XVI. The Window," p. 306; "XVII. A Memory," "XVIII. The Gardens of Yin," p. 307; "XIX. The Bells," "XX. Night-Gaunts," p. 308; "XXI. Nyarlathotep," "XXII. Azathoth," p. 309; "XXIII. Mirage," "XXIV. The Canal," p. 310; "XXV. St. Toad's," "XXVI. The Familiars," p. 311; "XXVII. The Elder Pharos," "XXVIII. Expectancy," p. 312; "XXIX. Nostalgia," "XXX. Background," p. 313; "XXXI. The Dweller," "XXXII. Alienation," p. 314; "XXXIII. Harbour Whistles," "XXXIV. Recapture," p. 315; "XXXV. Evening Star," "XXXVI. Continuity," p. 316); "The Messenger," p. 317; "The Ancient Track," pp. 317-18.

32. Derleth, August. *H. P. L.: A Memoir.* New York: Ben Abramson, 1945. 122 pp.

> Contains: "To Pan," p. 91; "Does 'Vulcan' Exist?" pp. 91-92; "The Cats of Ulthar," pp. 92-96; "Rudis Indigestaque Moles," pp. 96-99; "The Festival," pp. 99-110; "The Window," pp. 110-11.

33. Derleth, August, *The Lurker at the Threshold*. Sauk City,
    Wis.: Arkham House, 1945. [vi], 196 pp. London:
    Museum Press, [1948]. 224 pp. London: Victor
    Gollancz, Nov. 1968, Jan. 1969. [iv], 196 pp. New
    York: Beagle Books, March 1971, June 1971, 160 pp.
    New York: Ballantine Books, April 1976. [iv], 186
    pp. St. Albans, Eng.: Panther Books, 1970, 1973.
    160 pp.

    Contains: "Of Evill Sorceries done in New England," pp. 19-
    21, 23 (Arkham House, Gollancz); pp. 24-26, 28-29 (Museum
    Press); pp. 20-22, 23 (Beagle, Panther); pp. 16-18, 20
    (Ballantine).

    See I-E-i, I-E-i-14.

34. Derleth, August, ed. *New Worlds for Old*. London:
    Four Square, 1953, 1964. 126 pp.

    Contains: "From Beyond," pp. 77-84. Abridged edition of
    I-C-53.

35. Derleth, August, ed. *The Night Side: Masterpieces of the
    Strange and Terrible*. New York: Rinehart & Co., 1947.
    x, 372 pp. London: Four Square, 1963. 272 pp.

    Contains: "The Colour out of Space," pp. 3-30 (Rinehart); pp.
    12-37 (Four Square).

36. Derleth, August, ed. *Night's Yawning Peal: A Ghostly
    Company*. [New York:] Arkham House/Pellegrini &
    Cudahy, 1952. viii, 280 pp.

    Contains: "The Loved Dead," by C. M. Eddy, Jr., pp. 29-39;
    The Case of Charles Dexter Ward, pp. 156-280.

37. Derleth, August, ed. *Night's Yawning Peal: A Ghostly
    Company*. [Abridged edition.] New York: New
    American Library, Aug. 1974. 208 pp.

    Contains: *The Case of Charles Dexter Ward*, pp. 87-208.

38. Derleth, August, ed. *The Other Side of the Moon*. New York: Pellegrini & Cudahy, 1949. [xii], 461 pp.

    Contains: "Beyond the Wall of Sleep," pp. 130-44.

39. Derleth, August, ed. *The Other Side of the Moon*. [Abridged edition.] London: Grayson & Grayson, 1956. 239 pp.

    Contains: "Beyond the Wall of Sleep," pp. 52-63.

40. Derleth, August, ed. *The Other Side of the Moon*. [Abridged edition.] St. Albans, Eng.: Panther Books, 1963. 144 pp.

    Contains: "Beyond the Wall of Sleep," pp. 59-67.

41. Derleth, August, ed. *Sleep No More: Twenty Masterpieces of Horror for the Connoisseur*. New York: Farrar & Rinehart, 1944. x, 374 pp. [New York:] Editions for the Armed Services, [1944]. 384 pp.

    Contains: "Two Black Bottles," by Wilfred Blanch Talman, pp. 179-91 (Farrar); pp. 189-204 (Armed Services); "The Horror in the Burying Ground," by Hazel Heald, pp. 247-62 (Farrar); pp. 257-74 (Armed Services); "The Rats in the Walls," pp. 353-74 (Farrar); pp. 360-84 (Armed Services).

42. Derleth, August, ed. *Sleep No More*. [Abridged edition.] St. Albans, Eng.: Panther Books, Dec. 1964. 189 pp.

    Contains: "The Horror in the Burying Ground," by Hazel Heald, pp. 140-51.

43. Derleth, August, ed. *The Sleeping and the Dead: 30 Uncanny Tales*. New York: Pellegrini & Cudahy, 1947. [vi], 518 pp.

    Contains: "Out of the Eons," by Hazel Heald, pp. 85-114; "Deaf, Dumb and Blind," by C. M. Eddy, Jr., pp. 280-93; "The Dreams in the Witch House," pp. 472-513.

44. Derleth, August, ed. *The Sleeping and the Dead: Fifteen Uncanny Tales*. London: Four Square, 1963. 253 pp.

   Contains: "Out of the Eons," by Hazel Heald, pp. 57-83; "The Dreams in the Witch House," pp. 217-53.

45. Derleth, August. *Some Notes on H. P. Lovecraft*. [Sauk City, Wis.:] Arkham House, 1959; Folcroft, Pa.: Folcroft Press, 1971; [Norwood, Pa.:] Norwood Editions, 1976. xlii pp.

   Contains: "Four Letters" [to August Derleth]: [early December 1926], pp. xxxii-xxxiii; 20 February 1927, pp. xxxiv-xxxvii; 9 September 1931, pp. xxxvii-xxxix; 18 November 1936, pp. xxxix-xlii.

46. Derleth, August. *Strange Ports of Call*. New York: Pellegrini & Cudahy, 1948, Dec. 1949. [x], 393 pp.

   Contains: *At the Mountains of Madness*, pp. 63-165.

47. Derleth, August, ed. *Tales of the Cthulhu Mythos*. Sauk City, Wis.: Arkham House, 1969. xii, 407 pp.

   Contains: "The Call of Cthulhu," pp. 3-30; "The Haunter of the Dark," pp. 179-200.

48. Derleth, August, ed. *Tales of the Cthulhu Mythos: Volume 1*. New York: Beagle Books/Ballantine Books, May 1971 (5th printing Jan. 1975). xiv, 241 pp. St. Albans, Eng.: Panther Books, 1975. xvi, 239 pp.

   Contains: "The Call of Cthulhu," pp. 1-34 (Beagle); pp. 1-33 (Panther).

49. [Derleth, August, ed.] *Tales of the Cthulhu Mythos: Volume 2*. New York: Beagle Books/Ballantine Books, Aug. 1971 (5th printing Nov. 1975). 277 pp. St. Albans, Eng.: Panther Books, 1975. 254 pp.

   Contains: "The Haunter of the Dark," pp. 13-41 (Beagle); pp. 19-44 (Panther).

50. Derleth, August. *The Watchers out of Time and Others*.
    Sauk City, Wis.: Arkham House, 1974. 405 pp.

    Contains: "Of Evil Sorceries done in New England" (in *The
    Lurker at the Threshold*), pp. 14-16, 17-18.

    See I-E-i.

51. Derleth, August, ed. *When Evil Wakes: (A New
    Anthology of the Macabre)*. London: Souvenir Press,
    1963. 288 pp. London: Corgi, 1965. 223 pp. London:
    Sphere, 1977. 256 pp.

    Contains: "The Horror at Red Hook," pp. 163-86 (Souvenir);
    pp. 127-44 (Corgi); pp. 144-65 (Sphere).

52. Derleth, August, ed. *Who Knocks? Twenty Masterpieces of
    the Spectral for the Connoisseur*. New York: Rinehart &
    Co., 1946. ix, 391 pp.

    Contains: "The Shunned House," pp. 73-97.

53. Derleth, August, ed. *Worlds of Tomorrow: Science Fiction
    with a Difference*. New York: Pellegrini & Cudahy,
    1953. 351 pp.

    Contains: "From Beyond," pp. 217-26.

54. Derleth, August, ed. *Worlds of Tomorrow*. [Abridged
    edition.] London: Weidenfeld & Nicolson, 1954. 224
    pp.

    Contains: "From Beyond," pp. 124-31.

55. Dickie, James, ed. *The Undead*. Jersey, Eng.: Neville
    Spearman, 1971. 222 pp. London: Pan Books, 1973.
    224 pp. New York: Pocket Books, 1976. 220 pp.

    Contains: "The Hound," pp. 169-77 (Spearman); pp. 171-79
    (Pan); pp. 168-76 (Pocket).

56. Dickinson, Susan, ed. *Ghostly Experiences*. London:
    Collins (Armada Lions), 1972. 158 pp.

    Contains: "The Moon-Bog," pp. 75-85. Abridged edition of
    I-C-57.

57. Dickinson, Susan, ed. *The Restless Ghosts and Other Encounters and Experiences*. London: Collins, 1970; New York: E. P. Dutton, 1971 (as *The Usurping Ghost and Other Encounters and Experiences*). 318 pp.

    Contains: "The Moon-Bog," pp. 205-14.

58. Drake, G. E., and Sherry Taylor. *The Compleat Lovecraftian Bar Guide: A Compendium of Cthulhu Mythological, denomiacal [sic], and diabolical beverages: their preparation, uses, and history*. [Pekin, Il.:] The Golden Goblin Press, 1976. [vi], 13 pp.

    Contains: "Drinking Song from 'The Tomb' " (i.e., "Gaudeamus"), p. [v].

59. Dunsany, Lord. *Over the Hills and Far Away*. Edited, with an Introduction and Notes, by Lin Carter. New York: Ballantine Books, Apr. 1974. xii[+ii], 234 pp.

    Contains: "On Reading Lord Dunsany's 'Book of Wonder,' " p. [xiii].

60. Dunsany, Lord. *Tales of Three Hemispheres*. Philadelphia: Owlswick Press, 1976. xx, 140 pp.

    Contains: "Foreword" (i.e., "Lord Dunsany and His Work"), pp. vii-xviii.

61. Eddy, C. M., Jr. *Terror out of Time: Tales of Primitive People and Thrilling Experiments*. Providence: Dyer-Eddy, 1976. iv, 52 pp.

    Contains: "Ashes," by C. M. Eddy, Jr., pp. 3-11.

62. Elwood, Roger, and Vic Ghidalia, eds. *Androids, Time Machines and Blue Giraffes*. Chicago: Follet Publishing Co., 1973. 381 pp.

    Contains: "White Ape" (i.e., "Facts concerning the Late Arthur Jermyn and His Family"), pp. 207-17.

63. Elwood, Roger, and Vic Ghidalia, eds. *Horror Hunters.* New York: Macfadden-Bartell, 1971; New York: Manor Books, 1975. 192 pp.

> Contains: "The Unnamable," pp. 82-90.

64. Fabian, Stephen E. *Letters Lovecraftian: An Alphabet of Illuminated Letters Inspired by the Works of the Late Master of the Weird Tale, Howard Phillips Lovecraft (1890-1937).* Saddle River, N.J.: Gerry de la Ree, 1974. [28] leaves.

> Contains: "On the Death of a Rhyming Critic" (inside back cover [a facsimile of the original publication in the *Toledo Amateur* (I-B-iii-136)]).

65. Fiedler, Leslie A., ed. *In Dreams Awake: A Historical-Critical Anthology of Science Fiction.* New York: Dell, July 1975. 400 pp.

> Contains: "The Colour out of Space," pp. 90-118.

66. Foster, Dorothy, ed. *In Praise of Cats.* New York: Crown Publishers, 1974. x, 129 pp.

> Contains: "An Elegy to Oscar, a Dead Cat" (i.e., untitled poem included in a letter to James F. Morton, 28 June 1926), p. 124.

67. Galpin, Alfred, ed. *The Philosopher: A Casual Imperiodical.* [West Warwick, R.I.:] Necronomicon Press, 1977. 12 pp.

> Contains: "Polaris," pp. 3-5; "The House" (as by "Ward Phillips"), p. 6. Facsimile reproduction of the periodical.

68. Ghidalia, Vic, and Roger Elwood, eds. *Beware the Beasts.* New York: Macfadden-Bartell, July 1970, March 1971. 160 pp.

> Contains: "The Cats of Ulthar," pp. 19-22.

69. Goldberg, Gerry, ed. *A Strange Glory.* Toronto: McClelland & Stewart, 1975. 144 pp.

    Contains: "The Outsider," pp. 15-18.

70. Goldberg, Gerry, Stephen Storoschuk, and Fred Corbett, eds. *Nighttouch.* New York: St. Martin's Press, 1977. 160 pp.

    Contains: "The Curse of Yig," by Zealia Bishop, pp. 76-80, 82-85; "Cool Air," pp. 135-39.

71. Goodstone, Tony, ed. *The Pulps: Fifty Years of American Pop Culture.* New York: Bonanza Books, [1970]; New York: Chelsea Press, 1976. xvi, 239 pp.

    Contains: "Continuity," p. 200; "The Gardens of Yin," p. 200.

72. Haining, Peter, ed. *The Ancient Mysteries Reader.* Garden City, N.Y.: Doubleday & Co., 1975; London: Victor Gollancz, 1976. xi, 321 pp.

    Contains: "The Call of Cthulhu," pp. 86-113.

73. Haining, Peter, ed. *The Ancient Mysteries Reader, Book 1.* London: Sphere, 1978. 224 pp.

    Contains: "The Call of Cthulhu," pp. 110-43.

74. Haining, Peter, ed. *Christopher Lee's New Chamber of Horrors.* London: Souvenir Press, 1974. 316 pp.

    Contains: "The Thing on the Doorstep," pp. 165-96.

75. Haining, Peter, ed. *Dr. Caligari's Black Book.* London: W. H. Allen, 1968. 190 pp.

    Contains: "The Horror in the Museum," by Hazel Heald, pp. 143-76.

76. Haining, Peter, ed. *The Edgar Allan Poe Scrapbook.* New York: Schocken Books, 1977. 144 pp.

    Contains: "The Master of the Modern Horror Story" (i.e., Chapter VII ["Edgar Allan Poe"] of "Supernatural Horror in

Literature"), pp. 126-28; "Where Once Poe Walked: An Acrostic Sonnet" (i.e., "In a Sequestered Churchyard Where Once Poe Walked"), p. 127.

77. Haining, Peter, ed. *The Fantastic Pulps*. London: Victor Gollancz, 1975; New York: St. Martin's Press, 1976. 419 pp.

   Contains: "The Diary of Alonzo Typer," by "H. P. Lovecraft and William Lumley," pp. 292-314.

78. Haining, Peter, ed. *The Ghouls*. New York: Stein & Day, 1971, 1972. 383 pp. New York: Stein & Day (Book Club Edition), 1971. 382 pp. London: W. H. Allen, 1971. 383 pp. New York: Pocket Books, April 1972. xv, 400 pp.

   Contains: "Monster of Terror" (i.e., "The Colour out of Space"), pp. 322-49 (Stein & Day, W. H. Allen); pp. 321-47 (Stein & Day Book Club Ed.); pp. 335-63 (Pocket).

79. Haining, Peter, ed. *The Ghouls, Book 2*. London: Futura, 1974. 201 pp.

   Contains: "Monster of Terror" (i.e., "The Colour out of Space"), pp. 141-68.

80. Haining, Peter, ed. *The Hell of Mirrors*. London: Sidgwick & Jackson, 1965, 1974; London & New York: J. M. Dent & E. P. Dutton (Everyman's Library), 1976 (as *Everyman's Book of Classic Horror Stories*). xiii, 239 pp.

   Contains: "The Nameless City," pp. 166-80.

81. Haining, Peter, ed. *Legends for the Dark: Tales of Fantasy and Horror*. London: New English Library, Feb. 1968. 127 pp.

   Contains: "Beyond the Wall of Sleep," pp. 100-12.

82. Haining, Peter, ed. *The Monster Makers*. New York: Taplinger, 1974. 288 pp.

    Contains: "The Plague Demon" (Part II of "Herbert West—Reanimator"), pp. 149-55.

83. Haining, Peter, ed. *More of Christopher Lee's New Chamber of Horrors*. St. Albans, Eng.: Mayflower Books, 1976. 159 pp.

    Contains: "The Thing on the Doorstep," pp. 33-62.

84. Haining, Peter, ed. *The Nightmare Reader*. Garden City, N.Y.: Doubleday & Co., 1973; London: Victor Gollancz, 1973. xv, 340 pp.

    Contains: "The Evil Clergyman," pp. 272-76.

85. Haining, Peter, ed. *The Nightmare Reader: Volume Two*. London & Sydney: Pan Books, 1976. 192 pp.

    Contains: "The Evil Clergyman," pp. 118-22.

86. Haining, Peter, ed. *The Satanists*. Jersey, Eng.: Neville Spearman, 1969. 249 pp. New York: Taplinger, 1970. 249 pp. St. Albans, Eng.: Mayflower Books, 1971. 192 pp. New York: Pyramid, Feb. 1972. 255 pp.

    Contains: "The Festival," pp. 109-18 (Spearman, Taplinger); pp. 86-94 (Mayflower); pp. 112-22 (Pyramid).

87. Haining, Peter, ed. *The Second Book of Unknown Tales of Horror*. London: Sidgwick & Jackson, 1978. 208 pp.

    Contains: "The Challenge from Beyond" (Lovecraft portion only), pp. 97-104.

88. Haining, Peter, ed. *Summoned from the Tomb: Great Tales of Horror*. London: Brown, Watson, 1966. 159 pp. London: Sidgwick & Jackson, 1973. x, 213 pp.

    Contains: "Beyond the Wall of Sleep," pp. 104-16 (Sidgwick & Jackson). Brown, Watson ed. not seen.

89. Haining, Peter, ed. *The Unspeakable People: Being Twenty of the World's Most Horrible Horror Stories.* London: Leslie Frewin, 1969. 246 pp. New York: Popular Library, [1969]. 207 pp. London: Everest Books, 1975. 239 pp.

> Contains: "The Outsider," pp. 76-83 (Frewin); pp. 67-73 (Popular Lib.); pp. 75-82 (Everest); "The Loved Dead," by C. M. Eddy, Jr., pp. 84-96 (Frewin); pp. 74-84 (Popular Lib.); pp. 83-94 (Everest).

90. Haining, Peter, ed. *Weird Tales: A Facsimile of the World's Most Famous Fantasy Magazine.* Jersey, Eng.: Neville Spearman, 1976. 264 pp.

> Contains: "Beyond the Wall of Sleep," pp. 79-86; "The Familiars," p. 208; "The Pigeon-Flyers," p. 208.

91. Haining, Peter, ed. *Weird Tales: Volume 1.* London: Sphere, 1978.

> Contains: "Beyond the Wall of Sleep," pp. 137-50.

92. Haining, Peter, ed. *Weird Tales: Volume 2.* London: Sphere, 1978. 256 pp.

> Contains: "The Familiars," p. 161; "The Pigeon-Flyers," p. 163. Title on spine: *More Weird Tales.*

93. Haining, Peter, ed. *The Wild Night Company: Irish Stories of Fantasy and Horror.* London: Victor Gollancz, 1970; New York: Taplinger, 1971. 287 pp. London: Sphere, 1971, 317 pp.

> Contains: "The Moon-Bog," pp. 265-73 (Gollancz; Taplinger); pp. 291-301 (Sphere).

94. Hall, James B., and Joseph Langland, eds. *The Short Story.* New York: Macmillan & Co., 1956. x, 485 pp.

> Contains: "The Music of Erich Zann," pp. 150-57.

95. Hammett, Dashiell, ed. *Breakdown and Other Thrillers.*

London: New English Library, Jan. 1968. 128 pp.

Contains: "The Music of Erich Zann," pp. 19-27. Abridged edition of next entry.

96. Hammett, Dashiell, ed. *Creeps by Night: Chills and Thrills*. New York: John Day Co., 1931, Jan. 1932 (as by Tudor Publishing Company); New York: Blue Ribbon Books, 1931; Cleveland & New York: The World Publishing Co., Jan. 1944. 525 pp.

Contains: "The Music of Erich Zann," pp. 347-63.

97. Hammett, Dashiell, ed. *Modern Tales of Horror*. London: Victor Gollancz, 1932. 448 pp.

Contains: "The Music of Erich Zann," pp. 301-17. Abridged edition of preceding entry.

98. Hammett, Dashiell, ed. *The Red Brain, and Other Thrillers*. New York: Belmont Books, 1961. 144 pp. London: Four Square, Sept. 1965. 159 pp.

Contains: "The Music of Erich Zann," pp. 117-25 (Belmont); pp. 132-41 (Four Square). Abridged edition of I-C-96.

99. Harré, T. Everett, ed. *Beware after Dark: The World's Most Stupendous Tales of Mystery, Horror, Thrills and Terror*. New York: Macaulay, 1929; New York: Gold Label Books, 1929; New York: Emerson Books, [1942, 1945]. iii, [4-]461 pp.

Contains: "The Call of Cthulhu," pp. 223-59.

100. Herr, Dan, and Joel Wells, eds. *Bodies and Spirits*. Garden City, N.Y.: Doubleday & Co. (The Crime Club), 1964. 192 pp.

Contains: "The Haunter of the Dark," pp. 21-46.

101. Hoag, Jonathan E. *The Poetical Works of Jonathan E. Hoag*. New York: [Privately printed,] 1923. xi, 72 pp.

Contains: "Introduction," pp. iii-vii; "Prologue" to "Amid

Inspiring Scenes (Near Greenwich, N. Y.)" by Jonathan E. Hoag, p. 41; "Jonathan E. Hoag, Esq.: On His Eighty-seventh Birthday, February 10, 1918," pp. 61-63; "To Jonathan Hoag, Esq.: On His 88th Birthday, February 10, 1919," pp. 63-64; "Ad Scribam: Jonathan E. Hoag, Esq., Aetat LXXXIX: February 10, 1920," pp. 64-65; "To Mr. Hoag: On His Ninetieth Birthday, February 10, 1921," pp. 65-66; "On a Poet's Ninety-first Birthday: (To Jonathan Hoag, Esq., February 10, 1922)," p. 66; "To Mr. Hoag: Upon His Ninety-second Birthday, February 10, 1923," p. 67.

The "Prologue" on p. 41 is identical to I-B-iii-150. It is believed that Lovecraft himself, James F. Morton, and Samuel Loveman published the volume. A book entitled *The Complete Works of Jonathan E. Hoag* (New York, 1927), with an introduction by Lovecraft, has sometimes been listed in bibliographies. Such a volume does not exist.

102. Hoke, Helen, ed. *Monsters, Monsters, Monsters.* London: Franklin Watts, 1975. 187 pp.

Contains: "The Outsider," pp. 177-87.

103. Hoke, Helen, ed. *Spectres, Spooks, and Shuddery Shades.* London: Franklin Watts, 1977. 192 pp.

Contains: "The Music of Erich Zann," pp. 160-70.

104. Howard, Robert E. *The Coming of Conan.* New York: Gnome Press, 1953. 224 pp.

Contains: letter to Donald A. Wollheim, [ca. Sept. 1935] (introduction to *The Hyborian Age*), pp. 13-14.

105. Howard, Robert E. *The Hyborian Age.* And *A Probable Outline of Conan's Career* by P. Schuyler Miller and John D. Clark, Ph.D. Los Angeles: LANY Coöperative Publications, 1938. [vi], 22 pp.

Contains: "Introduction: A letter sent to Donald A. Wollheim, accompanying the manuscript of *The Hyborian Age*," [ca. Sept. 1935], p. [v].

106. Howard, Robert E. *Skull-Face and Others*. Sauk City, Wis.: Arkham House, 1946; Jersey, Eng.: Neville Spearman, 1974. xxvi, 475 pp.

> Contains: "Robert Ervin Howard: A Memoriam" (i.e., "In Memoriam: Robert Ervin Howard"), pp. xiii-xvi.

107. Howard, Robert E. *Skull-Face Omnibus*. St. Albans, Eng.: Panther Books, 1976. 3 vols.

> Contains: "Robert Ervin Howard: A Memoriam" (i.e., "In Memoriam: Robert Ervin Howard"), pp. 13-17 in all three volumes.

108. Howard, Robert E. [and others]. *The Garden of Fear and Other Stories of the Bizarre and Fantastic*. Los Angeles: Crawford Publishing House, 1945. 79 pp.

> Contains: "Celephais," pp. 33-38.

109. Hubler, Richard G., ed. *The World's Shortest Stories*. New York: Duell, Sloane and Pearce, 1961. 268 pp.

> Contains: "Nyarlathotep," pp. 153-56.

110. Jenkins, Alan C., ed. *Ghosts! An Anthology of Spectral Stories*. London & Glasgow: Blackie, 1971. 383 pp.

> Contains: "The Music of Erich Zann," pp. 239-49.

111. Karloff, Boris, ed. *And the Darkness Falls*. Cleveland: The World Publishing Co., April 1946. ix, 631 pp.

> Contains: "The Thing on the Doorstep," pp. 605-27.

112. Karloff, Boris, ed. *The Boris Karloff Horror Anthology*. London: Souvenir Press, 1965. 190 pp. New York: Avon, May 1965 (as *Boris Karloff's Favorite Horror Stories*). 176 pp. London: Corgi, 1967, 1969. 158 pp. Manchester, Eng.: World Distributors, 1974. 172 pp. London: Everest Books, 1975. 172 pp.

> Contains: "The Haunter of the Dark," pp. 165-90 (Souvenir); pp. 152-76 (Avon); pp. 138-58 (Corgi); pp. 150-72 (World Dist., Everest).

113. Karp, Marvin Allen, ed. *The Unhumans*. New York: Popular Library, 1965. 141 pp.

    Contains: "The Thing on the Doorstep," pp. 116-41.

114. Kelley, Leo, ed. *The Supernatural in Fiction*. New York: McGraw-Hill, 1973. [x], 313 pp.

    Contains: "The Outsider," pp. 308-13.

115. Knight, Damon, ed. *The Golden Road: Great Tales of Fantasy and the Supernatural*. New York: Simon & Schuster, 1973. 447 pp.

    Contains: *The Dream-Quest of Unknown Kadath*, pp. 307-411.

116. Kuntz, Eugene B., D.D. *Thoughts and Pictures*. Haverhill, Mass.: "Co-operatively published by H. P. Loveracft [sic] and C. W. Smith," Jan. 1932. [22] pp.

    Contains: "Foreword," pp. [1-2].

117. Lee, Christopher, and Michel Parry, eds. *From the Archives of Evil #2*. New York: Warner Books, Oct. 1976. 220 pp.

    Contains: "The Lurking Fear," pp. 36-59.

118. [Lee, Elizabeth, ed.] *Horror Stories*. London: Paul Elek (Bestseller Library), 1961, 1962; London: Arrow, 1965 (as *The Arrow Book of Horror Stories*). 256 pp.

    Contains: "The Dunwich Horror," pp. 85-129.

119. Lee, Elizabeth, ed. *Spine Chillers: An Anthology of Mystery and Horror*. London: Elek Books, 1961. 528 pp.

    Contains: "The Thing on the Doorstep," pp. 390-414; "Cool Air," pp. 415-22; "The Outsider," pp. 423-28.

120. Leonard, Sterling, and Harold Y. Moffett, eds. *Junior Literature: Book Two*. New York: The Macmillan Co., 1930, 1935. viii, 615 pp.

Contains: "Sleepy Hollow To-day," pp. 545-46. The essay is an excerpt from "Observations on Several Parts of America," which is itself part of a letter to Maurice W. Moe, who was an assistant editor of the *Junior Literature* series.

121. Long, Frank Belknap. *The Horror from the Hills.* Sauk City, Wis.: Arkham House, 1963. 114 pp.

Contains: letter to Frank Belknap Long, [Nov. 1927], pp. 65-74 (unsigned).

See I-B-v-b-32.

122. Long, Frank Belknap. *Odd Science Fiction.* New York: Belmont Books, 1964. 141 pp.

Contains: letter to Frank Belknap Long, [Nov. 1927], pp. 61-69 (in *The Horror from the Hills*; unsigned).

123. Lord, Glenn, ed. *The Last Celt: A Bio-Bibliography of Robert Ervin Howard.* West Kingston, R.I.: Donald M. Grant, 1976; New York: Berkley Publishing Corp., Nov. 1977. 416 pp.

Contains: "Robert Ervin Howard: A Memoriam" (i.e., "In Memoriam: Robert Ervin Howard"), pp. 67-70; "The Battle That Ended the Century," by H. P. Lovecraft and R. H. Barlow (as by "H. P. Lovecraft"), pp. 359-63.

124. Lucie-Smith, Edward, ed. *Holding Your Eight Hands: An Anthology of Science-Fiction Verse.* Garden City, N.Y.: Doubleday & Co., 1969; London: Rapp & Whiting, 1970. xix, 120 pp.

Contains: "Nyarlathotep" (sonnet), p. 59; "Harbour Whistles," p. 60.

125. McCauley, Kirby, ed. *Beyond Midnight.* New York: Berkley Medallion, Nov. 1976. xii, 210 pp.

Contains: "The Nameless City," pp. 2-16.

126. Manley, Seon, and Gogo Lewis, eds. *A Gathering of*

Ghosts. New York: Funk & Wagnall's, 1970. 217 pp.
Contains: "Cool Air," pp. 61-72.

127. Manley, Seon, and Gogo Lewis, eds. *Masters of Shades and Shadows: An Anthology of Ghost Stories*. Garden City, N.Y.: Doubleday & Co., 1978. 214 pp.
Contains: "The Thing in the Moonlight," pp. 164-65.

128. Manley, Seon, and Gogo Lewis, eds. *Shapes of the Supernatural*. Garden City, N.Y.: Doubleday & Co., 1969. 370 pp.
Contains: "The Ghost-Eater," by C. M. Eddy, Jr., pp. 17-26; "The Statement of Randolph Carter," pp. 77-83.

129. Margulies, Leo, ed. *Weird Tales: Stories of Fantasy*. New York: Pyramid, May 1964; New York: Jove/HBJ, 1978. 155 pp.
Contains: "The Strange High House in the Mist," pp. 91-100.

130. Masters, Anthony, ed. *Cries of Terror*. London: Arrow Books, 1976. 191 pp.
Contains: "In the Vault," pp. 32-41; "The Loved Dead," by C. M. Eddy, Jr., pp. 81-92.

131. Mazzeo, Henry, ed. *Hauntings: Tales of the Supernatural*. Garden City, N.Y.: Doubleday & Co., 1968. 318 pp. Garden City, N.Y.: Doubleday & Co. (Book Club Edition), 1968. 316 pp.
Contains: "In the Vault," pp. 27-35 (Doubleday); pp. 26-33 (Book Club Ed.).

132. Moskowitz, Sam, ed. *Horrors Unknown*. New York: Walker & Co., 1971; London: Faye & Ward, 1972. x, 214 pp. New York: Berkley Medallion, Feb. 1976. xi, 210 pp.
Contains: "The Challenge from Beyond," by H. P. Lovecraft, C. L. Moore, A. Merritt, Robert E. Howard, and Frank Belknap Long, pp. 4-19 (Walker, Faye & Ward); pp. 4-21 (Berkley).

133. Moskowitz, Sam, ed. *The Man Who Called Himself Poe.*
Garden City, N.Y.: Doubleday & Co., 1969. xvi, 244
pp. London: Victor Gollancz, 1970. 240 pp. London:
Sphere, 1972 (as *A Man Called Poe*). 223 pp.

Contains: "In a Sequestered Churchyard Where Once Poe
Walked," p. 237 (Doubleday); p. 233 (Gollancz); p. 216 (Sphere).

134. Moskowitz, Sam, ed. *Masterpieces of Science Fiction.*
Cleveland: The World Publishing Co., 1966;
Westport, Conn.: Hyperion Press, 1974. x, 552 pp.

Contains: "The Colour out of Space," pp. 436-68.

135. Moskowitz, Sam, and Elwood, Roger, eds. *Strange
Signposts.* New York: Holt, Rinehart & Winston,
1966. 319 pp.

Contains: "The Whisperer in Darkness," pp. 130-93.

136. Necker, Claire, ed. *Supernatural Cats.* Garden City,
N.Y.: Doubleday & Co., 1972. xiv, 439 pp. New
York: Warner Paperback Library, Jan. 1974. 446 pp.

Contains: "The Cats of Ulthar," pp. 329-32 (Doubleday); pp.
337-40 (Warner).

137. Nelson, James, ed. *The Complete Murder Sampler.*
Garden City, N.Y.: Doubleday & Co., 1946. xii, 368
pp. London: Macdonald, 1950. 335 pp.

Contains: "The Outsider," pp. 162-68 (Doubleday); pp. 123-
29 (Macdonald).

138. Netherwood, Bryan A., ed. *Medley Macabre: An
Anthology of Stories of the Supernatural, Being Ghosts,
Psychical Phenomena, Uncanny Mysteries.* London:
Hammond, Hammond, & Co., 1966, 1970, 1971,
1972. 544 pp.

Contains: "The Haunter of the Dark," pp. 525-44.

139. Netherwood, Bryan A., ed. *Terror! An Anthology of*

Blood-curdling Stories. London & Glasgow: Blackie, 1970. 392 pp.

> Contains: "The Colour out of Space," pp. 277-314.

140. Netherwood, Bryan A., ed. *Uncanny: Tales of the Spectral and Supernatural*. London: Blackie, 1974. [x], 306 pp.

> Contains: "The Statement of Randolph Carter," pp. 287-94.

141. Norton, Alden H., ed. *Hauntings and Horrors: Ten Grisly Tales*. New York: Berkley Medallion, Mar. 1969, Aug. 1969, Aug. 1969, Jan. 1972, Feb. 1972, June 1972. 171 pp.

> Contains: "The Temple," pp. 77-91.

142. Norton, Alden H., ed. *Horror Times Ten*. New York: Berkley Medallion, 1967, June 1968, Dec. 1968, July 1969, Sept. 1969, Sept. 1970, Nov. 1970, Dec. 1971, Feb. 1972. 175 pp.

> Contains: "Cool Air," pp. 31-39.

143. Norton, Alden H., and Sam Moskowitz, eds. *Great Untold Stories of Fantasy and Horror*. New York: Pyramid, Oct. 1969, Jan. 1970, Nov. 1970. 222 pp.

> Contains: "The Dreams in the Witch House," pp. 187-222.

144. O'Brien, Edward J., ed. *The Best Short Stories of 1928 and the Yearbook of the American Short Story*. New York: Dodd, Mead & Co., 1928. xiv, 429 pp.

> Contains: [Biographical Notice], p. 324.

145. Owen, Betty, ed. *Eleven Great Horror Stories*. New York: Scholastic Book Services, Nov. 1969 (7th printing Apr. 1973). 239 pp.

> Contains: "The Dunwich Horror," pp. 5-70.

146. Owings, Mark. *The Necronomicon: A Study*. Baltimore:

Mirage Associates (The Anthem Series), 1967. 30
pp.

Contains: "History and Chronology of the *Necronomicon*" (i.e.,
"History of the *Necronomicon*"), pp. 6-7.

147. Parry, Michel, ed. *Beware of the Cat: Weird Tales about
Cats.* London: Victor Gollancz, 1972; New York:
Taplinger, 1973 (with subtitle: *Stories of Feline Fantasy
and Horror*); London: Arrow, 1974. 192 pp.

Contains: "The Cats of Ulthar," pp. 162-65.

148. Parry, Michel, ed. *The Devil's Children: Tales of Demons
and Exorcists.* London: Futura, 1974; New York:
Taplinger, 1975. 213 pp. New York: Berkley
Medallion, Sept. 1976. [vi], 215 pp.

Contains: "The Thing on the Doorstep," pp. 70-98 (Futura,
Taplinger); pp. 67-96 (Berkley).

149. Parry, Michel, ed. *The Hounds of Hell: Stories of Canine
Fantasy and Horror.* London: Victor Gollancz, 1974;
New York: Taplinger, 1974; London: Arrow Books,
1975. 192 pp.

Contains: "The Hound," pp. 15-23.

150. Parry, Michel, ed. *The Rivals of Frankenstein: A Gallery
of Monsters.* London: Corgi (Transworld Publishers),
1977. 224 pp.

Contains: "Herbert West—Reanimator," pp. 126-57.

151. Parry, Michel, ed. *The Third Mayflower Book of Black
Magic Stories.* St. Albans, Eng.: Mayflower Books,
1975. 220 pp.

Contains: "The Dreams in the Witch House," pp. 144-86.

152. Parry, Michel, ed. *Waves of Terror: Weird Stories about
the Sea.* London: Victor Gollancz, 1976. 208 pp.

Contains: "Dagon," pp. 134-39.

153. Pepper, Elizabeth, and John Wilcock, eds. *The Witches' Almanac: Aries 1972-Pisces 1973*. New York: Grosset & Dunlap, 1973. 96 pp.

    Contains: "Expectancy," p. 5.

154. Pugmire, William H., ed. *Carl Jacobi: An Appreciation*. Pensacola, Fla.: Stellar Z Publications, 1977. 20 pp.

    Contains: H. P. Lovecraft to Carl Jacobi, 27 February 1932, p. 18.

155. Sanders, Thomas E., ed. *Speculations: An Introduction to Literature through Fantasy and Science Fiction*. Beverly Hills, Ca.: Glencoe Press, 1973. xvii, 621 pp.

    Contains: "The Outsider," pp. 348-53.

156. Saurès, Jean-Claude, and Seymore Chwast, eds. *The Literary Cat*. New York: Berkley Publishing Co., 1977. 128 pp.

    Contains: "An Elegy to Oscar, a Dead Cat" (i.e., untitled poem included in a letter to James F. Morton, 28 June 1926), p. 87.

157. Schweitzer, Darrell, ed. *Essays Lovecraftian*. Baltimore: T-K Graphics, 1976. iv, 114 pp.

    Contains: "Story-Writing: A Letter from HPL" (i.e., letter to Alvin Earl Perry, 4 October 1935), pp. 41-45.

158. Shreffler, Philip A. *The H. P. Lovecraft Companion*. Westport, Conn.: Greenwood Press, 1977. xvi, 198 pp.

    Contains: "The History and Chronology of the *Necronomicon*" (i.e., "History of the *Necronomicon*"), pp. 181-83.

159. Silverberg, Robert, ed. *Lost Worlds, Unknown Horizons: Nine Stories of Science Fiction*. Nashville: Thomas Nelson, 1978. 172 pp.

    Contains: "The Doom that Came to Sarnath." pp. 97-104.

160. Singer, Kurt [ed.]. *Horror Omnibus*. London: W. H. Allen, 1965. 317 pp. St. Albans, Eng.: Panther Books, 1966. 288 pp.

    Contains: "The Dreams in the Witch House," pp. 37-75 (Allen); pp. 34-68 (Panther).

161. Singer, Kurt, ed. *Satanic Omnibus*. London: W. H. Allen, 1973. ix, 293 pp.

    Contains: "The Shunned House," pp. 42-67.

162. Singer, Kurt [ed.]. *Shriek*. Sydney: Ure Smith, n.d. 607 pp.

    Contains: "The Shunned House," pp. 356-81.

163. Stickney, Corwin F., ed. *Amateur Correspondent: May-June 1937*. [West Warwick, R.I.: Necronomicon Press,] 1977. 30 pp.

    Contains: "Notes on Writing Weird Fiction," pp. 7-10. Facsimile reprinting of the periodical.

164. Stong, Phil, ed. *The Other Worlds*. New York: Wilfred Funk, 1941; Garden City, N.Y.: Garden City Publishing Co., 1942 (with subtitle: *25 Modern Stories of Mystery and Imagination*). vi, 466 pp.

    Contains: "In the Vault," pp. 335-44.

165. Symmes, Mrs. William B. *Old World Footprints*. With a Preface by Frank Belknap Long, Jr. Athol, Mass.: W. Paul Cook (The Recluse Press), 1928. 32 pp.

    Contains: "Preface," pp. [5-6] (as by "Frank Belknap Long, Jr."). The preface was written by Lovecraft at Long's suggestion, as Long himself has recently stated.

166. Talman, Wilfred B. [and others]. *The Normal Lovecraft*. Saddle River, N.J.: Gerry de la Ree, 1973. 32 pp.

    Contains: "Dirge of the Doomed" [poem], p. 9; postcard to Wilfred B. Talman, 18 August 1929, p. 10.

167. Thomson, Christine Campbell, ed. *By Daylight Only*. London: Selwyn & Blount, 1929. 286 pp.

> Contains: "Pickman's Model," pp. 37-52.

168. Thomson, Christine Campbell, ed. *Not at Night*. London: Arrow, 1960. 192 pp.

> Contains: "The Curse of Yig," by Zealia Bishop, pp. 57-75. This volume is different from the one of the same title and editor published by Selwyn & Blount (London), 1925.

169. Thomson, Christine Campbell, ed. *The "Not at Night" Omnibus*. London: Selwyn & Blount, [1937]. 511 pp.

> Contains: "The Curse of Yig," by Zealia Bishop, pp. 13-29; "Pickman's Model," pp. 119-31; "The Horror in the Museum," by Hazel Heald, pp. 279-307.

170. Thomson, Christine Campbell, ed. *Switch on the Light*. London: Selwyn & Blount, 1931. 256 pp.

> Contains: "The Curse of Yig," by Zealia Bishop, pp. 9-31; "The Rats in the Walls," pp. 141-65.

171. Thomson, Christine Campbell, ed. *Terror by Night*. London: Selwyn & Blount, [1934]. 252 pp.

> Contains: "The Horror in the Museum," by Hazel Heald, pp. 111-41.

172. Thomson, Christine Campbell, ed. *You'll Need a Night Light*. London: Selwyn & Blount, Sept. 1927, Sept. 1927, Oct. 1927, Nov. 1929. 254 pp.

> Contains: "The Horror at Red Hook," pp. 228-54.

173. Van Thal, Herbert, ed. *The Pan Book of Horror Stories*. London: Pan Books, 1959, 1960, 1960, 1961, 1961, 1962, 1962, 1963, 1964, 1964, 1965, 1965, 1969, 1970, 1970, 1972, 1972, 1973, 1974. 317 pp.

> Contains: "The Horror in the Museum," by Hazel Heald, pp. 123-55. In later printings the title is *The First Pan Book of Horror Stories*.

174. Ward, Don, ed. *Dark of the Soul*. New York: Tower Publications, 1970. 157 pp.

    Contains: "Cool Air," pp. 83-91.

175. Weinberg, Robert, ed. *The Weird Tales Story*. West Linn, Ore.: FAX Collector's Editions, 1977. ix, 134 pp.

    Contains: "In Memoriam: Henry St. Clair Whitehead," p. 126 (unsigned; facsimile of I-B-ii-150).

176. White, Michael, ed. *In Memoriam: Jennie E. T. Dowe*. Dorchester, Mass.: [W. Paul Cook,] Sept. 1921. 65 pp.

    Contains: "A Singer of Ethereal Moods and Fancies" [essay], p. 56; "In Memoriam: J. E. T. D." [poem], p. 56.

177. Whitehead, Henry S. *West India Lights*. Sauk City, Wis.: Arkham House, 1946. 367 pp.

    Contains: "The Trap," by Henry S. Whitehead, pp. 115-37; "Bothon," by Henry S. Whitehead, pp. 261-96.

178. [Williams, Herbert, ed.] *Avon Ghost Reader*. New York: Avon, 1946. 258 pp.

    Contains: "The Dunwich Horror," pp. 9-61.

179. Williams, Herbert, ed. *Terror at Night: 13 Tales of Mystery and Imagination*. New York: Avon, 1947. 194 pp.

    Contains: "The Haunter of the Dark," pp. 7-31.

180. Wise, Herbert A., and Phyllis Fraser, eds. *Great Tales of Terror and the Supernatural*. New York: Random House (The Modern Library), 1944, et seq. xix, 1080 pp. London: Hammond, Hammond & Co., 1947, 1954, 1957. 832 pp.

    Contains: "The Rats in the Walls," pp. 1010-30 (Random House); pp. 783-98 (Hammond, Hammond); "The Dunwich Horror," pp. 1031-76 (Random House); pp. 799-832 (Hammond, Hammond).

181. Wolf, Jack C., and Barbara H. Wolf, eds. *Ghosts, Castles, and Victims: Studies in Gothic Terror.* Greenwich, Conn.: Fawcett Crest, Aug. 1974. 576 pp.

     Contains: "From Beyond," pp. 561-69.

182. Wollheim, Donald A., ed. *Avon Fantasy Reader No. 1.* New York: Avon Book Co., 1947. 130 pp.

     Contains: "Nostalgia," p. 115.

183. Wollheim, Donald A., ed. *Avon Fantasy Reader No. 3.* New York: Avon Book Co., 1947. 128 pp.

     Contains: "The Silver Key," pp. 44-55.

184. Wollheim, Donald A., ed. *Avon Fantasy Reader No. 6.* New York: Avon Book Co., 1948. 121 pp.

     Contains: "Beyond the Wall of Sleep," pp. 21-30.

185. Wollheim, Donald A., ed. *Avon Fantasy Reader No. 8.* New York: Avon Publishing Co., 1948. 126 pp.

     Contains: "The Temple," pp. 89-99.

186. Wollheim, Donald A., ed. *Avon Fantasy Reader No. 10.* New York: Avon Publishing Co., 1949. 128 pp.

     Contains: "The Statement of Randolph Carter," pp. 53-58.

187. Wollheim, Donald A., ed. *Avon Fantasy Reader No. 14.* New York: Avon Publishing Co., 1950. 128 pp.

     Contains: "The Curse of Yig," by Zealia Bishop, pp. 66-78.

188. Wollheim, Donald A., ed. *Avon Fantasy Reader No. 17.* New York: Avon Publishing Co., 1951. 128 pp.

     Contains: "Through the Gates of the Silver Key," by H. P. Lovecraft and E. Hoffmann Price, pp. 76-103.

189. Wollheim, Donald A., ed. *Avon Fantasy Reader No. 18.* New York: Avon Publishing Co., 1952. 128 pp.

     Contains: "Out of the Eons," by Hazel Heald, pp. 62-81.

190. Wollheim, Donald A., ed. *Avon Science Fiction Reader No. 3*. New York: Avon Novels, 1952. 128 pp.

    Contains: "In the Walls of Eryx," by H. P. Lovecraft and Kenneth Sterling, pp. 59-80.

191. Wollheim, Donald A., ed. *The Macabre Reader*. New York: Ace Books, 1959. 223 pp. London: Brown, Watson (Digit Books), [1960]. 188 pp.

    Contains: "Night-Gaunts," p. 47 (Ace); p. 40 (Digit); "The Thing on the Doorstep," pp. 71-102 (Ace); pp. 60-85 (Digit); "The Curse of Yig," by Zealia Bishop, pp. 153-73 (Ace); pp. 129-45 (Digit); "The Dweller," p. 223 (Ace); p. 188 (Digit).

192. Wollheim, Donald A., ed. *Operation Phantasy*. Rego Park, N.Y.: The Phantagraph Press, 1967. 59 pp.

    Contains: "Harbour Whistles," p. 15; "Ex Oblivione," pp. 34-37.

193. Wollheim, Donald A., ed. *The Portable Novels of Science*. New York: Viking Press, 1945 (3rd printing 1950). xiii, 737 pp.

    Contains: "The Shadow out of Time," pp. 394-479.

194. Wollheim, Donald A., ed. *Terror in the Modern Vein*. Garden City, N.Y.: Hanover House, 1955. 315 pp.

    Contains: "He," pp. 123-33.

195. Wollheim, Donald A., ed. *Terror in the Modern Vein*. [Abridged edition.] London: Brown, Watson (Digit Books), [1961]. 156 pp.

    Contains: "He," pp. 101-14.

196. Wollheim, Donald A., and George Ernsberger, eds. *The Second Avon Fantasy Reader*. New York: Avon, Feb. 1969. 173 pp.

    Contains: "The Curse of Yig," by Zealia Bishop, pp. 74-90.

197. [Anonymous, ed.] *The Best Ghost Stories*. London: Hamlyn, 1977. 754 pp.

> Contains: "Pickman's Model," pp. 652-62; "The Dunwich Horror," pp. 663-99; "The Music of Erich Zann," pp. 700-06; "The Rats in the Walls," pp. 707-23.

198. [Anonymous, ed.] *In Memoriam: Hazel Pratt Adams*. [n.p.: privately printed,] 1927. 30 pp.

> Contains: "The Absent Leader," pp. 11-12. The volume appears to be a production of the Blue Pencil Club, an amateur journalism organization in Brooklyn, N.Y.

D. Works Edited by Lovecraft

i. Books

1. Bullen, John Ravenor. *White Fire*. Athol, Mass.: The Recluse Press, 1927. 86 pp.

2. Hoag, Jonathan E. *The Poetical Works of Jonathan E. Hoag: With Portrait and Autograph of the Author*. Biographical and Critical Preface by H. P. Lovecraft. New York: [privately printed] 1923. xi, 72 pp.

   It is believed that Lovecraft, James F. Morton, and Samuel Loveman published the volume.

3. Kuntz, Eugene, D.D. *Thoughts and Pictures*. Haverhill, Mass.: "Cooperatively published by H. P. Loveracft [sic] and C. W. Smith," Jan. 1932. [22] pp.

ii. Periodicals

1. *The Badger*, No. 2 (June 1915). Edited by George S. Schilling. Assistant eds.: Howard P. Lovecraft, et al. 16 [i.e., 20] pp.

2. *The Conservative*. Edited by H. P. Lovecraft. [As this is the most important magazine edited by Lovecraft, the complete contents of the thirteen issues are given.]

   1, No. 1 (April 1915), [8] pp.

   H. P. L[ovecraft], "The Simple Speller's Tale: (Translated into English)," p. [1]; [H. P. Lovecraft], "Introducing Mr. Chester Pierce Munroe," p. [2]; [H. P. Lovecraft], [Untitled], p. [2]; [H. P. Lovecraft], "The Morris Faction," p. [3]; [H. P. Lovecraft], "For President—Leo Fritter," p. [3]; H. P. Lovecraft, "The Crime of the Century," pp. [4-5]; [H. P. Lovecraft], "Editorial," pp. [5-6]; [H. P. Lovecraft], "The Question of the Day," p. [6]; [H. P. Lovecraft], [Untitled], pp. [7-8].

1, No. 2 (July 1915), 12 pp.

Ira A. Cole, "The Dream of a Golden Age" [poem], pp. 1-2.
H. P. Lovecraft, "Metrical Regularity," pp. 2-4; [H. P.
Lovecraft], "Editorial," pp. 4-5; [H. P. Lovecraft], "The
Conservative and His Critics," pp. 5-6; [H. P. Lovecraft], "Some
Political Phases," pp. 6-8; [H. P. Lovecraft], "Introducing Mr.
John Russell," pp. 8-9. [H. P. Lovecraft], "In a Major Key," pp.
9-11; [H. P. Lovecraft], "Amateur Notes," p. 11; Leo Fritter,
"An Open Letter," pp. 11-12.

1, No. 3 (October 1915), 16 pp.

H. P. Lovecraft, "The State of Poetry," pp. 1-3; H. P. Lovecraft,
"The Allowable Rhyme," pp. 3-6; [H. P. Lovecraft], "Editorial,"
pp. 6-7; [H. P. Lovecraft], "The Conservative and His Critics,"
pp. 7-8; [H. P. Lovecraft], "Gems from 'In a Minor Key': (With
Remarks by THE CONSERVATIVE)," p. 8; [H. P. Lovecraft],
"The Renaissance of Manhood," pp. 8-10; [H. P. Lovecraft],
"Liquor and Its Friends," pp. 10-11; [H. P. Lovecraft], "The
Youth of Today," pp. 11-12; [H. P. Lovecraft], "An Impartial
Spectator," p. 12; [H. P. Lovecraft], "Symphony and Stress,"
pp. 12-14; [H. P. Lovecraft], [Untitled], pp. 14-16.

1, No. 4 (January 1916), 4 pp.

Winifred Virginia Jordan [i.e., Jackson], "Song of the North
Wind" [poem], p. 1; [H. P. Lovecraft], "Introducing Mr. James
Pyke," pp. 1-2; Rheinhart Kleiner, "Consolation" [poem], p. 2;
Anne Tillery Renshaw, "The Horizon of Dreams" [poem], p. 2;
H. P. Lovecraft, "On Receiving a Picture of Swans," pp. 2-3;
Winifred Virginia Jordan [i.e., Jackson], "Galileo and
Swammerdam" [poem], p. 3; James T. Pyke, "Maia" [poem], p.
3; James T. Pyke, "The Poet" [poem], p. 3; Maude Kingsbury
Barton, "Departed" [poem], pp. 3-4; Rheinhart Kleiner, "To
Celia" [poem], p. 4.

2, No. 1 (April 1916), 4 pp.

Andrew Francis Lockhart, "Benediction" [poem], p. 1;
Rheinhart Kleiner, "Another Endless Day" [poem], p. 1;
Winifred Virginia Jordan, "April" [poem], pp. 1-2; Winifred
Virginia Jordan, "In Morven's Head" [poem], p. 2; Winifred
Virginia Jordan, "The Night Wind Bared My Heart" [poem], p.

2; H. P. Lovecraft, "R. Kleiner, Laureatus, in Heliconem," p. 2; William de Ryee, "The Best Wine" [poem], p. 3; H. P. Lovecraft, "Ye Ballade of Patrick von Flynn: Or, the Hibernio-German-American England-Hater," pp. 3-4 (as by "Lewis Theobald, Jun.").

2, No. 2 (July 1916), 4 pp.

Henry Clapham McGavack, "The American Proletariat Versus England" [essay], pp. 1-4.

2, No. 3 (October 1916), [12] pp.

Olive G. Owen, "The Mocking Bird" [poem], p. [1]; H. P. Lovecraft, "Old England and the 'Hyphen,' " pp. [1-2]; Winifred Virginia Jordan, "Insomnia" [poem], pp. [2-3]; William Thomas Harrington, "Prussianism" [essay], pp. [3-4]; Chester Pierce Munroe, "Twilight" [poem], p. [4]; David H. Whittier, "The Bond Invincible" [fiction], pp. [5-6]; H. P. Lovecraft, "Respite," pp. [6-7]; Eugene B. Kuntz, D.D., "By the Waters of the Brook" [poem], p. [7]; Winifred Virginia Jordan, "The Pool" [poem], p. [7]; [H. P. Lovecraft], "In the Editor's Study," pp. [7-11] (includes: "The Proposed Author's Union," pp. [7-9]; "Revolutionary Mythology," pp. [9-10]; "The Symphonic Ideal," pp. [10-11]); [H. P. Lovecraft], "Among the Amateurs," p. [11]; Winifred V. Jackson, "The Unknown" [poem], p. [12] (as by "Elizabeth Berkeley"); H. P. Lovecraft, "Inspiration," p. [12] (as by "Lewis Theobald, Jun.").

2, No. 4 (January 1917), [4] pp.

Winifred Virginia Jordan, "The Vagrant" [poem], p. [1]; Arthur W. Ashby, "The Unbreakable Link" [fiction], pp. [1-2]; H. P. Lovecraft, "Futurist Art," p. [2]; [H. P. Lovecraft], "In the Editor's Study," pp. [2-4] (includes: "The Vers Libre Epidemic," pp. [2-3]; "Amateur Standards," pp. [3-4]); Eugene B. Kuntz, D.D., "When New-year Comes" [poem], p. 4; [H. P. Lovecraft], "A Request," p. [4].

3, No. 1 (July 1917), [4] pp.

Ira A. Cole, "In Vita Elysium" [poem], p. [1]; Henry Clapham McGavack, "The Genesis of the Revolutionary War" [essay], pp. [1-3] (with "Editor's Note," p. [1]); Mary Henrietta Lehr,

"Sweet Frailty" [poem], p. [3]; [H. P. Lovecraft], "In the Editor's Study: A Remarkable Document," p. [4]; [H. P. Lovecraft], "The United's Problem," p. [4].

4, No. 1 (July 1918), 8 pp.

Wilfrid Kemble, "Lord Kitchener" [poem], p. 1; H. P. Lovecraft, "The Spirit of Summer," p. 1; H. P. Lovecraft, "The Despised Pastoral," p. 2; Winifred Virginia Jordan, "On Shore" [poem], p. 2; Philip B. McDonald, "Criticism of Amateur Journals," pp. 2-3; Alfred Galpin, Jr., "Selenaio-Phantasma" [poem], p. 3; H. P. Lovecraft, "Time and Space," pp. 3-4; Eugene B. Kuntz, D.D., "Upon the Brink" [poem], p. 4; H. P. Lovecraft, "Merlinus Redivivus," pp. 4-5; Ernest Lionel McKeag, R.N.R., "The Prodigal" [poem], p. 5; [H. P. Lovecraft], "In the Editor's Study," pp. 5-7 (includes: "Anglo-Saxondom," p. 5; "Amateur Criticism," pp. 5-6; "The United 1917-1918," p. 6; "The Amateur Press Club," pp. 6-7; "Grace," p. 7); [H. P. Lovecraft], "*Les Mouches Fantastiques*," pp. 7-8; Alfred Galpin, Jr., "Two Loves" [poem], p. 8 (as by "Consul Hasting").

5, No. 1 (July 1919), 12 pp.

Samuel Loveman, "Song" [poem], p. 1; James F. Morton, "Touching on Euphuism" [essay], pp. 1-4; Andrew Francis Lockhart, "Constancy" [poem], p. 4; Willis Tete Crossman (i.e., W. Paul Cook), "The Field of Night" [fiction], pp. 4-6; Arthur Goodenough, "The Joy of Books" [poem], p. 6; Maurice Winter Moe, "Imagism" [essay], pp. 6-7; Maurice Winter Moe, "Seven O'Clock" [poem], p. 7; Winifred Virginia Jordan, "April Shadows" [poem], p. 7; Agnes Richmond Arnold, "Bereft" [poem], p. 8; Ernest Lionel McKeag, "Mother Sea" [poem], p. 8; Rheinhart Kleiner, "At Providence in 1918" [poem], p. 8; Winifred Virginia Jordan, "Who Will Fare with Me?" [poem], p. 9; Wilfrid Kemble, "Disappointment" [poem], p. 9; [H. P. Lovecraft], "In the Editor's Study: The League," pp. 9-10; [H. P. Lovecraft], "Bolshevism," pp. 10-11; [H. P. Lovecraft], "For Official Editor-Anne Tillery Renshaw," pp. 11-12; [H. P. Lovecraft], "Amateurdom," p. 12.

No. 12 (March 1923), 8 pp.

Samuel Loveman, "Thomas Holley Chivers: (Buried at Decatur,

Georgia)" [poem], p. 1; Frank Belknap Long, "An American Humorist" [essay], pp. 2-5; [H. P. Lovecraft], "In the Editor's Study," pp. 5-8 (includes: "Rursus Adsumus," pp. 5-6; "Rudis Indigestaque Moles," pp. 6-8).

No. 13 (July 1923), 28 pp.

Samuel Loveman, "To Satan" [poem; dedicated "To H. P. L."], pp. 1-2; Frank Belknap Long, "Felis: A Prose Poem," pp. 3-4; Lilian Middleton, "The Crock o' Gold" [poem], p. 4; Alfred Galpin, Jr., "Intuition in the Philosophy of Bergson" [essay], pp. 5-9 (as by "A. T. Madison"); John Ravenor Bullen, "The Storm" [poem], pp. 9-10; Alfred Galpin, Jr., "Ennui" [prose poem], pp. 10-11 (as by "Anatol Kleinst"); James F. Morton, Jr., "Fause Murdoch" [poem], pp. 12-16; Betty Earle, "I Will Lead Thee" [compendium of prose and verse], pp. 16-19; Lilian Middleton, "Song XVIII Cent." [poem], pp. 20-21; [H. P. Lovecraft], "In the Editor's Study," pp. 21-24; [H. P. Lovecraft], [Untitled], pp. 24-28.

3. *The Credential*, 1, No. 1 (April 1920). Editor: Anne T. Renshaw. Assistant Editor: Howard P. Lovecraft. 21 pp.

4. *Driftwind*. Edited, printed, and published by Walter John Coates. 1926-1948. Associate Editors: H. P. Lovecraft, et al., for the issues: 9, No. 12 (June-July 1935), 373-406; 10, Nos. 1-2 (August-September 1935), 1-36; 10, Nos. 3-4 (September-October 1935), 37-74; 10, No. 5 (November 1935), 75-108; 10, No. 6 (December 1935), 109-46; 10, No. 7 (January 1936), 147-86; 10, No. 8 (February 1936), 187-226; 10, No. 9 (March 1936), 227-66; 10, No. 10 (April 1936), 267-304; 10, No. 11 (May-June 1936), 305-42; 11, No. 1 (July-August 1936), 1-40; 11, No. 2 (September 1936), 41-74; 11, No. 3 (October 1936), 75-116; 11, No. 4 (November 1936), 117-52; 11, No. 5 (December 1936), 153-94; 11, No. 6

(January 1937), 195-234; 11, No. 7 (February 1937), 235-74.

> The title varied in the earlier years of its publication (e.g., *The Drift-Wind*).

5. *The Inspiration*. Edited by Edna von der Heide. Assistant Editors: Howard Lovecraft, et. al. Tribute Number (April 1917), 16 pp.

> Other issues of the journal were not edited by Lovecraft.

6. *The Providence Amateur*. 1, No. 1 (June 1915), [12] pp.; 1, No. 2 (February 1916), 16 pp.

> For the first issue Lovecraft was "Literary Director"; for the second he was "Official Editor." No more issues were published. Both issues were reprinted in facsimile by Necronomicon Press (West Warwick, R.I.), the first in 1976 and the second in 1977, in an edition size of 200 and 500 copies, respectively.

7. *The United Amateur*. Official Editor: Miss Verna McGeoch. President: Howard P. Lovecraft for the issues: 17, No. 1 (September 1917), 1-20; 17, No. 2 (November 1917), 21-36; 17, No. 3 (January 1918), 37-60; 17, No. 4 (March 1918), 61-80; 17, No. 5 (May 1918), 81-108; 17, No. 6 (July 1918), 109-36.

8. *The United Amateur*. Official Editor: H. P. Lovecraft for the issues: 16, No. 9 (July 1917), 121-37; 20, No. 1 (September 1920), 1-16; 20, No. 2 (November 1920), 17-32; 20, No. 3 (January 1921), 33-44; 20, No. 4 (March 1921), 45-60; 20, No. 5 (May 1921), 61-68; 20, No. 6 (July 1921), 69-74; 21, No. 1 (September 1921), 1-12; 21, No. 2 (November 1921), 13-24; 21, No. 3 (January 1922), 25-36; 21, No. 4 (March 1922), 37-48; 21, No. 5 (May 1922), 49-56; 23, No. 1 (May 1924), 1-16; 24, No. 1 (July 1925), 1-14.

9. *The United Co-operative.* Edited by Winifred Virginia
   Jordan, H. P. Lovecraft, et al. 1, No. 1 (December
   1918), 8 pp.; 1, No. 2 (June 1919), 8 pp.; 1, No. 3
   (April 1921), 16 pp.

   No more issues published.

E. Apocrypha and Other Miscellany

i. Apocrypha

1. "Complete Chronology." In I-A-42, 48-49; II-A-45.

> This list was first printed in August Derleth's "Introduction" to I-A-42, pp. vii-viii. Derleth claimed that the list was from a letter by Lovecraft, but it was in fact fabricated (or hypothesized) by Derleth himself. The list resembles no surviving chronology of his fiction by Lovecraft (cf., e.g., "Tales of H. P. Lovecraft" in I-A-62), nor is it the list sent by Lovecraft to Derleth in a letter to him on 31 October 1926 (ms., WHS). The list makes the odd practice of alphabetizing titles when more than one tale has been written in a year. Needless to say, it is therefore quite inaccurate.

2. "The Cup Bearer." *Asmodeus*, No. 2 (Fall 1951), p. 15.

> This poem is not by Lovecraft but by Lilith Lorraine and is dedicated "To Clark Ashton Smith."

3. "Death." *The Silver Clarion*, 2, No. 8 (November 1918), 3. In Jonathan E. Hoag. *The Poetical Works of Jonathan E. Hoag*. New York: [privately printed] 1923, p. 50. *The Californian*, 5, No. 1 (Summer 1937), 25. I-A-25, 35.

> This poem seems clearly to be by Hoag (he is credited on the first two appearances), but may have been revised by Lovecraft. Hyman Bradofsky, editor of *The Californian*, has told the compiler that he reprinted the poem as by Lovecraft because Rheinhart Kleiner had told him that Lovecraft was the author. No explanation has been found as to why Kleiner conceived such an opinion.

4. "Downpour." *The Tryout*, October 1916.

> This poem was written by "H. S. Winterbone," which has frequently been assumed to be a pseudonym of Lovecraft's. But there was an actual British amateur journalist named H. J. Winterbone, and the poem (which is not noticeably

Lovecraftian) was probably written by him, the "S" being a stenographic error in a periodical known for its typographical inaccuracies.

5. "Excerpts from *The Necronomicon* of Abdul Alhazred." *Paragon*, No. 3 (1970), pp. 11, 13.

    As "Edited and annotated by H. P. Lovecraft." A hoax apparently perpetrated by the editors of *Paragon*.

6. "Who Ate Roger Williams?" *Vagabond*, No. 3 (Winter 1955-56), p. 20.

    Long believed to be a story by Lovecraft, it has now been determined that the author is Wilfred Blanch Talman. The ms. (in the Grill-Binkin collection [see III-G-iv-3]) was untitled, the present title having been given by Jack Grill.

The Lovecraft-Derleth "posthumous collaborations."

These stories (of which there are sixteen), listed as by "H. P. Lovecraft and August Derleth," were in fact written almost entirely by Derleth. In most cases, the stories were based on one or more ideas noted in Lovecraft's *Commonplace Book*; for example, "The Fisherman of Falcon Point" was based on this entry: "Fisherman casts his net into the sea by moonlight— what he finds." Plotting, description, dialogue, characterization, and other elements were entirely by Derleth. As such they cannot be classified as works by Lovecraft.

In some instances Derleth incorporated actual prose passages by Lovecraft into his stories. *The Lurker at the Threshold* (a 50,000-word novel) contains some 1,200 words by Lovecraft, taken from a fragment entitled "Of Evil Sorceries done in New England." This passage has been listed in this bibliography (I-C-33, 50; II-C-8, 9, 16). "The Survivor" was based on a comparatively lengthy plot sketch plus random notes for the story jotted down by Lovecraft in 1934. A descriptive passage of "The Lamp of Alhazred" was based on a portion of a letter by Lovecraft to James F. Morton, March [?] 1937. These extracts or paraphrases, however, have not been deemed significant enough to merit inclusion in this bibliography.

Listed below are first appearances of the sixteen

"collaborations," followed by a few collections in which they appear. There are many paperbound and foreign editions of these stories. Some give only Lovecraft as the author.

7. "The Ancestor." First published in *The Survivor and Others* (see I-E-i-22). Also in I-A-46.

> An accidental plagiarism of Leonard Cline's *The Dark Chamber* (1927); written up from a plot description of the novel in Lovecraft's *Commonplace Book*. Cf. "Supernatural Horror in Literature," Chap. viii.

8. "The Dark Brotherhood." First published in I-A-43. Also in I-A-46.

9. "The Fisherman of Falcon Point." First published in *The Survivor and Others* (see I-E-i-22). Also in I-A-46.

10. "The Gable Window." *Saturn*, 1, No. 2 (May 1957), 110-18 (as "The Murky Glass"). Also in I-A-46.

11. "The Horror from the Middle Span." First published in August Derleth, ed. *Travellers by Night*. Sauk City, Wis.: Arkham House, 1967, pp. 172-94 (as by "H. P. Lovecraft [completed by August Derleth]").

12. "Innsmouth Clay." First published in August Derleth, ed. *Dark Things*. Sauk City, Wis.: Arkham House, 1971, pp. 163-75 (as by "H. P. Lovecraft [completed by August Derleth]").

13. "The Lamp of Alhazred." *The Magazine of Fantasy and Science Fiction*, 13, No. 4 (October 1954), 44-53. Also in I-A-46.

14. *The Lurker at the Threshold.* See I-C-33, 50; II-C-8, 9, 16.

15. "The Peabody Heritage." First published in *The Survivor and Others* (see below). Also in I-A-46.

16. "The Shadow in the Attic." First published in August Derleth, ed. *Over the Edge*. Sauk City, Wis.: Arkham House, 1964, pp. 50-75 (as by "H. P. Lovecraft [completed by August Derleth]").

17. "The Shadow out of Space." First published in *The Survivor and Others* (see I-E-i-22). *Fantastic*, 11, No. 2 (February 1962), 86-106. Also in I-A-46.

     The second appearance contains a lengthy note (pp. 84-86) by Sam Moskowitz on Derleth's championing of Lovecraft and his penning the "posthumous collaborations."

18. "The Shuttered Room." First published in I-A-32. Also in I-A-46.

19. "The Survivor." *Weird Tales*, 46, No. 3 (July 1954), 2-21. Also in I-A-46.

20. "The Watchers out of Time." First published in *The Watchers out of Time and Others* (see I-E-i-22).

     An incomplete novel or novella.

21. "Wentworth's Day." First published in *The Survivor and Others* (see I-E-i-22). Also in I-A-46.

22. "Witches' Hollow." First published in August Derleth, ed. *Dark Mind, Dark Heart*. Sauk City, Wis.: Arkham House, 1962, pp. 161-78.

Collections:

   The Survivor and Others (Sauk City, Wis.: Arkham House, 1957). Seven stories.
   The Shuttered Room and Other Tales of Terror (New York: Beagle/Ballantine Books, 1971 et seq.). Six stories.
   The Watchers out of Time and Others (Sauk City, Wis.: Arkham House, 1974). All sixteen stories.

ii. Lost Works

1. [Astronomy articles and/or miscellany.] *The Pawtuxet Valley Gleaner*, 1907-08.

    Lovecraft stated (see letter to Rheinhart Kleiner, 16 Nov. 1916) that he wrote articles on astronomy and other subjects for *The Pawtuxet Valley Gleaner* from 1906 to 1908. Articles for the year 1906 have been found (I-B-ii-9-25), and evidence indicates that the weekly paper continued publication until at least the end of 1907, when it was apparently bought out by the rival *Pawtuxet Valley Daily Times*. No issues or clippings of the *Gleaner* for 1907 or 1908 seem to survive.

2. "Does 'Vulcan' Exist?" *The Providence Journal* (?), 1906 (?).

    August Derleth included this item in the appendix to *H. P. L.: A Memoir* (I-C-32), claiming that it was one of Lovecraft's earliest writings, and implying that it was (part of?) one of the columns of astronomical articles written by Lovecraft in his teens. Lovecraft, however, wrote no astronomical articles for the *Journal*. The article could be a letter to the editor (similar to I-B-v-a-1 and 3), but the letter columns of the *Journal* for 1906, 1907, and parts of 1908 have been checked with no result. The article is (from internal evidence) undoubtedly by Lovecraft, and must date from around 1906-15: in "April Skies" for April 1916 (I-B-ii-73) it was noted that the intra-Mercurial Vulcan "conclusively" does not exist, while in "Does 'Vulcan' Exist?" no firm denial of Vulcan's existence is made. The article may have appeared in the lost issues of *The Pawtuxet Valley Gleaner* (see I-E-ii-1).

3. [Essays on the works of Shakespeare.] ca. 1917-23.

    These essays—mentioned first by Alexander Ostrow in the letter column ("The Eyrie") of *Weird Tales*, Oct. 1933, and repeated in III-B-22, p. 10—were allegedly written "while [Lovecraft] was active in the affairs of the National Amateur Press Association" (Ostrow). It now seems certain that Lovecraft had no hand in writing them. Discussing Ostrow's letter in a letter to Clark Ashton Smith ([3 October 1933]; ms.,

JHL), Lovecraft completely denies having written the essays, and feels that Ostrow—an amateur journalist whose name Lovecraft had seen in the membership lists of the N.A.P.A.— had confused him with Samuel Loveman, who was a great enthusiast of Elizabethan literature.

4. Letters to Frank Belknap Long, 1931-37.

At some time in the possession of Samuel Loveman (who acquired them from Long), these letters were apparently sold by him to an unknown private collector. If they are in existence, their present owner has not publicized the fact. Lovecraft's letters to Long up to 1931 were published in the *Selected Letters* volumes (I-A-41, 45, 59) only because Donald Wandrei had managed to make copies of them before their dispersal. Loveman also owned the mss. of "The Shunned House" and "Under the Pyramids."

5. "Life and Death."

A prose poem written ca. 1919-20. An entry in the *Commonplace Book* (I-A-14, p. 19) reads: "Life and Death. Death— its desolation and horror—bleak spaces—sea-bottom—dead cities. But Life—the greater horror! Vast unheard-of reptiles and leviathans—hideous beasts of prehistoric jungle—rank slimy vegetation—evil instincts of primal man. Life is more horrible than Death." It was published in an amateur journal, and was located by George T. Wetzel in 1952 in the course of his bibliographic researches; but he then misplaced the reference and it has since not been located.

6. "The Mystery of Murdon Grange."

A "dime novel" partially or entirely written by Lovecraft, ca. 1918. It was "issued" in his typewritten magazine, *Hesperia*, but has never been seen.

7. [On Roman architecture.]

A 15,000-word essay written in 1935 but never typed. It was misplaced by Maurice W. Moe in late 1935; it has never been seen.

8. Review of *The Image-Maker of Thebes* (film).

> In late January 1917 Fay's Theatre (Providence, R.I.) offered a
> $25 prize for the best review of *The Image-Maker of Thebes*
> (playing Jan. 22-24). Lovecraft entered the contest with a
> review "covering four typewritten pages" (letter to Rheinhart
> Kleiner, 31 Jan. 1917) and won the prize. If the review is still in
> existence, its location has yet to be discovered; the files of Fay's
> Theatre have not been found.

9. "The Shadow out of Time." A.Ms., 65 pp.

> The whereabouts of the A.Ms. of this tale are not known.
> Lovecraft gave it to R. H. Barlow, who prepared a typescript of
> it for Lovecraft; it was one of the few mss. not given to the
> John Hay Library by Barlow after Lovecraft's death. If the ms.
> is still extant, it may be among Barlow's effects, which are
> scattered variously around the continent. Discovery of the ms.
> is important in that, according to one page of the ms. re-copied
> by Lovecraft (now in the John Hay Library), the story has
> never been printed as Lovecraft wrote it.

10. "Waste Paper: A Poem of Profound Insignificance."
    The Providence Journal (?), 1922-23 (?).

> Lovecraft wrote to J. Vernon Shea (24 March 1933) that his
> parody of T. S. Eliot's *The Waste Land* was published in "the
> newspaper," apparently shortly after Eliot's poem was
> published in *The Dial*, Nov. 1922. The appearance has never
> been found. The A.Ms. of the poem (as by "Humphry
> Littlewit, Gent.") survives in the John Hay Library.

11. [Title unknown.]

> A fiction tale based on a "true incident" about a hotel in
> Providence; probably written in the 1930s. Lovecraft made no
> copy of the story and it was lost in the mails. This matter was
> revealed by Lee Shaw (III-D-560), but it may be a hoax, for
> Lovecraft mentions no such tale in any of his correspondence
> seen by the compiler.

iii. Works Destroyed

The majority of the juvenile titles here listed are taken from the catalogues of his work appended to some of Lovecraft's surviving juvenile mss.; see John Hay Library.

a. Fiction

1. *The Club of the Seven Dreamers.*

    A novel idea, ca. March 1920. It may never have been begun.

2. "Gone—but Whither?"

    Juvenilia; ca. 1905. See Lovecraft to Maurice W. Moe, [6 April 1935].

3. "The Haunted House."

    Juvenilia; ca. 1897-1902.

4. *The House of the Worm.*

    A novel idea formed possibly in early 1923. It may never have been begun.

5. "John, the Detective."

    Juvenilia; ca. 1897-1902.

6. "The Noble Eavesdropper."

    Juvenilia; ca. 1897. Lovecraft's first attempt at short fiction. He describes it as the tale of "a boy who overheard some horrible conclave of subterranean beings in a cave" (letter to J. Vernon Shea, 19-31 July 1931).

7. "The Picture."

    Juvenilia; ca. 1907. Lovecraft describes this as follows: "I had a man in a Paris garret paint a mysterious canvas embodying the quintessential essence of all horror. He is found clawed & mangled one morning before his easel. The picture is destroyed, as in a titanic struggle—but in one corner of the frame a bit of canvas remains . . . & on it the coroner finds to his horror the painted counterpart of the sort of claw which evidently killed the artist" (letter to Robert Bloch, 1 June 1933; quoted in III-C-5). In the *Commonplace Book* (I-A-14) is this entry: "Revise 1907 tale—painting of ultimate horror." Perhaps the tale is a foreshadowing of "Pickman's Model."

8. "The Secret of the Grave."

Juvenilia; ca. 1897-1902.

Addendum:

Many juvenile "thrillers" were written between 1904 and 1908; only "The Beast in the Cave" and "The Alchemist" survived the destruction of this body of work in 1908.

b. Nonfiction

1. "Acids."

Juvenilia; ca. 1897-1902.

2. "Antarctic Atlas."

Juvenilia; ca. 1903. See Lovecraft to M. F. Bonner, 26 April 1936.

3. A Brief Course in Astronomy—Descriptive, Practical, and Observational; for Beginners and General Readers.

Juvenilia; ca. 1906. Lovecraft describes it as being ca. 150 pages in the "typed and hand-illustrated stage" (see letter to Maurice W. Moe, [6 April 1935]).

4. A Brief Course in Inorganic Chemistry.

Juvenilia; 1910. Lovecraft called this a "bulky manuscript" (letter to Alfred Galpin, 29 Aug. 1918).

5. Chemistry.

Juvenilia; ca. 1899. A work in six volumes of which four survive.

6. "Early Rhode Island."

Juvenilia; ca. 1897-1902.

7. "Egyptian Myths."

Juvenilia; ca. 1899.

8. "Explosives."

Juvenilia; ca. 1897-1902.

9. "An Historical Account of Last Year's War with SPAIN."

Juvenilia; ca. 1899.

10. "Iron Working."

Juvenilia; ca. 1897-1902.

11. Letters to Henry S. Whitehead.

Though somewhat of a mystery, these letters were apparently destroyed, along with other of Whitehead's papers, after his death in 1932. For more on the matter see R. H. Barlow's introduction to Whitehead's *West India Lights* (I-C-177).

12. "Mythology for the Young."

Juvenilia; ca. 1899.

13. *The Rhode Island Journal of Astronomy*. Issues for 1904-05, 1907-08.

There are gaps in the surviving issues of this juvenile periodical between Volume 1, No. 27 (31 Jan. 1904) and Volume 3, No. 1 (16 Apr. 1905), and between Volume 4, No. 9 (April 1907) and Volume 6, No. 6 (January 1909). Evidently Volumes 2 and 5 and parts of Volumes 4 and 6 have been lost or destroyed.

14. *The Science Library*.

Juvenilia; ca. 1904. A nine-volume series of which three survive. Non-extant volumes: "3. Life of Galileo"; "4. Life of Herschel (revised)"; "6. Selections from Author's 'Astronomy' "; "7. The Moon, Part I"; "8. The Moon, Part II"; "9. On Optics."

15. *The Scientific Gazette*. Issues for 1902-03.

> In *Poemata Minora*, Vol. 2 [Sept. 1902], Lovecraft "advertises"
> his *Scientific Gazette* in a catalogue of his works. No copies,
> however, survive between the New Issue of Vol. 1, No. 1 (12
> May 1902) and Vol. 3, No. 1 (16 August 1903); clearly volumes
> 1 and 2 were either lost or destroyed.

16. "Static Electricity."

> Juvenilia; ca. 1897-1902.

17. "Voyages of Capt. Ross, R.N."

> Juvenilia; ca. 1902. See Lovecraft to M. F. Bonner, 26 April
> 1936.

18. "Wilkes's Explorations."

> Juvenilia; ca. 1902. See Lovecraft to M. F. Bonner, 26 April
> 1936.

c. Poetry

1. "The Aeneid."

> Juvenilia; ca. 1898-1902. Like "The Poem of Ulysses," a
> retelling of the epic.

2. "The Argonauts."

> Juvenilia; ca. 1898-1902.

3. "The Hermit."

> Juvenilia; ca. 1898-1902.

4. "The Iliad."

> Juvenilia; ca. 1898-1902. A retelling of the epic.

5. *Poemata Minora*, Volume I.

> Juvenilia; ca. 1902. Volume II survives.

iv. Items Included within Published Works by Lovecraft

a. Poetry

1. "Despair." Included in a letter to Rheinhart Kleiner, 19 February 1919 (see I-A-41).

2. "An Epistle to Francis, Ld. Belknap, with a Volume of Proust, Presented to Him by his Aged Grandsire, Lewis Theobald, Jun. Christmas, MDCCCCX[X]VIII." Included in a letter to Maurice W. Moe, January 1929 (see I-A-45).

3. ["Fragment on Whitman."] Included in "In a Major Key" (I-B-ii-148), but untitled in that appearance; the title was bestowed later by Lovecraft himself (see letter to Rheinhart Kleiner, 4 April 1918).

4. "Gaudeamus." Included, without title, in all printings of "The Tomb." A manuscript of the poem, probably predating the story, survives and contains the title. The poem has appeared separately as "Drinking Song from The Tomb."

5. "Little Sam Perkins." Included in letter to James F. Morton, 24 September 1934; see I-A-69, I-B-v-b-54.

6. "The Messenger." Included in a letter to Clark Ashton Smith, 3 December 1929 (see I-A-59).

7. "A Mississippi Autumn." Twelve lines included (without title) in "October Skies" (I-B-ii-79).

8. "Nemesis." Last three lines of second stanza included as epigraph in all appearances of "The Haunter of the Dark." The first stanza is also included in a letter to Edwin Baird, [Sept.? 1923] (see I-B-v-b-24).

9. "Ode to Selene or Diana." Last stanza included in a
   letter to Edwin Baird, 3 February 1924; see I-A-41
   and 62. Also included in a letter to James F. Morton,
   Spring 1931 (see I-A-59).

10. "On Receiving a Picture of Swans." Included in a
    letter to Rheinhart Kleiner, 14 September 1915 (see
    I-A-41). Also included in "August Skies" (I-B-ii-77)
    (without title).

11. "The Pathetick History of Sir Wilful Wildrake."
    Included in a letter to Frank Belknap Long, 7
    February 1924 (as by "L. Theobald, Jun."); see
    I-A-41.

12. "The Poem of Ulysses, or, The Odyssey." First four
    lines included in a letter to Bernard Austin Dwyer,
    3 March 1927 (see I-A-45).

13. "Psychopompos." First eight lines included in a letter
    to Edwin Baird, [September? 1923]; see I-B-v-b-24.

14. "Recapture." Included in a letter to Clark Ashton
    Smith, 19 November 1929; see I-A-33.

15. "To Charlie of the Comics." Included in a letter to
    Rheinhart Kleiner, 30 September 1915 (see I-A-41).

16. "To Clark Ashton Smith, Esq., upon His Fantastic
    Tales, Verses, Pictures, and Sculptures." Included in
    a letter to James F. Morton, March [?] 1937 (see I-
    A-69; not included in I-B-v-b-68).

17. "To M. W. M." Included in "News Notes" for July
    1917 (see I-B-ii-202).

18. "To Mr. Finlay, upon His Drawing for Mr. Bloch's
    Tale, 'The Faceless God.' " Included in letters to

Virgil Finlay, 30 November 1936 (see I-B-v-a-5) and to James F. Morton, March [?] 1937 (see I-A-69; not included in I-B-v-b-68).

19. "To Mr. Hoag, upon His 93rd Birthday, February 10, 1924." Included in a letter to Edwin Baird, 3 February 1924; cf. I-A-62 (not included in I-A-41).

20. "To Zara: Inscribed to Miss Sarah Longhurst—June 1829." (As by "Edgar Allan Poe (?).") Included in a letter to Maurice W. Moe, [August? 1922]; see I-A-41.

21. "Unda, or, the Bride of the Sea . . ." Included in a letter to Rheinhart Kleiner, 30 September 1915 (see I-A-41).

22. "Unity." Included in a letter to James F. Morton, 18 January 1931 (see I-A-59).

23. [Untitled: "Alone in space, I view'd a feeble flock . . ."]. Included in "May Skies" (I-B-ii-86). This poem, 13 lines long, is a recasting of ll. 142-60 of "The Poe-et's Nightmare."

24. [Untitled: "But (past belief) a dolphin's arched back . . ."]. Included in "The July Skies" (I-B-ii-64).

25. [Untitled: "Damn'd be this harsh mechanick age . . ."]. Included in a letter to James F. Morton, 28 June 1926 (see I-A-45).

26. [Untitled: "Far as the eye can see, behold outspread . . ."]. Included in a letter to Frank Belknap Long, 8 November 1923 (see I-A-41).

27. [Untitled: "If, as you start toward Lillie's festive spread, . . ."]. Included in a letter to Sarah Phillips Lovecraft, 30 November 1911 (see I-A-41).

28. [Untitled: "Slang is the life of speech, the critics say, . . ."]. Included in [Untitled] (I-B-ii-251), p. [2].

29. [Untitled: "Slumber, watcher, till the spheres, . . ."]. Included in all printings of "Polaris."

30. [Untitled: "What! shall th' aspiring Blood of Lancaster . . ."]. Included in letter to Miss M. F. Bonner, 26 April 1936 (see I-A-69).

31. [Untitled: "When Gallant LEEDS auspiciously shall wed . . ."]. Included in all printings of "A Reminiscence of Dr. Samuel Johnson."

32. [Untitled: "When the bright Blue assaults the chaulk-white Strand, . . ."]. Included in a letter to Annie E. Phillips Gamwell, 17 September 1927 (see I-A-45).

33. [Untitled: "Whilst town astronomers, with straining eyes, . . ."]. Included in "September Skies" (I-B-ii-78).

34. [Untitled: "The winged steed above th' horizon flies, . . ."]. Included in "October Skies" (I-B-ii-67).

b. Letter

1. To Lee Alexander Stone, M. D., 18 September 1930. Included in a letter to James F. Morton, 26 September 1930 (see I-A-59).

v. Award-Winning Stories by H. P. Lovecraft

1. *The Best Short Stories . . . and the Yearbook of the American Short Story.* Ed. Edward J. O'Brien. Boston: Small,

Maynard & Co., 1915-25; New York: Dodd, Mead & Co., 1926-32.

1924: "The Picture in the House" (1 star); see p. 346 (index).
1928: "The Colour out of Space" (3-star); see pp. 312 ("Roll of Honor"), 324 ("Biographical Notices"), 404 (index).
1929: "The Dunwich Horror" (3-star), "The Silver Key" (1-star); see pp. 280 ("Roll of Honor"), 371 (index).

2. *O. Henry Memorial Award Prize Stories.* Ed. Blanche Colton Williams. Garden City, N.Y.: Doubleday, Doran & Co., 1919f.

1928: "Pickman's Model," p. 294 ("Stories Ranking Third").
1929: "The Silver Key," p. 358 ("Stories Ranking Second").
1932: "The Strange High House in the Mist," p. 274 ("Stories Ranking Highest"); "In the Vault," p. 283 ("Stories Ranking Second").

vi. Miscellany

1. "The Favorite Weird Stories of H. P. Lovecraft." *The Fantasy Fan*, 2, No. 2 (October 1934), 22.

A list of ten tales; apparently taken from a letter from Lovecraft to H. C. Koenig.

2. "Map of the Principal Parts of Arkham, Massachusetts." *The Acolyte*, 1, No. 1 (Fall 1942), 26 (as "Map of Arkham").

A reproduction of a hand-drawn map by Lovecraft.

3. "Official Organ Fund." *The United Amateur*, 20, No. 1 (September 1920), 11; 20, No. 3 (January 1921), 42; 20, No. 4 (March 1921), 60; 21, No. 2 (November 1921), 24; 21, No. 4 (March 1922), 46; 21, No. 5 (May 1922), 56.

A list of contributions to the U.A.P.A.; signed "H. P. Lovecraft, Custodian."

II. Works by Lovecraft in Translation

A. Books by Lovecraft

1. *La Couleur tombée du ciel* (1954)
   a. H.-P. LOVECRAFT / LA COULEUR /
   TOMBÉE / DU CIEL / Traduit de l'américain
   par / JACQUES PAPY / *PRÉSENCE DU
   FUTUR* / ÉDITIONS DENOËL / 19, RUE
   AMÉLIE——PARIS VIIe [colophon page:] 3
   September 1954

   > [1]^{16} 2-8^{16} [1-7] 8 [9] 10-42 [43] 44-91 [92-93] 94-166
   > [167] 168-239 [240-44]
   > [1-2]: blank; [3]: half-title; [4]: blank; [5]: title; [6]:
   > copyright page; [7]-8: "H.-P. Lovecraft (1890-1937)," by
   > Jacques Bergier; [9]-42: "La Couleur tombée du ciel" (CS);
   > [43]-91: "L'Abomination de Dunwich" (DH); [92]: blank;
   > [93]-166: "Le Cauchemar d'Innsmouth" (SOI); [167]-239:
   > "Celui qui chuchotait dans les ténèbres" (WD); [240]: blank;
   > [241]: contents list; [242]: colophon; [243-44]: blank.
   > Bound in paper; 20.8 × 14 cm.
   > *Notes.* Présence du futur No. 4.

   b.1. *Second(?) Edition.* Paris: Éditions Denoël, 5 January 1971.
   233[+7] pp.

   b.2. *Reprint.* Paris. Éditions Denoël, 20 June 1975. New cover
   by J. J. Boyer.

   c. *Hardbound Edition.* Paris: Éditions Denoël, 1973. 248[+8] pp.
   Bound in white cloth; spine stamped in black, violet, and
   maroon; no dust jacket. Illustrations by Jean Gourmelin.

2. *Dans l'abime du temps* (1954)
   a. H. P. LOVECRAFT / DANS L'ABIME / DU
   TEMPS / *Traduit de l'américain par* / JACQUES
   PAPY / PRÉSENCE DU FUTUR / ÉDITIONS

DENOËL / 19, RUE AMÉLIE—PARIS VIIe
[colophon page:] 25 October 1954

Perfect-bound: [1-7] 8-79 [80-81] 82-119 [120-21] 122-55 [156-57] 158-244 [245-48]

[1-2]: blank; [3]: half-title; [4]: list of books by Lovecraft; [5]: title; [6]: copyright page; [7]-77: "Dans l'abime du temps" (SOOT); [80]: blank; [81]-119: "La Maison de la sorcière" (DWH); [120]: blank; [121]-55: "L'Appel de Cthulhu" (CC); [156]: blank; [157]-244: *Les Montagnes hallucinées* (ATMOM); [245]: contents list and erratum; [246]: blank; [247]: colophon; [248]: blank.

Bound in paper; 17.8 × 12.2 cm.

Notes. Présence du futur No. 5.

b.1. *Second(?) Edition.* Paris: Éditions Denoël, 6 October 1970. 221[+3] pp.

b.2. *Reprint.* Paris: Éditions Denoël, 21 June 1976. New cover design by N. Rondet and S. Dumont.

c. *Hardbound Edition.* Paris: Éditions Denoël, 1973. 248[+8] pp. Bound in white cloth; spine stamped in orange, black, and brown. Illustrations by Jean Gourmelin.

3. *Démons et merveilles* (1955)

a. "LUMIÈRE INTERDITE" / COLLECTION DIRIGÉE PAR LOUIS PAUWELS / H. P. LOVECRAFT / DÉMONS / ET / MERVEILLES / *Roman* / Traduction de Bernard Noël / *Avec une* / Introduction de Jacques Bergier / DEUX [publisher's device] RIVES [colophon page:] Paris . . . November 1955

[1]^8 2-13^8 [1-7] 8-12 [13-15] 16-21 [22-25] 26-38 [39-41] 42-48 [49] 50-51 [52-53] 54-61 [62-63] 64-66 [67] 68-73 [74-75] 76-80 [81] 82-84 [85] 86-90 [91-93] 94-121 [122-23] 124-46 [147] 148-76 [177] 178-203 [204-08]

[1-2]: blank; [3]: half-title; [4]: publisher's note; [5]: title; [6]: list of volumes in the "Lumière Interdite" series; [7]-12: "H.-P. Lovecraft, ce grand génie venu d'ailleurs" by Bergier; [13]: half-title to following story (similarly for succeeding

works); [14]: blank; [15]-21: "Le Témoignage de Randolph Carter" (SRC); [22]: blank; [23]: half-title; [24]: blank; [25]-38: "La Clé d'argent" (SK); [39]: half-title; [40]: blank; [41]-51, [53]-61, [63]-73, [75]-90: "À travers les portes de la clé d'argent" (TGSK); [52, 62, 74]: blank; [91]: half-title; [92]: blank; [93]-121, [123]-203: *À la recherche de Kadath* (DQ); [122, 204]: blank; [205]: contents list; [206]: blank; [207]: colophon; [208]: blank.

    Bound in paper; 19.1 × 14.4 cm.

    Notes. Lumière Interdite No. 5 (?). The stories are presented as if they were four parts of a novel ("*roman*"); DQ is divided into three chapters and conclusion.

  b. *Second Edition.* Paris: Bibliotheque Mondiale, ca. 1958. Not seen.

  c.1. *Third Edition.* Paris: Union Générale d'Éditions (Christian Bourgois), 1963. 250[+6] pp. Cover design by Alain Maylan.

  c.2. *Reprint.* Paris: Union Générale d'Éditions, 1 April 1970. New cover art by Pierre Bernard.

  c.3. *Reprint.* Paris: Union Générale d'Éditions, 10 April 1977.

  d. *Deluxe Edition.* Paris: Éditions Opta/André Sauret, 1976. 248 [+5] pp. Bound in light brown leather; spine stamped in black; gold edges; no dust jacket. Illustrations in color and black and white by Philippe Druillet. Two thousand numbered copies; 1-190 each have an original illustration by Druillet, who also signed the books.

4. *Par delà le mur du sommeil* (1956)

  a. H. P. LOVECRAFT / PAR DELÀ / LE MUR / DU SOMMEIL / *Traduit* de l'américain par / JACQUES PAPY / PRÉSENCE DU FUTUR / ÉDITIONS DENOËL / 19, rue Amélie, Paris—7ᵉ [colophon page:] 19 October 1956

    Perfect-bound: [1-9] 10-22 [23-25] 26-49 [50-53] 54-80 [81-83] 84-105 [106-09] 110-19 [120] 121-52 [153] 154-80 [181] 182-204 [205] 206-37 [238-40]

    [1-2]: blank; [3]: half-title; [4]: blank; [5]: title; [6]: copyright page; [7]: half-title to following story (similarly for succeeding works); [8]: blank; [9]-22: "Par delà le mur du

sommeil" (BWS); [23]: half-title; [24]: blank; [25]-49: "Les
Rats dans les murs" (RW); [50]: blank; [51]: half-title; [52]:
blank; [53]-80: "Le Monstre sur le seuil" (TD); [81]: half-
title; [82]: blank; [83]-105: "Celui qui hantait les ténèbres"
(HD); [106]: blank; [107]: half-title to CDW and quotation
from Borellus; [108]: blank; [109]-237: *L'Affaire Charles Dexter
Ward* (CDW); [238]: blank; [239]: contents list; [240]:
colophon.
    Bound in paper; 18 × 12.3 cm.
    Notes. Présence du futur No. 16.

b.1.   *Second(?) Edition*. Paris: Éditions Denoël, 5 June 1970.
       219[+5] pp. Dust jacket over paper covers bears title "La
       Malédiction d'Arkham" (the French adaptation of the film,
       The Haunted Palace, based upon CDW) and a photograph of
       a scene from the film.

b.2.   *Reprint*. Paris: Éditions Denoël, 20 February 1975. No
       dust jacket.

b.3.   *Reprint*. Paris: Éditions Denoël, 9 January 1978.

5. *El color que cayó del cielo* (1957)

a.1.   h. p. lovecraft / el color / que cayó / del
       cielo / [publisher's device] / ediciones /
       minotauro / buenos aires [colophon page:]
       20 March 1957

           [1-2]¹⁶ [3]⁸ [4-5]¹⁶ [6]⁸ [7-8]¹⁶ [9]⁸ [10-11]¹⁶ [12]⁸ [1-6] 7-
       55 [56] 57-185 [186] 187-315 [316-20]
           [1-2]: blank; [3]: half-title; [4]: blank; [5]: title; [6]:
       copyright page; 7-14: "Prólogo," by Ricardo Gosseyn; 15-
       55: "El llamado de Cthulhu" (CC); [56]: blank; 57-96: "El
       color que cayó del cielo" (CS); 97-185: "El que susurraba
       en las tinieblas" (WD); [186]: blank; 187-315: *En las
       montañas alucinantes* (ATMOM); [316]: blank; [317]:
       contents list; [318]: blank; [319]: colophon; [320]: blank.
           Bound in paper; 19.8 × 11.5 cm.
           Notes. Translations by Ricardo Gosseyn.

a.2.   *Second Printing*. Not seen. Dated July 1964.

b.1.   *Second Edition*. Buenos Aires: Ediciones Minotauro, 5 April
       1974. 261[+7] pp. Cover art by Domingo Ferreira.

b.2.   *Second Printing*. Buenos Aires: Ediciones Minotauro,
       10 June 1975.

6. *Os mortos podem voltar* (1958?)

H. P. LOVECRAFT / OS MORTOS / PODEM
VOLTAR / [ornament] / TRADUÇÃO DE / SILAS
CERQUEIRA / [rectangular rule around all the
above] / [publisher's device] / 103 [copyright page:]
Livros do Brasil Lda. . . . Lisboa

[1]⁶ 2-6¹⁶ 7⁸ [1-8] 9-22 [23-24] 25-67 [68-70] 71-107 [108-10]
111-42 [143-44] 145-92 [193-96] [I-II] III-IX [X-XII]

[1]: blurb; [2]: list of books by the publishers; [3]: title; [4]:
copyright page; [5]: quotation from Borellus; [6]: blank; [7]:
half-title to Part I; [8]: blank; 9-22: Part I of CDW; [23]: half-
title to Part II; [24]: blank; 25-67: Part II; [68]: blank; [69]: half-
title to Part III; [70]: blank; 71-107: Part III; [108]: blank; [109]:
half-title to Part IV; [110]: blank; 111-42: Part IV; [143]: half-
title to Part V; [144]: blank; 145-[93]: Part V; [194]: blank;
[195]: publisher's note; [196]: blank; [I]: title page to excerpts
from George Simenon's *O Revólver de Maigret* (tr. L. de Almeida
Campos); [II]: blank; III-[X]: excerpts from the novel; [XI-XII]:
blank.

Bound in paper; 16.1 × 10.8 cm.; cover art by Cândido Costa
Pinto.

Notes. The book is not dated, but was probably published ca.
1958. "Collecção Vampiro" No. 103 (Simenon's novel is No.
104). Presumably excerpts of CDW were printed in the
previous volume (No. 102), but this has not been located.

7. *Je suis d'ailleurs* (1961)

a.1. *H. P. LOVECRAFT / Je suis d'ailleurs / Nouvelles
traduites* par Yves Rivière / DENOËL [copyright
page:] Paris . . . 1961

[1]¹⁶ 2-5¹⁶ [6]¹⁶ 7¹⁶ [1-7] 8-17 [18-19] 20-32 [33] 34-46
[47] 48-61 [62-63] 64-75 [76-77] 78-116 [117] 118-28
[129] 130-42 [143] 144-63 [164-65] 166-83 [184-85] 186-
216 [217-24]

[1]: series title; [2]: blank; [3]: half-title; [4]: other books
from the publisher; [5]: title; [6]: copyright page; [7]-17:
"Je suis d'ailleurs" (O); [18]: blank; [19]-32: "La Musique
d'Erich Zann" (MEZ); [33]-46: "L'Indicible" (U); [47]-61:

"Air froid" (CA); [62]: blank; [63]-75: "Le Molosse" (H);
[76]: blank; [77]-116: "La Maison maudite" (SH); [117]-28:
"La Tourbière hantée" (MB); [129]-42: "Arthur Jermyn"
(FAJ); [143]-63: "Le Modèle de Pickman" (PM); [164]:
blank; [165]-83: "La Cité sans nom" (NC); [184]: blank;
[185]-216: "La Peur qui rôde" (LF); [217]: half-title to
contents list; [218]: blank; [219]: contents list; [220]:
blank; [221]: advertisements; [222-24]: blank.

Bound in paper; 17.9 × 11.4 cm.

Notes. Printed on 5 February 1961 (see colophon).
Présence du futur No. 45.

a.2. *Reprint.* Paris: Éditions Denoël, 10 March 1971.

a.3. *Reprint.* Paris: Éditions Denoël, 21 June 1976.

8. *12 grusel Stories* (1965)

12 / GRUSEL STORIES / von / H. P.
Lovecraft / [publisher's device] / WILHELM
HEYNE VERLAG / MÜNCHEN [copyright page:]
1965

Perfect-bound: [1-6] 7-17 [18] 19-26 [27] 28-39 [40] 41-66
[67] 68-89 [90] 91-137 [138] 139-46 [147] 148-210 [211] 212-14
[215] 216-41 [242] 243-95 [296] 297-301 [302-04]

[1]: publisher's note and device; [2]: list of books from the
publisher; [3]: title; [4]: copyright page; [5]: contents list; [6]:
blank; 7-[18]: "H. P. Lovecraft und sein Werk" ("H. P. Lovecraft
and His Work"), by August Derleth; 19-[27]: "In der Gruft"
(IV); 28-[40]: "Pickmans Modell" (PM); 41-[67]: "Die Farbe aus
dem All" (CS); 68-[90]: "Der dunkle Alptraum" (HD); 91-98:
"Das Bild in dem Haus" (PH); 99-[138]: "Der Schrecken von
Dunwich" (DH); 139-[47]: "Kuhle Lüft" (CA); 148-[211]: "Das
Flüstern im Dunkeln" (WD); 212-[15]: "Der schreckliche Alte"
(TOM); 216-[42]: "Das Ding auf der Schwelle" (TD); 243-[96]:
"Der Schatten über Innsmouth" (SOI); 297-[203]: "Der
Aussenseiter" (O); [303-04]: advertisements.

Bound in paper; 19.4 × 13.6 cm.

Notes. Translations by Wulf H. Bergner. Text printed in two
columns on each page. Heyne-Anthologie No. 12.

9. *Le montagne della follia* (1966)

a. H. P. Lovecraft / LE MONTAGNE DELLA

FOLLIA / due romanzi / e / due
raconti / SUGAR [publisher's device] EDITORE
[colophon page:] Milan . . . January 1966

[1-20]⁸ [21]² [1-8] 9-130 [131-32] 133-276 [277-78] 279-
309 [310-12] 313-19 [320-24]

[1-2]: blank; [3]: series title; [4]: copyright page; [5]: title;
[6]: blank; [7]: half-title to following story (similarly for
succeeding works); [8]: blank; 9-130: *Le montagne della follia*
(ATMOM); [131]: half-title; [132]: blank; 133-276: *Il caso di
Charles Dexter Ward* (CDW); [277]: half-title; [278]: blank;
279-309: "La casa sfuggita" (SH); [310]: blank; [311]: half-
title; [312]: blank; 313-19: "La dichiarazione di Randolph
Carter" (SRC); [320]: blank; [321]: contents list; [322]:
blank; [323]: list of books from the publisher; [324]:
colophon.

Bound in green cloth; spine stamped in black; 21.4 × 13.8
cm.; dust jacket art by Angelo Torres.

Notes. Translations by Giovanni De Luca. Most of the
edition was bound in paper covers, with cover art different
from the hardcover dust jacket. I giorni No. 15.

b. *Second Edition*. Milan: Longanesi & C., November 1974.
339[+9] pp. I Libri Pocket Italiani No. 480.

10. *I mostri all'angolo della strada* (1966)

a.1. H. P. Lovecraft / I MOSTRI [in
red] / ALL'ANGOLO DELLA STRADA [in
red] / a cura di / Carlo Fruttero   Franco
Lucentini / ARNOLDO MONDADORI
EDITORE [copyright page:] Verona . . . I
edition June 1966

[1-28]⁸ [1-7] 8-13 [14-19] 20-24 [25-27] 28-35 [36] 37-47
[48] 49-57 [58-61] 62-89 [90-93] 94-96 [97] 98-100 [101]
102-04 [105] 106-08 [109] 110-12 [113] 114-16 [117] 118-
20 [121] 122-24 [125] 126-33 [134-37] 138-89 [190-93]
194-203 [204] 205-17 [218] 219-33 [234] 235-61 [262-65]
266-88 [289-91] 292-310 [311-13] 314-22 [323-25] 326-27
[328-33] 334-39 [340-43] 344-51 [352-55] 356-60 [361]
362 [363] 364-67 [368] 369-72 [373] 374-76 [377-79] 380-

99 [400-03] 404-12 [413-15] 416-23 [424-27] 428-39 [440-48]

[1-2]: blank; [3]: title; [4]: copyright page; [5]: half-title to introduction; [6]: blank; [7]-13: "Introduzione: Storia della storie di Lovecraft" by Fruttero and Lucentini; [14]: blank; [15]: half-title to Part I; [16]: blank; [17]: half-title to following story (similarly for succeeding works); [18]: original title and name of translator (hereafter abbreviated as "o.t., tr."); [19]-24: "Dagon" (tr. Maria Luisa Bonfanti); [25]: half-title; [26]: o.t., tr.; [27]-57: "Il richiamo di Cthulhu" (CC; tr. Elena Linfossi); [58]: blank; [59]: half-title; [60]: o.t., tr.; [61]-89: "Il colore venuto dallo spazio" (CS; tr. Sarah Cantoni); [90]: blank; [91]: half-title; [92]: o.t., tr.; [93]-133: "L'orrore di Dunwich" (DH; tr. Floriana Bossi); [134]: blank; [135]: half-title; [136]: o.t., tr.; [137]-89: "Colui che susurrava nelle tenebre" (WD; tr. Cantoni); [190]: blank; [191]: half-title; [192]: o.t., tr.; [193]-261: "La maschera di Innsmouth" (SOI; tr. Cantoni); [262]: blank; [263]: half-title; [264]: o.t., tr.; [265]-88: "La cosa sulla soglia" (TD; tr. Bonfanti); [289]: half-title; [290]: o.t., tr.; [291]-310: "L'abitatore del buio" (HD; tr. Bonfanti); [311]: half-title; [312]: o.t., tr.; [313]-22: "La finestra della soffita" ("The Gable Window" [by August Derleth; see I-E-i-10]; tr. Bonfanti); [323]: half-title; [324]: o.t., tr.; [325]-27: "Nyarlathotep" (tr. Bonfanti); [328]: blank; [329]: half-title to Part II; [330]: blank; [331]: half-title; [332]: o.t., tr.; [333]-39: "L'estraneo" (O; tr. Bonfanti); [340]: blank; [341]: half-title; [342]: o.t., tr.; [343]-51: "La musica di Erich Zann" (MEZ; tr. Bonfanti); [352]: blank; [353]: half-title; [354]: o.t., tr.; [355]-76: "Herbert West, reanimatore" (HWB; tr. Bonfanti); [377]: half-title; [378]: o.t., tr.; [379]-99: "I ratti nel muro" (RW; tr. Bonfanti); [400]: blank; [401]: half-title; [402]: o.t., tr.; [403]-12: "Nella cripta" (IV; tr. Ludovico Terzi); [413]: half-title; [414]: o.t., tr.; [415]-23: "Aria fredda" (CA; tr. Bonfanti); [424]: blank; [425]: half-title; [426]: o.t., tr.; [427]-39: "Il modello di Pickman" (PM; tr. Roberto Mauro); [440]: blank; [441]: half-title to contents list; [442]: blank; [443]: contents list; [444]:

blank; [445-46]: additional copyright pages; [447]: blank; [448]: colophon.

Bound in black cloth; spine stamped in white; 21.6 × 15.8 cm.; cover art by Karel Thole.

a.2. *Second Printing.* Verona: Arnoldo Mondadori, April 1974. New dust jacket. P. [448] blank.

11. *Obras escogidas (I)* (1966)

a.1. H. P. LOVECRAFT / OBRAS ESCOGIDAS / EDICIONES ACERVO / Apartado 5319 / BARCELONA [copyright page:] 1966

[1]⁸ 2-28⁸ [1-5] 6-9 [10-11] 12-15 [26-27] 28-37 [38-39] 40-68 [69] 70-79 [80-81] 82-118 [119] 120-232 [233] 234-42 [243] 244-90 [291] 292-427 [428-40]

[1]: half-title; [2]: blank; [3]: title; [4]: copyright page; [5]-9: "H. P. Lovecraft y su obra," by [José A. Llorens Borrás?]; [10]: blank; [11]-25: "El modelo de Pickman" (PM); [26]: blank; [27]-37: "La tumba" (T); [38]: blank; [39]-68: "La casa encantada" (SH); [69]-79: "Arthur Jermyn" (FAJ); [80]: blank; [81]-118: "Los sueños en la casa de la bruja" (DWH); [119]-232: *En las montañas de la locura* (ATMOM); [233]-42: "En la cripta" (IV); [243]-90: "El horror de Dunwich" (DH); [291]-427: *El caso de Charles Dexter Ward* (CDW); [428]: blank; [429]: contents list; [430]: blank; [431-34]: advertisements; [435]: colophon; [436-40]: blank.

Bound in green, red, and gold cloth; spine stamped in gold; 20.2 × 14.6 cm.; white dust jacket.

Notes. Selection is by José A. Llorens Borrás; translations by José M. Aroca.

a.2. *Second Printing.* Barcelona: Ediciones Acervo, 1975. Subtitle added: "(Primera Seleccion)" (see II-A-44).

12. *O que sussurrava nas trevas* (1966)

h. p. lovecraft / o que / sussurrava / nas trevas / *Tradução de* / GEORGE GURJAN / EDIÇÕES G R D / RIO DE JANEIRO—GB / 1966

[1]¹⁰ 2-9⁸ [1-6] 7-39 [40-41] 42-111 [112-13] 114-43 [144-48]

[1-2]: blank; [3]: half-title and publisher's device; [4]: other books from the publisher; [5]: title; [6]: copyright page; 7-39: "O chamado de Cthulhu" (CC); [40]: blank; [41]-111: "O que sussurrava nas trevas" (WD); [112]: blank; [113]-43: "A côr que vieo de espaço" (CS); [144]: blank; [145]: contents list; [146]: blank; [147]: colophon; [148]: blank.

Bound in paper; 18.6 × 13.4 cm.

Notes. Literatura fantástica No. 3.

13. *La casa delle streghe* (1967)

a. H. P. Lovecraft / LA CASA / DELLE STREGHE / e altri raconti / SUGAR [publisher's device] EDITORE [colophon page:] Milan . . . April 1967

   1-21⁸ [1-8] 9-71 [72-74] 75-95 [96-98] 99-164 [165-66] 167-337 [338-40]

   [1-2]: blank; [3]: series title: "Week-end / 17"; [4]: copyright page; [5]: title; [6]: blank; [7]: half-title to following story (similarly for succeeding works); [8]: name of original title (similarly for succeeding works); 9-71: "La casa delle streghe" (DWH); [72]: blank; [73]: half-title; [74]: original title; 75-95: "La chiave d'argento" (SK); [96]: blank; [97]: half-title; [98]: original title; 99-164: "Attraverso le porte della chiave d'argento" (TGSK); [165]: half-title; [166]: original title; 167-337: *Il mirraggio dello sconosciuto Kadath* (DQ); [338]: blank; [339]: contents list and colophon; [340]: advertisements.

   Bound in paper; 21.4 × 13.5 cm.

   Notes. Translations by Giovanni De Luca.

b.1. *Second Edition.* Milan: Longanesi & C., July 1974. 229[+7] pp. I Libri Pocket Italiani No. 457.

b.2. *Second Printing.* Milan: Longanesi & C., May 1977. Cover art (different from above) by O. Berni.

14. *Macabere Verhalen* (1967)

a.1, 2. The first (1967) and second (date unknown) printings of this book not seen. Described below are later printings.

a.3. H. J. [sic] LOVECRAFT / MACABERE

VERHALEN / [publisher's device] UITGEVERIJ
CONTACT   AMSTERDAM [copyright
page:] First printing 1967 / Third printing 1973

Perfect-bound: [1-4] 5-80 77-80 81-118 [119-20]
[1]: half-title; [2]: list of books from the publisher; [3]:
title; [4]: copyright page; 5-40: "De kleur uit de ruimte"
(CS); 41-70: "De bezoeker uit de duisternis" (HD); 71-77:
"Dagon"; 78-80: beginning of "Het onzienbare" (FB); 77:
last page of "Dagon"; 78-87: "Het onzienbare"; 88-101:
"Hij" (He); 102-18: "De tempel" (Te); [119]: contents list;
[120]: blank.

Bound in paper; 20.2 × 12.5 cm.; cover design by
Herbert Binneweg.

Notes. Translations by Jean A. Schalekamp. In all copies
seen pp. 77-80 were printed twice.

a.4. *Fourth Printing.* Amsterdam: Uitgeverij Contact, 1974.
Author's name on the title page has been corrected. Pp.
77-80 not printed twice.

15. *Cthulhu: Gespenstergeschichten* (1968)

Cthulhu / Gespenstergeschichten / von H. P.
Lovecraft / Deutsch von H. C. Artmann / Vorwort
von Giorgio Manganelli / Leseesemplar / Insel
Verlag [copyright page:] Frankfurt am
Main . . . 1968

Perfect-bound: [1-4] 5-27 [28] 29-66 [67] 68-81 [82-84]
[1]: publisher's device; [2]: blank; [3]: title; [4]: copyright page;
5-[28]: "Pickmans Modell" (PM); 29-[67]: "Der leuchtende
Trapezoeder" (HD); 68-[82]: "Die Musik des Erich Zann"
(MEZ); [83-84]: blank.

Bound in paper; 19 × 11.3 cm.; dust jacket as for A-16.

Notes. A review copy (part of II-A-16) sent out by the
publisher.

16. *Cthulhu: Geistergeschichten* (1968)

a. Cthulhu / Geistergeschichten von H. P.
Lovecraft / Deutsch von H. C. Artmann /
Vorwort von Giorgio Manganelli / Insel Verlag

[copyright page:] Frankfurt am Main . . . 1968

[1-15]⁸ [1-4] 5-13 [14] 15-123 [124] 125-91 [192] 193-238 [239-44]

[1]: publisher's device; [2]: blank; [3]: title; [4]: copyright page; 5-13: "Vorwort" by Manganelli; [14]: blank; 15-38: "Pickmans Modell" (PM); 39-71: "Die Ratten im Gemäuer" (RW); 72-85: "Die Musik des Erich Zann" (MEZ); 86-[124]: "Der leuchtende Trapezoeder" (HD); 125-[92]: "Das Grauen von Dunwich" (DH); 193-[239]: "Cthulhus Ruf" (CC); [240]: blank; [241]: contents list; [242]: additional copyright page; [243-44]: blank.

Bound in black-and-white cloth; spine stamped in blue and black; 19.1 × 12.1 cm.; dust jacket art by Heinz Edelmann.

Notes. Foreword translated from the Italian by Gerald Bisinger.

b.1. *Second Edition.* Berlin: Suhrkamp, 1972. 238[+18] pp. Cover by Hans Ulrich and Ute Osterwalder. Suhrkamp Taschenbuch No. 29.

b.2. *Second Printing.* Berlin: Suhrkamp, 1972.

b.3. *Third Printing.* Not seen.

b.4. *Fourth Printing.* Berlin: Suhrkamp, 1977. Part of the "Phantastiche Bibliothek" series (No. 19).

17. *En las montañas de la locura* (1968)

a.1. First printing (1968) not seen. Later printings described below.

a.2. H. P. LOVECRAFT / EN LAS MONTAÑAS / DE LA LOCURA / [publisher's device] / BIBLIOTECA BREVE / EDITORIAL SEIX BARRAL, S. A. / BARCELONA [copyright page:] Second printing: 1973

[1]⁸ 2-11⁸ 12² [1-6] 7-175 [176-80]

[1-2]: blank; [3]: half-title; [4]: blank; [5]: title; [6]: copyright page; 7-175: *En las montañas de la locura* (ATMOM); [176]: blank; [177]: colophon; [178-80]: blank.

Bound in paper; 19.6 × 12.6 cm.; grey paper dust jacket (with illustration by Bosch).

Notes. Translation by Calvert Casey; 3,000 copies. Actually published January 1974 (see colophon).

a.3. *Third Printing.* Barcelona: Editorial Seix Barral, March 1975. Dust jacket design of above reproduced here on the paper covers.

a.4. *Fourth Printing.* Barcelona: Editorial Seix Barral, March 1977.

18. *Het gefluister in de duisternis* (1968)

a. Howard Phillips Lovecraft / Het gefluister in de duisternis / GRIEZELVERHALEN / [publisher's device] / A. W. Bruna & Zoon   Utrecht/ Antwerpen [copyright page:] 1968

Perfect-bound: [1-6] 7-185 [186] 187-89 [190-92]
[1]: half-title; [2]: publisher's note; [3]: title; [4]: copyright page; [5]: contents list; [6]: illustration by Frank Utpatel (from I-A-35, p. 114); 7-9: "Tot ziens in de maalstroom van Azathoth," by Aart C. Prins; 10-29: "De visioenen van Richard Pickman" (PM); 30-73: "De lokroep van Cthulhu" (CC); 73-84: "De muziek van Erich Zann" (MEZ); 85-94: "De buitenstaander" (O); 95-185: "Het gefluister in de duisternis" (WD); [186]: blank; 187-89: "De verboden boeken van H. P. Lovecraft" by Prins; [190]: blank; [191-92]: advertisements.
Bound in paper; 17.5 × 11.4 cm.; cover art by Dick Bruna.
Notes. Translations by R. Germeraad. Zwarte Beertjes No. 1166.

b. *Second Edition.* Utrecht and Antwerp: A. W. Bruna, 1975. Contains new afterword by Prins; preface eliminated. Cover art by Bob van Blommestein. Bruna Fantasy & Horror No. 24.

19. *Heksensabbat* (1969)

HOWARD PHILLIPS / LOVECRAFT / *Heksensabbat* / griezelverhalen / [publisher's device] / A. W. Bruna   Utrecht/Antwerp [copyright page:] 1969

Perfect-bound: [1-6] 7-158 [159-60]
[1]: half-title; [2]: publisher's note; [3]: title; [4]: copyright

page; [5]: contents list; [6]: illustration by Frank Utpatel (from I-A-35, p. 128); 7-16: "Koelte" (CA); 17-63: "Heksensabbat" (DWH); 64-78: "Het maanmoeras" (MB); 75-81: "De verklaring van Randolph Carter" (SRC); 82-89: "De hund" (H); 90-158: "De schaduw uit de tijd" (SOOT); [159-60]: "De 'verboden' boeken van H. P. Lovecraft," by Aart C. Prins.

  Bound in paper; 17.5 × 11.5 cm.; cover art by Dick Bruna.
  Notes. Translations by C. A. G. van der Broek. Zwarte Beertjes No. 1298.

20. *Das Ding auf der Schwelle* (1969)

  a.1. H. P. Lovecraft / Das Ding / auf der Schwelle / Unheimliche Geschichten / Insel Verlag [copyright page:] Frankfurt am Main . . . 1969

   [1-13]⁸ [14]⁴ [1-4] 5-213 [214-16]
   [1]: publisher's devices; [2]: blank; [3]: title; [4]: copyright page; 5-39: "Das Ding auf der Schwelle" (TD); 40-47: "Der Aussenseiter" (O); 48-84: "Die Farbe aus dem All" (CS); 85-113: "Träume im Hexenhaus" (DWH); 132-[214]: "Der Schatten aus der Zeit" (SOOT); [215]: contents list; [216]: additional copyright page.

   Bound in black cloth; spine stamped in white; 21.2 × 12.3 cm.; dust jacket art and design by Hans Ulrich and Ute Osterwalder.

   Notes. Translations by Rudolf Hermstein. Paper tinted light green. Part of the Bibliothek des Hauses Usher series.

  a.2. *Second Printing.* Frankfurt am Main: Insel Verlag, 1973.

  b.1. *Second Edition.* Berlin: Suhrkamp, 1976. 210[+14] pp. Contains an afterword by Kalju Kirde. Cover design by Willy Fleckhaus and Rolf Staudt. Suhrkamp Taschenbuch 357.

  b.2. *Second Printing.* Not seen. Dated 1977.

21. *Épouvante et surnaturel en littérature* (1969)
   H. P. LOVECRAFT / ÉPOUVANTE ET / SURNATUREL / EN LITTÉRATURE /

(Supernatural Horror in Literature) / traduit de
l'américain / par J. BERGIER et F. TRUCHAUD /
CHRISTIAN BOURGOIS EDITEUR [copyright
page:] Paris . . . 1969

[1]¹⁶ 2-5¹⁶ 6⁸ [1-6] 7 [8] 9-33 [34] 35-40 [41-42] 43-48 [49-50]
51-59 [60] 61-67 [68] 69-79 [80] 81-88 [89-90] 91-100 [101-02]
103-22 [123-24] 125-37 [138] 139-63 [164-76]

[1-2]: blank; [3]: half-title; [4]: blank; [5]: title; [6]: copyright
page; 7-[8]: "Note" by Truchaud (d'après August Derleth); 9-
[34]: "H. P. Lovecraft et la creation fantastique" by Truchaud;
35-[41], 43-[49], 51-[89], 91-[101], 103-[64]: SHiL; [42, 50, 90,
102, 124]: blank; [165]: half-title to contents list; [166]: blank;
[167]: contents list; [168]: blank; [169]: colophon; [170]: blank;
[171-72]: list of books edited by Bergier and Truchaud; [173-
76]: blank.

Bound in paper; 20.2 × 12 cm.

22. *Dagon et autres récits de terreur* (1969)

a. H. P. LOVECRAFT / DAGON / ET AUTRES
RÉCITS DE TERREUR / Préface
de / FRANCOIS TRUCHAUD / Traduction
de / PAULE PÉREZ / ÉDITIONS PIERRE
BELFOND / 10, rue du Regard / PARIS—VIᵉ
[copyright page:] 1969

[1-11]¹⁶ [1-7] 8-14 [15] 16-21 [22-23] 24-35 [36-37] 38-41
[42-43] 44-49 [50-51] 52-58 [59] 60-62 [63] 64-69 [70] 71-79
[80-81] 82-95 [96-97] 98-101 [102-03] 104-08 [109] 110-16
[117] 118-51 [152-53] 154-61 [162-63] 164-72 [173] 174-200
[201] 202-12 [213] 214-37 [238-39] 240-49 [250-51] 252-81
[282-83] 284-87 [288-89] 290-94 [295] 296-304 [305] 306-12
[313] 314-19 [320-21] 322-29 [330-31] 332 [333] 334-37
[338-39] 340-41 [342-43] 344-45 [346-47] 348 [349-52]

[1-2]: blank; [3]: half-title; [4]: blank; [5]: title; [6]:
copyright page; [7]-14: "H. P. Lovecraft ou: Dire
l'invincible" by Truchaud; [15]-21: "Dagon"; [22]: blank;
[23]-35: "La Tombe" (T); [36]: blank; [37]-41: "Polaris"; [42]:
blank; [43]-49: "La Malédiction de Sarnath" (DS); [50]:
blank; [51]-62: "Le Bateau blanc" (WS); [63]-69: "Celephais";

[70]: blank; [71]-79: "De l'au-dela" (FB); [80]: blank; [81]-95:
"Le Temple" (Te); [96]: blank; [97]-101: "L'Arbre" (Tr);
[102]: blank; [103]-08: "Les Autres Dieux" (OG); [109]-16:
"La Quête d'Iranon" (QI); [117]-51: "Herbert West,
réanimateur" (HWR); [152]: blank; [153]-61: "Hypnos";
[162]: blank; [163]-72: "Le Festival" (F); [173]-200:
"Prisonnier des Pharaohs" (UP); [201]-12: "Lui" (He); [213]-
37: "Horreur à Red Hook" (HRH); [238]: blank; [239]-49:
"L'Etrange Maison haute dans la brume" (SHH); [250]:
blank; [251]-81: "Dans les murs d'Eryx" (IWE); [282]: blank;
[283]-87: "Le Clergyman maudit" (EC); [288]: blank; [289]-
94: "La Bête de la caverne" (BC); [295]-304: "L'Alchemiste"
(A); [305]-12: "La Poésie et les dieux" (PG); [313]-19: "La
Rue" (S); [320]: blank; [321]-29: "La Transition de Juan
Romero" (TJR); [330]: blank; [331]-32: "Azathoth"; [333]-37:
"Le Descendant" (De); [338]: blank; [339]-42: "Le Livre" (B);
[343]-45: "La Chose dans le clarté lunaire" (TM); [346]:
blank; [347]-48: contents list; [349]: colophon; [350-52]:
blank.

Bound in paper; 24.2 × 16.3 cm.

Notes. Actually published on 15 January 1970 (see
colophon).

b.1. *Second Edition.* Paris: Éditions J'ai Lu, 1972. 433[+5] pp. "Les
Chats d'Ulthar" (CU) has been added, Truchaud's preface
deleted. Cover art by Tibor Csernus. J'ai Lu No. 459.

b.2. *Reprint.* Paris: Éditions J'ai Lu, 1973.

b.3. *Reprint.* Paris: Éditions J'ai Lu, 20 April 1978. New front
cover art by Philippe Druillet.

23. *Berge des Wahnsinns* (1970)

a. H. P. Lovecraft / Berge des Wahnsinns / Zwei
Horrorgeschichten / Insel Verlag [copyright
page:] Frankfurt am Main . . . 1970

[1]⁴ [2-15]⁸ [1-4] 5-138 [139] 140-223 [224-28]
[1]: publisher's devices; [2]: blank; [3]: title; [4]: copyright
page; [5]-139: *Berge des Wahnsinns* (ATMOM); 140-[224]:
"Der Flüsterer im Dunkeln" (WD); [225]: contents list;
[226]: blank; [227]: additional copyright page; [228]: blank.

Bound in black cloth; spine stamped in white; 21.4 × 12.2

cm.; dust jacket art and design by Hans Ulrich and Ute Osterwalder.

Notes. Translations by Rudolf Hermstein. Paper tinted light green. Part of the Bibliothek des Hauses Usher series.

b.1. *Second Edition.* Berlin: Suhrkamp, 1975. 214[+10] pp. Cover design by Willy Fleckhaus and Rolf Staudt. Suhrkamp Taschenbuch No. 220.

b.2. *Second Printing.* Berlin: Suhrkamp, 1975.

24. *Der Fall Charles Dexter Ward* (1971)

a. H. P. Lovecraft / Der Fall / Charles Dexter Ward / Zwei Horrorgeschichten / Insel Verlag [copyright page:] Frankfurt am Main . . . 1971

[1-16]⁸ [1-4] 5-166 [167] 168-250 [251-56]

[1]: publisher's devices; [2]: blank; [3]: title; [4]: copyright page; 5-[167]: *Der Fall Charles Dexter Ward* (CDW); 168-[251]: "Schatten über Innsmouth" (SOI); [255]: additional copyright page; [256]: blank.

Bound in black cloth; spine stamped in white; 21.4 × 12.2 cm.; dust jacket art and design by Hans Ulrich and Ute Osterwalder.

Notes. Translations by Rudolf Hermstein. Paper tinted light green. Part of the Bibliothek des Hauses Usher series.

b.1. *Second Edition.* Berlin: Surhkamp, 1977. Afterword by Marek Wydmuch added. Cover design by Willy Fleckhaus and Rolf Staudt. Suhrkamp Taschenbuch No. 391.

b.2. *Second Printing.* Not seen. Dated 1978.

25. *El caso de Charles Dexter Ward* (1971)

a.1. EL CASO DE / CHARLES DEXTER WARD / H. P. LOVECRAFT / [publisher's device] / BARRAL EDITORES / BARCELONA / 1971

[1]¹⁶ 2-5¹⁶ [1-6] 7-111 [112] 113-55 [156-68]

[1]: publisher's device; [2]: blank; [3]: half-title; [4]: blank; [5]: title; [6]: copyright page; 7-111, 113-55: text (CDW); [112, 156]: blank; [157]: half-title to contents list; [158]: blank; [159]: contents list; [160]: blank; [161]:

colophon; [162]: blank; [163-66]: advertisements; [167-68]:
blank.

Bound in paper; 18.6 × 11.5 cm.; cover art and design
by José Miguel Tola.

Notes. Published in April 1971 (cf. colophon).
Translations by José Maria Aroca.

a.2. *Second Printing.* Barcelona: Barral Editores, 1977. New
cover art.

b. *First Argentine Printing.* Buenos Aires: Barral Editores, 15
April 1974.

26. *Viajes al otro mundo* (1971)

a.1. First printing (1971) not seen. Description of second
printing follows.

a.2. Howard Phillips Lovecraft / E. Hoffmann
Price / y Thomas Owen: / Viajes al otro
mundo / (Ciclo de aventuras oníricas de
Randolph Carter) / Edición al cuidado de Rafael
Llopis / El Libro de Bolsillo / Alianza
Editorial / Madrid / [publisher's device, to the
right of last three lines] [copyright page:]
second edition: 1973

Perfect-bound: [1-6] 7-205 [206] 207 [208]

[1-2]: blank; [3]: half-title; [4]: publisher's note; [5]: title;
[6]: copyright page; 7-24: "Introducción: En busca del
paraíso perdido" by Llopis; 25-32: "La declaración de
Randolph Carter" (SRC); 32-45: "La llave de plata" (SK);
46-86: "A través de las puertas de la llava de plata"
(TGSK); 87-203: *En busca de la ciudad del sol poniente* (DQ);
204-05: "Testimonio" ("Témoignage" [fiction]), by
Thomas Owen; [206]: blank; 207: contents list; [208]:
blank.

Bound in paper; 18 × 11.1 cm.

Notes. Translations by F. Torres Oliver.

27. *Épouvante et surnaturel en littérature* (1971)
ÉPOUVANTE / ET SURNATUREL / EN

LITTÉRATURE / Traduit de l'anglais par /
Bernard DA COSTA / [publisher's device] /
CHRISTIAN BOURGOIS / DOMINIQUE DE
ROUX [colophon page:] 1971

Perfect-bound: [1-8] 9-165 [166] 167-79 [180] 181-84
[185-92]

[1-4]: blank; [5]: publisher's note; [6]: blank; [7]: title; [8]:
copyright page; 9-[166]: "L'Horreur surnaturelle dans la
littérature" (SHiL); 167-[80]: "Index des noms avec
compléments biographiques"; 181-[85]: "Bibliographie des
romans et nouvelles traduits en francais et actuellement
disponibles en librarie"; [186]: blank; [187-90]: advertisements;
[191]: colophon; [192]: blank.

Bound in paper; 17.7 × 10.7 cm.; cover art by Pierre Bernard.
Notes. Part of the Union Générale d'Éditions of Christian
Bourgois.

28. *Träume im Hexenhaus* (1971)

H. P. LOVECRAFT [in red] / Träume im
Hexenhaus / Mit 6 reproduzierten
Radierungen / von Peter Collien / [publisher's
device in red] / ANABIS VERLAG / BERLIN 1971

Perfect-bound: [i-vi] 1-46 [47-56]

[i-ii]: blank; [iii]: publisher's notes; [iv]: "motto" (from Edgar
Allan Poe); [v]: title; [vi]: copyright page; 1-46: text (DWH);
[47]: blank; [48]: biographical and bibliographical notes on
Lovecraft; [49]: colophon; [50]: blank; [51-55]: advertisements;
[56]: blank.

Bound in paper; 29.1 × 20.6 cm.

Notes. Illustrations by Collien appear on the cover (detail of
the illustration facing p. 38), and facing pp. 8, 16, 24, 32, 38,
and 44. Translator not identified. Of the 470 copies, fifty
included a plate with the "Witch with Child" drawing signed by
Collien (numbered, in Roman capitals, I to L), and twenty
carried all six Collien drawings as signed plates, numbered
1/100 to 20/100 (separate plates numbered 21/100 to 100/100
could be ordered from the publisher).

29. *L'Affaire Charles Dexter Ward* (1972)

a.1. [publisher's device] / L'affaire Charles / Dexter Ward / HOWARD PHILIPS [sic] LOVECRAFT / Traduit de l'américain / par Jacques PAPY [colophon page:] 1972

> 1-6¹⁶ [1-6] 7-19 [20] 21-64 [65-66] 67-102 [103-04] 105-36 [137-38] 139-81 [181-92]
>
> [1]: half-title; [2]: list of books by Lovecraft; [3]: title; [4]: copyright page; [5]: quotation from Borellus; [6]: blank; 7-[65], 67-[103], 105-[37], 139-[82]: text (CDW); [66, 104, 138]: blank; [183-92]: advertisements.
>
> Bound in paper; 16.5 × 11.4 cm.; cover art by Alexis Oussenko.
>
> *Notes.* Published by Éditions J'ai Lu, Paris. J'ai Lu No. 410.

a.2. Reprint. Paris: Éditions J'ai Lu, 10 November 1975.

30. *De droomwereld van Kadath* (1972)

howard phillips lovecraft / [rule] / de droomwereld / van kadath / *vertaald door pé hawinkels* / [rule] / a. w. bruna & zoon   utrecht/ antwerpen [copyright page:] 1972

> Perfect-bound: [1-6] 7-9 [10-12] 13-173 [174-76]
>
> [1]: half-title; [2]: publisher's device and note; [3]: title; [4]: copyright page; [5]: contents list; [6]: illustration by Frank Utpatel (from I-A-35, p. 116); 7-9: "De droomwereld van H. P. Lovecraft," by Aart C. Prins; [10]: blank; [11]: part-title; [12]: blank; 13-173: text (DQ); [174]: blank; [175-76]: advertisements.
>
> Bound in paper; 17.5 × 11.4 cm.; cover art by Bob van Blommestein.
>
> *Notes.* Bruna Fantasy & Horror No. 1.

31. *Lovecraft kessakushu* (1972)

[LOVECRAFT KESSAKUSHU] / [ANGOKU NO HIGI] / [publisher's device] / [SODOSHA] [all the above in Japanese characters]

[1-28]⁸ [3-10] 11-445 [446-52]

[3]: title; [4]: photograph of Lovecraft; [5]: half-title; [6]: blank; [7-8]: contents list; [9]: part-title; [10]: blank; 11-19: "Kaijin Dagon" (D); 20-29: "Shiroi hansen" (WS); 30-40: "Yume no toshi Celephais" (C); 41-61: "Kaitei no chinden" (Te); 62-75: "Erich Zann no ongaku" (MEZ); 76-88: "Outsider" (O); 87-102: "Angoku no higi" (F); 103-15: "Nokanjo no nakade" (IV); 116-62: "Cthulhu no yobigoe" (CC); 163-207: "Toguchi no kaibutsu" (TD); 208-22: "Reiki" (CA); 223-322: "Chojikan no kage" (SOOT); 323-35: "Tsuki no numa" (MB); 336-98: "Kofu shosetsu no keifu" (SHiL; abridged); 399-416: "Howard Phillips Lovecraft no shogai" (biography), by Katsuo Jinka; 417-20: "Sakuhin kaisetsu" (commentary), by Jinka; 421-23: "Howard Phillips Lovecraft sakuhin list" (chronology of tales); 424-40: "Kaisetsu" (commentary), by Hiroshi Aramata; 441-43: "Atogaki" (afterword), by Jinka; 444-45: list of books from publisher; [446]: note about Jinka; [447]: colophon; [448-52]: advertisements.

Bound in black cloth; spine stamped in silver; 18.7 × 13.7 cm.; boxed in brown and white cardboard slipcase.

Notes. Published in 1972 by Sodosha, Tokyo. Translations by Katsuo Jinka.

32. *La casa encantada* (1973)

a.1. H. P. LOVECRAFT / La Casa Encantada / Editorial MERLIN [colophon page:] Buenos Aires . . . 30 March 1973

[1-4]¹⁶ [1-6] 7-71 [72] 73-126 [127-28]

[1-2]: blank; [3]: half-title; [4]: blank; [5]: title; [6]: copyright page; 7-34: "La casa encantada" (SH); 35-71: "Los sueños en la casa de la bruja" (DWH); [72]: blank; 73-118: "El horror de Dunwich" (DH); 119-26: "El extraño" (O); [127]: contents list; [128]: colophon.

Bound in paper; 19.8 × 13.8 cm.; cover art by Sergio Camporeale.

Notes. Translations by José M. Aroca. Cover prints author's name as "H. P. Lovekraft."

a.1(a) There is a variant state (perhaps a new edition) which is reset from the above. Cover design as above. Colophon

reads "30 March 1973" as does the above, but this seems
to be of later date.

33. *De bergen van de waanzin* (1973)

howard phillips lovecraft / [rule] / de bergen van de
waanzin / [rule] / a. w. bruna & zoon   utrecht/
antwerpen [copyright page:] 1973

> Perfect-bound: [1-4] 5-159 [160]
>
> [1]: half-title; [2]: publisher's device and note; [3]: title; [4]:
> copyright page; 5-159: text (ATMOM); [160]: advertisement
> for A-30.
>
> Bound in paper; 17.5 × 11.4 cm.; cover art by Bob van
> Blommestein.
>
> *Notes.* Translation by Heleen ten Holt. Bruna Fantasy en
> Horror No. 12.

34. *El color surgido del espacio* (1973)

el color / surgido / del espacio / H. P. Lovecraft /
[publisher's device] VERON | *editor* / *Barcelona - España*
[copyright page:] 1973

> Perfect-bound: [i-x] 1-83 [84] 85-95 [96] 97-175 [176] 177-
> 264 [265-78]
>
> [i-ii]: blank; [iii]: publisher's device; [iv]: blank; [v]: half-title;
> [vi]: blank; [vii]: title; [viii]: copyright page; [ix]: contents list;
> [x]: blank; 1-34: "El color surgido del espacio" (CS); 35-44: "La
> casa de las imágenes" (PH); 45-83: "El llamado de Cthulhu"
> (CC); [84]: blank; 85-95: "Aire frío" (CA); [96]: blank; 97-175:
> "El que susurraba en las tinieblas" (WD); [176]: blank; 177-80:
> "El terrible viejo" (TOM); 181-[265]: "La sombra surgida del
> tiempo" (SOOT); [266-68]: blank; [269-71, 273, 275-76]:
> advertisements; [272, 274, 277-78]: blank.
>
> Bound in paper; 17.2 × 11.7 cm.; cover art and design by
> Estudio F. Bas and J. Gracia.
>
> *Notes.* Edited by M. Salvatella and R. Zendrera.

35. *Opere complete* (1973)

a. HOWARD PHILLIPS / LOVECRAFT / opere /
complete / sugar editore &c. [copyright page:]
Milan . . . 1973

[1-30]¹⁶ [31]⁸ [1-6] 7-13 [14-16] 17-66 [67-68] 69-74 [75-76] 77-84 [85-86] 87-90 [91-92] 93-97 [98-100] 101-05 [106-08] 109-13 [114-16] 117-19 [120-22] 123-24 [125-26] 127-29 [130-32] 133-35 [136-38] 139-41 [142-44] 145-50 [151-52] 153-59 [160-62] 163-67 [168-70] 171-99 [200-02] 203-07 [208-10] 211-16 [217-18] 219-31 [232-34] 235-41 [242-44] 245-49 [250-52] 253-61 [262-64] 265-70 [271-72] 273-77 [278-80] 281-86 [287-88] 289-96 [297-98] 299-307 [308-10] 311-27 [328-30] 331-48 [349-50] 351-58 [359-60] 361-81 [382-84] 385-90 [391-92] 393-401 [402-04] 405-34 [435-36] 437-72 [473-74] 475-81 [482-84] 485-510 [511-12] 513-16 [517-18] 519-24 [525-26] 527-33 [534-36] 537-41 [542-44] 545-618 [619-20] 621-64 [665-66] 667-79 [680-82] 683-98 [699-700] 701-19 [720-22] 723-25 [726-28] 729-818 [819-20] 821-61 [862-64] 865-933 [934] 935-39 [940-44]

[1-2]: blank; [3]: half-title; [4]: copyright page; [5]: title; [6]: blank; 7-13: "Nota biografia," by August Derleth (excerpts from Chap. I of III-C-6); [14]: blank; [15]: half-title to following work (similarly for succeeding works); [16]: original title and name of translator (hereafter abbreviated as "o.t., tr."); 17-66: "L'orrore soprannaturale nella letteratura" (SHiL; tr. Alda Carrer); [67]: half-title; [68]: o.t., tr.; 69-74: "L'illustrazione nella casa" (PH; tr. Carrer); [75]: half-title; [76]: o.t., tr.; 77-84: "Oltre il muro del sonno" (BWS; tr. Carrer); [85]: half-title; [86]: o.t., tr.; 87-90: "Dagon" (tr. Maria Luisa Bonfanti); [91]: half-title; [92]: o.t., tr.; 93-97: "La nave bianca" (WS; tr. Carrer); [98]: blank; [99]: half-title; [100]: o.t., tr.; 101-05: "La dichiarazione di Randolph Carter" (SRC; tr. Giovanni De Luca); [106]: blank; [107]: half-title; [108]: o.t., tr.; 109-13: "La funesta sorte che colpì Sarnath" (DS; tr. Carrer); [114]: blank; [115]: half-title; [116]: o.t., tr.; 117-19: "I gatti di Ulthar" (CU; tr. Carrer); [120]: blank; [121]: half-title; [122]: o.t., tr.; 123-24: "Nyarlathotep" (tr. Bonfanti); [125]: half-title; [126]: o.t., tr.; 127-29: "La stella polare" (P; tr. Carrer); [130]: blank; [131]: half-title; [132]: o.t., tr.; 133-35: "Il vecchio terribile" (TOM; tr. Carrer); [136]: blank; [137]: half-title; [138]: o.t., tr.; 139-41: "L'albero" (Tr; tr. Carrer); [142]: blank; [143]: half-title; [144]: o.t.,

tr.; 145-50: "La musica di Erich Zann" (MEZ; tr.
Bonfanti); [151]: half-title; [152]: o.t., tr.; 153-59: "La
tomba di famiglia" (T; tr. Carrer); [160]: blank; [161]: half-
title; [162]: o.t., tr.; 163-67: "Celephais" (tr. Carrer); [168]:
blank; [169]: half-title; [170]: o.t., tr.; 171-82: "Herbert
West, rianimatore" (HWR; tr. Bonfanti); [183]: half-title;
[184]: o.t., tr.; 185-99: "La paura in agguato" (LF; tr.
Carrer); [200]: blank; [201]: half-title; [202]: o.t., tr.; 203-
07: "Hypnos" (tr. Carrer); [208]: blank; [209]: half-title;
[210]: o.t., tr.; 211-16: "Il cane" (H; tr. Carrer); [217]: half-
title; [218]: o.t., tr.; 219-31: "I ratti nel muro" (RW; tr.
Bonfanti); [232]: blank; [233]: half-title; [234]: o.t., tr.;
235-41: "La celebrazione" (F; tr. Carrer); [242]: blank;
[243]: half-title; [244]: o.t., tr.; 245-50: "L'innominabile"
(U; tr. Carrer); [251]: half-title; [252]: o.t., tr.; 253-61: "Il
tempio" (Te; tr. Carrer); [262]: blank; [263]: half-title;
[264]: o.t., tr.; 265-70: "Nel deposito murtuario" (IV; tr.
Carrer); [271]: half-title; [272]: o.t., tr.; 273-77:
"L'estraneo" (O; tr. Bonfanti); [278]: blank; [279]: half-
title; [280]: o.t., tr.; 281-86: "La palade lunare" (MB; tr.
Carrer); [287]: half-title; [288]: o.t., tr.; 289-96: "Lui" (He;
tr. Carrer); [297]: half-title; [298]: o.t., tr.; 299-307: "La
città senza nome" (NC; tr. Carrer); [308]: blank; [309]:
half-title; [310]: o.t., tr.; 311-27: "Orrore a Red Hook"
(HRH; tr. Maurizio Belloti); [328]: blank; [329]: half-title;
[330]: o.t., tr.; 331-48: "Il colore venuto dello spazio" (CS;
tr. Sarah Cantoni); [349]: half-title; [350]: o.t., tr.; 351-58:
"Il modello di Pickman" (PM; tr. Roberto Mauro); [359]:
half-title; [360]: o.t., tr.; 361-81: "Il richiamo di Cthulhu"
(CC; tr. Carrer); [382]: blank; [383]: half-title; [384]: o.t.,
tr.; 385-90: "Aria fredda" (CA; tr. Bonfanti); [391]: half-
title; [392]: o.t., tr.; 393-401: "La chiave d'argento" (SK;
tr. De Luca); [402]: blank; [403]: half-title; [404]: o.t., tr.;
405-34: "L'orrore di Dunwich" (DH; tr. Carrer); [435]:
half-title; [436]: o.t., tr.; 437-72: "Colui che sussurrava
nelle tenebre" (WD; tr. Cantoni); [473]: half-title; [474]:
o.t., tr.; 475-81: "La casa misteriosa appollaiata nella
nebbia" (SHH; tr. Carrer); [482]: blank; [483]: half-title;
[484]: o.t., tr.; 485-510: "La casa delle streghe" (DWH; tr.
De Luca); [511]: half-title; [512]: o.t., tr.; 513-16: "Gli altri

dei" (OG; tr. Carrer); [517]: half-title; [518]: o.t., tr.; 519-
24: "Dall'ignoto" (FB; tr. Carrer); [525]: half-title; [526]:
o.t., tr.; 527-33: "Arthur Jermyn" (FAJ; tr. Carrer); [534]:
blank; [535]: half-title; [536]: o.t., tr.; 537-41: "La ricerca
di Iranon" (QI; tr. Carrer); [542]: blank; [543]: half-title;
[544]: o.t., tr.; 545-618: *Le montagne della follia* (ATMOM; tr.
De Luca); [619]: half-title; [620]: o.t., tr.; 621-64: "L'ombre
fuori del tempo" (SOOT; tr. Carrer); [665]: half-title;
[666]: o.t., tr.; 667-79: "L'abitatore del buio" (HD; tr.
Bonfanti); [680]: blank; [681]: half-title; [682]: o.t., tr.;
683-98: "La cosa sulla soglia" (TD; tr. Bonfanti); [699]:
half-title; [700]: o.t., tr.; 701-19: "La casa sfuggita" (SH;
tr. De Luca); [720]: blank; [721]: half-title; [722]: o.t., tr.;
723-25: "Il prete malvagio" (EC; tr. Carrer); [726]: blank;
[727]: half-title; [728]: o.t., tr.; 729-818: *Il caso di Charles
Dexter Ward* (CDW; tr. De Luca); [819]: half-title; [820]:
o.t., tr.; 821-61: "La maschera di Innsmouth" (SOI; tr.
Cantoni); [862]: blank; [863]: half-title; [864]: o.t., tr.; 865-
933: *Il miraggio dello sconosciuto Kadath* (DQ; tr. De Luca);
[934]: blank; 935-36: contents list; 937-39: additional
copyright pages; [940]: blank; [941]: colophon; [942-44]:
blank.

Bound in paper; 21.2 × 15.5 cm.; cover design by
Claudio Baini.

Notes. Between pp. 448 and 449 are reproductions of 21
photographs of Lovecraft and illustrations by Lovecraft,
Philippe Druillet, Yak Rivais, Frank Utpatel, Virgil Finlay,
Hannes Bok, and Neil Austin.

b.   *Second Edition.* Milan: Sugar Edizioni, November 1978. [6] + viii
+ 7-949[+3] pp. With a new preface and bibliographic
appendixes by Giuseppe Lippi. New cover art by Spazio 3
Associati.

36. *Skräckens labyrinter* (1973)

H. P. Lovecraft / Skräckens labyrinter / Noveller i
urval av / Sam J. Lundwall / Askild & Kärnekull /
[rule] / ISBN 91 7008 141 7 [copyright page:]
Stockholm . . . 1973

[1]⁸ 2-14⁸ [1-6] 7-221 [222-24]

[1]: half-title; [2]: blank; [3]: title; [4]: copyright page; [5]: contents; [6]: blank; 7-10: "Inledning" by Lundwall; 11-22: "Hunden" (H); 23-54: "Den lurande skräcken" (LF); 55-68: "I gravkammaren" (IV); 69-113: "Färg bortom tid och rum" (CS); 114-44: "Råttorna i muren" (RW); 145-54: "Återkomsten" (O); 155-76: "Pickmans modell" (PM); 177-89: "Träsket" (MB); 190-209: "Den namnlösa staden" (NC); 210-17: "De andra gudarna" (OG); 218-[22]: "Nyarlathotep"; [223-24]: blank.

Bound in paper; 21 × 12 cm.; cover art by Tom Hultgren.

Notes. Translations by Sam J. Lundwall.

37. *Tingen på terskelen* (1973)

H. P. Lovecraft / TINGEN PÅ TERSKELEN / og andre hårreisende historier / UTVALG OG OVERSETTELSE / VED ØYVIND MYHRE OG EINAR ENGSTAD / J. W. CAPPENELS FORLAG A·S [copyright page:] Oslo . . . 1973

[1]⁸ 2-9⁸ [1-6] 7-35 [36] 37-50 [51] 52-54 [55] 56-60 [61] 62-135 [136] 137-39 [140-44]

[1]: publisher's device; [2]: list of other books by the publisher; [3]: title; [4]: copyright page; [5]: contents list; [6]: blank; 7-[36]: "Tingen på terskelen" (TD); 37-[51]: "Pickmans modell" (PM); 52-[55]: "Ulthars katter" (CU); 56-[61]: "De andre gudene" (OG); 62-[136]: "Hrisk i mørket" (WD); 137-[40]: "Etterord" (afterword) by Myhre; [141-44]: blank.

Bound in paper; 18.6 × 12.3 cm.; cover art by Omar Andréen.

Notes. Edited and translated by Øyvind Myhre and Einar Engstad. Ugelbøkene No. 86.

38. *Stadt ohne Namen* (1973)

H. P. Lovecraft / Stadt ohne Namen / Horrorgeschichten / Insel Verlag [copyright page:] Frankfurt am Main . . . 1973

[1-16]⁸ [1-4] 5-19 [20] 21-26 [27] 28-36 [37] 38-48 [49] 50-59 [60] 61-87 [88] 89-98 [99] 100-37 [138] 139-54 [155] 156-68 [169] 170-95 [196] 197-207 [208] 209-11 [212] 213-47 [248-56]

[1]: publisher's devices; [2]: blank; [3]: title; [4]: copyright page; 5-[20]: "Stadt ohne Namen" (NC); 21-[27]: "Dagon"; 28-[37]: "Der Hund" (H); 38-[49]: "Das Fest" (F); 50-[60]: "Das

merkwürdige hochgelegene Haus im Nebel" (SHH); 61-[88]:
"Grauen in Red Hook" (HRH); 89-[97]: "Das Bild im Haus"
(PH); 100-[38]: "Herbert West—der Wiedererwecker" (HWR);
139-[55]: "Der Tempel" (Te); 156-[69]: "Er" (He); 170-[96]: "Die
lauernde Furcht" (LF); 197-[208]: "Arthur Jermyn" (FAJ); 209-
[12]: "Nyarlathotep"; 213-[47]: "Das gemiedene Haus" (SH);
[248]: blank; [249]: contents list; [250]: blank; [251]: additional
copyright page; [252]: blank; [253-54]: advertisements; [256]:
blank.

Bound in black cloth; spine stamped in white; 21.2 × 12.3 cm.;
dust jacket art and design by Hans Ulrich and Ute Osterwalder.

Notes. Translations by Charlotte Gräfin von Klinckowstroem.
Paper tinted light green. Part of the Bibliothek des Hauses
Usher series.

39. *Lovecraft kessakushu 1* (1974)

[LOVECRAFT KESSAKUSHU 1] / [H. P.
LOVECRAFT] / [TADAAKI ONISHI] / [rule
around title, author, and translator] / [publisher's
device] / [SOGENSUIRI BUNKO] / [all the above in
Japanese characters]

[1-5]¹⁶ [1-9] 10-130 [131] 132-70 [171] 172-86 [187] 188-317
[318-20]

[1]: half-title; [2]: blank; [3]: title; [4]: English title of
collection: "The Shadow over Innsmouth and Other Stories";
[5]: contents list; [6]: blank; [7]: part-title; [8]: blank; [9]: half-
title to following story (similarly for succeeding works); 10-130:
"Innsmouth no kage" (SOI); [131]: half-title; 132-70: "Kabe no
naka no nezuni" (RW); [171]: half-title; 172-86: "Shitai anchisho
nite" (IV); [187]: half-title; 188-307: "Yamini sasayaku mono"
(WD); 308-17: "Yakusha atogaki" (translator's afterword);
[318]: blank; [319-20]: advertisements.

Bound in paper; 14.9 × 10.5 cm.

Notes. Translations by Tadaaki Onishi. Published in 1974 by
Sogensha, Tokyo.

40. *De zaak Charles Dexter Ward* (1974)

howard phillips lovecraft / [rule] / de zaak / charles
dexter ward / [rule] / a.w. bruna & zoon

utrecht/antwerpen [copyright page:] 1974

Perfect-bound: [1-4] 5-160

[1]: half-title; [2]: publisher's device and note; [3]: title; [4]: copyright page; 5-160: text (CDW).

Bound in paper; 17.5 × 11.5 cm.; cover art by Bob van Blommestein.

Notes. Translation by J. F. Niessen-Hossele. Bruna Fantasy & Horror No. 15.

41. *La tumba y otros relatos* (1974)

a. H. P. LOVECRAFT / LA TUMBA / Y OTROS RELATOS / EDITORIAL MERLIN / BUENOS AIRES [copyright page:] 1974

[1-5]⁸ [6]¹⁰ [1-8] 9-24 [25-26] 27-41 [42-44] 45-65 [66-68] 69-82 [83-84] 85-97 [98] 99 [100]

[1-2]: blank; [3]: half-title; [4]: blank; [5]: title; [6]: copyright page; [7]: half-title to following story (similarly for succeeding works); [8]: blank; 9-24: "La tumba" (T); [25]: half-title; [26]: blank; 27-41: "Arthur Jermyn" (FAJ); [42]: blank; [43]: half-title; [44]: blank; 45-65: "El modelo de Pickman" (PM); [66]: blank; [67]: half-title; [68]: blank; 69-82: "En la cripta" (IV); [83]: half-title; [84]: blank; 85-97: "Aire frío" (CA); [98]: blank; 99: contents list; [100]: colophon.

Bound in paper; 19.5 × 11.2 cm.; cover design by Sergio Camporeale.

Notes. Translations by José M. Aroca. Published on 5 June 1974 (see colophon); 3,000 copies.

b. *Second Edition.* Buenos Aires: Ediciones Fantaciencia, January 1968. New cover; 3,000 copies.

42. *Los horrores de Dunwich* (1974)

a.1. H. P. LOVECRAFT / NECRONOMICON I / LOS HORRORES / DE DUNWICH / Y OTROS RELATOS / [publisher's device] / BARRAL EDITORES / BARCELONA / 1974

[1-9]¹⁶ [10]⁸ [1-10] 11-51 [52-54] 55-87 [88-90] 91-132 [133-34] 135-93 [194-96] 197-288 [289-304]

[1-2]: blank; [3]: half-title; [4]: blank; [5]: title; [6]: copyright page; [7]: biographical sketch of Lovecraft; [8]: blank; [9]: half-title to following story (similarly for succeeding works); [10]: blank; 11-51: "El color allende del espacio" (CS); [52]: blank; [53]: half-title; [54]: blank; 55-87: "El duende de las tinieblas" (HD); [88]: blank; [89]: half-title; [90]: blank; 91-132: "La voz de Cthulhu" (CC); [133]: half-title; [134]: blank; 135-93: "Los horrores de Dunwich" (DH); [194]: blank; [195]: half-title; [196]: blank; 197-288: "El murmurador en las tinieblas" (WD); [289]: half-title to contents list; [290]: blank; [291]: contents list; [292]: blank; [293-301]: advertisements; [302]: blank; [303]: colophon; [304]: blank.

Bound in paper; 18.5 × 11.4 cm.; cover art by Jordi Vives.

Notes. Translations by Melitón Bustamente Díaz. Published in July 1974 (see colophon). Ediciones de Bolsillo No. 375.

a.2. *Second Printing.* Barcelona: Barral Editores, January 1976. New cover art by Julio Vivas.

43. *La sombra más allá del tiempo* (1974)

a.1. H. P. LOVECRAFT / NECRONOMICON II / LA SOMBRA MAS ALLA / DEL TIEMPO / Y OTROS CUENTOS / con el ensayo: EL HORROR SOBRE- / NATURAL EN LA LITERATURA / [publisher's device] / BARRAL EDITORES / BARCELONA / 1974

[1-8]¹⁶ [9]⁸ [1-8] 9-45 [46-48] 49-141 [142-44] 145-55 [156-58] 159-254 [255-72]

[1-2]: blank; [3]: half-title; [4]: blank; [5]: title; [6]: copyright page; [7]: half-title for following work (similarly for succeeding works); [8]: blank; 9-45: "El ser en el umbral" (TD); [46]: blank; [47]: half-title; [48]: blank; 49-141: "La sombra más allá del tiempo" (SOOT); [142]: blank; [143]: half-title; [144]: blank; 145-55: "El sabueso" (H); [156]: blank; [157]: half-title; [158]: blank; 159-254: "El horror sobrenatural en la literatura" (SHiL); [255]: half-title to contents list; [256]: blank; [257-58]:

advertisements; [259]: contents list; [260]: blank; [261-65, 267-68]: advertisements; [266, 269-70]: blank; [271]: colophon; [272]: blank.

Bound in paper; 18.5 × 11.2 cm.; cover art by Jordi Vives.

Notes. Translations by Melitón Bustamente Díaz. Published in July 1974 (see colophon). Ediciones de Bolsillo No. 376.

a.2. *Second Printing.* Barcelona: Barral Editores, January 1976. New cover art by Julio Vivas.

44. *Obras escogidas (II)* (1974)

H. P. LOVECRAFT / OBRAS ESCOGIDAS / (SEGUNDA SELECCION) / EDICIONES ACERVO / Apartado 5319 — Julio Verne, 5-7 / BARCELONA [copyright page:] October 1974

[1]¹⁶ 2-14¹⁶ [15]⁴ [1-5] 6-8 [9] 10-32 [33] 34-61 [62-63] 64-73 [74-75] 76-154 [155] 156-235 [236-37] 238-44 [245] 246-339 [340-41] 342-54 [355] 356-99 [400-01] 402-07 [408-09] 410-12 [413] 414-21 [422-23] 424-32 [433] 434-46 [447-56]

[1]: half-title; [2]: blank; [3]: title; [4]: copyright page; [5]-8: "Introducción," by [José A. Llorens Borras?]; [9]-32: "Las ratas en las parades" (RW); [33]-61: "El frecuentador de la oscuridad" (HD); [62]: blank; [63]-73: "El grabado en la casa" (PH); [74]: blank; [75]-154: "La sombra sobre Innsmouth" (SOI); [155]-235: "La sombra fuera del tiempo" (SOOT); [236]: blank; [237]-44: "La declaracion de Randolph Carter" (SRC); [245]-339: *La onirica busqueda de desconocida Kadath* (DQ); [340]: blank; [341]-54: "La llave de plata" (SK); [355]-99: "A través de las puertas de la llave de plata" (TGSK); [400]: blank; [401]-07: "Dagon"; [408]: blank; [409]-12: "Los gatos de Ulthar" (CU); [413]-21: "Lo innominable" (U); [422]: blank; [423]-32: "La extraña casa en la niebla" (SHH); [433]-46: "El" (He); [447]: contents list; [448]: blank; [449]-53: advertisements; [454-56]: blank.

Bound in green, gold, and red cloth; spine stamped in gold; 20.3 × 14.5 cm.; white dust jacket.

Notes. Selection is by José A. Llorens Borrás; translations by "J. M. A." (José M. Aroca).

45. *El sepulcro y otros relatos* (1974)

    a.1. H. P. LOVECRAFT / EL SEPULCRO / Y
OTROS RELATOS / Prólogo, tradducción y
notas de / EDUARDO HARO IBARS / LA
VELA LATINA / [publisher's device] /
EDICIONES JUCAR [copyright page:] Madrid
. . . November 1974

        [1-19]^8 [20]^4 [1-8] 9-19 [20-22] 23-39 [40] 41-55 [56] 57-
99 [100] 101-69 [170] 171-223 [224] 225-81 [282] 283
[284] 285-303 [304-12]

        [1-2]: blank; [3]: half-title; [4]: blank; [5]: title; [6]:
copyright page; [7]: half-title to introduction; [8]: blank; 9-
19: "Las máscaras de la nada: (Notas possibles a una
lectura de Lovecraft)" by Ibars; [20]: blank; [21]: part-title;
[22]: blank; 23-39: "El sepulcro" (T); [40]: blank; 41-55:
"La festividad" (F); [56]: blank; 57-99: "Encerrado con los
faraones" (UP); [100]: blank; 101-18: "El" (He); 119-54: "El
horror de Red Hook" (HRH); 155-69: "La extraña casa alta
en la niebla" (SHH); [170]: blank; 171-216: "En los muros
de Eryx" (IWE): 217-23: "El malvado clérigo" (EC); [224]:
blank; 225-26: "Cuentos primerizos" (note by August
Derleth); 227-36: "La bestia en la cueva" (BC); 237-50: "El
alquimista" (A) 251-61: "La poesía y los dioses" (PG); 262-
70: "La calle" (S); 271-81: "La trasición de Juan Romero"
(TJR); [282]: blank; 283: "Cuatro fragmentos" (note by
August Derleth); [284]: blank; 285-87: "Asathoth" [sic];
287-93: "El descendiente" (De); 293-97: "El libro" (B); 298-
300: "La cosa en la claro de luna" (TM); 301-03:
chronology of tales (see I-E-i-1); [304]: blank; [305]: half-
title to contents list; [306]: blank; [307]: contents list;
[308]: blank; [309]: colophon; [310]: blank; [311]: other
books from the publisher; [312]: blank.

        Bound in paper; 20.2 × 12.6 cm.; cover art by Roberto
Cabrera.

        Notes. Translation of I-A-49.

    a.2. *Second Printing.* Madrid: Ediciones Jucar, 1976. New cover
by J. M. Domínguez.

    a.3. *Third Printing.* Madrid: Ediciones Jucar, October 1979. New
cover by M. Domínguez.

46. *Lettres d'Arkham* (1975)

   a.1. marginalia / LOVECRAFT / lettres d'arkham /
      Correspondence choisie, / traduite et présentée
      par / Yves Rivière / éditions / jacques
      glénat / 4, rue de la liberté / 38000 grenoble
      [copyright page:] June 1975

> Unsigned: [1-2] 3-19 [20] 21-77 [78] 79 [80]
> [1]: title; [2]: quotations from Lovecraft and Philip
> Herrera (see III-F-i-4), copyright; 3-14: "Lovecraft, un
> cauchemar américain" by Rivière; 15-16: "Repères
> bibliographiques" (chronology of Lovecraft's life); 17-19:
> "Notes sur quelques auteurs cités par Lovecraft"; [20]:
> blank; 21-77: excerpts of letters; [78]: cover and art
> credits; 79: "Bibliographie francaise"; [80]: colophon.
> Bound in paper; 20 × 10.9 cm.; cover art by Moebius.
> *Notes.* Very brief and random excerpts from the first
> two volumes of *Selected Letters* (I-A-41, 45); dates of writing
> and addresses are almost never identified. Interior
> lettering by Floc'h.

   a.2. *Second Printing.* Grenoble: Éditions Jacques Glénat, October
      1976.

47. *L'Horreur dans le musée*, Volume I (1975)

   a. LES RÉVISIONS DE LOVECRAFT /
     L'HORREUR / DANS LE MUSÉE / *Traduction de*
     Jacques PARSONS / *Préface d'August DERLETH* /
     Introduction de Francis LACASSIN / TOME
     I / CHRISTIAN BOURGOIS EDITEUR / 8, rue
     Garancière / PARIS VIe [copyright page:] 1975

> [1-9][16] [1-4] 5-7 [8] 9-29 [30] 31-39 [40] 41-47 [48] 49-55
> [56] 57-61 [62] 63-81 [82] 83-88 [89] 90-101 [102] 103-15
> [116] 117-29 [130] 131-44 [145-46] 147-57 [158] 159-69
> [170] 171-86 [187] 188-205 [206] 207-12 [213] 214-38 [239-
> 40] 241-43 [244] 245-66 [267-68] 269-84 [285-88]
> [1]: half-title; [2]: list of books by Lovecraft; [3]: title; [4]:
> copyright page; 5-[8]: "Préface: Les 'Révisions' de Lovecraft"
> ("Lovecraft's 'Revisions' "), by Derleth; 9-[30]:

"Introduction: H. P. Lovecraft 'nègre' littéraire ou accoucher de talents?" by Lacassin; 31-[40]: "En rampant dans le chaos" (CrC); 41-47: "La Verte Prairie" (GM); [48]: blank; 49-[56]: "Le Monstre invisible" (HMB); 57-[62]: "Quatres heures" (FO); 63-[82]: "L'Homme de pierre" (MS); 83-[116]: "La Mort ailée" (WiD); 117-29: "Le Nécrophile" (LD); [130]: blank; 131-[45]: "Sourd, muet et aveugle" (DDB); [146]: blank; 147-[58]: "Le Manguer des spectres" (GE); 159-69: " 'Jusqu'a ce que toutes les mers . . .' " (TAS); [170]: blank; 171-[206]: "L'Horreur dans le musée" (HM); 207-[39]: "Surgi du fond des siècles" (OE); [240]: blank; 241-[67]: "Le Journal d'Alonso Typer" (DAT); [268]: blank; 269-[85]: L'Horreur dans le cimetière" (HB); [286]: blank; [287]: contents list; [288]: colophon.

Bound in paper; 24 × 15.7 cm.

Notes. Published in July 1975 (see colophon).

b. *Second Edition.* Paris: France Loisirs, 1977. 286[+2] pp. Bound in grey cloth; spine stamped in black; dust jacket art by Benjamin Baltimore.

48. *L'Horreur dans le musée,* Volume II (1975)
a. LES RÉVISIONS DE H. P. LOVECRAFT / L'HORREUR / DANS LE MUSÉE / Traduction de Jacques PARSONS / TOME II / CHRISTIAN BOURGOIS EDITEUR / 8, rue Garancière / PARIS VIᵉ [copyright page:] 1975

[1-8]¹⁶ [9]⁴ [10]⁸ [1-4] 5-64 [65-66] 67-89 [90] 91-111 [112] 113-59 [160] 161-86 [187] 188-205 [206] 207-18 [219] 220-30 [231] 232-42 [243] 244-54 [255-56] 257-70 [271-72] 273-74 [275-80]

[1]: half-title; [2]: list of other books by Lovecraft; [3]: title; [4]: copyright page; 5-[65]: "Le Dernier Examen" (LT); [66]: blank; 67-[90]: L'Exécuteur des hautes oeuvres" (EE); 91-[112]: "La Malédiction de Yig" (CY); 113-[60]: "La Chevelure de Méduse" (MC); 161-[255]: "Le Tertre" (Mo); [256]: blank; 257-[71]: "Deux bouteilles noires" (TBB); [272]: blank; 273-[75]: "Bibliographie des 'révisions' de Lovecraft"; [276]: blank; [277]: half-title to contents list; [278]: blank; [279]: contents list; [280]: blank.

Bound in paper; 24 × 15.7 cm.
Notes. Published in September 1975 (see colophon).

b. *Second Edition.* Paris: France Loisirs, 1977. 279[+5] pp. Bound in grey cloth; spine stamped in violet; dust jacket art by Benjamin Baltimore.

49. *Gengångaren* (1975)

H. P. Lovecraft / Gengångaren / Delta Förlags AB / [rule] / ISBN 91 7228 038 [copyright page:] Bromma [Sweden] . . . 1975

[1]⁸ 2-13⁸ [1-4] 5-205 [206-08]
[1]: half-title; [2]: blank; [3]: title; [4]: copyright page; 5-205: text (CDW); [206]: blank; [207]: advertisements; [208]: blank.
Bound in paper; 19.5 × 12.4 cm.; cover art by Henri Lievens.
Notes. Translation by Gunnar Gällmo. Skräckens klassiker No. 3.

50. *Lovecraft zenshu 1* (1975)

HPL / [rule] / [LOVECRAFT ZENSHU] / [rule] / I / [publisher's device] / [SODOSHA] [Name of title and publisher in Japanese characters]

[1-32]⁸ [1-12] 13-27 [28-30] 31-37 [38-40] 41-56 [57-58] 59-94 [95-96] 97-131 [132-34] 135-83 [184-86] 187-211 [212-14] 215-69 [270-72] 273-78 [278-80] 281-326 [327-28] 329-40 [341-42] 343-63 [364-66] 367-439 [440-42] 443-63 [464-65] 466-78 [479-80] 481-92 [493] 494-95 [496] 497-513 [514-18]
[1]: title; [2]: blank; [3-6]: photographs of Lovecraft and his work; [7]: half-title; [8]: blank; [9-10]: contents list; [11]: half-title to following story (similarly for succeeding works); [12]: blank; 13-27: "Renkinjutsushi" (A); [28]: blank; [29]: half-title; [30]: blank; 31-37: "Polaris" (tr. Hiroshi Aramata and Mikikazu Mori); [38]: blank; [39]: half-title; [40]: blank; 41-56: "Yoken" (H); [57]: half-title; [58]: blank; 59-94: "Hisomisumu kyofu" (LF; tr. Aramata and Mori); [95]: half-title; [96]: blank; 97-131: "Kabe no naka no mezumi" (RW; tr. Aramata and Mori); [132]: blank; [133]: half-title; [134]: blank; 135-83: "Imareta ie" (SH); [184]: blank; [185]: half-title; [186]: blank; 187-211: "Pickman no model" (PM; tr. Aramata and Akira Takegami); [212]: blank; [213]: half-title; [214]: blank; 215-69: "Ijigen no shikisai" (CS);

[270]: blank; [271]: half-title; [272]: blank; 273-78: "Nyarlathotep"; [279]: half-title; [280]: blank; 281-326: "Yami ni hau mono" (HD); [327]: half-title; [328]: blank; 329-40: "Randolph Carter no benmei" (SRC); [341]: half-title; [342]: blank; 343-63: "Gin no kagi" (SK; tr. Aramata and Hitoshi Yasuda); [364]: blank; [365]: half-title; [366]: blank; 367-439: "Gin no kagi no mon o koete" (TGSK); [440]: blank; [441]: half-title; [442]: blank; 443-63: "Kaikishosetsu no Copernicus" ("A Literary Copernicus"), by Fritz Leiber (tr. Aramata and Mori); [464]: blank; [465]: half-title; [466]: blank; 467-68, 470-76, 478: letter to M. W. Moe, 1 January 1915 (as "Waga yonenki o kataru"); 469, 477: photographs of Lovecraft; [479]: half-title; [480]: blank; 481-92, 494-95, 497: "Bunkagensho toshiteno Lovecraft" by Aramata; 493, 496: photographs of Lovecraft and his work; 498-513: "Sakuhin kaitai" (commentary) by Aramata; [514]: note about Aramata; [515]: colophon; [516]: advertisements; [517-18]: blank.

Bound in black cloth; spine stamped in silver; boxed in a black and silver cardboard slipcase; 19 × 14 cm.

Notes. Volume 1 of the Collection of H. P. Lovecraft's Fiction (first volume of short fiction). Published in 1975 by Sodosha, Tokyo. Edited and translated, save where indicated, by Hiroshi Aramata.

51. *Nelle spire di Medusa* (1976)

H. P. Lovecraft / NELLE SPIRE / DI MEDUSA / *serie completa, 1* / Con due illustrazioni nel testo / FANUCCI [copyright page:] Rome . . . March 1976

[1]⁸ 2-17⁸ [1-4] 5-15 [16] 17-19 [20] 21-29 [30] 31-47 [48] 49-57 [58] 59-79 [80] 81-91 [92] 93-135 [136] 137-270 [271-74]

[1]: publisher's note; [2]: blank; [3]: title; [4]: copyright page; 5-10: "Introduzione," by Gianfranco de Turris and Sebastiano Fusco; 11-15: "Il gentiluomo di Providence," by Dirk W. Mosig; [16]: blank; 17-19: "Le 'revisioni' di Lovecraft" ("Lovecraft's 'Revisions' "), by August Derleth; [20]: blank; 21: reproduction of Virgil Finlay's portrait of Lovecraft; [22]: note about Finlay by de Turris and Fusco; 23-29: "Il caos che monta" (CrC); [30]: blank; 31-36: "Il prato verde" (GM); 37-42: "La minaccia

invisibile" (HMB); 43-47: "Alle quattro del mattino" (FO); 49-
57: "Il divoratore di spettri" (GE); [58]: blank; 59-68: "I cari
estini" (LD); 69-79: "Cieco, sordo e muto" (DDB); [80]: blank;
81-91: "Due bottiglie nere" (TBB); [92]: blank; [93]-135:
"L'ultimo esperimento" (LT); [136]: blank; 137-54: "Il boia
elettrico" (EE); 155-70: "La maledizione di Yig" (CY); 171:
illustration by Philippe Druillet; 172: note about Druillet by de
Turris and Fusco; 173-236: "Xinaian" (Mo); 237-70: "Nelle spire
di Medusa" (MC); [271]: contents list; [272]: colophon; [273-74]:
advertisements.
   Bound in paper; 21.1 × 14.8 cm.; dust jacket art by Glauco
Cartocci.
   Notes. Translations by Roberta Rambelli.

52. *Sfida dall'infinito* (1976)
   H. P. Lovecraft / SFIDA / DALL'INFINITO /
   serie completa, 2 / Con quattro illustrazioni nel
   testo / FANUCCI [copyright page:] Rome . . .
   September 1976

   [1]⁸ 2-21⁸ [1-4] 5-20 [21-22] 21-61 [62] 63-107 [108] 109-21
   [122] 123-50 [151-52] 153-59 [160-62] 163-87 [188] 189-203
   [204-06] 207-36 [237-38] 239-60 [261-62] 263-71 [272] 273-78
   [279] 280-85 [286] 287-301 [302] 303-35 [336] 337 [338-40]

   [1]: publisher's note; [2]: blank; [3]: title; [4]: copyright,
   acknowledgments; 5-6: "Introduzione," by Gianfranco de
   Turris and Sebastiano Fusco; 7-20: "Dall'orrore alla
   fantascienza" ("H. P. Lovecraft: A Study in Horror"), by Sam
   Moskowitz; [21]: reproduction of cover illustration to *H. P.
   Lovecraft: A Portrait* (III-C-4); [22]: note about illustration by de
   Turris and Fusco; 23-36: "L'uomo di pietra" (MS); 37-61:
   "L'orrore nel museo" (HM); [62]: blank; 63-84: "La morte alata"
   (WiD); 85-107: "Reliquia di un mondo perduto" (OE); [108]:
   blank; 109-21: "La casa dalle finestre sbarrate" (HB); [122]:
   blank; 123-42: "Il diario de Alonzo Typer" (DAT); 143-50:
   "L'erede della terra" (TAS); [151]: half-title: "Narrativa"; [152]:
   editors' note; 153-59: "Il sogno degli dèi" (PG); [160]: blank;
   [161]: illustration by Virgil Finlay; [162]: note about illustration
   by de Turris and Fusco; 163-87: "Prigioniero dei faraoni" (UP);
   [188]: blank; 189-203: "Sfida dall' infinito" (CB); [204]: blank;

[205]: illustration by Carlos Giménez; [206]: note about
illustration by de Turris and Fusco; 207-34: "Nel labirinto di
Eryx" (IWE); 235-36: "Universi in sfacelo" ("Collapsing
Cosmoses"); [237]: facsimile of letter by Lovecraft to Hyman
Bradofsky indicating revision of NO; [238]: editors' note on
letter; 239-60: "L'oceano di notte" (NO); [261]: half-title to
Appendix II; [262]: editors' note; 263-64: "Il saggio di College
Street" ("The Sage of College Street"), by E. Hoffmann Price;
265-71: "Il vento che è tra l'erba" ("The Wind That Is in the
Grass"), by R. H. Barlow; [272]: blank; 273-85: "Il Lovecraft
normale" ("The Normal Lovecraft"), by Wilfred B. Talman (pp.
278-[79]: "Dirge of the Doomed," by Lovecraft, both in English
and in Italian); [286]: blank; 287-301: "Abissi smisurati per
l'uomo" ("Caverns Measureless to Man"), by Kenneth Sterling;
[302]: blank; 303-35: "Guida alla lettura di Lovecraft"
(chronology of fiction with commentary), by de Turris and
Fusco; [336]: blank; 337: contents list; [338]: blank; [339-40]:
advertisements.

Bound in paper; 21.3 × 15.1 cm.; dust jacket art by Glauco
Cartocci.

Notes. Translations by Roberta Rambelli. NO was reprinted
here for the first time; it was discovered by Hyman Bradofsky
and Dirk W. Mosig.

53. *Het huis in de nevel* (1976)

H. P. Lovecraft / Het huis in de nevel / A. W.
BRUNA & ZOON   Utrecht/Antwerpen
[copyright page:] 1976

Perfect-bound: [1-6] 7-221 [222-24]

[1]: half-title; [2]: series title; [3]: title; [4]: copyright page and
note on original title: "A Collection of Short Stories © H. P.
Lovecraft" (!); [5]: contents list; [6]: blank; 7-92: "Schaduwen
boven Innsmouth" (SOI); 93-122: "De verschrikking in Red
Hook" (HRH); 123-34: "Het huis in de nevel" (SHH); 135-38:
"De verschrikkelijke oude man" (TOM); 139-46: "De
verdoemenis die over Sarnath kwam" (DS); 147-85: "De muren
van Eryx" (IWE); 186-221: "Het gemeden huis" (SH); [222-24]:
advertisements.

Bound in paper; 17.3 × 11.4 cm.; cover art by Karel Thole.
Notes. Translations by Pon Ruiter. Zwarte Beertjes No. 1752.

54. *Lovecraft kessakushu 2* (1976)

[LOVECRAFT KESSAKUSHU 2] / [H. P.
LOVECRAFT] / [TOSHIYASU UNO] / [rule
around all the above] / [publisher's device] /
[SOGENSUIRI BUNKO] [all the above in Japanese
characters]

[1-19]⁸ [1-9] 10-61 [62-63] 64-78 [79] 80-301 [302-04]
[1]: half-title; [2]: blank; [3]: title; [4]: English title of
collection: "The Case of Charles Dexter Ward and Other
Stories"; [5]: contents list; [6]: blank; [7]: part-title; [8]: blank;
[9]: half-title to following story (similarly for succeeding
works); 10-61: "Cthulhu no yobigoe" (CC); [62]: blank; [63]:
half-title; 64-78: "Erich Zann no ongaku" (MEZ); [79]: half-title;
80-296: *Charles Dexter Ward no kikai na jiken* (CDW); 297-301:
"Yakusha atogaki" (translator's afterword); [302]: blank; [303-
04]: advertisements.
Bound in paper; 14.8 × 10.7 cm.
Notes. Translation by Toshiyasu Uno. Published in 1976 by
Sogensha, Tokyo.

55. *La sombra sobre Innsmouth* (1977)

LA SOMBRA / SOBRE / INNSMOUTH / H. P.
Lovecraft / EDITORIAL / BRUGUERA, S. A.
[copyright page:] Barcelona . . . 1977

Perfect-bound: [1-4] 5-219 [220-24]
[1]: half-title; [2]: blank; [3]: title; [4]: copyright page; 5-6:
"Presentación," by Carlo Frabetti; 7-33: "El horror oculto" (LF);
34-40: "Dagón"; 41-54: "Más allá del muro de los sueños"
(BWS); 55-62: "La nave blanca" (WS); 63-74: "Arthur Jermyn"
(FAJ); 75-84: "Desde el más allá" (FB); 85-101: "El templo" (Te);
102-12: "El pantano de la diosa luna" (MB); 113-22: "El
sabueso" (H); 123-32: "Lo innominable" (U); 133-40: "El
intruso" (O); 141-[220]: "La sombra sobre Innsmouth" (SOI);
[221]: contents list; [222]: blank; [223-24]: advertisements.
Bound in paper; 17.3 × 10.4 cm.; cover art by Jorge Sanchez.
Notes. Translations by Maria Teresa Segur. Libro Amigo No.
527.

56. *El que susurra en la oscuridad* (1977)
EL QUE / SUSURRA EN / LA OSCURIDAD /
H. P. Lovecraft / EDITORIAL / BRUGUERA, S. A.
[copyright page:] Barcelona . . . 1st edition:
November 1977

    Perfect-bound: [1-4] 5-11 [12] 13-280 [281-88]
    [1]: half-title; [2]: blank; [3]: title; [4]: copyright page; 5-6:
"Presentación," by Carlo Frabetti; 7-11: "Introducción a H. P.
Lovecraft" ("An Introduction to H. P. Lovecraft"), by August
Derleth; [12]: blank; 13-38: "Las ratas en las paredes" (RW); 39-
56: "El modelo de Pickman" (PM); 57-114: "El horror de
Dunwich" (DH); 115-98: "El que susurra en la oscuridad" (WD);
199-235: "El color que cayó del cielo" (CS); 236-70: "La criatura
tras la puerta" (TD); 271-[81]: "La musica de Erich Zann"
(MEZ); [282]: blank; [283]: contents list; [284]: blank; [285-88]:
advertisements.
    Bound in paper; 17.5 × 10.5 cm.; cover art by Jorge Sanchez.
    Notes. Translations by Maria Teresa Segur. Libro Amigo No.
548.

57. *Horror en el museo* (1978)
H. P. Lovecraft / y otros / HORROR EN EL
MUSEO / y otras colaboraciones / [rule] /
Introducción de / Antonio Prometeo Moya [copyright
page:] Luis de Caralt Editor, S. A. . . . Barcelona,
. . . January 1978

    [1]¹⁶ 2-6¹⁶ 7⁶ [1-4] 5-45 [46] 47-53 [54] 55-75 [76] 77-91 [92]
93-103 [104] 105-15 [116] 117-98 [199-208]
    [1]: publisher's device and series title; [2]: series subheading:
"Serie Novela"; [3]: title; [4]: copyright page; 5-14:
"Introducción" by Moya; 15-45: "Horror en el museo" (HM);
[46]: blank; 57-53: "La pradera verde" (GM); [54]: blank; 55-66:
"Amor a la muerte" (LD); 67-75: "El caos reptante" (CrC); [76]:
blank; 77-91: "El horror del cementerio" (HB); [92]: blank; 93-
103: "Hasta la ultima gota del oceano" (TAS); [104]: blank; 105-
15: "El zampaespectros" (GE); [116]: blank; 117-22: "Cuatro en
punto" (FO); 123-36: "Sordo, mudo y ciego" (DDB); 137-44: "El
monstruo invisible" (HMB); 145-74: "Fuera del tiempo" (OE);

175-98: "El diario de Alonso Typer" (DAT); [199]: contents list;
[200]: blank; [201-04]: advertisements; [205-08]: blank.
Bound in paper; 18 × 11.6 cm.; cover design by Balaguer.
Notes. Translations by Antonio Prometeo Moya. No. 121 in
the Biblioteca Universal Caralt.

58. *Muerte con alas* (1978)

H. P. Lovecraft / y otros / MUERTE CON ALAS / y
otras colaboraciones / [rule] / *Introducción
de* / Antonio Prometeo Moya [copyright page:] Luis
de Caralt Editor S. A. . . . Barcelona . . . May
1978

[1-9]¹⁶ [10]⁸ [1-4] 5-290 [291-304]

[1]: publisher's device and series title; [2]: series subheading:
"Serie Novela"; [3]: title; [4]: copyright page; 5-9:
"Introducción" by Moya; 10-37: "Muerte con alas" (WiD); 38-
120: "El montículo" (Mo); 121-37: "El hombre de piedra" (MS);
138-91: "La última prueba" (LT); 192-210: "La maldicción de
Yig" (CY); 211-32: "El verdugo eléctrico" (EE); 233-76: "La
cabellera de Medusa" (MC); 277-90: "Dos botellas negras"
(TBB); [291]: half-title to contents list; [292]: blank; [293]:
contents list; [294]: blank; [295-99]: advertisements; [300-04]:
blank.
Bound in paper; 18 × 11.6 cm.; cover photograph by Media
Press.
Notes. Translations by Antonio Prometeo Moya. No. 135 in
the Biblioteca Universal Caralt.

59. *Lettres*, Volume 1 (1978)

H. P. LOVECRAFT / LETTRES / *Recueillies par
August Derleth and Donald Wandrei* / *Choix, préface,
chronologie, bibliographie et notes* / *par* Francis
LACASSIN / *Traduit de l'américain par* Jacques
PARSONS / Tome I / (1914 - 1926) / CHRISTIAN
BOURGOIS EDITEUR / 8, rue Garancière, PARIS
VIᵉ [colophon page:] 31 May 1978

[1]¹⁶ 2-13¹⁶ [1-8] 9-33 [34] 35-39 [40-42] 43-56 [57-60] 61-402
[403-06] 407-09 [410-12] 413 [414-16]

[1-2]: blank; [3]: half-title; [4]: list of books by Lovecraft; [5]:
title; [6]: copyright page; [7]: dedication by Lacassin; [8]: blank;
9-[34]: "Préface: Lovecraft ou l'acteur vaincu par son
personnage" by Lacassin; 35-[40]: "Chronologie de H. P.
Lovecraft"; [41]: "Note de l'editeur francais"; 43-63: "Prologue:
Lovecraft raconté par Lovecraft" (excerpts from letters); 64-
[403]: letters; [404]: blank; [405]: half-title to bibliography;
[406]: blank; 407-10: "Bibliographie des contes et nouvelles";
[411]: half-title to contents list; [412]: blank; 413-14: contents
list; [415]: colophon; [416]: blank.

Bound in paper; 24 × 15.5 cm.; cover art by Studio Briat.

Notes. A selection and translation of Volume I and part of
Volume II of the Selected Letters (I-A-41 and 45). Most letters are
extensively annotated by Lacassin.

60. Lovecraft zenshu IV (1978)

HPL / [rule] / [LOVECRAFT ZENSHU] / [rule] /
IV / [publisher's device] / [SODOSHA] [Name of
title and publisher in Japanese characters]

[1]¹⁰ [2-33]⁸ [a-b] [1-10] 11-190 [191-192] 193-257 [258-60]
261-381 [382-84] 385-492 [493-94] 495-516 [517] 518-21 [522-
24] 525-32 [533-36]

[a]: title; [b]: blank; [1-4]: illustrations; [5]: half-title; [6]:
blank; [7]: contents list; [8]: blank; [9]: half-title to following
work (similarly for succeeding works); [10]: blank; 11-190: Kyoki
no yama nite (ATMOM); [191]: half-title; [192]: blank; 193-257:
"Majo no ie de mita yume" (DWH); [258]: blank; [259]: half-
title; [260]: blank; 261-381: "Yami ni sasayaku mono" (WD);
[382]: blank; [383]: half-title; [384]: blank; 385-492: "Chojikan
no kage" (SOOT); [493]: half-title; [494]: blank; 495-516:
"Brown Jenkin totomoni jiku o meguru" ("Through Hyperspace
with Brown Jenkin"), by Fritz Leiber; [517, 522-24]:
illustrations for ATMOM from Astounding Stories; 518-21, 525-
32: [Commentary], by Hiroshi Aramata; [533]: blank; [534]:
colophon; [535-36]: advertisements.

Bound in black cloth; spine stamped in silver; 19 × 14 cm.;
boxed in a black and silver cardboard slipcase.

Notes. Volume 4 of the Collection of H. P. Lovecraft's Fiction
(second volume of novels). Published in 1978 by Sodosha,
Tokyo. Edited and translated by Horoshi Aramata. Pp. [1-4]
contain reproductions of art by Nicholas Roerich (mentioned in
ATMOM).

B.   Contributions to Periodicals

i. Fiction

1. "Azathoth." *Ganymed Horror*, Nos. 10/11/12 (1974), pp. 47-48 (tr. Heinz W. Kloos).

2. "The Beast in the Cave." *Il Re in Giallo*, 1, No. 2 [1976], 87-92 (as "L'essere nella caverna"; tr. Giuseppe Lippi). *Crypt Horror Tales*, No. 8 (April 1976), pp. 6-10 (as "Dokutsu no kaiju"; tr. Katsuhiro Suzuki).

3. "Beyond the Wall of Sleep." *Crypt Horror Tales*, No. 8 (April 1976), pp. 17-25 (as "Nemuri no tobari o koete"; tr. Hiroaki Hazu).

4. "The Book." *Ganymed Horror*, Nos. 10/11/12 (1974), pp. 51-54 (as "Das Buch"; tr. Heinz W. Kloos). *Arcanda*, No. 2 (1977), pp. 4-7 (as "Boken"; tr. Tor Skarv).

5. "The Call of Cthulhu." *Hayakawa's Mystery Magazine*, No. 188 (December 1971), pp. 132-38; No. 189 (January 1972), pp. 149-59; No. 190 (February 1972), pp. 47-56 (as "Cthulhu yobigoe"; tr. Kozaburo Yano).

6. "The Cats of Ulthar." *Hayakawa's Mystery Magazine*, No. 208 (August 1973), pp. 51-53 (as "Ulthar no neko"; tr. Katsuo Jinka).

7. "The Colour out of Space." *Urania*, No. 310 (16 June 1963), pp. 80-82, 84-110 (as "Il colore venuto del cielo"; tr. Sarah Cantoni). *Little Weird*, No. 11 (November 1968) (as "Ijigen no shikisai"; tr. Hiroshi Aramata). *Secolul 20*, No. 4 (1973), pp. 45-66 (as "Culoara căzută din cer"; tr. M[ircea] I[vănesco]).

   Also appeared in the Polish *Przekrój*, but no information available on date of appearance.

8. "Cool Air." *Los Cuentos Fantasticos*, 2, No. 18 (15 August 1949), 60-66 (as "Aire frio"; tr. [Antonio Mejia?]). *Galassia*, No. 178 (15 November 1972), pp. 91-100 (as "Aria fredda"; tr. Giampaolo Cossato and Sandro Sandrelli). *Nueva Dimensión*, Special issue No. 6 (May 1975), pp. 89-94 (as "Aire frio"; tr. anon.). *Przekrój*, No. 855 (date unknown).

9. "Dagon." *Hayakawa's Mystery Magazine*, No. 180 (April 1971), pp. 142-45 (as "Gyojin Dagon"; tr. Hiroyuki Akitsu). *Nueva Dimensión*, No. 27 (December 1971), 84-90 (tr. L. Vigil). *Simplizissimus*, No. 3 (January-February-March-April 1972), pp. 43-52 (tr. Volker Diefenbach). *Nueva Dimensión*, Special issue No. 6 (May 1975), pp. 63-67 (tr. [L. Vigil]).

   Also appeared in the Polish *Ta i Ja*, but no further information available.

10. "The Descendant." *Ganymed Horror*, Nos. 10/11/12 (1974), pp. 48-51 (as "Der Nachkomme"; tr. Heinz W. Kloos).

11. "The Doom that Came to Sarnath." *Nova*, 4, No. 3 (1974), 36-38 (as "Sarnaths undergang"; tr. Øyvind Myhre). *Crypt Horror Tales*, No. 8 (April 1976), pp. 11-16 (as "Kyoun no miyako Sarnath"; tr. Toshio Akai [as "Gufu Akai"]).

12. "The Dreams in the Witch House." *Les Lettres Nouvelles*, No. 21 (November 1954), pp. 641-63 (1st part; as "La maison de la sorcière"; tr. Jacques Papy). *Ullstein Kriminalmagazin*, No. 19 (1971), pp. 7-66 (as "Träume im Hexenhaus"; tr. Bodo Baumann).

13. "The Dunwich Horror." *Historias Para No Dormir*, 2, No. 5 (1968), pp. 5-64 (as "El horror de Dunwich"; tr. anon.). *Luther's Grusel-Magazin*, No. 11 (n.d.), pp.

83-90, 92-100, 102-12, 114-21 (as "Horror in
Dunwich"; tr. anon.). *Przekrój*, Nos. 1,145-46 (date
unknown), pp. 11,101-100,000 (binary); No. 1,147
(date unknown), pp. 13-14; No. 1,148 (date
unknown), pp. 10-11 (as "Okropność w Dunwich";
tr. Franciszek Welczar; abridged).

Also appeared in the Japanese *Hoseki* in the 1940s.

14. "The Evil Clergyman." *Ganymed Horror*, Nos. 10/11/12
(1974), pp. 43-46 (as "Metamorphose"; tr. Uwe
Anton).

15. "Ex Oblivione." *Nova SF*, No. 18 (1971).

16. "Facts concerning the Late Arthur Jermyn and His
Family." *Nova*, 6, No. 4 (1976), 19-23 (as "Arthur
jermyn"; tr. Øyvind Myhre).

17. "The Festival." *Drab*, 1, No. 3 (n.d.), [11-14] (as "Yule
Ritus"; tr. Roeland de Vust).

18. "From Beyond." *Drab*, 4, No. 3 (October 1978), 12-
14, 16-17 (as "Van wat daarbuiten is"; tr. Tamme
Tams).

19. "The Haunter of the Dark." *Luther's Grusel-Magazin*,
No. 17 (n.d.), pp. 100-12, 114-27 (as "Dämon der
Finsternis"; tr. anon.). *S-F Magazine*, No. 164 (Special
Summer issue [September 1976]), pp. 344-66 (as
"Yamini hau mono"; tr. Hiroshi Aramata [as "Seiji
Dan"]).

20. "He." *Nueva Dimensión*, No. 24 (July 1971), pp. 69-78.
Nueva Dimensión, Special issue No. 6 (May 1975), pp.
143-51.

Both as "El"; tr. anon.

21. "The Horror at Red Hook." *Nueva Dimensión*, Special

issue No. 6 (May 1975), pp. 71-86 (as "Horror in Red Hook"; tr. anon.).

22. "The Hound." *Genso to Kaiki*, No. 1 (April 1973), pp. 106-13 (as "Yoken"; tr. Hiroshi Aramata [as "Seiji Dan"]).

23. "Hypnos." *Planète*, No. 1 (October-November 1961), pp. 47-51 (tr. Louis Pauwels and Jacques Bergier). *Nueva Dimensión*, Special issue No. 6 (May 1975), pp. 137-40 (as "Hipnos"; tr. anon.).

24. "In the Vault." *L'Herne*, No. 12 (1969), pp. 263-69 (as "Dans le caveau"; tr. Jacques Parsons).
    Also appeared in the Japanese *Hoseki* in the 1940s.

25. "Memory." *L'Herne*, No. 12 (1969), pp. 251-52 (as "Souvenir"; tr. Jacques Parsons). *Genso to Kaiki*, No. 7 (May 1974), pp. 8-9 (as "Haikyo no kioku"; tr. Junichiro Kida). *Oltre il Cielo*, No. 155 (30 September 1975), p. 3 (as "Ricordo"; tr. anon.).

26. "The Music of Erich Zann." *Pianeta*, No. 7 (April-May 1965), pp. 55-60 (as "La musica di Erich Zann"; tr. anon.). *Luther's Grusel-Magazin*, No. 9 [1974], pp. 73-76, 78-83 (as "Die Musik von Erich Zann"; tr. anon.).
    Also appeared in the Japanese *Hoseki* in the 1940s.

27. "Nyarlathotep." *Fiction*, No. 183 (March 1969), pp. 130-33 (tr. Jacques Parsons). *L'Herne*, No. 12 (1969), pp. 248-50 (tr. Jacques Parsons).

28. "Of Evill Sorceries done in New England." *Nueva Dimensión*, No. 55 (May 1974), pp. 17-20, 21 (in *El que acecha en el umbral* [*The Lurker at the Threshold*], by August Derleth; tr. E. Lomino).
    See I-E-i, I-E-i-14.

29. "The Other Gods." *Hayakawa's Mystery Magazine*, No.
    175 (November 1970), pp. 29-33 (as "Kamigami no
    yama"; tr. Takeko Sumita). *Science-Fiction Stories*, No.
    21 (1972), pp. 42-47 (as "Die anderen Götter"; tr.
    Ingrid Rothman). *Deije Shits*, No. 2 (1977), pp. 13-15
    (as "De andre gudene"; tr. Robert Ommundsen).

30. "The Outsider." *Romanzi e Racconti*, 1, No. 3 (1965),
    158-64 (as "L'estraneo"; tr. anon.). *Cero*, Nos. 5/6
    (June 1966), pp. 19-22 (as "El extraño"; tr. José M.
    Aroca). *Drab*, 1, No. 1 [1974], [12-14] (as "De
    buitenstaender"; tr. R. Germeraad). *Nova*, 5, No. 1
    (1975), 27-29 (as "Den utstøtte"; tr. Øyvind
    Myhre).
    Also appeared in the Japanese *Hoseki* in the 1940s.

31. "Pickman's Model." *Urania*, No. 310 (16 June 1963),
    pp. 65-74, 76-79 (as "Il modello di Pickman"; tr.
    Adalberto Chiesa). *Jules Verne-Magasinet*, No. 3
    (September 1972), pp. 10, 12-15 (as "Pickmans
    modell"; tr. anon.). *Luther's Grusel-Magazin*, No. 9
    [1974], pp. 51-54, 56-50, 62-66 (as "Pickman's
    Modell"; tr. anon.).

32. "The Picture in the House." *L'Herne*, No. 12 (1969),
    pp. 256-62 (as "L'Image dans la maison déserte"; tr.
    Jacques Parsons). *Nova*, 3, No. 3 (1973), 21, 24-27 (as
    "Bildet i huset"; tr. Øyvind Myhre). *La Opinión*, No.
    681 (5 August 1973), Cultural Supplement, pp. 6-7
    (as "El grabado en la casa"; tr. anon.). *Crypt Horror
    Tales*, No. 13 (Summer 1978), pp. 46-53 (as "Ichimai
    no sashie"; tr. Kunichika Takagi).

33. "Polaris." *Little Weird*, No. 8 (March 1968) (as
    "Polarisu"; tr. Hiroshi Aramata). *Crypt Horror Tales*,
    No. 1 (1973), pp. 4-12 (as "Hokkyokusei"; tr.
    Tetsuya Imamura [as "Sakae Kuroki"]).

34. "The Quest of Iranon." *Little Weird*, No. 6 (August 1967), pp. 5-9 (as "Ushinawareta rakuen o motomete"; tr. Hiroshi Aramata). *Hayakawa's Mystery Magazine*, No. 182 (June 1971), pp. 135-40 (as "Horo no oji Iranon"; tr. Takeko Sumita).

35. "The Rats in the Walls." *I Racconti del Terrore*, Nos. 3/4 (August-September 1962). *Luther's Grusel-Magazin*, No. 12 [1975], pp. 5-6, 10-19, 22-28 (as "Die Ratten in der Wand"; tr. anon.).

36. "The Shadow out of Time." *Nueva Dimensión*, Special issue No. 6 (May 1975), pp. 7-59 (as "El abismo en el tiempo"; tr. anon.).

37. "The Shadow over Innsmouth." *Przekrój*, Nos. 766/768 (December 1959), pp. 17-23; No. 769 (3 January 1960), pp. 10-11; No. 770 (10 January 1960), pp. 10-11; No. 771 (17 January 1960), pp. 10-11 (as "Koszmar z Innsmouth"; tr. Andrzej Wermer).

38. "The Shunned House." *Maxi Hoho*, No. 234 (n.d.), pp. 7-11, 20-22, 30-33, 41-44 (as "Het huis van verderf"; tr. anon.).

39. "The Statement of Randolph Carter." *Hayakawa's Mystery Magazine*, No. 194 (June 1972), pp. 146-51 (as "Randolph Carter no shogen"; tr. Kazuburo Yano).

40. "The Strange High House in the Mist." *Ullstein Kriminalmagazin*, No. 10 (1967), pp. 101-12 (as "Visionen im Nebel"; tr. Udo Schwager). *Nova*, 3, No. 4 (1973), 13-16 (as "Det underlige høye huset i tåken"; tr. Øyvind Myhre).

41. "The Temple." *Planète*, No. 5 (June-July-August 1962), pp. 101-06 (tr. Louis Pauwels and Jacques

Bergier). *Pianeta*, No. 2 (May-June 1964), pp. 89-94
(as "Il tempio"; tr. anon.). *Nueva Dimensión*, Special
issue No. 6 (May 1975), pp. 97-107 (as "El templo";
tr. anon.).

42. "The Terrible Old Man." *L'Herne*, No. 12 (1969), pp.
253-55 (as "Le Terrible Vieillard"; tr. Jacques
Parsons). *La Opinión*, No. 681 (5 August 1973),
Cultural Supplement, p. 12 (as "El anciano terrible";
tr. anon.). *Weird Fiction Times*, No. 48 (February
1977), pp. 29-30 (as "Der Schreckliche Alte"; tr.
Heinz W. Kloos).

43. "The Thing in the Moonlight." *Ganymed Horror*,
Nos. 10/11/12 (1974), pp. 54-55 (as "Das Ding
im Mondlicht"; tr. Heinz W. Kloos).

44. "The Thing on the Doorstep."
Appeared in the Polish *Przekrój*, but no further information
available.

45. "The Tomb." *Fiction*, No. 183 (March 1969), pp. 119-
29 (as "La tombe"; tr. Paule Pérez).

46. "The Whisperer in Darkness." *Urania*, No. 310 (16
June 1973), pp. 4-10, 12-18, 20-26, 28-34, 36-42, 44-
52, 54-62 (as "Colui che sussurrava nel buio"; tr.
Sarah Cantoni).

47. "The White Ship." *Deije Shits*, No. 1 (1977), pp. 52-54
(as "Det kvite skipet"; tr. Dave Jørgensen).

ii. Nonfiction

1. "In Memoriam: Robert Ervin Howard." *Il Re in Giallo*,
1, No. 2 [1976], 107-10 (as "In memoria di Robert
Ervin Howard"; tr. Giuseppe Lippi).

2. "Lord Dunsany and His Work." *Quarber Merkur*, 4, No. 1 (March 1966), 36-43 (as "Lord Dunsany und sein Werk"; tr. Franz Rottensteiner).

3. "Some Notes on Interplanetary Fiction." *Quarber Merkur*, 7, No. 2 (August 1969), 34-38. *Simplizissimus*, No. 1 (May-June 1971), pp. [58-67].

   Both as "Einige Bemerkungen über interplanetarische Erzählungen"; tr. Franz Rottensteiner (uncredited in second appearance).

4. "Suggestions for a Reading Guide." *L'Herne*, No. 12 (1969), pp. 217-38 (as "Suggestions pour un guide du lecteur"; tr. Jacques Parsons).

5. "Supernatural Horror in Literature." *Hayakawa's Mystery Magazine*, No. 172 (August 1970), pp. 42-49; No. 209 (September 1973); No. 222 (October 1974) (as "Kyofushusetsu no keifu"; tr. Katsuo Jinka [as "Hiroyuki Akitsu"]; abridged). *Secolul 20*, No. 4 (1973), pp. 69-72 (as "Nasterea povestirii fantastice"; tr. anon.; abridged).

6. "What Belongs in Verse." *L'Herne*, No. 12 (1969), pp. 239-41 (as "Ce qui doit se dire en vers"; tr. Jacques Parsons). *Il Re in Giallo*, 1, No. 2 [1976], 100-02 (as "Quello che si deve dire in versi"; tr. Giuseppe Lippi).

iii. Poetry

1. *Fungi from Yuggoth. Ides . . . et Autres*, Special issue (15 April 1978), pp. ii-ix as follows:

   "The Book" ("Le Livre"), "Pursuit" ("Poursuite"), "The Key" ("La Clé"), "Recognition," p. ii; "Homecoming" ("Le Retour"), pp. ii-iii; "The Lamp" ("La Lampe"), "Zaman's Hill" ("La Colline de Zaman"), "The Port" ("La Port"), "The Courtyard" ("La Cour murée"), p. iii; "The Pigeon-Flyers" ("Vols de pigeons"), "The Well" ("L'Aven"), "The Howler" ("Le Hurleur"), "Hesperia," "Star-Winds" ("Vents venus des étoiles"), p. iv; "Antarktos," "The Window" ("La Finetre"), "A Memory" ("Les Souvenirs"), "The Gardens of Yin" ("Les Jardins de Yin"), "The Bells" ("Les Cloches"), p. v; "Night-Gaunts" ("Maigres créatures de la nuit"), "Nyarlathotep," "Azathoth" ("Azatoth"), "Mirage," p. vi; "The Canal" ("Le Canal"), pp. vi-vii; "St. Toad's" ("Saint-Toad"), "The Familiars" ("Les Familiers"), "The Elder Pharos" ("L'Ancien Pharos"), "Expectancy" ("Attente"), p. vii; "Nostalgia" ("Nostalgie"), "Background" ("Toile de fond"), "The Dweller" ("L'Habitant"), "Alienation" ("Aliénation"), p. viii; "Harbour Whistles" ("Murmures de port"), pp. viii-ix; "Recapture" ("Reprise"), "Evening Star" ("Étoile du soir"), "Continuity" ("Continuité"), p. ix. Prose translation; tr. anon.

Individual publications:

2. VIII. "The Port." *Il Re in Giallo*, 1, No. 2 [1976], 103-04 (both in English and in an Italian translation by Giuseppe Lippi).

3. XX. "Night-Gaunts." *L'Herne*, No. 12 (1969), pp. 208-09 (both in English and in a French translation [as "Les Decharnes de la nuit"] by Jacques Parsons).

4. XXXVI. "Continuity." *Il Re in Giallo*, 1, No. 2 [1976], 104 (both in English and in an Italian translation by Giuseppe Lippi).

---

5. "In a Sequestered Churchyard Where Once Poe Walked." *Drab*, 4, No. 3 (October 1978), 6 (as "Waar eens Poe wandelde"; tr. Roeland de Vust).

6. "Oceanus." *Il Re in Giallo*, 1, No. 2 [1976], 103 (both in English and in an Italian translation by Giuseppe Lippi).

iv. **Revisions and Collaborations**

1. [With Barlow, R. H.] "The Battle That Ended the Century." *L'Herne*, No. 12 (1969), pp. 212-16 (as "Le combat qui marqua la fin de siècle"; as by "H. P. Lovecraft"; tr. Jacques Parsons).

2. Barlow, R. H. " 'Till A' the Seas.' " *Drab*, 3, No. 2 (n.d.), 13-19 (as "En de zee was niet meer"; tr. Roeland de Vust).

3. Bishop, Zealia. "The Curse of Yig." *Ganymed Horror*, Nos. 10/11/12 (1974), pp. 27-40 (as "Der Fluch des Yig"; tr. Heinz W. Kloos).

4. Heald, Hazel. "The Man of Stone." *Genso to Kaiki*, No. 4 (November 1973), pp. 46-59 (as "Ishi no tami"; tr. Masafumi Ayase).

5. Heald, Hazel. "Out of the Eons." *S-F Magazine*, No. 164 (Special Summer number [September 1972]), pp. 324-40 (as "Eigo yori"; tr. Jiro Ono). *Little Weird*, No. 13 (date unknown) (as "Eigo yori"; tr. Jiro Ono?).

6. With Moore, C. L.; Merritt, A.; Howard, Robert E.; and Long, Frank Belknap, Jr. "The Challenge from Beyond." *Univers*, No. 01 (June 1975), pp. 132-50 (as "Le Défi de l'au-delà"; tr. France-Marie Watkins; Lovecraft portion on pp. 137-45).

7. With Price, E. Hoffmann. "Through the Gates of the Silver Key." *Genso to Kaiki*, No. 3 (September 1973), pp. 160-91 (as "Gin no kagi no mon o koete"; as by "H. P. Lovecraft"; tr. Hiroshi Aramata [as "Seiji Dan"]).

8. With Sterling, Kenneth. "In the Walls of Eryx." *Nueva Dimensión*, No. 32 (May 1972), pp. 98-124. *Nueva*

Dimensión, Special issue No. 6 (May 1975), pp. 111-34.

> Both as "El muro de Eryx"; tr. B. Samarbete.

v. Letters

a. Multiple Publication

1. "Lettres." *L'Herne*, No. 12 (1969), pp. 196-208 (tr. Jacques Parsons).

> Letters: to Alfred Galpin and Maurice W. Moe [i.e., the Gallomo], 11 December 1919, pp. 196-99; to Rheinhart Kleiner, 14 December 1921 [i.e., 1920], pp. 199-200; to Clark Ashton Smith, 29 November 1933, pp. 200-03; to Alfred Galpin and Maurice W. Moe [i.e., the Gallomo], 11 December 1934, pp. 203-07; to Virgil Finlay, 24 October 1936, p. 208.

b. Individual Publications

1. To the Gallomo, 11 December 1919. *Hayakawa's Mystery Magazine*, No. 194 (June 1972), pp. 152-55 (as " 'Randolph Carter no shogen' ni kansuru sakusha shokan"; tr. Kazuburo Yano). *La Opinión*, No. 681 (5 August 1973), Cultural Supplement, p. 5 (tr. anon.).

2. To Frank Belknap Long, 8 November 1923. *Genso to Kaiki*, No. 2 (July 1973), pp. 179-89 (as "Waga kaikishosetsu o kataru"; tr. Hiroshi Aramata [as "Seiji Dan"]).

3. To Maurice W. Moe, 5 April 1931. *Il Re in Giallo*, 1, No. 2 [1976], 93-99 (tr. Giuseppe Lippi).

C. Material Included in Books by Others

1. Ackerman, Forrest J., ed. *Las mejores historias de horror.* Barcelona: Editorial Bruguera, Feb. 1969, June 1970, Aug. 1971, Dec. 1971, Jan. 1972, Apr. 1973, Apr. 1974, Jan. 1975. 669 pp.

    Contains: "El desafío del más allá" ("The Challenge from Beyond"), by C. L. Moore, A. Merritt, H. P. Lovecraft, Robert E. Howard, and Frank Belknap Long, pp. 629-47 (tr. Fernando Corripio).

2. Aramata, Hiroshi, ed. *Cthulhu shinwashu.* Tokyo: Kokusho-kankokai, 1976. 376 pp.

    Contains: "Eigoyori" ("Out of the Eons"), by Hazel Heald, pp. 35-70 (tr. Kunio Namura); "Yig no noroi" ("The Curse of Yig"), by Zealia Bishop, pp. 129-57 (tr. Ryusuke Doi); "Hakubutsukan no kyofu" ("The Horror in the Museum"), by Hazel Heald, pp. 159-204 (tr. Kunio Namura).

3. Brandstätter, Christian, ed. *Phantastica: 24 Geschichten der Weltliteratur illustriert von Hans Fronius: Eine Hommage für E. T. A. Hoffmann.* Vienna: Verlag Fritz Molden, 1976. 208 pp.

    Contains: "Die Musik des Erich Zann" ("The Music of Erich Zann"), pp. 140, 142-46, 148-51 (tr. H. C. Artmann).

4. Carter, Lin, ed. *Die Zaubergärten.* Rastatt/Baden: Pabel Verlag, 1978. 162 pp.

    Contains: "Die Katzen von Ulthar" ("The Cats of Ulthar"), pp. 69-73 (tr. Lore Strassl). Partial translation of *The Young Magicians* (I-C-10).

5. Conklin, Groff, ed. *Con los pelos de punta.* Barcelona: Editorial Molino, 1965. 192 pp.

    Contains: "La casa apartada" ("The Shunned House"), pp. 151-74 (tr. E. de Obregon). Translation of *Twisted* (I-C-20).

6. Dario, Argento, ed. *12 racconti sanguinari*. Milan: Edizioni Profundo Rosso, 1976. 200 pp.

> Contains: "Nel deposito mortuario" ("In the Vault"), pp. 49-55 (tr. Ettore Tempini).

7. De Bruijn, A., and A. Van Der Hoek, eds. *Griezelverhalen*. Utrecht & Antwerp: Prisma-Boeken, 1958. 216 pp.

> Contains: "Ratten" ("The Rats in the Walls"), pp. 130-49 (tr. W. Wielek-Berg).

8. Derleth, August. *El que acecha en el umbral* [*The Lurker at the Threshold*]. Buenos Aires: Editorial Molino, 1946. 228 pp. Caracas: Aucallin, 1972 (as by "H. P. Lovecraft"). 181 pp. Buenos Aires: Ediciones Fantaciencia, 1976 (as by "H. P. Lovecraft"), 1977 (as by "H. P. Lovecraft and A. Derleth"). 147 pp. Barcelona: Bruguera, 1977. 192 pp.

> Contains: "Of Evill Sorceries done in New England," pp. 22-25, 27 (Molino; tr. Delia Piquerez); pp. 21-23, 24 (Aucallin; tr. Casiano S. Martinez); pp. 18-20, 21 (Fantaciencia; tr. Lester del Río); pp. 24-26, 28 (Bruguera; tr. Eladio Lomino).
> See I-E-i, I-E-i-14.

9. Derleth, August. *Il guardiano della soglia* [*The Lurker at the Threshold*]. Rome: Fanucci, 1977. 236 pp.

> Contains: "La mia formazione culturale" (excerpts of letters to Maurice W. Moe, Jan. 1915; to Bernard Austin Dwyer, 3 March 1927), pp. 11-18; "Of Evill Sorceries done in New England," pp. 35-37, 39 (tr. Alfredo Pollini).
> See I-E-i, I-E-i-14.

10. Derleth, August, ed. *Légendes du mythe de Cthulhu*. Paris: Christian Bourgois, 1975. 419 pp.

> Contains: "L'Appel de Cthulhu" ("The Call of Cthulhu"), pp. 15-54; "L'Habitué des ténèbres" ("The Haunter of the Dark"), pp. 261-92; tr. Claude Gilbert. Partial translation of *Tales of the Cthulhu Mythos* (I-C-47).

11. Derleth, August, ed. *Légendes du mythe de Cthulhu*
    [Volume 1]. Paris: France Loisirs, 1975. 214 pp.

    Contains: "L'Appel de Cthulhu" ("The Call of Cthulhu"), pp.
    15-54 (tr. Claude Gilbert). Translation of *Tales of the Cthulhu
    Mythos, Volume 1* (I-C-48).

12. Derleth, August, ed. *Légendes du mythe de Cthulhu*
    [Volume 2]. Paris: France Loisirs, 1975. 215 pp.

    Contains: "L'Habitué des ténèbres" ("The Haunter of the
    Dark"), pp. 57-88 (tr. Claude Gilbert). Partial translation of
    Tales of the Cthulhu Mythos, Volume 2 (I-C-49).

13. Derleth, August, ed. *I miti di Cthulhu*. Rome: Fanucci,
    Oct. 1975. 486 pp.

    Contains: "I magri notturni" ("Night-Gaunts"), p. 33; "Storia
    e cronologia del 'Necronomicon' " ("History of the
    Necronomicon"), pp. 35-41 (both a facsimile of the A.Ms. and a
    printed text); "L'abitatore" ("The Dweller"), p. 453;
    "L'immagine sensa nom," pp. 455-62 (letters to Clark Ashton
    Smith, 7 Oct. 1930, 18 Nov. 1930, 25 Dec. 1930, Dec. 1931,
    Dec. 1931, 24 Dec. 1931, 16 Jan. 1932, 28 Jan. 1932, 8 Feb.
    1932, 31 May 1933, 14 June 1933, 29 June 1933); "Azathoth,"
    pp. 463-64; "Il successore" ("The Descendant"), pp. 464-68; "Il
    libro" ("The Book"), pp. 468-71; tr. Alfredo Pollini and
    Sebastiano Fusco.

14. [Derleth, August, ed.] *Relatos de los mitos de Cthulhu (I)*.
    Barcelona: Editorial Bruguera, Jan. 1977, June
    1978. 269 pp.

    Contains: "La llamada de Cthulhu" ("The Call of Cthulhu"),
    pp. 23-69 (tr. Francisco Torres Oliver). Partial translation of
    Tales of the Cthulhu Mythos (I-C-47).

15. [Derleth, August, ed.] *Relatos de los mitos de Cthulhu (II)*.
    Barcelona: Editorial Bruguera, Feb. 1977, July
    1978. 217 pp.

    Contains: "El huesped de la negrura" ("The Haunter of the
    Dark"), pp. 117-51 (tr. Francisco Torres Oliver). Partial
    translation of *Tales of the Cthulhu Mythos* (I-C-47).

16. [Derleth, August.] *Le rôdeur devant le seuil* [*The Lurker at the Threshold*]. Paris: Christian Bourgois, 1971. 337[+11] pp. Paris: Editions J'ai Lu, 1973, 1975. 309 pp.

> Contains: "Of Evill Sorceries done in New England," pp. 36-40, 43 (Bourgois); pp. 30-34, 37 (J'ai Lu); tr. Claude Gilbert. See I-E-i, I-E-i-14.

17. Dickie, James, ed. *14 Horror-Stories*. Munich: Wilhelm Heyne Verlag, 1973. 255 pp.

> Contains: "Das Amulett des Grabäubers" ("The Hound"), pp. 92-101 (tr. Maikell Michael). Translation of *The Undead* (I-C-55).

18. Doi, Ryusuke, ed. *Cthulhu no hitsugi*. [Tokyo: Ryusuke Doi, 1975.]

> Contains: Lovecraft to August Derleth, 1 Jan. 1930, p. 74 (tr. Ryusuke Doi).

19. Edogawa, Ranpo, ed. *Kaiki shosetsu kessakushu 1*. Tokyo: Sogensha, 1957.

> Contains: "Outsider" ("The Outsider"), pp. 285-97 (tr. Teiichi Hirai).

20. Finné, Jacques, ed. *L'Amerique fantastique de Poe à Lovecraft*. Verviers, Belgium: André Gerard & Co., 1973. 383 pp.

> Contains: "La maison de la sorcière" ("The Dreams in the Witch House"), pp. 357-82 (tr. Jacques Papy).

21. Fruttero, Carlo, and Franco Lucentini, eds. *Storie di fantasmi*. Turin: Einaudi, 1960, 1975; Milan: Club degli Editori, 1978. xvi, 416 pp.

> Contains: "L'orrore di Dunwich" ("The Dunwich Horror"), pp. 29-66 (tr. Floriano Bossi); "Il richiamo di Cthulhu" ("The Call of Cthulhu"), pp. 215-46 (tr. Elena Linfossi); "Nella cripta" ("In the Vault"), pp. 305-14 (tr. Lodovico Terzi).

22. Fruttero, Carlo, and Franco Lucentini, eds. *Universo a sette incognite: Antologia di capolavori della fantascienza*.

[Milan:] Arnoldo Mondadori, June 1963, June 1968. xi, 915[+5] pp.

Contains: "La maschera di Innsmouth" ("The Shadow over Innsmouth"), pp. 637-708 (tr. Sarah Cantoni).

23. Fukushima, Masami, Masahiro Noda, and Sadao Itoh, eds. *Sekai no SF (Danhenshu): Kodenhen.* Tokyo: Asakawa Shoho, 1971. 671 pp.

Contains: "Ijigen no sekisai" ("The Colour out of Space"), pp. 203-38 (tr. "Seiji Dan" [i.e., Hiroshi Aramata]).

24. Gandolfo, Elvio E., and Samuel Wolpin, eds. *45 cuentos siniestros 45* [sic]. Buenos Aires: Ediciones de la Flor S.R.L., 1974. 313 pp.

Contains: "El sabueso" ("The Hound"), pp. 123-25 (tr. anon.). Only a few paragraphs of the tale are printed.

25. Ghidalia, Vic, and Roger Elwood, eds. *Skrekkjegere.* Oslo: Fredhøis Forlag, 1976. 156 pp.

Contains: "Den unevnelige" ("The Unnamable"), pp. 51-58 (tr. Per Glad). Translation of *Horror Hunters* (I-C-63).

26. Goimard, Jacques, and Roland Stragliati, eds. *Histoires d'aberrations.* Paris: Presses Pocket, 1977. 416 pp.

Contains: "Les rêves dans la maison de la sorcière" ("The Dreams in the Witch House"), pp. 139-81 (tr. Jacques Papy).

27. Goimard, Jacques, and Roland Stragliati, eds. *Histoires d'occultisme.* Paris: Presses Pocket, 1977. 448 pp.

Contains: "Lui" ("He"), pp. 401-14 (tr. Paule Pérez).

28. Gutierrez, Nestor R., ed. *Historias de horror.* Buenos Aires: Ediciones Dronte Argentina, 1975. 124 + 7-126 + 7-124 + 7-121 pp. (i.e., 4 vols. in 1).

Contains: "El templo" ("The Temple"), I, 17-34 (tr. P. Castillo); "El muro de Eryx" ("In the Walls of Eryx"), by H. P. Lovecraft and Kenneth Sterling, II, 33-73 (tr. B. Samarbete).

29. Haining, Peter, ed. *I classici della magia nera.* Milan:
    Longanesi & C., 1971, 1972. 382 pp.

    Contains: "La festa" ("The Festival"), pp. 165-82 (tr. Tullio
    Dobner). Translation of *The Satanists* (I-C-86).

30. Haining, Peter, ed. *15 Satan-Stories.* Munich: Wilhelm
    Heyne Verlag, 1975. 255 pp.

    Contains: "Teufels-Weihnacht" ("The Festival"), pp. 101-09
    (tr. [Wulf H. Bergner]). Partial translation of *The Satanists*
    (I-C-86).

31. Haining, Peter, ed. *17 Horror-Stories.* Munich: Wilhelm
    Heyne Verlag, 1974. 255 pp.

    Contains: "Das Ungeheuer aus dem Weltram" ("The Colour
    out of Space"), pp. 217-32 (tr. Hans Maeter). Partial translation
    of *The Ghouls* (I-C-78).

32. Haining, Peter, ed. *22 Alptraum-Stories.* Munich:
    Wilhelm Heyne Verlag, 1975. 256 pp.

    Contains: "Der Geistliche" ("The Evil Clergyman"), pp. 213-
    17 (tr. Maikell Michael). Partial translation of *The Nightmare
    Reader* (I-C-84).

33. Hirai, Teiichi, ed. *Kaiki shosetsu kessakushu 3.* Tokyo:
    Sogensha, 1969 (18th printing 1974). 403 pp.

    Contains: "Dunwich no kai" ("The Dunwich Horror"), pp.
    238-314 (tr. Tadaaki Onishi).

34. Hutardo, Carlos, ed. *Narraciones de ciencia ficción.*
    Madrid: Miguel Castellote, 1971, 1973. 452 pp.

    Contains: "El llamado de Cthulhu" ("The Call of Cthulhu"),
    pp. 357-95 (tr. Ricardo Gosseyn).

35. Ibor, Juan J. Lopéz, ed. *Antología de cuentos de misterio y
    terror.* Barcelona: Editorial Labor, 1958. 2 vols.; 1324
    pp. (numbered consecutively).

    Contains: "El horror de Dunwich" ("The Dunwich Horror"),
    II, 981-1011; tr. anon.

36. Juin, Hubert, ed. *Les 20 Meilleurs Récits de Science-Fiction.*

Verviers, Belgium: Editions Gérard & Co., 1964. 448 pp.

Contains: "Hypnos," pp. 295-302 (tr. Louis Pauwels and Jacques Bergier).

37. Jungstedt, Torsten, ed. *Mannen i svart: En antologi.* [Stockholm:] Rabén & Sjögren, 1955. 439 pp. [Stockholm:] Rabén & Sjögren, 1972. 300 pp.

Contains: "Främlingen" ("The Outsider"), pp. 347-55 (1955 ed.); pp. 237-42 (1972 ed.); "Bilden i huset" ("The Picture in the House"), pp. 356-66 (1955 ed.); pp. 243-49 (1972 ed.); tr. Torsten Jungstedt. The contents of the two editions are only slightly different.

38. Jungstedt, Torsten, ed. *Stora skräckboken: En antologi.* Stockholm: Rabén & Sjögren, 1959. 439 pp. Stockholm: Rabén & Sjögren, 1972. 318 pp.

Contains: "I gravokret" ("In the Vault"), pp. 183-93 (1959 ed.), pp. 129-36 (1972 ed.); "Färg bortom tid och rum" ("The Colour out of Space"), pp. 194-228 (1959 ed.), pp. 137-62 (1972 ed.); tr. Torsten Jungstedt.

39. [Kida, Junichiro, and Hiroshi Aramata, eds.] *Kaiki genso no bungaku II: Ankoku no saigi.* Tokyo: Shinjinbutsu Oraisha, 1969, 1977.

Contains: "Ankoku no higi" ("The Festival"), pp. 197-208 (tr. Katsuo Jinka).

40. [Kida, Junichiro, and Hiroshi Aramata, eds.] *Kaiki genso no bungaku III: Senritsu no sozo.* Tokyo: Shinjinbutsu Oraisha, 1970, 1977.

Contains: *Charles Dexter Ward no kikai na jiken* (*The Case of Charles Dexter Ward*), pp. 167-316 (tr. Toshiyasu Uno).

41. [Kida, Junichiro, and Hiroshi Aramata, eds.] *Kaiki genso no bungaku V: Kaibutsu no jidai.* Tokyo: Shinjinbutsu Oraisha, 1977.

Contains: "Red Hook gai kaijiken" ("The Horror at Red Hook"), pp. 109-35 (tr. Toshio Akai).

42. Kluge, Manfred, ed. *Die besten Gespenstergeschichten aus aller Welt*. Munich: Wilhelm Heyne Verlag, 1976. 159 pp.

> Contains: "Der Aussenseiter" ("The Outsider"), pp. 149-56 (tr. Rudolf Hermstein).

43. Kluge, Manfred, ed. *13 PSI Stories*. Munich: Wilhelm Heyne Verlag, 1976. 254 pp.

> Contains: "Der Schrecken von Dunwich" ("The Dunwich Horror"), pp. 15-51 (tr. [Wulf H. Bergner]).

44. Kluge, Manfred, ed. *17 Dämonen Stories*. Munich: Heyne, 1978. 256 pp.

> Contains: "Der dunkle Alptraum" ("The Haunter of the Dark"), pp. 92-115 (tr. anon.).

45. Kluge, Manfred, ed. *17 Horror-Stories*. Munich: Wilhelm Heyne Verlag, 1976.

> Contains: "Das Ding auf der Schwelle" ("The Thing on the Doorstep"), pp. 11-36 (tr. Wulf H. Bergner).

46. Kluge, Manfred, ed. *18 Gänsehaut Stories*. Munich: Wilhelm Heyne Verlag, 1976. 239 pp.

> Contains: "In der Gruft" ("In the Vault"), pp. 126-34 (tr. [Wulf H. Bergner]).

47. La Cour, Tage, ed. *Spøgelses Historier fra hele verden*. [n.p.:] Carit Andersens Forlag, [n.d.]. 336 pp.

> Contains: "Rotterne i murene" ("The Rats in the Walls"), pp. 41-59 (tr. Poul Ib Liebe).

48. La Cour, Tage, ed. *Verdens beste spøkelses historier*. Oslo: Helge Erichsens Forlag, [n.d.].

> Contains: "Rottene i muren" ("The Rats in the Walls"), pp. 277-95 (tr. Lotte Holmboe).

49. Llopis Paret, Rafael, ed. *Cuentos de terror*. Madrid: Taurus, 1963. 608 pp.

Contains: "Las ratas de las paredes" ("The Rats in the Walls"), pp. 531-47; "El extraño" ("The Outsider"), pp. 549-54; "La ciudad sin nombre" ("The Nameless City"), pp. 555-65; tr. Rafael Llopis Paret.

50. Llopis, Rafael, ed. *Los mitos de Cthulhu: Tales of Cosmic Horror*. Madrid: Alianza Editorial, 1969, 1970, 1975, 1976. 532 pp.

Contains: "La maldición que cayó sobre Sarnath" ("The Doom that Came to Sarnath"), pp. 149-55 (tr. Rafael Llopis); "El ceremonial" ("The Festival"), pp. 163-72 (tr. F. Torres Oliver); "La sombra sobre Innsmouth" ("The Shadow over Innsmouth"), pp. 189-251 (tr. F. Torres Oliver); "En la noche de los tiempos" ("The Shadow out of Time"), pp. 287-353 (tr. F. Torres Oliver); "Reliquia de un mundo olvidado" ("Out of the Eons"), by Hazel Heald, pp. 354-80 (tr. F. Torres Oliver); "El morador de las tinieblas" ("The Haunter of the Dark"), pp. 398-421 (tr. F. Torres Oliver).

51. Llorens, José A., ed. *Narraciones terroríficas: Fourth Selection*. Barcelona: Ediciones Acervo, 1964. 420 pp.

Contains: "El extraño" ("The Outsider"), pp. 201-08; "Aire frio" ("Cool Air"), pp. 209-19; "El susurrador en la oscuridad" ("The Whisperer in Darkness"), pp. 221-98; tr. anon.

52. Llorens, José A., ed. *Narraciones terroríficas: Fifth Selection*. Barcelona: Ediciones Acervo, 1964, 1969. 418 pp.

Contains: "La cosa en al umbral" ("The Thing on the Doorstep"), pp. 67-98 (tr. anon.).

53. Llorens, José A., ed. *Narraciones terroríficas: Seventh Selection*. Barcelona: Ediciones Acervo, 1966, 1973. 420 pp.

Contains: "El pantano-luna" ("The Moon-Bog"), pp. 41-50; "Herbert West, reanimador" ("Herbert West—Reanimator"), pp. 51-88; "Horror en Red Hook" ("The Horror at Red Hook"), pp. 89-113; tr. anon.

54. Llorens Borrás, José A., ed. *Narraciones terroríficas: Eighth Selection.* Barcelona: Ediciones Acervo, 1968, 1975. 388 pp.

    Contains: "El sabueso" ("The Hound"), pp. 95-103 (tr. anon.).

55. Lobo, B. Jessurun, ed. *50 beroemde griezelverhalen.* Amsterdam & Brussels: Elsevier, 1974. 432 pp.

    Contains: "Het ding op de drempel" ("The Thing on the Doorstep"), pp. 270-94 (tr. A. Verhoeff).

56. Lobo, B. Jessurun, ed. *Voor en na middernacht.* Antwerp: Elsevier, 1949, 1954.

    Contains: "Het ding op de drempel" ("The Thing on the Doorstep") (tr. A. Verhoeff). Not seen.

57. Lugones, Piri, ed. *El libro de los autores.* Buenos Aires: Ediciones de la Flor, 1967. 176 pp.

    Contains: "El terror de Dunwich" ("The Dunwich Horror"), pp. 45-102 (tr. J. Davis).

58. Lundwall, Sam J., ed. *Den fantastiska Romanen: Gotisk Skräckromantik från Horace Walpole till H. P. Lovecraft.* Stockholm: Gummessons Grafiska, 1973. 336 pp.

    Contains: "Råttorna i Muren" ("The Rats in the Walls"), pp. 292-314 (tr. anon.). Title on spine: *Den fantastiska Romanen 2.*

59. Mommers, H. W., and A. D. Kraus, ed. *22 Horror Stories.* Munich: Wilhelm Heyne Verlag, 1966.

    Contains: "Die Ratten in den Mauern" ("The Rats in the Walls"), pp. 93-115 (tr. Ingrid Neumann).

60. Nippon Uni Agency, ed. *Anthology: Kyofu to genso 2.* Tokyo: Gekkan pen sha, 1971, 1973. 244 pp.

    Contains: "Reibo sochi no akumu" ("Cool Air"), pp. 131-43.

61. Nippon Uni Agency, ed. *Anthology: Kyofu to genso 3.* Tokyo: Gekkan pan sha, 1971, 1973. 304 pp.

258 **II–C–61**

Contains: "Majo no ie no kai" ("The Dreams in the Witch House"), pp. 241-97 (tr. Makoto Sawa).

62. Norton, Alden H., and Sam Moskowitz, eds. *Las más grandes historias jamás antes contadas de fantasía y horror*. Mexico City: Editorial Novaro, Aug. 1972. 288 pp.

Contains: "Sueños en la casa embrujada" ("The Dreams in the Witch House"), pp. 242-86 (tr. Miguel Ángel Arila). Translation of *Great Untold Stories of Fantasy and Horror* (I-C-143).

63. Parry, Michel, ed. *Die Hunde der Hölle: 13 unheimliche Geschichten*. Frankfurt am Main: Fischer Taschenbuch Verlag, May 1977. 156 pp.

Contains: "Der Bluthund" ("The Hound"), pp. 7-15 (tr. Karl H. Kosmehl). Translation of *The Hounds of Hell* (I-C-149).

64. Parry, Michel, ed. *Lautlos schleicht das Grauen*. Rastatt/Baden: Erich Pabel Verlag, 1975. 143 pp.

Contains: "Das Grauen pocht an meine Tür" ("The Thing on the Doorstep"), pp. 25-55 (tr. Werner Gronwold). Partial translation of *The Devil's Children* (I-C-148).

65. Perales, Ana M., ed. *Antología de novelas de anticipación: Third Selection*. Barcelona: Ediciones Acervo, 1964, 1967, 1971. 436 pp.

Contains: "El color surgido del espacio" ("The Colour out of Space"), pp. 147-81 (tr. anon.).

66. Perales, Ana M., ed. *Antologia de novelas de anticipación: Sixth Selection*. Barcelona: Ediciones Acervo, 1966, 1968. 431 pp.

Contains: "Desde más allá" ("From Beyond"), pp. 121-29; "Más allá de la pared del sueño" ("Beyond the Wall of Sleep"), pp. 131-43; tr. anon.

67. Prins, A. C., ed. *Het monster in de lift en andere griezelverhalen*. Utrecht & Antwerp: A. W. Bruna, 1966. 223 pp.

Contains: "De verschrikking in het museum" ("The Horror in the Museum"), by "Hazel Heald and Howard Phillips Lovecraft," pp. 182-222 (tr. A. C. Prins).

68. Rottensteiner, Franz, ed. *Insel Almanach auf das Jahr 1972: Pfade ins Unendliche.* Frankfurt am Main: Insel Verlag, 1971. 179 pp.

Contains: "Autobiographies—Bemerkungen über einen unbedeutenden Menschen" ("Autobiography—Some Notes on a Nonentity"), pp. 124-36 (with annotations by August Derleth); "Der Untergang Sarnaths" ("The Doom that Came to Sarnath"), pp. 137-45; tr. Michael Maier.

69. Sadoul, Jacques, ed. *Les Meilleurs Récits de Weird Tales: Tome I (1925-1932).* Paris: Editions J'ai Lu, 1975. 249 pp.

Contains: "La Piste très ancienne" ("The Ancient Track"), pp. 209-10 (tr. France-Marie Watkins).

70. Sadoul, Jacques, ed. *Les Meilleurs Récits de Weird Tales: Tome II (1933-1937).* Paris: Editions J'ai Lu, 1975. 286 pp.

Contains: "Hors du temps" ("Out of the Eons"), by Hazel Heald, pp. 27-63; "Psychopompos," pp. 219-27; tr. France-Marie Watkins.

71. Singer, Kurt, ed. *Antología del horror.* Mexico City: Organizacion Editorial Novaro, June 1966. 206 pp.

Contains: "Los sueños en la casa de la bruja" ("The Dreams in the Witch House"), pp. 49-100 (tr. Juan José Utrilla). Partial translation of *Horror Omnibus* (I-C-160).

72. Singer, Kurt, ed. *Horror.* Stuttgart & Hamburg: Wolfgang Krüger, 1969. 192 pp.

Contains: "Träume im Hexenhaus" ("The Dreams in the Witch House"), pp. 57-92 (tr. Joachim A. Frank). Partial translation of *Horror Omnibus* (I-C-160).

73. Singer, Kurt, ed. *Horror*. Frankfurt am Main: Büchergilde Gutenberg, 1971.

> Contains: "Träume im Hexenhaus" ("The Dreams in the Witch House"), pp. 241-76 (tr. Joachim A. Frank). Partial translation of *Horror Omnibus* (I-C-160).

74. Singer, Kurt, ed. *Horror 2*. Munich: Wilhelm Heyne Verlag, 1972. 190 pp.

> Contains: "Träume im Hexenhaus" ("The Dreams in the Witch House"), pp. 34-66 (tr. Joachim A. Frank). Partial translation of *Horror Omnibus* (I-C-160).

75. Singer, Kurt, ed. *Horror 6*. Barcelona: Editorial Bruguera, Sept. 1976. 185 pp.

> Contains: "Sueños en la casa de brujas" ("The Dreams in the Witch House"), pp. 55-114 (tr. Carlos M. Sánchez-Rodrigo). Partial translation of *Horror Omnibus* (I-C-160).

76. Singer, Kurt, ed. *Satansbraten à la Carte*. Rastatt/Baden: Erich Pabel Verlag, 1978. 162 pp.

> Contains: "Das gemiedene Haus" ("The Shunned House"), pp. 69-106 (tr. Annegret Gross-Hermann). Partial translation of *Satanic Omnibus* (I-C-161).

77. Sternberg, Jacques, ed. *Les Chef-d'oeuvres de la science-fiction*. Paris: Editorial Planète, 1970, 458 pp.

> Contains: "Dans les murs d'Eryx" ("In the Walls of Eryx"), by H. P. Lovecraft and Kenneth Sterling (as by "H. P. Lovecraft"), pp. 271-88 (tr. Pierre Chapelot).

78. Tasso, Bruno, ed. *Il breviario del brivido*. Rome: Sugar, 1967.

> Contains: "I topi nel muro" ("The Rats in the Walls") (tr. Bruno Tasso). Not seen.

79. Tasso, Bruno, ed. *Un secolo di terrore*. Rome: Sugar, 1960.

> Contains: "I topi nel muro" ("The Rats in the Walls"), pp. 237-66 (tr. Bruno Tasso).

80. Van Hageland, A., ed. *Land van de griezel*. Alsemberg, Belgium: D. A. P. Reinaert Uitgaven, 1976. 415 pp.

    Contains: "Het huis van verderf" ("The Shunned House"), pp. 349-84 (tr. anon.).

81. Ward, Don, ed. *Chi di vampiro ferisce*. Piacenza: Casa Editrice la Tribuna, 1972. 176 pp.

    Contains: "Aria fredda" ("Cool Air"), pp. 91-100 (tr. G. Cossato and S. Sandrelli). Translation of *Dark of the Soul* (I-C-174).

82. Yano, Kozaburo, ed. *Sekai kaiki mystery kessakusen*. Tokyo: Bancho Shobo, 1977.

    Contains: "Cthulhu no yobigoe" ("The Call of Cthulhu"), pp. 197-248 (tr. Kozaburo Yano).

83. [Anonymous, ed.] *Breviario del estremecimiento: Relatos*. Caracas: Monte Avila Editores, 1970. 185 pp.

    Contains: "El llamado de Cthulhu" ("The Call of Cthulhu"), pp. 55-91 (tr. Maria Esther Vazquez).

84. [Anonymous, ed.] *Fem Öppna Gravar*. Falun, Sweden: B. Wahlströms, 1976. 159 pp.

    Contains: "Sträcken i brunnen" ("Monster of Terror" [i.e., "The Colour out of Space"]), pp. 72-117 (tr. Peter Gissy).

85. [Anonymous, ed.] *Genso to kaiki 2*. Tokyo: Hayakawa Shobo, 1969, 1974. 234 pp.

    Contains: "Dunwich no kai" ("The Dunwich Horror"), pp. 75-131 (tr. Takeshi Shiota).

86. [Anonymous, ed.] *Die Höllenkatze*. Sasbachwalden, West Ger.: Wolfhart Luther Verlag, 1972. 190 pp.

    Contains: "Rache in der Gruft" ("In the Vault"), pp. 164-71 (tr. Ernst Heyda and Hella Unruh).

87. [Anonymous, ed.] *Horror I*. Milan: Sugar, March 1965. 605 pp.

Contains: "Orrore a Red Hook" ("The Horror at Red Hook"), pp. 365-402 (tr. Maurizio Belloti).

88. [Anonymous, ed.] *Kaidan (2)*. Tokyo: Kodansha, 1972 (6th printing 1974). 214 pp.

Contains: "Reibo o osoreru otoko" ("Cool Air"), pp. 4-24 (tr. Shigeru Shiraki).

89. [Anonymous, ed.] *Kaidan (3)*. Tokyo: Kodansha, 1974. 200 pp.

Contains: "Dunwich no kaibutsu" ("The Dunwich Horror"), pp. 127-94 (tr. Michio Tsuzuki).

90. [Anonymous, ed.] *Monster*. Falun, Sweden: B. Wahlströms Bokförlag, 1974. 160 pp.

Contains: "Monstret utifrån" ("The Outsider"), pp. 105-14 (tr. Alf Agdler).

91. [Anonymous, ed.] *Relatos de terror y espanto 1*. Barcelona: Ediciones Dronte, 1972. 128 pp.

Contains: "El abismo en el tiempo" ("The Shadow out of Time"), pp. 9-102 (tr. P. Castillo).

92. [Anonymous, ed.] *Sekai kyofu shosetsu zenshu 5*. Tokyo: Sogensha, 1958.

Contains: "Kabe no naka no nezumi" ("The Rats in the Walls"), pp. 7-41; "Innsmouth no kage" ("The Shadow over Innsmouth"), pp. 43-149; "Dunwich no kai" ("The Dunwich Horror"), pp. 151-222; tr. Tadaaki Onishi.

III. Works about Lovecraft

A. News Items and Encyclopedias

1. Ash, Brian. *Who's Who in Science Fiction*. New York: Taplinger, 1976, pp. 138-39.

2. Ashley, Mike. *Who's Who in Horror and Fantasy Fiction*. New York: Taplinger, 1977, pp. 121-22.

3. Burke, W. J., and Will D. Howe. *American Authors and Books: 1640 to the Present Day*. Augmented and revised by Irving R. Weiss. New York: Crown Publishers, 1962, p. 451.

4. Coates, Walter John. "Howard Phillips Lovecraft [1890-1937]." *Driftwind*, 11, No. 9 (April 1937), 343-44.

   Death notice by Lovecraft's friend, appearing in the magazine of which he was associate editor (see I-D-ii-4).

5. De Turris, Gianfranco. "Il mago della litteratura fantastica." *Vita*, 19, No. 66 (15 March 1977), 3.

6. De Turris, Gianfranco. "Uno straniero nel cosmo." *Roma*, 116, No. 64 (15 March 1977), 3.

7. [De Turris, Gianfranco, and Sebastiano Fusco.] "Lovecraft, Howard Phillips (1890-1937)." *Arcana: Il meraviglioso l'erotica il surreale il nero l'insolite nelle litterature di tutti i tempi e paesi*. Milan: Sugar, 1970, pp. 440-48.

8. Franklin, H. Bruce. "Lovecraft, H. P." *Encyclopedia Americana*. New York: Americana Corp., 1973. XVII, 808.

9. [Gillings, Walter?] "Fantasy Loses Lovecraft." *Scientifiction* [1937].

10. Hart, James D., ed. *The Oxford Companion to American Literature*. 4th ed. New York: Oxford Univ. Press, 1965, p. 497.

11. Herzberg, Max J., and the staff of the Thomas Y. Crowell Co. *The Reader's Encyclopedia of American Literature*. New York: Thomas Y. Crowell Co., 1962, p. 657.

12. Jones, Agnes, et al. *A Selected Biographical and Bibliographical List of Rhode Island Authors*. [Providence:] Providence Public Library, 1967, pp. 19-20.

13. Kellar, Mark M. "The Horrible Truth about Rhode Island." *Fresh Fruit*, 4, No. 24 (31 October 1976), 4-5.

14. Kincaid, Dorothy. "Lovecraft Cult Growing." *Milwaukee Sentinel*, April 1975.

15. Kunitz, Stanley J., ed. *Twentieth Century Authors: First Supplement: A Biographical Dictionary of Modern Literature*. New York: The H. W. Wilson Co., 1955, pp. 596-98.

16. Moore, Violet. "Lovecraft Legend Lives." *The Atlanta Journal*, 22 April 1974, p. 3.

17. *The New Encyclopaedia Britannica*. 15th ed. Chicago: Encyclopaedia Britannica, Inc., 1974. Micropaedia, VI, 355.

18. Valla, Ricardo. "I mostri nascono dalla cattiva coscienza: Riscoperta di Lovecraft a 40 anni della morte." *Stampa Sera*, 22 June 1977, pp. 12-13.

19. Van Doren, Charles, ed.; Robert McHenry, associate ed. *Webster's American Biographies*. Springfield, Mass.: G. & C. Merriam Co., 1974, p. 650.

20. Van Tieghem, Philippe, and Pierre Josserand, eds.

Dictionnaire des Littératures. Paris: Presses
Universitaires de France, 1968. II, 2414-15.

21. Versins, Pierre. *Encyclopédie de l'utopie, des voyages
    extraordinaries, et de la science fiction.* Lausanne: l'Age
    d'Homme, 1972, pp. 550-53.

22. [Unsigned.] "Attualità di Howard Lovecraft." *Roma*,
    116, No. 134 (27 May 1977), 3.

23. [Unsigned.] "Un convegno su Lovecraft." *Secolo
    d'Italia*, 26, No. 137 (15 June 1977), 3.

24. [Unsigned.] "The Day that Lovecraft's House Was
    Moved." *Brown Alumni Monthly*, 72, No. 5 (February
    1972), 29.

25. [Unsigned.] "House Shunned No Longer." *Pawtucket
    [R.I.] Times*, 353, No. 49 (27 November 1975), 16.

26. [Unsigned.] "H.P.L. Was a Loner." *The Rhode Islander
    (The Providence Sunday Journal Magazine)*, 26 October
    1975, pp. 10-11.

27. [Unsigned.] "H. P. Lovecraft at the John Hay."
    Weekend (The Providence Sunday Journal magazine), 61,
    No. 43 (1 November 1975), 5.

28. [Unsigned.] "H. P. Lovecraft, Author, Is Dead:
    Student and Writer about Supernatural Things Was
    46 Years of Age: Wrote about Astronomy: Native
    of This City Kept Accurate Daily Account of
    Incapacity until He Went to Hospital." *The Providence
    Journal*, 59, No. 64 (16 March 1937), 18.

29. [Unsigned.] "H. P. Lovecraft Dead in Hospital." *The
    Providence Evening Bulletin*, 75, No. 62 (15 March
    1937), 26.

30. [Unsigned.] "Literary Persons Meet in Guilford." *Brattleboro* [Vt.] *Reformer*, 18 June 1928, p. 1.

31. [Unsigned.] "Local Writer Discussed: Journal Editor Lectures on Life of H. P. Lovecraft." *The Providence Journal*, 66, No. 52 (1 March 1944), 4.

    On a lecture by W. T. Scott at the Providence Public Library.

32. [Unsigned.] "Lovecraft narratore cosmico: A Trieste un convegno internazionale." *La Repubblica*, 2, No. 133 (11 June 1977), 13.

33. [Unsigned.] "Lovecraft's Family Had Rochester Ties." *The* [Rochester, N.Y.] *Democrat and Chronicle*, 20 April 1975.

34. [Unsigned.] "Masters of Fantasy: Howard Phillips Lovecraft—'The Outsider'—1890-1937." *Famous Fantastic Mysteries*, 8, No. 6 (August 1947), 113.

35. [Unsigned.] "Nell'inquitante universo dello scrittore Lovecraft: Concluso a Trieste il convegno sui maestro americano della litteratura 'gotica.' " *L'Unità*, 14 June 1977.

36. [Unsigned.] [Obituary.] *The Providence Journal*, 109, No. 64 (16 March 1937), 3; 109, No. 65 (17 March 1937), 3; 109, No. 66 (18 March 1937), 3.

37. [Unsigned.] [Obituary.] *The* [Providence] *News-Tribune*, 35, No. 62 (16 March 1937), 2.

38. [Unsigned.] "Old East Side House Ends Trip Up Hill." *The Providence Journal*, 131, No. 226 (21 September 1959), 1, 17.

39. [Unsigned.] "Old House Will Get New View." *The Providence Sunday Journal*, 75, No. 6 (9 August 1959), 23.

40. [Unsigned.] "Un personaggio straordinario." *Il Meridiano di Trieste*, 1, No. 23 (9 June 1977), 4.

41. [Unsigned.] "Writer Charts Fatal Malady." *The New York Times*, No. 28,906 (16 March 1937), p. 5.

    This obituary, circulated by A.P., was picked up by many newspapers across the country.

B. Bibliographies and Glossaries

1. Berglund, E. P. "Addenda to HPL Story Listing."
   Nyctalops, 1, No. 3 (February 1971), 8; 1, No. 4 (June
   1971), 21-25; 1, No. 5 (October 1971), 13, 47.
   Additions and corrections to Morris' list (see III-B-25).

2. Berglund, E. P. "Foreign Publications of Howard
   Phillips Lovecraft." *Nyctalops*, 1, No. 5 (October
   1971), 42-47.

3. Bertin, Eddy C. "Additions to the Complete Index to
   Lovecraft, Published by Arkham House in 'The
   Dark Brotherhood and Other Pieces' (1966) by Jack
   L. Chalker." *Shadow*, No. 7 (September 1969), pp.
   16-21.

4. Bertin, Eddy C. "H. P. Lovecraft: A Checklist of His
   Books." *Cahier*, No. 1 (1976), pp. 11-15.

5. Bertin, Eddy C. "H. P. Lovecraft: A Listing of His
   Fiction." *Cahier*, No. 1 (1976), pp. 17-20.

6. Bertin, Eddy C. "Lovecraft in Dutch-Language
   Books." *Cahier*, No. 1 (1976), pp. 9-10.

7. Brennan, Joseph Payne. *H. P. Lovecraft: A Bibliography.*
   Washington, D.C.: Biblio Press, 1952. 14 pp.
   Revised version of III-B-8.

8. Brennan, Joseph Payne. *A Select Bibliography of H. P.
   Lovecraft.* [New Haven, Conn.: Joseph Payne
   Brennan,] 1952. [8] pp.

9. Chalker, Jack L., compiler and editor. *The New H. P.
   Lovecraft Bibliography.* Baltimore: The Anthem Press,
   1962. 40 pp.
   See III-D-396 for an updated version.

10. Cochran, Donald. "Innsmouth." *Decal*, No. 4 (December 1973), pp. 11-14.

    Glossary of terms in "The Shadow over Innsmouth."

11. Cochran, Donald E. *Lovecraft: The Fiction.* [Jackson, Miss.:] Eidolon Press, 1974. 15 pp.

    Index of proper names in the Arkham House 3-volume edition of Lovecraft's fiction (I-A-34, 39, 42).

12. Cochran, Don. *Lovecraft: The Revisions: An Index to* The Horror in the Museum and Other Revisions. Jackson, Miss.: Eidolon Press, 1975. 5 pp.

13. Cochran, Donald. "The Palaeological Lovecraft." *Decal*, No. 3 (18 May 1973), 14-17.

    Glossary of terms in "The Shadow out of Time" and *At the Mountains of Madness.*

14. Cockcroft, T. G. L. "Random Notes on H. P. Lovecraft." *Bacchanalia*, 1, No. 1 (April 1953). *Nyctalops*, 2, No. 1 (April 1973), 20 (as "Articles about H. P. Lovecraft in Amateur Journals").

15. Cortoos, Josiane. "Bibliografie." *Rigel*, No. 3 (November 1976), pp. [18-31].

16. Eisner, Steven. "A Bibliography of H. P. Lovecraft." *Fresco*, 8, No. 3 (Spring 1958), 52-53.

17. Emmons, Winfred S., Jr. "A Bibliography of H. P. Lovecraft." *Extrapolation*, No. 3 (December 1961), pp. 2-25.

18. Faig, Kenneth W. "HPL: The Early Years[:] A Bibliography." *Nyctalops*, 2, No. 3 (January-February 1975), 46-49, 54.

    Invaluable research on Lovecraft's early publications in the Providence newspapers.

19. Faig, Kenneth W. "The Lovecraft Fiction
    Manuscripts: A Listing." *Nyctalops*, 1, No. 5 (October
    1971), 28-36; 1, No. 6 (February 1972), 35-39.

20. Hill, L. W. "The Owings Bibliography: Addenda and
    Corrigenda." *Myrrdin*, 1, No. 1 (Winter 1975), 15-20.

21. Hillman, Arthur F., Kenneth E. Slater, and Peter W.
    Campbell. "Lovecraft's Proffesionally [sic] Published
    Works." *Operation Fantast*, 2, Nos. 1-2 (Winter 1952),
    40-42.

22. Laney, Francis T., and William H. Evans, compilers
    and editors. *Howard Phillips Lovecraft (1890-1937): A
    Tentative Bibliography*. [Los Angeles:] Acolyte—FAPA
    Publications, 1943. 12 pp.

    The first Lovecraft bibliography.

23. Lippi, Giuseppe. "Appendice I: Breve indirezzario
    lovecraftiano." *Il Re in Giallo*, 1, No. 2 [1976], 124.

24. Lippi, Giuseppe. "Appendice II: H. P. Lovecraft:
    Bibliografia essenziale." *Il Re in Giallo*, 1, No. 2
    [1976], 125-26.

25. [Morris, Harry O.] "H. P. Lovecraft: A Story
    Listing." *Nyctalops*, 1, No. 2 (October 1970), 7-10; 1,
    No. 3 (February 1971), 9-12; 1, No. 4 (June 1971),
    25-27.

26. Morris, Harry O. "Listing from *The Dream-Quest of
    Unknown Kadath*." *Tamlacht*, 2, No. 2 (n.d.), 27-31.

    Glossary of names used in the novel.

27. Owings, Mark, with Jack L. Chalker. *The Revised H. P.
    Lovecraft Bibliography*. Baltimore: Mirage Press, 1973.
    vii, 43 pp.

    Updating of Chalker's 1966 bibliography (see III-D-396).

Review

a. [Schiff, Stuart D.] *Whispers*, 1, No. 2 (December 1973), 49.

28. Sutton, David A., ed. *Bibliotheca: H. P. Lovecraft.* Birmingham, Eng.: David A. Sutton, 1971. 41 pp.

Contains: David A. Sutton, "Introduction," p. 2; Eddy C. Bertin, "Howard Phillips Lovecraft: A Complete Chronological Checklist of His Stories and Novels," pp. 3-9; E. P. Berglund, "A Chronological Listing of the Cthulhu Mythos Stories," pp. 10-12, 14-18; Eddy C. Bertin, "Additions to the Chalker Index," pp. 19-24, 26-27; Ted Ball, "Additions & Corrections to the Chalker Index," pp. 28-30; E. P. Berglund, "Addenda to 'H. P. Lovecraft: The Books' [by Lin Carter]," pp. 31-34, 36-41, 18.

Review

a. [Unsigned.] *Ambrosia*, No. 1 (24 June 1972), p. 45.

29. Tuck, Donald. *The Encyclopedia of Science Fiction and Fantasy through 1968.* Chicago: Advent Publishers, Inc., 1974, pp. 281-85.

30. Van Herp, Jacques [et al.]. "Bibliographie." *L'Herne*, No. 12 (1969), pp. 359-79.

Adapted from Chalker (III-D-396), but listing additional foreign Lovecraftiana.

31. Vetter, John E. "Howard Phillips Lovecraft: Poetic Tributes: A Tentative Bibliography." *Mirage*, 1, No. 5 (Summer 1962), 42-43.

32. Weinberg, R. E., and E. P. Berglund, compilers. *Reader's Guide to the Cthulhu Mythos.* 2nd rev. ed. Albuquerque, N.M.: The Silver Scarab Press, 1973. 88 pp.

Lists tales of the "Cthulhu Mythos" by Lovecraft and other writers.

Review

a. [Schiff, Stuart D.] *Whispers*, 2, No. 1 (November 1974), 19.

33. Wetzel, George T. "Howard Phillips Lovecraft in the Amateur Magazines." *Vagabond*, No. 1 (Spring 1955); No. 2 (Summer 1955).

Chronological listing of the alphabetical listing printed in III-B-35.

34. Wetzel, George T. "Lovecraft in the Ashville [sic] Gazette-News." *Renaissance*, 2, No. 2 (March 1953), 12-13.

35. Wetzel, George [T.], ed. *The Lovecraft Collectors Library, Volume Seven: Bibliographies.* North Tonawanda, N.Y.: SSR Publications, 1955. v, [6-]42 pp.

Contains: George [T.] Wetzel, "Amateur Press Works," pp. v-17; Robert E. Briney, "Professional Works and Miscellany," pp. 18-42.

A landmark in Lovecraft bibliography, giving the first extensive listing of Lovecraft's amateur press works. The foundation for all subsequent work in the field.
See also III-C-26.

36. Wetzel, George T. "Lovecraft's Amateur Press Works." *Destiny*, 1, No. 4-5 (Summer-Fall 1951), 23-25. *Operation Fantast*, 2, No. 1-2 (Winter 1952), 39-40.

37. [Unsigned.] "A Listing of Some Lovecraft Manuscripts." *Nyctalops*, 1, No. 3 (February 1971), 13-14.

C.   Books and Pamphlets about Lovecraft

1. Brennan, Joseph Payne. *H. P. Lovecraft: An Evaluation.*
   New Haven, Conn.: Macabre House, 1955. 8 pp.

2. Carter, Lin. *Lovecraft: A Look Behind the "Cthulhu Mythos."*
   New York: Ballantine Books, Feb. 1972, Dec. 1976.
   xvi, 198 pp. St. Albans, Eng.: Panther Books, 1975.
   189 pp.

   Although full of serious factual errors and misinterpretations
   (e.g., an acceptance of Derleth's view of the myth-cycle), the
   volume provides a reasonable history of the "Cthulhu Mythos"
   tradition, particularly after Lovecraft's death. The literary
   criticism is amateurish.

Reviews

a. Ball, Ted. *Shadow*, No. 18 (November 1972), pp.
   14-18.

b. Bertin, Eddy C. "A Pair from R'lyeh." *Ambrosia*, No. 2
   (August 1973), p. 27

c. Bryant, Roger. "Looking Behind—but not *at*—the
   Mythos." *Nyctalops*, 2, No. 1 (April 1973), 26-28.

d. Campbell, Ramsey. *Shadow*, No. 18 (November 1972),
   pp. 18-19.

e. Egan, Thomas M. *Delap's Fantasy and Science Fiction
   Review*, 3, No. 4 (April 1977). 37-38.

f. Leiber, Fritz. *Fantastic*, 22, No. 1 (October 1972),
   113-14.

g. Rottensteiner, Franz. *Quarber Merkur*, 11, No. 2 (July
   1973), 62-64.

h. Williamson, Chet. *Nyctalops*, 2, No. 1 (April 1973), 28.

3. Chalker, Jack L., ed. *Mirage on Lovecraft: A Literary View*.
   Baltimore: Jack L. Chalker and Mark Owings (The
   Anthem Series), 1965. ix, 46 pp.

   > Contains: [Jack L. Chalker], "Foreword," p. ix; H. P.
   > Lovecraft, "Autobiography: Some Notes on a Nonentity," pp.
   > 3-10 (annotated by August Derleth); H. P. Lovecraft, "Notes on
   > the Writing of Weird Fiction" (i.e., "Notes on Writing Weird
   > Fiction"), pp. 13-15; H. P. Lovecraft, "Some Notes on
   > Interplanetary Fiction," pp. 19-23; David H. Keller, "Notes on
   > Lovecraft," pp. 29-35; August Derleth, "A Rebuttal to
   > Lovecraft Criticism," pp. 37-39; Jack L. Chalker, "And a
   > Conclusion That Isn't," pp. 41-43; Jack L. Chalker, "The Books
   > of H. P. Lovecraft: A Checklist," pp. 45-46.

Review

a. Bertin, Eddy C. *Shadow*, No. 7 (September 1969), pp.
   52-53. *Nyctalops*, 1, No. 2 (October 1970), 14.

4. Cook, W. Paul. *In Memoriam: Howard Phillips Lovecraft:
   Recollections, Appreciations, Estimates*. North Montpelier,
   Vt.: The Driftwind Press, 1941. [ii], 76 pp.
   Baltimore: Mirage Press, 1968 (as *H. P. Lovecraft: A
   Portrait*). iii, 66 pp. West Warwick, R. I.:
   Necronomicon Press, 1977. [iv], 76 pp.

   > Still the best memoir of Lovecraft, from which many classic
   > tales about him have arisen. Cook is particularly strong on
   > Lovecraft's early involvement with amateur journalism and on
   > his travels through New England.

Reviews

a. Bertin, Eddy C. *Shadow*, No. 7 (September 1969), pp.
   53-54. *Nyctalops*, 1, No. 2 (October 1970), 14-15.

b. Orton, Vrest. "Seems If: A Weekly Column." *Bellows
   Falls* [Vt.] *Times*, 3 July 1941.

5. de Camp, L. Sprague. *Lovecraft: A Biography*. Garden
   City, N.Y.: Doubleday & Co., 1975, 1975, 1976;

London: New English Library, 1976. xvi, 510 pp.
New York: Ballantine Books, Aug. 1976. xiv. 480
pp.

The first full-length biography, containing a wealth of
factual data (although with many errors), but weakened by
value judgments upon Lovecraft's character and very crude
attempts at literary criticism. The volume is useful for
reference and for providing a rough chronology of the whole of
Lovecraft's life, but is generally superficial and its author's lack
of sympathy for his subject causes him often to misinterpret
Lovecraft's ideals and motives. The English edition follows the
American third edition, which is slightly revised; the Ballantine
edition is "abridged by the author": thirteen thousand words, as
well as the bibliography, notes, and index, have been omitted.

Reviews

a. Adams, Phoebe. *The Atlantic*, 235, No. 3 (March
    1975), 146.

b. Ball, Ted. *The British Fantasy Society Bulletin*, 3, No. 1
    (March-April 1975), 4.

c. Barkham, John. "A Master of the Macabre." *SF
    Chronicle*, 30 January 1975.

d. Bertin, Eddy C. *SF-Gids*, 4, No. 5 (September 1975),
    14.

e. Biggers, Cliff. "The HPL Revival." *Future Perspective*,
    No. 8 (September 1976), pp. 5-6.

f. Blistein, Elmer M. "Posthumously He Lost His
    Amateur Standing." *The Providence Sunday Journal*, 90,
    No. 47 (25 May 1975), Sec. H, p. 30.

g. Brennan, Joseph Payne. *Connecticut Fireside Magazine*, 4,
    No. IV, 1 (Spring 1976), 14-15.

h. Budrys, Algis. "H. P. Lovecraft and Others." *The

Magazine of Fantasy and Science Fiction, 49, No. 3 (September 1975), 32-38.

i. Collins, Tom. "Lovecraft: Man and Myth." *Mythologies*, No. 6 (July-August 1975), pp. 10-15. *Moebius Trip Library's SF Echo*, Nos. 23-24 (August-December 1975), pp. 62-70. *SF Booklog*, No. 7 (January-February 1976), pp. 2-3 (without title).

j. Delap, Richard. *Delap's Fantasy and Science Fiction Review*, 1, No. 2 (May 1975), 8-9.

k. del Rey, Lester. *Analog*, 95, No. 8 (August 1975), 170.

l. Dettro, Chris. "Weird Tales Pioneer Subject of Biography." *Springfield* [Ill.] *State Journal-Register*, 16 February 1976, p. 20.

m. de Vust, Roeland. *Drab*, 3, No. 2 (n.d.), 42-43.

n. Ellis, James. *Nyctalops*, 2, Nos. 4-5 (April 1976), 27-28.

o. Gingrich, Arnold. "The Greatest Character H. P. Lovecraft Ever Created." *Chicago Tribune*, 2 February 1975.

p. Hartmann, Matthew. *Library Journal*, 100, No. 4 (15 February 1975), 387.

q. Heffelfinger, Charles. "Providence's Ghostly Gentleman." *Bombastium*, No. 32 (August 1975), pp. [9-11].

r. Jonas, Gerald. "Of Things to Come." *New York Times Book Review*, 29 June 1975, pp. 25-27.

s. Kurland, Michael. *Locus*, No. 13 (10 May 1975), p. 7.

t. Lamanna, Jim, Jr. "He Was One of Us." *People Watcher*, No. 39 (February 1976), pp. [1-2].

u. Le Guin, Ursula. "New England Gothic." *The Times Literary Supplement*, No. 3863 (26 March 1976), p. 335.

v. Lehmann-Haupt, Christopher. "The New England Horror." *The New York Times*, No. 42,739 (29 January 1975), p. 15. *Fort Lauderdale* [Fl.] *News and Sun-Sentinel*, 9 February 1975.

w. Leiber, Fritz. *Fantastic*, 24, No. 6 (October 1975), 115-18, 128.

x. Lovecraft, H. P. *Mask*, January 1977, p. 6. [Excerpts from I-A-59, pp. 290, 312, and 326.]

y. McMurtry, Larry. " 'Master of the Turgid.' " *The Washington Post*, 98, No. 74 (17 February 1975), Sec. D, p. 4. *Rocky Mountain News*, 14 March 1975.

z. Meschkow, Sanford Zane. *Amra*, 2, No. 63 (April 1975), 15-16.

aa. Millar, Jeff. *The Houston Chronicle*, 23 February 1975.

bb. Miller, Dan. "Lovecraft, Petrified Ghoulmaster of Horror Tales." *Chicago Daily News*, 100, No. 33 (8-9 February 1975), *Panorama* sec., p. 5.

cc. Mosig, Dirk W. *SFRA Newsletter*, No. 38 (March 1975), pp. 1-2.

dd. Mosig, Dirk W. "Lovecraft: A Parody." *Fantasy Crossroads*, 1, Nos. 4-5 (August 1975), 5-8. *Nyctalops*, 2, Nos. 4-5 (April 1976), 26-27. *The Fossil*, No. 215 (July 1976), pp. 8-10. *Weird Fiction Times*, No. 47 (January 1977), pp. 35-41 (as "Lovecraft: Eine Parodie"; tr. anon.).

ee. M[ullen], R. D. "The Great Futilitarian: De Camp's Biography of Lovecraft." *Science-Fiction Studies*, No. 5 (March 1975), pp. 89-91.

ff. Price, E. Hoffmann. *Nyctalops*, 2, Nos. 4-5 (April 1976), 28-29. [Excerpt of a letter to L. Sprague de Camp.]

gg. Rottensteiner, Franz. *Quarber Merkur*, 14, No. 3 (December 1976), 78-81.

hh. Schiff, Stuart D. "Two on Lovecraft and Others." *Whispers*, 2, Nos. 2-3 (June 1975), 58-60.

ii. Schlueter, Paul. "The Demons of Lovecraft." *Chicago Sunday Sun-Times Book Week*, 28, No. 20 (16 February 1975), 7.

jj. Schweitzer, Darrell. *Concert*, April 1975. *Ash-Wing*, No. 18 (n.d.), pp. 22-23.

kk. Searles, Baird. *The Science Fiction Book Review*, No. 1 (March 1975).

ll. Shreffler, Philip A. *St. Louis Post-Dispatch*, 117, No. 90 (1 April 1975), 3B.

mm. Sinclair, David. "Five Dollar Fruit Cake." *The Times* (London), No. 59,662 (25 March 1976), p. 13.

nn. Thomas, William V. "A Spaced-Out Cult Figure." *The Chronicle of Higher Education*, 19 July 1976, p. 10.

oo. Thompson, Dan. "Two Labors of Lovecraft." *Cleveland Press*, 23 January 1976. *Reader's Guide*, No. 125 (9 April 1976), p. 30.

pp. Young, Jack. *Fosfax*, No. 20 (14 April 1975), pp. 1, 4.

qq. [Unsigned.] *Kirkus*, December 1974.

rr. [Unsigned.] *Publishers' Weekly*, 206, No. 25 (16 December 1974), 47.

ss. [Unsigned.] *Starling*, No. 31 (May 1975), pp. 21-23.

6. Derleth, August. *H. P. L.: A Memoir.* New York: Ben
   Abramson, 1945. 122 pp.

   Review

   a. Cole, Edward H. *The Fossil*, No. 109 (January 1946),
      pp. 24-25.

7. Derleth, August. *Some Notes on H. P. Lovecraft.* [Sauk
   City, Wis.:] Arkham House, 1959; Folcroft, Pa.:
   Folcroft Press, 1971; [Norwood, Pa.:] Norwood
   Editions, 1976. xliii pp.

   Review

   a. Bertin, Eddy C. *Shadow*, No. 7 (September 1969), p.
      54. *Nyctalops*, 1, No. 2 (October 1970), 15.

8. Eddy, Muriel E. *The Gentleman from Angell Street.*
   [Providence: Privately printed,] 1961, 1977. 25 pp.

9. Eddy, Muriel E. *H. P. Lovecraft Esquire: Gentleman.*
   [Providence: Privately printed, n.d.] 6 pp.

10. Eddy, Muriel E. *The Howard Phillips Lovecraft We Knew.*
    [Providence: Privately printed, n.d.] [10] pp.

    Review

    a. Bertin, Eddy C. *Shadow*, No. 7 (September 1969), pp.
       54-55. *Nyctalops*, 1, No. 3 (February 1971), 15.

11. Eddy, Muriel E. *Howard Phillips Lovecraft: The Man and
    the Image.* [Providence:] Muriel E. Eddy (Studio Guild
    Press), 1969. 8 pp.

12. Frierson, Meade, III, and Penny Frierson, eds. *HPL.*
    [Birmingham, Al.: The Editors, 1972, 1975.] 143 pp.

    Contains: Robert Bloch, "The Lovecraft Mythos," p. 5;
    Joseph Payne Brennan, "A Haunter of the Night," p. 6; Stuart
    D. Schiff, "An Interview with Frank Belknap Long," pp. 7-11; E.

Hoffman[n] Price, "HPL: An Astrological Analysis," pp. 12-16; E. Hoffman[n] Price, "Reminiscences of HPL," pp. 16-17; Fritz Leiber, "A Few Short Comments on the Writings of HPL," p. 18; R. Alain Everts, "Ira A. Cole and Howard Phillips Lovecraft: A Brief Friendship," pp.19-21; excerpts from *Order of Assassins*, by Colin Wilson, pp. 22-23; [Unsigned], "An Early HPL Publisher," p. 24; George T. Wetzel, "Bibliographic Notes on Lovecraft," pp. 25-27; J. Vernon Shea, "HPL and Films," pp. 28-30; Gerry de la Ree, "An Unknown HPL Artist," p. 30; William Scott Home, "The Horror Theme After HPL," pp. 32-34; George T. Wetzel, "The Cthulhu Mythos: A Study" (revised), pp. 35-41; Roger Bryant, "Stalking the Elusive Necronomicon," pp. 42-43; Stuart D. Schiff, "Notes on Collecting Lovecraftiana," pp. 44-45; John L. McInnis III, "Notes on Researching Lovecraftiana," pp. 46-47; Bill Wallace, "HPL on *Night Gallery*: A Review," p. 50; J. Vernon Shea, Review of *Lovecraft's Follies*, by James Schevill, p. 51; James Wade, Review of *Selected Letters III*, by H. P. Lovecraft, p. 52; Richard L. Tierney, "The Derleth Mythos," p. 53; James Wade, "My Life with the Greatest Old One," p. 54; Don Walsh, Jr., "Gruden Itza: The Evolution of a Sub-Mythos," pp. 55. [The rest of the volume contains fiction and poetry save the following:] "Contributors' Notes," pp. 135-40; "Special Announcements," p. 141; Emil Petaja, "Hannes Bok and HPL," p. 141; [Meade Frierson III], "Survey of Current Publications in the Field of the Macabre with Special Emphasis on H. P. Lovecraft," p. 143.

A notable collection of essays about Lovecraft both from his own correspondents (Bloch, Shea, Price) and recent scholars. Tierney's article exposes Derleth's misconceptions of Lovecraft's myth-cycle, while in Everts' article is reprinted a long fantasy poem by Ira A. Cole which explains Lovecraft's admiration for his "cosmicism." The volume also contains some outstanding illustrations.

Reviews

a. Brown, Gary. "We Love You HPL!" *The Monster Times*, No. 15 (6 September 1972), p. 18.

b. [Unsigned.] *Ambrosia*, No. 1 (24 June 1972), pp. 46-47.

13. Gatto, John Taylor. *The Major Works of H. P. Lovecraft: A Critical Commentary.* Monarch Notes No. 00982. New York: Monarch Press, 1977. [vi], 100[+12] pp.

> Superficial and idiosyncratic study whose value is almost nil. His assertion that "The Whisperer in Darkness" is a pornographic tale is as novel as it is absurd.

14. Grant, Donald M., and Thomas P. Hadley, eds. *Rhode Island on Lovecraft.* Providence: Grant-Hadley, 1945, Dec. 1945. 26 pp.

> Contains: The Editors, "Foreword," pp. 1-2; Winfield Townley Scott, "Lovecraft as a Poet," pp. 3-7; Dorothy C. Walter, "Lovecraft and Benefit Street," pp. 8-13; Mrs. Clifford [Muriel E.] Eddy, "Howard Phillips Lovecraft," pp. 14-22; Marion F. Barner [i.e., Bonner], "Miscellaneous Impressions of H.P.L.," pp. 23-24; Mary V. Dana, "A Glimpse of H.P.L.," pp. 25-26.
>
> Mrs. Eddy's article discusses her memories and associations with Lovecraft; the last two articles are memoirs by very minor acquaintances. Scott's article is still an important study of influences upon Lovecraft's poetry, although his hypothesis that E. A. Robinson inspired the *Fungi from Yuggoth* (echoed by Edmund Wilson) has no external support. For the Walter article, see III-C-25.

15. *H. P. Lovecraft: A Symposium.* Panelists: Fritz Leiber, Robert Bloch, Sam Russell, Arthur Jean Cox, Leland Sapiro. Annotated by August Derleth. [Los Angeles:] The Riverside Quarterly/Los Angeles Science Fantasy Society, 1963. 17 pp.

> The five panelists discuss such aspects of Lovecraft's work as the themes of "psychic displacement" and hereditary degeneration, his use of overstatement, and whether Lovecraft's tales are actually frightening.

16. Joshi, S. T., ed. *H. P. Lovecraft: Four Decades of Criticism.* Athens, Ohio: Ohio Univ. Press, 1980. xv, 247 pp.

> Contains: S. T. Joshi, "Preface," pp. xiii-xv; Kenneth W. Faig,

Jr. and S. T. Joshi, "H. P. Lovecraft: His Life and Work," pp. 1-19; S. T. Joshi, "Lovecraft Criticism: A Study," pp. 20-26; S. T. Joshi, "A Chronology of Selected Works by H. P. Lovecraft," pp. 27-41; T. O. Mabbott, "H. P. Lovecraft: An Appreciation," pp. 43-45; Edmund Wilson, "Tales of the Marvellous and the Ridiculous," pp. 46-49; Fritz Leiber, Jr., "A Literary Copernicus," pp. 50-62; Peter Penzoldt, excerpts from *The Supernatural in Fiction*, pp. 63-77; George T. Wetzel, "The Cthulhu Mythos: A Study" (revised), pp. 79-95; Edward Lauterbach, "Some Notes on Cthulhuian Pseudobiblia," pp. 96-103; Dirk W. Mosig, "H. P. Lovecraft: Myth-Maker," pp. 104-12; J. Vernon Shea, "On the Literary Influences Which Shaped Lovecraft's Writings," pp. 113-39; Fritz Leiber, Jr., "Through Hyperspace with Brown Jenkin: Lovecraft's Contribution to Speculative Fiction," pp. 140-52; Peter Cannon, "The Influence of *Vathek* on H. P. Lovecraft's *The Dream-Quest of Unknown Kadath*," pp. 153-57; Robert Bloch, "Poe and Lovecraft," pp. 158-60; Peter Cannon, "H. P. Lovecraft in Hawthornian Perspective," pp. 161-65; Barton L. St. Armand, "Facts in the Case of H. P. Lovecraft," pp. 166-85; Dirk W. Mosig, " 'The White Ship': A Psychological Odyssey," pp. 186-90; Richard L. Tierney, "Lovecraft and the Cosmic Quality in Fiction," pp. 191-95; Paul Buhle, "Dystopia as Utopia: Howard Phillips Lovecraft and the Unknown Content of American Horror Literature," pp. 196-210; Winfield Townley Scott, "A Parenthesis on Lovecraft as Poet," pp. 211-16; R. Boerem, "A Lovecraftian Nightmare," pp. 217-21; R. Boerem, "The Continuity of the *Fungi from Yuggoth*," pp. 222-25; Clark Ashton Smith, "To Howard Phillips Lovecraft" [poem], pp. 227-28; Appendix I: The Collected Works of H. P. Lovecraft (Arkham House edition), pp. 229-31; Appendix II: Supplementary Readings, pp. 232-37.

17. Lévy, Maurice. *Lovecraft ou du fantastique*. Paris: Christian Bourgois (Union Générale d'Éditions), 1972. 189 pp.

A revision of his doctoral dissertation (III-E-7). Outstanding study discussing Lovecraft's use of landscape, monsters, the theme of hereditary degeneration, his myth-cycle, and many other points. Lévy's distinction between Lovecraft's work and

science fiction is particularly valuable; his biographical chapter
is rather weaker. Still perhaps the finest critical study of
Lovecraft.

Reviews

a. Nolane, Derek. *Horizons du fantastique*, No. 23 (1973),
p. 89.

b. S., I. M. *Fantasiae*, 3, No. 3 (March 1975), 5.

c. Wegener, Manfred. *Quarber Merkur*, 11, No. 1 (April
1973), 61-63.

18. Long, Frank Belknap. *Howard Phillips Lovecraft: Dreamer
on the Nightside*. Sauk City, Wis.: Arkham House,
1975. xiv, 237 pp.

Notable memoir by one who perhaps knew Lovecraft best
and longest. Aside from recounting Lovecraft's trips to New
York and his marriage, Long also includes some valuable
interpretation of his work. The memoir is marred by a lack of
real substance and by unsuccessful attempts to record
Lovecraft's precise words uttered 50 years previously.

Reviews

a. Ambrose, Michael E. "H. P. Lovecraft Revenant."
Macabre, 2, No. 1 (Summer 1976), 6-8.

b. Connors, Scott. "The Long View." *Fantasy Crossroads*,
No. 8 (May 1976), p. 7.

c. de Camp, L. Sprague. *Amra*, 2, No. 65 (1976), 10-11.

d. Hall, Loay H. *Fantasy Crossroads*, No. 8 (May 1976),
pp. 6-7.

e. Kloos, Heinz W. *Weird Fiction Times*, No. 47 (January
1977), p. 44.

f. Leiber, Fritz. *Fantastic*, 26, No. 2 (June 1977), 116.

g. Lovecraft, H. P. *Mask,* January 1977, p. 6. [See III-C-5x.]

h. Lupoff, Richard. *Algol,* 14, No. 2 (Spring 1977), 49-52.

i. Mosig, Dirk W. *SFRA Newsletter,* No. 49 (June 1976), pp. 5-7. *Evermist,* 2, No. 4 (Fall 1976), 14-18.

j. Orven, J. *Bakka,* No. 4 (Summer 1976), p. 42.

k. [Unsigned.] *Quarber Merkur,* 14, No. 2 (July 1976), pp. 76-77.

19. St. Armand, Barton Levi. *The Roots of Horror in the Fiction of H. P. Lovecraft.* Elizabethtown, N.Y.: Dragon Press, 1977. viii[+iv], 102 pp.

> Powerful psychological study of "The Rats in the Walls" and its relation to the theories of Jung. Although sometimes making self-evident conclusions and using glib scholarly rhetoric rather too often, the work remains one of the finest modern critical works on Lovecraft.

Reviews

a. Coale, Sam. "In His Providence 'Dream Sanctuary' Lovecraft Found His Nightmares." *The Providence Sunday Journal,* 7 January 1979.

b. Fredericks, S. C. "The Horrors of Lovecraft." *Science-Fiction Studies,* 5, No. 2 (July 1978), 196-97.

c. Morris, Harry, Jr. *Nyctalops,* 2, No. 7 (March 1978), 35.

20. Schweitzer, Darrell. *The Dream Quest of H. P. Lovecraft.* San Bernardino, Ca.: R. Reginald (The Borgo Press), May 1978. 63 pp.

> Error-ridden and amateurish.

21. Schweitzer, Darrell, ed. *Essays Lovecraftian*. Baltimore:
     T-K Graphics, 1976. iv, 114 pp.

>   Contains: Darrell Schweitzer, "Introduction," pp. iii-iv;
>   Robert Bloch, "Notes on an Entity," pp. 1-3; Fritz Leiber, "A
>   Literary Copernicus," pp. 5-15; Dirk W. Mosig, "The Four Faces
>   of 'The Outsider,' " pp. 17-34; R. Boerem, "The First Lewis
>   Theobald," pp. 36-39; H. P. Lovecraft, letter to Alvin Earl
>   Perry, 4 October 1935, pp. 41-45 (as "Story-Writing: A Letter
>   from HPL"); Darrell Schweitzer, "Character Gullibility in
>   Weird Fiction," pp. 47-49; Arthur Jean Cox, "Some Thoughts
>   on Lovecraft," pp. 51-55; Richard L. Tierney, "The Derleth
>   Mythos," pp. 57-59; Marion Zimmer Bradley, "The (Bastard)
>   Children of Hastur," pp. 60-65; George Wetzel, "Genesis of the
>   Cthulhu Mythos," pp. 67-75; Bill Wallace, "The Untravelled
>   Roads 'Round Arkham," pp. 76-78; Ben P. Indick, "Lovecraft's
>   Ladies," pp. 80-83; Richard L. Tierney, "When the Stars Are
>   Right," pp. 84-89; Darrell Schweitzer, "Lovecraft and Lord
>   Dunsany," pp. 91-107; Robert Weinberg, "H. P. Lovecraft and
>   Pseudomathematics," pp. 109-12; [Notes on contributors], pp.
>   113-14.

Reviews

  a. Delap, Richard. *Delap's Fantasy and Science Fiction
     Review*, 3, No. 4 (April 1977), 19-20.

  b. Post, J. B. *Luna Monthly*, No. 67 (Spring 1977), p. 26.

22. Schweitzer, Darrell. *Lovecraft in the Cinema*. [Baltimore:
     T-K Graphics], 1975. [26] pp.

>   Contains: "Introduction," p. [3]; "Lovecraft in the Movies,"
>   pp. [5-12]; "Lovecraft on Television," pp. [13-18]; "Filming 'The
>   Outsider,' " pp. [19-26].

Review

  a. Delap, Richard. *Delap's Fantasy and Science Fiction
     Review*, 2, No. 7 (July 1976), 23.

23. Shreffler, Philip A. *The H. P. Lovecraft Companion*.

Westport, Conn.: Greenwood Press, 1977. xvi, 198 pp.

Interesting index of places and characters in Lovecraft's fiction (excluding revisions), with some valuable (though at times erroneous or speculative) research as to local sources for Lovecraft's tales. The first chapter, on Lovecraft's place in fantasy, has many questionable assumptions and interpretations, and throughout there is an amusing attempt to link Lovecraft and occultism.

24. Talman, Wilfred B. [and others]. *The Normal Lovecraft* [etc.]. Saddle River, N.J.: Gerry de la Ree, 1973. 32 pp.

Contains: [Gerry de la Ree], "Preface," p. 3; Wilfred B. Talman, "The Normal Lovecraft: A Few Memories to Restore Balance to the Shade of a Man of Delightful Character," pp. 5-11, 13-14, 16-17; L. Sprague de Camp, "Sonia and H.P.L.," pp. 24-25, 27; Gerry de la Ree, "When Sonia Sizzled: Letters Heretofore Unpublished," pp. 28-32. [Inside back cover prints obituary from *The* [Providence] *Evening Bulletin* (III-A-29).]

Talman's essay attempts to depict Lovecraft as far more "normal" a human being than is often allowed by his critics, while de la Ree has unearthed letters from Lovecraft's wife revealing her disputes with August Derleth in the 1940s.

Reviews

a. N., L. *Fantasiae*, 1, No. 8 (November 1973), 9.

b. [Unsigned.] *Aurora*, 1, No. 1 (March 1974), 48-49.

25. Walter, Dorothy C. *Lovecraft and Benefit Street*. North Montpelier, Vt.: W. Paul Cook (Driftwind Press), [1943]. [14] pp.

Lovecraft "relied much too often on references to things distasteful to himself that he assumed would produce similar feelings of aversion or fear or disgust in others." Although Walter "misses humor in his stories" and believes that "his stories suffer . . . from similarity in the method of producing a weird atmosphere," she feels that Lovecraft had a great imagination.

26. Wetzel, George, ed. *Howard Phillips Lovecraft: Memoirs,
    Critiques, and Bibliographies.* North Tonawanda, N.Y.:
    SSR Publications, 1955. iii, [4-]83 pp.

    Contains: E. A. Edkins, "Idiosyncrasies of HPL," pp. 5-7;
    James F. Morton, "A Few Memories," pp. 8-9; Edward H. Cole,
    "Ave atque Vale!" pp. 10-17; George Wetzel, "The Cthulhu
    Mythos: A Study," pp. 18-27; Matthew H. Onderdonk, "The
    Lord of R'lyeh," pp. 28-37; Lin Carter, "HPL: The History," pp.
    38-40; George Wetzel, "The Research of a Biblio," pp. 41-46;
    George Wetzel, "Amateur Press Works," pp. 47-57; Robert E.
    Briney, "Professional Works and Miscellany," pp. 59-83.

    Combination of *The Lovecraft Collectors Library,* Vols. VI and VII
    (see III-B-35 and III-C-27), with the addition of the Carter article
    and Wetzel's "Research of a Biblio."

27. Wetzel, George, ed. *The Lovecraft Collectors Library,
    Volume Six: Commentaries.* North Tonawanda, N.Y.:
    SSR Publications, 1955. iii, [4-]37 pp.

    Contains: E. A. Edkins, "Idiosyncrasies of HPL," pp. 5-7;
    James F. Morton, "A Few Memories," pp. 8-9; Edward H. Cole,
    "Ave atque Vale!" pp. 10-17; George Wetzel, "The Cthulhu
    Mythos: A Study," pp. 18-27; Matthew H. Onderdonk, "The
    Lord of R'lyeh," pp. 28-37.

D.   Criticism in Books or Periodicals

1. Akai, Toshio. "Private Lovecraft kara image Lovecraft he." *Crypt Horror Tales*, No. 8 (April 1976), pp. 39-46 (as by "Gufu Akai").

2. Aldiss, Brian W. *Billion Year Spree: The True History of Science Fiction*. London: Weidenfeld & Nicolson, 1973; Garden City, N.Y.: Doubleday & Co., 1973; New York: Schocken Books, 1974, pp. 176-78.

3. Anton, Uwe. "Howard Philips [sic] Lovecraft— Biographie und Werk." *Ganymed Horror*, No. 1 (1972), pp. 8-9.

4. Anton, Uwe. "Lovecraft & Weird Fiction in der BRD." *Weird Fiction Times*, No. 47 (January 1977), pp. 42-43.

5. Aquino, Michael A. "Lovecraftian Ritual: Ceremony of the Nine Angles: The Call of Cthulhu." *Nyctalops*, No. 13 (May 1977), pp. 13-15.

6. Aramata, Hiroshi. "Cosmic horror no fukkatsu." *S-F Magazine*, No. 164 (Special Summer issue [September 1972]), pp. 291-92 (as by "Seiji Dan").

7. Aramata, Hiroshi, ed. *Cthulhu shinwashu*. Tokyo: Kokushokankokai, 1976.

     Contains: ["Foreword"], pp. 7-10; "Hottan" ["Opening"], pp. 11-12; "Chouchu no jashin," pp. 33-34; "Masho no keiji," pp. 205-06; "Kaibutsu no shinko," pp. 313-14; all by Hiroshi Aramata.

8. Aramata, Hiroshi. "Katsuji de kunda bohimei." *S-F Magazine*, No. 154 (December 1971), pp. 122-25 (as by "Seiji Dan").

9. Aramata, Hiroshi. "Lovecraft to kare no kurai yuaidan." *Genso to Kaiki*, No. 4 (November 1973), pp. 70-82.

10. Armand, Frédéric. "Spaziergänge im Dunkel: Der unamerikanische Kosmos des Howard Phillips Lovecraft." *Die Weltwoche*, No. 37 (11 September 1970).

11. Arthos, Giorgio, and Lorenzo Tibaldi, eds. "Il 'Necronomicon,' libro maledetto." *G sera*, NS 1, No. 98 (19 October 1976), 3.

    A page of the A.Ms. of "History of the *Necronomicon*" is reproduced.

12. Ash, Brian, ed. *The Visual Encyclopedia of Science Fiction.* London: Trewin Copplestone Publishing Ltd.; New York: Harmony Books, 1977, passim.

13. Autolycus. "What of H. P. Lovecraft?" *The Science Fiction Fan*, 4, No. 6 (January 1940), 11-15. *Crucified Toad*, 1 (Winter 1970).

14. Babcock, Mitchel. "Lovecraft vs. Poe." *Mirth and Irony*, [1962], pp. 26-27.

15. Bailey, J. O. *Pilgrims through Space and Time: Trends and Patterns in Scientific and Utopian Fiction.* New York: Argus Books, 1947; Westport, Conn.: Greenwood Press, 1972, pp. 178-81.

    Sympathetic if superficial discussion of *At the Mountains of Madness* and "The Shadow out of Time."

16. Baldwin, F. Lee. "H. P. Lovecraft: A Biographical Sketch." *Fantasy Magazine*, 4, No. 5 (April 1935), 108-10, 132.

    Brief biography written by one of Lovecraft's correspondents.

17. Baldwin, F. Lee. "Some Lovecraft Sidelights." *Fantasy Commentator*, 2, No. 6 (Spring 1948), 219-20.

    Revised version of III-D-16.

18. Banks, Ann. "Lovecraftimania at Brown." *Brown Alumni Monthly*, 72, No. 5 (February 1972), 22-24, 26-28.

19. Barclay, Glen St. John. "The Myth That Never Was: Howard P. Lovecraft." In *Anatomy of Horror*. London: Weidenfeld & Nicolson, 1978, pp. 81-96.

20. Barlow, Robert H. "Footnote to The Round Tower." *Golden Atom*, 1, No. 10 (Winter 1943).

21. Barlow, Robert H. "Pseudonyms of Lovecraft." *The Acolyte*, 1, No. 4 (Summer 1943), 18.

22. Barlow, Robert H. "Three Letters on H. P. Lovecraft." *Golden Atom*, 1, No. 10 (Winter 1943), 31-32.

23. Baronian, Jean-Baptiste. *Un Nouveau Fantastique*. Lausanne: Editions l'Age d'Homme, 1977, pp. 74-76.

24. Béaler, Marcel. "Une Multitude d'immensités par delà la porte de profond sommeil." *L'Herne*, No. 12 (1969), pp. 177-78.

25. Beardson, W. E. "The Mound of Yig?" *Etchings and Odysseys*, No. 1 (1973), pp. 10-13.

26. Beck, Claire P. "A Note from the Editor." *The Science Fiction Critic*, 1, No. 9 (May 1937), 1-2.
    Includes a letter by Clark Ashton Smith; see III-D-665.

27. Behnke, Rolf-Ingo. "H. P. Lovecraft." *Quarber Merkur*, 10, No. 2 (April 1972), 43-58.

28. Belevan, H. *Teoria de la fantastico*. Barcelona: Editorial Anagrama, 1976.

29. Benét, William Rose. "My Brother Steve." *The Saturday Review of Literature*, 24, No. 30 (15 November

1941), 3-4, 22-26.

Stephen Vincent Benét "was entirely familiar with the work of H. P. Lovecraft long before that little-known master of horror was brought to the attention of the critics."

30. Benét, William Rose. "The Phoenix Nest." *The Saturday Review of Literature*, 28, No. 1 (17 March 1945), 32-33.

31. Bergier, Jacques. "H.-P. Lovecraft (1890-1937)." In II-A-1.

32. Bergier, Jacques. Letters. *Weird Tales*, 27, No. 3 (March 1936), 381; 30, No. 3 (September 1937), 382.

33. Bergier, Jacques. *Los libros condenados*. Barcelona: Plaza & Janés, 1976.

34. Bergier, Jacques. "Lovecraft, ce grand génie venu d'ailleurs." *Planète*, No. 1 (October-November 1961), pp. 43-46. *Pianeta*, No. 2 (May-June 1964), pp. 85-88 (as "Lovecraft, questo genio venuto da fuori"; tr. anon.). *L'Herne*, No. 12 (1969), pp. 121-25.

First published in II-A-3. The magazine appearances represent an altered version.

35. Bergier, Jacques. "Mysteries in overloed." *Bres*, No. 38 (December 1972-January 1973), pp. 54-71 (esp. 70-71).

36. Berthel, Werner. "H. P. L. oder Cthulhus Ruf: Skizzen zu einem Porträt des Horror-Erzählers Lovecraft." *Frankfurter Rundschau*, No. 280 (2 December 1972), p. 2.

37. Bertin, Eddy C. "The Cthulhu Mythos." *Shadow*, Nos. 6/7 (1969). *Nyctalops*, 1, No. 4 (June 1971), 3-6, 43 (with subtitle: "A Review and Analysis"). *Drab*, 4, No. 3 (October 1978), 18-20, 22-24.

38. Bertin, Eddy C. "The Followers of Cthulhu." *Shadow*, No. 9 (January-February 1970). *Nyctalops*, 1, No. 5 (October 1971), 5-12, 58 (as "In the Trail of Lovecraft: The Followers of Cthulhu").

39. Bertin, Eddy C. "H. P. Lovecraft: The Critics." *Shadow*, No. 7 (September 1969), pp. 28-31. *Nyctalops*, 1, No. 3 (February 1971), 4-7.

40. Bertin, Eddy C. "H. P. Lovecraft Did Not Write SF . . . By His Own Standards." *Shadow*, No. 7 (September 1969), pp. 42-44. *Nyctalops*, 1, No. 2 (October 1970), 3-5. *Drab*, 4, No. 3 (October 1978), 7-9, 11.

41. Bertin, Eddy C. "Lovecraft in Comic Form." *Shadow*, No. 10 (April-May 1970), p. 10.

42. Bertin, Eddy C. "Lovecraft in Europe." *Shadow*, No. 10 (April-May 1970), pp. 13-16, 26.

43. Bertin, Eddy C. "Lovecraft in Screen Screams." *Mystification & Terror*, 4, No. 3 (July 1969). *Maniac*, No. 2 (July 1969).

44. Bertin, Eddy C. "The Lovecraftian Works of Colin Wilson." *Tamlacht*, 2, No. 2 (n.d.), 16-18, 22. *Ganymed Horror*, No. 18 [i.e., *Weird Fiction Times*, No. 43] (1976), pp. 22-25 (as "Colin Wilson—auf Lovecrafts Spur"; tr. Uwe Anton).

45. Bishop, Zealia. "H. P. Lovecraft: A Pupil's View." In I-A-29.

46. Blanck, Jacob. "News from the Rare Book Sellers." *Publishers' Weekly*, 148, No. 25 (22 December 1945), 2726-27.

    Notes on a hoax involving the *Necronomicon*.

47. Bleiler, E. F. "Introduction to the Dover Edition" of
I-A-21.

48. Blish, James. Letter. *Haunted*, 1, No. 3 (June 1968),
107-08.

There follows a long reply to the letter (pp. 108-09) by
Samuel D. Russell.

49. Bloch, Robert. "As a Small Boy . . ." *L'Herne*, No. 12
(1969), pp. 285-86 (tr. into French by Francois
Truchaud).

50. Bloch, Robert. "Inside the Outsider." *Xenophile*, 2, No.
6 (October 1975), 4-5.

The contradictions in Lovecraft's character simply indicate
that he was a human being like any one of us.

51. Bloch, Robert. "Introduction." In *The Disciples of
Cthulhu*. Ed. Edward P. Berglund. New York: DAW
Books, Oct. 1976, pp. 9-14.

52. Bloch, Robert. "Notes on an Entity." *Tamlacht*, 2, No.
2 (n.d.), 14-15.

53. Bloch, Robert. "Poe and Lovecraft." *Ambrosia*, No. 2
(August 1973), pp. 4-5.

The work of both writers is "in many particulars removed
and remote from the main current of American life"; yet both
related to their times by keeping abreast of current scientific
discoveries.

54. Boerem, R. "On the *Fungi from Yuggoth*." *The Dark
Brotherhood Journal*, 1, No. 1 (June 1971), 2-5.

55. Boerem, R. "A Lovecraftian Nightmare." *Nyctalops*, 2,
No. 4-5 (April 1976), 22-24.

A study of "The Poe-et's Nightmare" and its expression of
the "central Lovecraftian theme" of man's insignificance in the
cosmos.

56. Bogdanoff, Igor, and Gritchko Bogdanoff. *Clefs pour la science-fiction.* Paris: Seghers, 1976, pp. 81, 218-20, passim.

57. Boggs, Redd. "Leaves: A Botanical Rarity." *Fantasy Commentator*, 3, No. 1 (Winter 1948-49), 14-19.

58. Boggs, Redd. "Lovecraft: 25 Years After." *The Lovecraftsman*, No. 1 (May 1963), pp. [1-2].

59. Boland, Stuart. "Interlude with Lovecraft." *The Acolyte*, 3, No. 3 (Summer 1945), 15-18.

    Reminiscences by a late correspondent of Lovecraft's.

60. Bolitho, William. "Pulp Magazines" [?]. *The New York World*, ca. 1929-30.

    This article discusses Lovecraft briefly; the original appearance has not been located, but the article was quoted extensively in the editor's column of *Weird Tales*, April 1930.

61. Borges, Jorge Luis, and Esther Zemborain de Torres. *An Introduction to American Literature.* New York: Schocken Books, 1971, pp. 83-84.

62. [Boruta, Victor.] "Appreciation of H. P. Lovecraft (1890-1937)." *Tamlacht*, 2, No. 2 (n.d.), [2-3].

63. B[radley], C[hester] P. "An Appreciation . . ." *The Perspective Review*, Winter 1934 (Fourth Anniversary Number), p. 14.

    Thanks Lovecraft for his aid in developing this magazine to its then-present status.

64. Bradley, Marion Zimmer. "The (Bastard) Children of Hastur: An Irrelevant Inquiry into the Ancestry and Progeny of the Hasturs." *Nyctalops*, 1, No. 6 (February 1972), 3-6.

65. Bradley, Marion Zimmer. "Two Worlds of Fantasy."
    Haunted, 1, No. 3 (June 1968), 82-85.

66. Bradley, Marion Zimmer, and Robert Carson.
    "Lovecraftian Sonnetry." *Astra's Tower*, No. 2
    (December 1947).

67. Bradofsky, Hyman. "Amateur Affairs." *The
    Californian*, 5, No. 1 (Summer 1937), 28-31.

    > "Great as was Howard Lovecraft in heart and mind, we of
    > today are unable to evaluate him at his true worth. Time and
    > the march of events will bring increased understanding of him
    > and of his tangible legacies."

68. Brennan, Joseph Payne. "H. P. L.: An Informal
    Commentary." *Fresco*, 8, No. 3 (Spring 1958), 5-8.

69. Brennan, Joseph Payne. "Lovecraft and the O'Brien
    Annuals." *Macabre*, No. 23 (1976), pp. 30-32.

70. Brennan, Joseph Payne. "Lovecraft on the Subways."
    Macabre, No. 22 (1973), pp. 7-9.

71. Brennan, Joseph Payne. "Lovecraft's 'Brick Row.' "
    Macabre, No. 5 (Summer 1959), pp. 21-22.

72. Brennan, Joseph Payne. "The Terror of Time." *Astral
    Dimensions*, No. 6 (Fall 1977), p. 34.

73. Brennan, Joseph Payne. "Three Footnotes on H. P.
    Lovecraft: I. An Overlooked Lovecraft Article; II.
    Lovecraft in Anthologies; III. Necrophilism, Poe and
    Lovecraft." *Macabre*, No. 9 (Summer 1961), pp.
    19-22.

74. Brennan, Joseph Payne. "Time and H. P. L." *Macabre*,
    No. 7 (Summer 1960), pp. 8-9.

75. Brown, David J. "The Search for Lovecraft's
    'Outsider.' " *Nyctalops*, 2, No. 1 (April 1973), 46-47.

Brown determines that the unnamed character in "The Outsider" (1921) is Richard Upton Pickman, the central character in "Pickman's Model" (1926).

76. Brown, M. E. "Lovecraft in the Brown University Library." *Books at Brown*, 11, Nos. 1-2 (February 1949), 14.

77. Brunner, John. "Rusty Chains." *Inside and Science Fiction Advertiser*, No. 14 (March 1956), pp. 17-21.

78. Bryant, Roger. "The Alchemist and the Scientist: Borellus and the Lovecraftian Imagination." *Nyctalops*, 2, No. 3 (January-February 1975), 26-29, 43.

Biography of Giovanni Borelli, whom Bryant incorrectly believes is the "Borellus" mentioned in *The Case of Charles Dexter Ward.* The actual "Borellus," as Robert Marten has discovered, was the 12th-century Frenchman Pierre Borel.

79. Bryant, Roger. "Necronomicon." *Tamlacht*, 2, No. 2 (n.d.), 10-13, 15.

80. Buhle, Paul. "Dystopia as Utopia: Howard Phillips Lovecraft and the Unknown Content of American Horror Literature." *The Minnesota Review*, NS 6 (Spring 1976), pp. 118-31.

Profound essay exploring Lovecraft's philosophical thought and its relation to political and cultural history. "If Lovecraft . . . continually reminded humanity of its fragility and slightness in the scale of the Universe, it was not to diminish human striving but to reopen the vents to the imagination increasingly closed since the rise of formal society, the State, and private property."

81. Burgin, Richard. *Conversations with Jorge Luis Borges.* New York: Avon Book Co. (Discus), Sept. 1970, p. 79.

82. Butman, Robert. "Modern Mythological Fiction." *The
Reader and Collector*, 3, No. 5 (October 1945), 1-12; 3,
No. 6 (January 1946), 13-27; 4, No. 1 (April 1946),
6-39.

83. Cabos, Lew. "Continuing the Mythos." *Antithesis*,
1974, pp. 21-25.

84. Caen, Michel. "Lovecraft/Cinéma." *L'Herne*, No. 12
(1969), pp. 182-84. *Il Re in Giallo*, 1, No. 2 [1976], 68-
69 (as "Il cinema e Lovecraft"; tr. Fabio Calabrese).

85. Campbell, J. Ramsey. "Cthulhu in Celluloid." *The
Arkham Collector*, No. 3 (Summer 1968), pp. 72-77.
Studies of three films made from Lovecraft's tales.

86. Campbell, J. Ramsey. "Lovecraft in Retrospect."
Shadow, No. 7 (September 1969), pp. 15, 48. *L'Herne*,
No. 12 (1969), pp. 357-58 (tr. Francois Truchaud).

87. Campbell, J. Ramsey. "On Juvenilia and 'The Face in
the Desert.' " *Weird Fantasy*, No. 1 (December 1969),
p. 20.

88. Cannon, Peter. " 'You Have Been in Providence, I
Perceive.' " *Nyctalops*, 2, No. 7 (March 1978), 45-46.
On the Sherlock Holmes influence upon Lovecraft.

89. Capanna, Pablo. *El sentido de la ciencia-ficción*. Buenos
Aires: Columba, 1966, pp. 242-43.

90. Carneiro, André. *Introdução ao estudo da "science-fiction."*
Sao Pablo: Conselho Estodual de Cultura/Comissão
de Litteratura, 1967, pp. 37-38, passim.

91. Carter, Lin. "The Cthulhu Mythos." In Lin Carter,
ed. *The Spawn of Cthulhu*. New York: Ballantine
Books, Oct. 1971, pp. 1-4. *Nueva Dimensión*, No. 79

(July 1976), pp. 30-31 (as "Los mitos de Cthulhu"; tr. anon.).

92. Carter, Lin. "Der Cthulhu-Mythos." *Ganymed Horror*, Nos. 3/4 (1973), pp. 40-62 (tr. Heinz W. Kloos).

Compendium of Carter's critical comments in *The Spawn of Cthulhu* (see III-D-91).

93. Carter, Lin. "HPL: The History." *Fantasy Advertiser*, 4, No. 1 (March 1950), 8-10.

Outlines the "colossal and complex history of the Earth" as mapped out in *At the Mountains of Madness* and "The Shadow out of Time."

94. Carter, Lin. "H. P. Lovecraft: The Books." *Inside and Science Fiction Advertiser*, No. 14 (March 1956), pp. 11-16; Nos. 15/49 (May 1956), pp. 13-23; Nos. 16/50 (September 1956), pp. 24-31. In [Hiroshi Aramata, ed.?] *Lloigor no fukkatsu*. Tokyo: Hayakawa Shobo, 1977, pp. 131-38 (as "Necronomicon no rekishu"; abridged; tr. Hiroshi Aramata [as "Seiji Dan"]).

Study of the real and mythical books used by Lovecraft and his associates in their tales.

95. Carter, Lin. "H. P. Lovecraft: The Gods." *Inside Science Fiction*, No. 52 (October 1957), pp. 49-59. *Genso to Kaiki*, No. 4 (November 1973), pp. 12-28 (as "Cthulhu shinwa no kamigami"; tr. Keisuke Otaki).

96. Carter, Lin. *Imaginary Worlds: The Art of Fantasy*. New York: Ballantine Books, 1973, pp. 55-58, passim.

97. Carter, Lin. *A Look behind the Cthulhu Mythos. Crypt Horror Tales*, No. 2 (July 1973), pp. 37-56; No. 4 (November 1974), pp. 50-60; No. 5 (March 1975), pp. 23-35; No. 7 (November 1975), pp. 57-71; No. 9 (June 1976), pp. 97-114 (as "Cthulhu shinwa nottaikei").

The first four installments were translated by Tetsuya Imamura; the last by Toshio Akai.

98. Carter, Lin. "Omissions, Corrections and Errata to H. P. Lovecraft: The Books." *Inside Science Fiction*, No. 52 (October 1957), pp. 47-48.

99. Carter, Lin. "Through the Gates of Deeper Slumber." In I-A-51.

100. Carter, Paul A. *The Creation of Tomorrow*. New York: Columbia Univ. Press, pp. 7-8, 18, 67, 93-96, 111, 137-39, 259, 291-92, 298.

101. Chalker, Jack L., and Mark Owings. "The Necronomicon: A Bibliography." *Mirage*, No. 9 (1970), pp. 17-26.

102. Circulo H. P. Lovecraft di Torino, ed. "Lovecraft magico." *Il Re in Giallo*, 1, No. 2 [1976], 49-53.

103. Cirlot, Juan-Eduardo. "El pensamiento de Lovecraft." *Horizonte*, No. 4 (1969), pp. 45-49.

104. Clements, Jack. "Howard Phillips Lovecraft—Pro and Con." *Spacewarp* (February 1949).

105. Cockcroft, T. G. L. Letter. *Nyctalops*, 1, No. 5 (October 1971), 48-49.

106. Cockcroft, T. G. L. "Notes on the Works of H. P. Lovecraft." *Woomera*, No. 2 (September 1951), pp. 22-28.

107. Cockcroft, T. G. L. "Random Notes." *Nyctalops*, 2, No. 1 (April 1973), 20-21, 32.

   Literary and bibliographical remarks.

108. Cohen, Daniël. "De schittering in de duisternis: H. P. Lovecraft op film." *Drab*, 4, No. 3 (October 1978), 25-26, 28, 30.

109. Cole, Edward H. "Ave atque Vale!" *The Olympian*,
No. 35 (Autumn 1940), pp. 7-22.

> Random memories by a long-time associate of Lovecraft's.

110. [Cole, Edward H.] "The Bureau of Critics: *The
Conservative*." *The National Amateur*, 41, No. 1
(September 1918), 7-8.

111. Cole, Edward H. "A View behind the Veil." *The
Fossil*, No. 157 (April 1958), pp. 45, 61-63.

> Briefly touches upon Lovecraft's relations with W. Paul
> Cook.

112. Cole, Ira A. "A Tribute from the Past." *The O-Wash-
Ta-Nong*, [2, No. 2] [1937], [4].

113. Cole, Ira A. [Untitled.] *The Plainsman*, 1, No. 4
(December 1915), 2-3.

> On "On the Cowboys of the West."

114. Coletti, Lina. "I mostri sono con noi." *L'Europeo*, 33,
No. 46 (18 November 1977), 98-100.

> Lovecraft is quoted on p. 100.

115. Collins, Charles. "Bookman's Holidays." *Chicago
Sunday Tribune*, 102, No. 52 (26 December 1943), Sec.
6, p. 12; 103, No. 24 (11 June 1944), Sec. 6, p. 12;
103, No. 25 (18 June 1944), Sec. 6, p. 13; 103, No.
28 (9 July 1944), Sec. 6.

116. Collins, Tom. "Afterword" to I-A-66.

117. Condra, Cyrus B. "The Sailor Lopez and Kindred
Musings." *Ausländer*, No. 3 (June 1966), pp. 20-24.

> On "The Call of Cthulhu" and other matters.

118. Conover, Willis. "The Call of Lovecraft." *Xenophile*,
2, No. 6 (October 1975), 15-16.

> On the production of *Lovecraft at Last* (I-A-62).

119. Conover, Willis. Letter. *Weird Tales*, 34, No. 6 (December 1939), 120-21.

120. Conover, Willis. "Observations and Otherwise." *The* [Cambridge, Md.] *Democrat and News* (8 July 1937).

   Announces the death of Lovecraft and includes complete texts of the poems, "The Pigeon-Flyers," "Homecoming," "A Memory," and "Night-Gaunts"; the first appearance in print for the first and third of these.

121. Conte, Rafael. "Howard Phillips Lovecraft, maestro de ceremonias." *Nueva Dimensión*, No. 13 (1970), pp. 145-49.

122. Cook, W. Paul. "H. P. Lovecraft." *The Olympian*, No. 35 (Autumn 1940), pp. 28-35.

   Later incorporated almost verbatim into his book (III-C-4).

123. Cook, W. Paul. "A Plea for Lovecraft." *The Ghost*, No. 3 (May 1945), pp. 55-56.

   Lovecraft's admirers should keep "one foot on the ground."

124. Copper, Basil. *The Vampire in Legend, Fact and Art.* Secaucus, N.J.: The Citadel Press, 1974, pp. 109-10. Munich: Goldmann Verlag, 1974 (as *Der Vampir in Legende, Kunst und Wirklichkeit*), p. 98.

125. Corliss, Richard. "Movies: Lit Crit." *New Times*, 8, No. 5 (4 March 1977), 57-58, 62.

   On Lovecraft's influence upon Alain Resnais' recent film, *Providence.*

126. Cox, Arthur Jean. "The Call of Nature: A Note on 'The Call of Cthulhu' by Howard Phillips Lovecraft." *Science Fiction Review*, No. 40 (October 1970), p. 35.

127. Cox, Arthur Jean. "H. P. L.: The Automatic Ghost." *The Lovecraftsman*, No. 4 (Autumn 1965), p. [1].

128. Cox, Arthur Jean. "Lovecrap." *The Lovecraftsman*, No. 3 (Spring 1964), pp. [1-2].

129. Cox, Arthur Jean. "Some Thoughts on Lovecraft." *Haunted*, 1, No. 2 (December 1964), 26-30. *Quarber Merkur*, 7, No. 2 (August 1969), 29-33. *Simplizissimus*, No. 1 (May-June 1971), pp. [47-54].

   In the last two appearances as "Gedanken über Lovecraft"; tr. Franz Rottensteiner.

130. Daniels, Les. "The Bizarre World of H. P. Lovecraft." *Fusion*, No. 66 (12 November 1971), pp. 14-17, 19. In *Living in Fear: A History of Horror in the Mass Media*. New York: Charles Scribner's Sons, 1975, pp. 116-21 (revised; without title).

131. Davenport, Basil. Letter. *The Acolyte*, 2, No. 3 (Summer 1944), 28.

132. Davis, Graeme. "Mere Musings." *The Lingerer*, No. 2 (Winter 1917), pp. 1-10.

   Part of the article deals with Lovecraft's magazine, *The Conservative*.

133. Davis, Graeme. "With Consideration for the Conservative." *The Lingerer*, No. 3 (Summer 1917), pp. 9-18.

134. Davis, Sonia H. "Howard Phillips Lovecraft as His Wife Remembers Him." *The Providence Journal*, 64, No. 8 (22 August 1948), Sec. VI, p. 8. *Books at Brown*, 11, Nos. 1/2 (February 1949), 3-13.

135. Davis, Sonia H. "Memories of Lovecraft: I." *The Arkham Collector*, No. 4 (Winter 1969), pp. 116-17.

Excerpts of Mrs. Davis' letters, as she discusses Poe, Lovecraft's appearance, his mother, and other subjects.

136. deAngelis, Michael. "H. P. Lovecraft: A Revaluation." *Asmodeus*, No. 2 (Fall 1951), p. 30.

137. de Camp, L. Sprague. "Eldritch Yankee Gentleman." *Fantastic*, 20, No. 6 (August 1971), 98-106; 21, No. 1 (October 1971), 100-08, 114. In *Literary Swordsmen and Sorcerers: The Makers of Heroic Fantasy*. Sauk City, Wis.: Arkham House, 1976, pp. 64-113.

138. de Camp, L. Sprague. "H. P. Lovecraft: Maestro de la fantasia." *Nueva Dimensión*, No. 79 (July 1976), pp. 93-98 (tr. anon.).

Excerpts from his biography (III-C-5).

139. de Camp, L. Sprague. "H. P. Lovecraft and H. S. Chamberlain." *Amra*, 2, No. 57 (June 1972), 3-9.

Makes the unfounded claim that Lovecraft derived his racial views from Chamberlain (T. H. Huxley is the more probable source).

140. de Camp, L. Sprague. Letters. *Fantasy Crossroads*, 1, Nos. 4/5 (August 1975); 1, No. 6 (November 1975), 20; 1, No. 7 (February 1976), 1.

Rebuttals to Dirk W. Mosig's comments on his biography (III-D-470).

141. de Camp, L. Sprague. Letter. *Nyctalops*, 2, No. 3 (January-February 1975), 38.

Comments on the state of Lovecraft's health.

142. de Camp, L. Sprague. "Lovecraft: Failed Aristocrat." *The Magazine of Fantasy and Science Fiction*, 48, No. 1 (January 1975), 84-97.

143. de Camp, L. Sprague. "Lovecraft and the Aryans."
In *Blond Barbarians and Noble Savages*. [Brooklyn, N.Y.:]
LUNA Publications, 1975, pp. 6-20.

144. de Camp, L. Sprague. *The Miscast Barbarian: A Biography of Robert E. Howard (1906-1936)*. Saddle River,
N.J.: Gerry de la Ree, 1975, pp. 13-14, 24-25, 37-38.

145. de Camp, L. Sprague. *Science-Fiction Handbook: The
Writing of Imaginative Fiction*. New York: Hermitage
House, 1953, pp. 76-79. Philadelphia: Owlswick
Press, 1975 (revised; as *Science Fiction Handbook,
Revised*; with Catherine Crook de Camp), pp. 29-32.

146. de Camp, L. Sprague. *Scribblings*. Boston: The
NESFA Press, 1975.

> Contains: "Three Thirds of a Hero," pp. 63-72; "Books That
> Never Were" (i.e., "The Unwritten Classics"), pp. 73-85.
>
> In the first article de Camp talks about Lovecraft's "reclusive
> life," his "hatred of foreigners and ethnics," and his
> "xenophobia." See III-D-148 for the second.

147. de Camp, L. Sprague. "Sesquithoughts on
Lovecraft." *Nyctalops*, 2, No. 7 (March 1978), 40.

148. de Camp, L. Sprague. "The Unwritten Classics." *The
Saturday Review of Literature*, 30, No. 13 (29 March
1947), 7-8, 25-26. *The Magazine of Fantasy and Science
Fiction*, 43, No. 6 (December 1972), 78-85 (as "Books
That Never Were").

> Part of the article discusses the *Necronomicon* and other books
> invented by Lovecraft and his colleagues.

149. de Camp, L. Sprague. "Young Man Lovecraft."
Xenophile, 2, No. 6 (October 1975), 8.

> De Camp interviews the Rev. John T. Dunn, who knew
> Lovecraft in his twenties.

150. Derleth, August. "Arkham House: A Thumbnail Sketch." *The Fossil*, No. 128 (October 1950), pp. 240-41, 247.

151. Derleth, August. *Arkham House: The First 20 Years, 1939-1959*. Sauk City, Wis.: Arkham House, 1959, pp. i-vi, passim.

    Includes a history of the publishing firm and a bibliography of all books published under its own and its subsidiary imprints.

152. Derleth, August. "The Arkham House Story." *Fantastic Worlds*, 1, No. 1 (Summer 1952), 7-12.

153. Derleth, August. "The Building of Arkham House." *Fantasy Review*, 1, No. 3 (June-July 1947), 6-8.

154. Derleth, August. "The Cthulhu Mythos." In I-C-47, 48; II-C-10, 11. In *De Cthulhu-Mythologie: Lovecraftiaanse Verhalen*. Ed. August Derleth. Utrecht/Antwerp: A. W. Bruna & Zoon, 1974, pp. 7-13 (as "De Cthulhu-Mythologie"; tr. Meta Beukema).

155. Derleth, August. "Foreword" to I-A-21.

156. [Derleth, August.] *Il guardiano della soglia* [*The Lurker at the Threshold*]. Rome: Fanucci, 1977.

    Contains: Gianfranco de Turris and Sebastiano Fusco, "Introduzione," pp. 5-10; Claudio De Nardi, "Alla ricerca della chiave d'argento," pp. 167-204; Giuseppe Lippi, "Il triplice fascino de H. P. Lovecraft," pp. 205-28.

157. Derleth, August. "H. P. L.—Two Decades After." *Fresco*, 8, No. 3 (Spring 1958), 9-11.

158. Derleth, August. "H. P. Lovecraft: The Making of a Literary Reputation, 1937-1971." *Books at Brown*, 25 (1977), 13-25.

    Outlines the publishing and recognition of Lovecraft after his death.

159. Derleth, August. "H. P. Lovecraft and His Work."
In I-A-34, 37. II-A-8. *La Opinión*, No. 681 (5 August
1973), Cultural Supplement, pp. 2-3 (as "La vida de
un alucinado"; Part I only; tr. anon.).

Revised and expanded version of Chapter iii of III-C-6.

160. [Derleth, August.] "H. P. Lovecraft & Science
Fiction." *The Arkham Collector*, No. 1 (Summer 1967),
pp. 3-5.

Quoting "Some Notes on Interplanetary Fiction," Derleth
tries to show that Lovecraft was not primarily a science-fiction
writer.

161. Derleth, August. "H. P. Lovecraft, Outsider." *River*,
1, No. 3 (June 1937), 88-89.

162. Derleth, August. "H. P. Lovecraft's Novels." In I-A-
39, 47. *Ganymed Horror*, Nos. 3/4 (1973), pp. 76-78 (as
"H. P. Lovecrafts Novellen"; tr. Heinz W. Kloos).

163. Derleth, August. "Introduction" to I-A-42.

Prints a chronology of Lovecraft's tales which he falsely
attributes to Lovecraft (see I-E-i-1).

164. Derleth, August. "Introduction" to I-A-33.

165. Derleth, August. "Introduction" to I-A-20.

166. Derleth, August. "An Introduction to H. P.
Lovecraft." In I-A-26; II-A-56. *Ganymed Horror*, Nos.
3/4 (1973), pp. 73-75 (as "H. P. Lovecraft"; tr. Heinz
W. Kloos).

167. Derleth, August. Letter. *Haunted*, 1, No. 3 (June
1968), 114.

168. Derleth, August. "Lovecraft and Music." *Utopia*, 1,
No. 1 (May 1945), 3-7.

Incorporated into III-C-6.

169. Derleth, August. "Lovecraft and 'The Pacer.' "
     Magazine of Horror, 1, No. 6 (November 1964), 91-92.
     Excerpt from "Lovecraft as Mentor" (III-D-409).

170. Derleth, August. "Lovecraft's 'Revisions.' " In I-A-
     52, 64-65. II-A-47, 51.

171. Derleth, August. "The Making of a Hoax." *L'Herne*,
     No. 12 (1969), 279-82 (as "Genèse d'une
     mystification"; tr. Jacques Parsons). *La Opinión*, No.
     681 (5 August 1973), Cultural Supplement, p. 4 (as
     "Genesis de una mistificacion"; tr. anon.).
     Quotes the entire "History of the *Necronomicon*" in explaining
     how that mythical tome came to be regarded by many as
     authentic.

172. Derleth, August. "A Master of the Macabre."
     Reading and Collecting, 1, No. 9 (August 1937), 9-10.

173. Derleth, August, ed. *I miti de Cthulhu*. Rome: Fanucci,
     Oct. 1975.
     Contains: August Derleth, "Genesi e struttura dei 'miti di
     Cthulhu' " ("The Cthulhu Mythos"), pp. 15-21; Dirk W. Mosig,
     "Lovecraft mitografo" ("H. P. Lovecraft: Myth-Maker"), pp.
     23-31.

174. Derleth, August. "Myths About Lovecraft." *The
     Lovecraft Collector*, No. 2 (May 1949), pp. 1, 3-4.
     An early version of III-C-7.

175. Derleth, August. "New HPL Pseudonyms Rejected
     by Derleth." *The Fossil*, No. 159 (October 1958), p.
     90.
     Corrections to Willametta Keffer's article (III-D-316).

176. Derleth, August. "A Note About the Outsider." *The
     Alchemist* (December 1940).

177. Derleth, August. "Nota biografia." In II-A-35.

> Excerpts of Chapter i of III-C-6.

178. Derleth, August. "A Note on the Cthulhu Mythos." In *The Trail of Cthulhu*. Sauk City, Wis.: Arkham House, 1962, pp. 245-48. New York: Ballantine Books, July 1971, June 1976; Jersey, Eng.: Neville Spearman, 1974, pp. 213-16.

179. [Derleth, August.] "The Origin of a Lovecraft Essay." *The Arkham Collector*, No. 2 (Winter 1968), p. 41.

> States that "Cats and Dogs" was written in rebuttal to an obscure essay by Robert E. Howard, "The Beast in the Abyss"; actually, it was the other way round.

180. Derleth, August. "Précisions biographiques." *L'Herne*, No. 12 (1969), pp. 272-78 (tr. Jacques Parsons).

> Excerpt from Chapter I of III-C-6.

181. Derleth, August. "Random Notes: On The Lurker at the Threshold." *The Arkham Sampler*, 1, No. 2 (Spring 1948), 49-50.

> Later incorporated into III-C-7.

182. Derleth, August. "A Rebuttal to Lovecraft Criticism: A Group of Letters." *Mirage*, No. 4 (Winter 1961-62), pp. 12-14.

183. Derleth, August. "Something about Howard Phillips Lovecraft." In I-A-22.

184. Derleth, August. *Thirty Years of Arkham House*. Sauk City, Wis.: Arkham House, 1970, pp. 1-6, passim.

> Updating of III-D-151.

185. Derleth, August. "The Weird Tale in English since

1890." *The Ghost*, No. 3 (May 1945), pp. 5-32 (esp. 15-18).

186. Derleth, August. "A Wreath for Lovecraft." *Frontier* (February 1941).

187. Derleth, August. *Writing Fiction*. Boston: The Writer, Inc., 1946, pp. 102-05, passim.

188. Derleth, August, and Donald Wandrei. "H. P. Lovecraft: Outsider." In I-A-15.

189. Derleth, August, and Donald Wandrei. Letter. *Weird Tales*, 35, No. 9 (May 1941), 120-21 (as "The Lovecraft Tradition").

   Explains how Derleth and Wandrei re-discovered the text of *The Case of Charles Dexter Ward*, which had been lost after Lovecraft's death.

190. Derleth, August, and Donald Wandrei. "The Lovecraft Memorial: A Note on Work in Progress." *Scienti-Snaps*, 3, No. 1 (February 1940), 12-13.

191. Derleth, August, and Donald Wandrei. "Preface" to I-A-41.

   Prints the complete text of Lovecraft's letter of application, [ca. Sept. 1924].

192. Derleth, August, and Donald Wandrei. "Preface" to I-A-45.

193. Derleth, August, and Donald Wandrei. "Preface" to I-A-59.

194. de Turris, Gianfranco. "Howard P. Lovecraft." *Sgt. Kirk*, No. 40 (November-December 1974), pp. 12-15.

195. de Turris, Gianfranco. "H. P. Lovecraft, l'ultimo demiurgo." *La Destra*, 2, No. 5 (May 1972), 67-75.

196. de Turris, Gianfranco. "Gli illustratori di Lovecraft." *Sgt. Kirk*, No. 44 (July-August 1975), pp. 331-35.

197. d[e] T[urris], G[ianfranco], and S[ebastiano] F[usco]. "Conversazione con Dirk W. Mosig." *Futuro Notizie* (Fanucci Editore), 2, Nos. 2/3 (1977), [16-17].

198. de Turris, Gianfranco, and Sebastiano Fusco. "Del 'Necronomicon' e di altre abominazione." *Pianeta*, No. 57 (March-April 1974), pp. 109-19.

> Reprints (in Italian translation) the complete text of "History of the *Necronomicon*" (as "Storia e cronologia del 'Necronomicon' "), pp. 111-14.

199. d[e] T[urris], G[ianfranco], and S[ebastiano] F[usco]. "HPL: Un apprezzamento." *Futuro Notizie* (Fanucci Editore), 2, Nos. 2/3 (1977), [12].

200. de Turris, G[ianfranco], and S[ebastiano] Fusco. "H. P. Lovecraft e il suo universo fantastico." *Playmen*, July 1971 (as by "G. de Turris"; abridged). *Il Re in Giallo*, 1, No. 2 [1976], 7-28.

201. de Turris, Gianfranco, and Sebastiano Fusco. "Lovecraft a fumetti." *Sgt. Kirk*, No. 46 (November-December 1975), 563-65.

202. de Turris, G[ianfranco], and S[ebastiano] Fusco. "Le traduzione Italiane di Lovecraft." *Il Re in Giallo*, 1, No. 2 [1976], 55-64.

203. Deutsch, Michel. "Lovecraft ou la mythologie." *Esprit*, No. 253 (September 1957), pp. 256-66.

204. Dillard, R. H. W. "Dagon" [by Fred Chappell]. *Masterplots: 1969 Annual: Magill's Literary Annual: Essay-Reviews of 100 Outstanding Books Published in the*

United States during 1968. New York: Salem Press, 1970, pp. 82-86.

> Touches upon Lovecraft's influence on Chappell's novel (see III-G-iv-4).

205. Doi, Ryusuke. "Ankokuma." *Crypt Horror Tales*, No. 8 (April 1976), pp. 32-33.

206. Doi, Ryusuke, ed. *Cthulhu no hitsugi.* [Tokyo: Ryusuke Doi, 1975.]

> Contains: Ryusuke Doi, "R'lyeh ibun," pp. 4-5; August Derleth, "Kaisetsu: Cthulhu shinwa" ("The Cthulhu Mythos"), pp. 37-43 (tr. Hideaki Hazu).

207. Dorflas, Gillo. "Racconti dell'orrore all'esame di letteratura: Meritano maggiore o minore attenzione le novelle alla Lovecraft?" *Corriere della sera*, 102, No. 147 (29 June 1977), 3.

208. Douglas, Drake. "Rhode Island Recluse: H. P. Lovecraft." In *Horror!* New York: Macmillan & Co., 1966, Dec. 1966, pp. 263-76. London: John Baker, 1967, pp. 287-307. New York: Collier, 1969, pp. 236-48.

209. Duperray, Max. "Villes fantastiques: Les Fantasmes de l'identité chez Dunsany et Lovecraft." *Confluents*, No. 2 (1975), pp. 39-53.

210. Eber, Robert M. "A Comparison of the Usage of Cats in the Fiction of Edgar Allan Poe and H. P. Lovecraft." *Fandom Unlimited*, No. 3 (Spring 1977), pp. 29-30.

211. Eddy, Clifford M. Letter. *The Providence Journal*, 138, No. 283 (26 November 1966), 21 (as "Knew Lovecraft").

212. Eddy, C[lifford] M., Jr. "Walks with H. P. Lovecraft." *L'Herne*, No. 12 (1969), pp. 354-56 (as "Promenades avec H. P. Lovecraft"; tr. Jacques Parsons).

213. Eddy, Muriel E. "H. P. Lovecraft among the Demons." *The Rhode Islander* (the *Providence Sunday Journal Magazine*), 8 March 1970, pp. 23-26.

214. Eddy, Muriel E. Letter. *Magazine of Horror*, 6, No. 2 (May 1970), 115-16.

215. Eddy, Muriel E. Letters. *The Providence Journal*, 59, No. 27 (2 January 1944), Sec. III, p. 1; 120, No. 205 (26 August 1948), 11; 130, No. 129 (30 May 1958), 23.

216. Eddy, Muriel E. "Lovecraft's Marriage and Divorce." *Haunted*, 1, No. 3 (June 1968), 86, 93.

217. Eddy, Muriel E. "Memories of H. P. L." *Magazine of Horror*, 2, No. 6 (Winter 1965-66), 83-84.

218. Eddy, Ruth. "The Man Who Came at Midnight." *Fantasy Commentator*, 3, No. 3 (Summer-Fall 1949), 71.

219. Edkins, E. A. "Idiosyncrasies of HPL." *The Olympian*, No. 35 (Autumn 1940), pp. 1-7.

> "I think that the most lasting impression Lovecraft left me was one of essential nobility, of dauntless integrity . . . he remains enshrined in my memory as a great gentleman, in the truest sense of that much abused term."

220. Edkins, Ernest A. "Musings and Miscellanea: Of Lovecraft." *The Aonian*, 2, No. 4 (Winter 1944), 187-88.

221. Edogawa, Ranpo. "Kaidan nyomon." *Hoseki*, June 1948-July 1949. *Edogawa Ranpo Zenshu*, No. 15 (1970), pp. 138-67.

222. Edwards, Jay. "Lovecraftiana." *Lethe*, No. 7 (August 1947), pp. 1-5; No. 8 (February-March 1948), pp. 2-5; No. 9 (September 1948), pp. 2-3, 5.

223. Eekhaut, Guido. "Leven & Werken." *Rigel*, No. 3 (November 1968), pp. [8-16].

224. Eisner, Steven. "H. P. L.—Imagination's Envoy to Literature (Some Introductory Remarks)." *Fresco*, 8, No. 3 (Spring 1958), 2-4.

225. Eizykman, Boris. *Science-fiction et capitalisme: Critique de la position de désir de la science*. [Paris:] Maison Mame, 1973.

> Contains: "Lovecraft et la fantastique comme figure judaïque," pp. 31-41; "Démons et merveilles," pp. 215-23.

226. Elflandsson, Galad. "H. P. Lovecraft: Master of the Macabre." *The Montreal Star*, 2 April 1977, Sec. D, p. 1.

227. Elliott, Gordon. "Lovecraft's Unsung Masterpiece." *Dream-Quest*, 1, No. 5 (April 1948), 20-22.

228. Emmons, Wilfred S., Jr. "H. P. Lovecraft as a Mythmaker." *Extrapolation*, No. 1 (May 1960), pp. 35-37.

229. Ennis, Clifford D. Letter. *The Argosy*, [74], No. 4 (March 1914), 956 (as "Wants Jackson Stories").

> Rebuttal to Lovecraft's comments (see I-B-v-b-7).

230. Ernoult, Claude. "Lovecraft ou le mythe en révolution." *Les Lettres Nouvelles*, No. 21 (1954), pp. 664-71.

231. Errigo, Angela M. "The Haunted Dreamer." *Fate & Fortune*, No. 6 (1974), pp. 44-48.

> An occultist view of Lovecraft.

232. Ertal, Claude. "Démons et merveilles: Rêve ou écriture." *L'Herne*, No. 12 (1969), pp. 75-90.

233. Everts, R. Alain. "Howard Phillips Lovecraft and Sex: or The Sex Life of a Gentleman." *Nyctalops*, 2, No. 2 (July 1974), 19.

      Lovecraft had a low sex drive but was not impotent or homosexual.

234. Everts, R. Alain. "Introduction" to I-A-9.

235. Everts, R. Alain. Introduction to I-A-75.

236. Everts, R. Alain. "Lovecraft and Lord Dunsany." *The* HPL *Supplement*, No. 2 (July 1973), pp. 2-3.

237. Everts, R. Alain. "The Lovecraft Family in America." *Xenophile*, 2, No. 6 (October 1975), 7, 16.

      Sketches of Lovecraft's paternal ancestors.

238. Everts, R. Alain. "Mrs. Howard Phillips Lovecraft." *Nyctalops*, 2, No. 1 (April 1973), 45.

239. Everts, R. Alain, and Phillips Gamwell, III [sic]. "The Death of a Gentleman; the Last Days of Howard Phillips Lovecraft." *Nyctalops*, 2, No. 1 (April 1973), 24-25.

      Painstaking account of Lovecraft's terminal illness and his final days in the hospital.

240. Faig, Kenneth W., Jr. "Howard Phillips Lovecraft: The Early Years, 1890-1914." *Nyctalops*, 2, No. 1 (April 1973), 3-9, 13-15; 2, No. 2 (July 1974), 34-44.

      Comprehensive article covering not only Lovecraft's life but his writings—fiction, poetry, science, etc.—during his early years.

241. Faig, Kenneth W., Jr. "HPL: The Book That Nearly Was." *Xenophile*, No. 11 (March 1975), pp. 118-23.

On R. H. Barlow's stillborn edition of Lovecraft's *Fungi from Yuggoth*.

242. Faig, Kenneth W., Jr. Letter. *Nyctalops*, 1, No. 5 (October 1971), 49-51.

Discussion of the unity of Lovecraft's myth-cycle.

243. Faig, Kenneth W., Jr. "The Lovecraft Circle: A Glossary." *Mirage*, No. 10 (1971), pp. 27-40.

Sketches of Lovecraft's correspondents and associates.

244. Faig, Kenneth W., Jr. "A Lovecraftian Note." *The Dark Brotherhood Journal*, 1, No. 1 (June 1971), 10-12.

Lovecraft as mentioned in his high-school yearbooks.

245. Faig, Kenneth W., Jr. "Lovecraft's Own Book of Weird Fiction." *The* HPL *Supplement*, No. 2 (July 1973), pp. 4-14.

Quotes the entire poem, "The Messenger" (without title), p. 6.

246. Faig, Kenneth W., Jr. "Lovecraft's Providence." *Tamlacht*, 2, No. 2 (n.d.), 4-9.

Description of Lovecraft's favorite sites in Providence.

247. Faig, Kenneth W., Jr. "A Note and an Anecdote." *Myrrdin*, No. 3 (1976), pp. 24-27.

On the Driftwind Press edition of *The Materialist Today*.

248. Faig, Kenneth W., Jr. "A Note Regarding the Harold Farnese Musical Pieces." *The Dark Brotherhood Journal*, 1, No. 1 (June 1971), 12-14.

249. Faig, Kenneth W., Jr. "Robert H. Barlow and H. P. Lovecraft: A Reflection." In Robert H. Barlow. *Annals of the Jinns*. West Warwick, R.I.: Necronomicon Press, 1978, pp. 1-6.

250. Farber, Marjorie. "Subjectivity in Modern Fiction." *The Kenyon Review*, 7, No. 4 (Autumn 1945), 645-52.

  An attempt to psychoanalyze Lovecraft through his fiction.

251. Faussone, Bruno. "La grande paura." *Tuttolibri*, 2, No. 3 (24 June 1976), 8.

252. Finné, Jacques. *Les Grandes Mystifications*. Verviers, Belg.: Bibliotheque Marabout, 1975, pp. 176-78.

253. Fisher, H. M. Letter. *The Argosy*, [74], No. 4 (March 1914), 959 (as "Congratulates Fred Jackson").

  Rebuttal to Lovecraft's remarks (see I-B-v-b).

254. Forsey, Paul. "H. P. Lovecraft: The Man and His Works." *Gothique Era*, March [?] 1972, pp. 9-15.

255. Frabetti, Carlo. "Presentación." In II-A-55, 56.

256. Frabetti, Carlo. "Presentación: En el umbral de la cordura." In II-C-8 (Bruguera ed.).

257. Frost, Brian J. "H. P. Lovecraft: A Stranger in This Century." *Shadow*, No. 7 (September 1969), pp. 5-7. *Fantasycon* (The British Fantasy Society), 22 February 1975, pp. 3-5.

258. Fruttero, Carlo, and Franco Lucentini. "Storia della storie di Lovecraft." In II-A-10.

259. Fryer, Donald S. "Klarkash-Ton & Ech Pi El: Or the Alleged Influence of H. P. Lovecraft on Clark Ashton Smith." *Mirage*, 1, No. 6 (Winter 1963-64), 30-33.

260. Fulwiler, William. "E. R. B. and H. P. L." *ERB-dom*, No. 80 (February 1975), pp. 41, 44.

  On Edgar Rice Burroughs' influence upon Lovecraft.

261. Fusco, Sebastiano. "Lovecraft: fantasia e politica." *L'Italiano*, June 1971, pp. 460-64.

262. Gaddes, Vincent H. "The Genius Who Lived Backwards." *Writer's Forum*, No. 2 (February 1954), pp. 5-7, 9, 59-60.

263. Garci, José Luis. *Ray Bradbury, humanista del futuro*. Madrid: Helios, 1971, p. 37.

> Brief comment by the critic who allegedly ranked Lovecraft among the world's ten greatest authors (see III-D-571).

264. Gatto, John Taylor. "Lovecraft and the Grotesque Tradition." *Nyctalops*, 2, No. 6 (May 1977), 7-11.

> Incorporated into his book (III-C-13).

265. Gehman, Richard B. "Imagination Runs Wild." *New Republic*, 120, No. 3 (17 January 1949), 15-18. *Fantasy Review*, 3, No. [3] (Summer 1949), 9-11.

> On Lovecraft's influence in fantasy fiction.

266. Glut, Donald F. *The Frankenstein Legend: A Tribute to Mary Shelley and Boris Karloff*. Metuchen, N.J.: The Scarecrow Press, 1973, p. 299.

> On "Herbert West—Reanimator."

267. Golowin, Sergius. "Sagenerzähler von heute." In *Hexen, Hippies, Rosenkreuzer*. Hamburg: Merlin Verlag, 1977, pp. 251-55.

268. Goodenough, Arthur Henry. "Further Recollections of Amateur Journalism. [Written in 1920.]" *The Vagrant*, [Spring 1927], pp. 100-06 [i.e., 24-30].

> On Goodenough's encounters and assessments of Lovecraft in amateur journalism. Includes Goodenough's poem, "Lovecraft—an Appreciation" (pp. 101-02 [i.e., 25-26]), and Lovecraft's reply, "To Mr. Arthur Goodenough of New England, on His Most Meritorious Poetrie" (pp. 104-05 [i.e., 28-29]).

269. Gosseyn, Ricardo. "Prologo" to II-A-5.

270. Gould, Bartlett. "Rhode Island's Genius of Grue."
   Yankee, 33, No. 10 (October 1969), 95-97, 156-59.

   A remarkably sane general analysis of Lovecraft's life and
   work.

271. Grant, Kenneth. "Dreaming out of Space." *Man,
   Myth & Magic: An Illustrated Encyclopedia of the
   Supernatural*. New York: Marshall Cavendish Corp.,
   1970. XXIII, 3214-15.

   Lovecraft's myth-cycle may not be entirely fictional.

272. Grant, Kenneth. *The Magical Revival*. London:
   Frederick Muller, 1972, pp. 114-17.

273. Grover, Roy M. Letter. *The Argosy*, [74], No. 4
   (March 1914), 960 (as "Praises Lovecraft's Poetry").

   Comment on I-B-v-b-7.

274. Guinn, Gerald. "The Cthulhu Mythos Revisited."
   The Dragon, 2, No. 8 (May 1978), 22.

275. Gullette, Alan D. "The Colour out of Cygnus."
   Nyctalops, 1, No. 6 (February 1972), 8.

   "The Colour out of Space" may have been inspired by a
   curious explosion in Siberia in 1908.

276. Gunn, James. *Alternate Worlds: The Illustrated History of
   Science Fiction*. [Englewood Cliffs, N.J.:] A & W Visual
   Library, [1975], pp. 141-43.

277. Haining, Peter. *Terror! A History of Horror Illustrations
   from the Pulp Magazines*. [Englewood Cliffs, N.J.:] A &
   W Visual Library, 1976, pp. 124-29.

278. Hall, Loay, Terry Dale, and Randall Larson. "A
   History of the Cthulhu Mythos." *Fandom Unlimited*,
   No. 2 (Spring 1977), pp. 21-28; No. 3 (Summer
   1977), pp. 8-14.

279. Harris, Mason. "Lovecraft and the Horror of Darkness." *Entropy*, No. 3 (1971); No. 4 (October 1971), pp. [21-25].

> Amateurish psychological study.

280. Harrison, Michael. "Howard Phillips Lovecraft." *The Phoenix*, 5, No. 5 (May 1946), 355-58. *Fantasy Advertiser*, 2, No. 4 (November 1947), 21-23.

281. Hart, B. K. "The Sideshow." *The Providence Journal*, 101, No. 280 (23 November 1929); 101, No. 281 (25 November 1929), 2; 101, No. 286 (30 November 1929), 10; 101, No. 288 (3 December 1929), 14; 102, No. 66 (18 March 1930), 12.

> A regular column by a correspondent of Lovecraft's. The fourth article prints "The Messenger" (inspired by a remark of Hart's) for the first time; the last prints a letter by Lovecraft.

282. Hart, Philomena. "A Lovecraft Postscript Based on Barnes Street Letters.—The Providence Poe and His Decade of Mail to 'The Sideshow.' " *The Providence Sunday Journal*, 59, No. 28 (9 January 1944), Sec. IV, p. 2.

> Quotes the entire text of "The Messenger."

283. Hart, Philomena, ed. *The Sideshow of B. K. Hart: A Selection of Columns Written for the Providence Journal 1929-1941.* Providence: The Roger Williams Press, 1941, pp. 56-58.

284. Hartmann, J. F. Letters. *The* [Providence] *Evening News*, 45, No. 119 (7 October 1914), 12; 46, No. 22 (14 December 1914), 3 (as "A Defense of Astrology").

> Rebuttal to Lovecraft's comments (see I-B-v-b).

285. Hartwell, David G. "Howard Phillips Lovecraft." *Whispers*, 2, No. 1 (November 1974), 48-51.

286. Heald, Hazel. Letter. *Weird Tales*, 30, No. 2 (August 1937), 248.

287. Hebron, C. C. "From Oyo to Arkham." *Mirage*, No. 10 (1971), pp. 55-59.

288. Heins, Charles W. "Lovecraft, Addenda." *The Phoenix*, 3, No. 1 (September 1943), 74-75.

     Announcement of Arkham House's plans to publish Lovecraft's works.

289. Henneberger, J. C. "Out of Space, out of Time." *Deeper Than You Think*, 1, No. 2 (July 1968), 3-5.

290. Hetzel, Frederick A. "The Squamous Factor." *Pittsburgh*, 7, No. 12 (December 1976), 8-9.

     On Lovecraft's growing fame and reputation.

291. Hewetson, Alan. "The Legend of an 18th Century Gentleman: H. P. Lovecraft." *Psycho*, No. 10 (January 1973), pp. 31-33.

292. Hillman, Arthur F. "The Lovecraft Cult." *Fantasy Review*, 1, No. 4 (August-September 1947), 2-4.

     Discusses Lovecraft's "increasing recognition" and "Supernatural Horror in Literature."

293. Hillman, Arthur F. "The Poet of Science Fiction." *Fantasy Review*, 3, No. [2] (April-May 1949), 14-16.

     On Clark Ashton Smith; the author quotes from "Some Notes on Interplanetary Fiction" and "Supernatural Horror in Literature."

294. Holmes, J. Eric. "A Rebuttal to 'The Cthulhu Mythos Revisited' by Gerald Guinn." *The Dragon*, 3, No. 2 (July 1978), 3.

295. Home, William Scott. "The Lovecraft 'Books': Some Addenda and Corrigenda." *L'Herne*, No. 12 (1969),

pp. 300-11 (as "Les 'Livres' de Lovecraft: Quelques
addenda et corrigenda"; tr. Jacques Parsons).

Examination of some of the real and mythical books used by
Lovecraft in his fiction. Home also linguistically explores "The
Rats in the Walls."

296. Home, William Scott. "What's in a Nom?" *Nyctalops*,
2, No. 6 (May 1977), 35-36.

On the *Necronomicon*.

297. [Hornig, Charles D.] "Startling Fact." *The Fantasy
Fan*, 1, No. 3 (November 1933), 38.

On fictitious books invented by Lovecraft and Clark Ashton
Smith.

298. Houtain, George Julian. "20 Webster Street:
Lovecraft." *The Zenith*, January 1921, p. 5.

299. Howard, Robert E. Letter. *Weird Tales*, 11, No. 5
(May 1928), 711-12.

300. [Howard, Robert E.] *Runes of Ahrh-eih-eche*. [Lamoni,
Iowa: Stygian Isle Press,] 1976.

Contains letters by Robert E. Howard: To Farnsworth
Wright, August 1930, p. 9; to H. P. Lovecraft, July 1933, p. 14.

301. Huber, Richard, Jr. "Nodens and the Elder Gods."
Nyctalops, 2, No. 7 (March 1978), 11.

302. Hutin, Serge. "L'Ecrivain Lovecraft: Ses Clefs
initiatiques et son secret." *Lunatique*, No. 41
(November 1968), pp. 35-44.

303. Ibars, Eduardo Haro. "Las máscaras de la nada:
(Notas possibles a una lectura de Lovecraft)." In
II-A-45.

304. Indick, Ben P. "Lovecraft's Ladies." *Xenophile*, 2, No.
6 (October 1975), 10-11.

Studies of Lovecraft works involving women.

305. Ioakimidis, Demètre, and Pierre Strinati. " 'Tekeli-li': La Posterité littéraire d'Arthur Gordon Pym." *Fiction*, No. 74 (January 1960), pp. 123-29.

306. Isaacson, Charles D. "Concerning the Conservative." *In a Minor Key*, No. 2 [1915], pp. [10-11].

307. Ivănescu, Mircea. "Lovecraft vizionarul." *Secolul 20*, No. 4 (1973), pp. 78-80.

308. Jacob, John. "*The Commonplace Book* of H. P. Lovecraft." *Tamlacht*, 1, No. 6 (n.d.), 16-20, 26; 1, No. 10 (n.d.), 2-5; 2, No. 2 (n.d.), 23-25, 15.

309. Jinka, Katsuo. "Arkham House no junin 2: H. P. Lovecraft." *Hayakawa's Mystery Magazine*, No. 208 (August 1973), pp. 44-50.

310. Joshi, S. T. "Introduction" to I-A-83.

311. Joshi, S. T. "Lovecraft Criticism: A Study." *Rigel Magazine*, No. 59 (November 1977), pp. 9-16 (as "Een studie: Lovecraft-kritiek"; tr. anon.).

   A history of Lovecraft criticism from his death to the present and an exploration of the causes for his lack of recognition.

312. Joshi, S. T. "Who Wrote 'The Mound'?" *Nyctalops*, 2, No. 7 (March 1978), 41-42.

   Proves that Lovecraft ghost-wrote "The Mound" without assistance from Frank Belknap Long, as has often been believed.

313. Juin, Hubert. "Les potences de Salem." *L'Herne*, No. 12 (1969), pp. 111-16.

314. Kałużyński, Zygmunt. "Alpträume der neuen Welt." In *Listy zza Oceanu*. Warsaw, 1956.

315. Keel, Billy. "Astronomy and the Cthulhu Mythos." *Ambrosia*, No. 1 (24 June 1972), pp. 16-19; No. 2 (August 1973), pp. 6-8.

316. Keffer, Willametta. "Howard P(seudonym) Lovecraft: The Many Names of HPL." *The Fossil*, No. 158 (July 1958), pp. 82-84.

   Strong article on Lovecraft's pseudonymous authorship of work in the amateur journals. She was the first to suggest that "El Imparcial" was a pseudonym of Lovecraft's.

317. [Keffer, Willametta.] "More on HPL Pseudonyms." *The Fossil*, No. 161 (April 1959), p. 118.

   Rebuttal to III-D-175.

318. Keil, Paul Livingston. "I Met Lovecraft." *The Phoenix*, 3, No. 6 (July 1944), 149.

319. Kellar, Michael. Letter. *Fantasy Crossroads*, No. 6 (November 1975), pp. 1-3.

320. Keller, David H. "Lovecraft's Astronomical Notebook." *The Lovecraft Collector*, No. 3 (October 1949), pp. 1-4.

   Studies the astronomical notebook kept by Lovecraft from 1909 to 1915. "This notebook shows more than Lovecraft's interest in astronomy. There is an evident love of the beauty of the skies. . . ."

321. Keller, David H. "Notes on Lovecraft." *Mirage*, No. 3 (Summer 1961), pp. 12-18.

322. Keller, David H. "Shadows over Lovecraft." *Fantasy Commentator*, 2, No. 7 (Summer 1948), 237-46. *Fresco*, 8, No. 3 (Spring 1958), 12-27.

   In explaining Lovecraft's literary theme of hereditary degeneration, Keller tries to prove that Lovecraft had syphilis, acquired from his parents. The second appearance contains the noted rebuttal by Kenneth Sterling (see III-D-583).

323. Keller, Georges. "Le Royaume noir." *L'Herne*, No. 12 (1969), pp. 139-40.

324. Keller, Georges, and Francois Kienzle. "Essai de synopsis." *L'Herne*, No. 12 (1969), pp. 191-94.

325. Ketterer, David. *New Worlds for Old: The Apocalyptic Imagination, Science Fiction, and American Literature.* Bloomington: Indiana University Press, 1974; Garden City, N.Y.: Doubleday & Co. (Anchor Books), 1974, pp. 261-63.

326. Kienzle, Francois. "Lovecraftiana." *L'Herne*, No. 12 (1969), pp. 135-36.

327. Kirde, Kalju. *Bemerkungen über Weird Fiction.* Kitzingen: C. C. Schaef, 1967, pp. 54-59. Also in *Quarber Merkur*, 4, No. 2 (August 1966), 34-39.

328. Kirde, Kalju. "H. P. Lovecraft—Schöpfer kosmischer Mythen." In II-A-20.

329. Klein, Gérard. "Entre le fantastique et la science-fiction, Lovecraft." *L'Herne*, No. 12 (1969), pp. 47-74. *Secolul 20*, No. 4 (1973), pp. 75-76 (as "Lovecraft—o tentativă de abordare sociologică"; tr. Tea Preda; abridged).

330. Kleiner, Rheinhart. "After a Decade and the Kalem Club." *The Californian*, 4, No. 2 (Fall 1936), 45-47.

331. Kleiner, Rheinhart. "Bards and Bibliophiles." *The Aonian*, 2, No. 4 (Winter 1944), 169-74.

332. Kleiner, Rheinhart. "Bards of Passion and of Mirth." *The Aonian*, 2, No. 1 (Spring 1944), 106-09.

333. Kleiner, Rheinhart. "Discourse on H. P. Lovecraft." *The Amateur Scribe*, No. 15 (June 1951), pp. 12-19.

334. Kleiner, Rheinhart. "Howard Phillips Lovecraft."
     The Californian, 5, No. 1 (Summer 1937), 5-8.

335. Kleiner, Rheinhart. "Howard Phillips Lovecraft."
     The Phoenix, 3, No. 1 (September 1943), 73-74.

     Aspects of Lovecraft's involvement with amateur journalism.

336. Kleiner, Rheinhart. "A Memoir of Lovecraft." *The
     Arkham Sampler*, 1, No. 2 (Spring 1948), 52-61.

337. Kleiner, Rheinhart. "A Note on Howard P.
     Lovecraft's Verse." *The United Amateur*, 18, No. 4
     (March 1919), 76.

     The first assessment of Lovecraft's poetry. Kleiner admires
     Lovecraft's sharp satirical verse.

338. Knight, Damon. "Iä! Yog-Sothoth! Yah, yah, yah!"
     The Magazine of Fantasy and Science Fiction, 18, No. 5
     (May 1960), 79-80.

339. Knight, Damon. "The Tedious Mr. Lovecraft." *The
     Magazine of Fantasy and Science Fiction*, 19, No. 2
     (August 1960), 100-02. In Knight, *In Search of
     Wonder: Essays on Modern Science Fiction*. Rev. and
     enlarged ed. Chicago: Advent Publishers, 1967, pp.
     223-24 (without title).

     Shows an ignorance of the difference between Lovecraft's
     works and Derleth's "posthumous collaborations."

340. Kuntz, Rob. "The Lovecraftian Mythos in
     Dungeons & Dragons." *The Dragon*, 2, No. 6
     (February 1978), 18, 20-21.

341. Kyle, David A., ed. *The Illustrated History of Science
     Fiction Ideas and Dreams*. London: Hamlyn Publishing
     Group, 1977, pp. 132-33, 150.

342. Kyle, David A. *A Pictorial History of Science Fiction*.

London: Hamlyn Publishing group, 1976, pp. 52-54, 69, 124.

343. Kynell, K. S. "The Craft of H. P. Lovecraft." In *The Dissonant Eye: A Collection of Critical Essays*. Ed. Laurence Goldstein, Lawrence S. Dietz, Harry Shearer, and Digby Diehl. Los Angeles: Associated Students, Univ. of California, 1965, pp. 41-47.

344. Lacassin, Francis. "Lovecraft et les trous de la toile peinte." *L'Herne*, No. 12 (1969), pp. 106-10.

345. Lacassin, Francis. "Préface: Lovecraft ou l'acteur vaincu par son personnage." In II-A-47.

346. Ladd, Thyril L. "Did Lovecraft Miss This?" *Fantasy Commentator*, 2, No. 7 (Summer 1948), 234-35.

347. Lampo, Hubert. "Het fantastisch genie van H. P. Lovecraft." *Bres*, No. 39 (February-March 1973), pp. 105-23.

348. Lampo, Hubert. "H. P. Lovecraft of: Een andere manier van denken." *De Nieuwe Gazet*, 28 February-1 March 1970, p. 2.

349. Lampo, Hubert. "Lovecraft's vriendenkring, of het ontstaan van een mythe." In *De heus van Cleopatra*. Amsterdam: Meulenhoff, 1975, pp. 268-88.

350. Lampo, Hubert. "Zelf een kosmos scheppen: Howard Phillips Lovecraft." In *De zwanen van Stonehenge*. Amsterdam: Meulenhoff, Jan. 1972, April 1972, pp. 309-39.

351. Laney, Francis T. *Ah! Sweet Idiocy!* Los Angeles: Francis T. Laney/Charles Burbee, 1948, passim.

In this autobiography Laney records his growing disgust with Lovecraft and with fantasy fandom.

352. Laney, Francis T. "The Cthulhu Mythology: A Glossary." *The Acolyte*, 1, No. 2 (Winter 1942), 6-12.

353. Langley, Lloyd R. "Even for the Damned There Are Ways . . . Said H. P. Lovecraft." *Connecticut Fireside Magazine*, 4, No. 1 (Spring 1976), 10-14.

354. La Polla, Franco. "Lovecraft, il gotico e i segni cosmici." *Il Verri*, No. 37 (October 1971), pp. 68-75.

355. Larnach, S. L. "H. P. Lovecraft—a Master of the Uncanny." *Biblionews* (September-October 1948).

356. Lauterbach, Edward S. "Lovecraft in the British Thriller." *Armchair Detective*, No. 2 (January 1969), p. 102. *The Dark Brotherhood Journal*, 2, No. 1 (July 1973), 2-3.

357. LaVey, Anton Szandor. *The Satanic Rituals*. New York: Avon Books, Dec. 1972.
    Contains: "The Metaphysics of Lovecraft," pp. 175-78; "The Call to Cthulhu," pp. 197-201.
    Occultist view of Lovecraft.

358. Lawson, Horace L. "Lovecraft Was My Mentor." *Amateur Offerings*, No. 28 (December 1977), pp. 5-6. *The Fossil* (April 1978), pp. 11-12.
    Memoir by an amateur journalist associate of Lovecraft's.

359. Le Bris, Michel. "La Lettre et le désir." *L'Herne*, No. 12 (1969), pp. 91-105.

360. Leiber, Fritz, Jr. "Butman's Essay." *The Reader and Collector* (October 1946).
    Comments on III-D-82.

361. Leiber, Fritz, Jr. "The Cthulhu Mythos: Wondrous and Terrible." *Fantastic*, 24, No. 4 (June 1975), 118-21.

362. Leiber, Fritz, Jr. "The Grisly Universe and H.P.L." *Shangri-L'Affaires*, No. 63 (January 1963), p. 18.

> On Lovecraft's philosophical thought.

363. Leiber, Fritz, Jr. "Lovecraft in My Life." *Journal of the H. P. Lovecraft Society*, No. 1 (1976), pp. [5-9].

364. Leiber, Fritz, Jr. "My Correspondence with Lovecraft." *Fresco*, 8, No. 3 (Spring 1958), 30-33.

365. Leiber, Fritz, Jr. "The Sails of Fancy." *Whispers*, 4, No. 4 (July 1974), 19-20.

366. Leiber, Fritz, Jr. "Some Random Thoughts about Lovecraft's Writings." *The Acolyte*, 3, No. 1 (Winter 1945), 20-21.

367. Leiber, Fritz, Jr. "Through Hyperspace with Brown Jenkin: Lovecraft's Contribution to Speculative Fiction." *Shangri-L'Affaires*, No. 66 (September 1963), pp. 8-12. In *The Second Book of Fritz Leiber*. New York: DAW Books, 1975, pp. 182-98 (revised).

> Strong article showing how "Lovecraft helped lead the way to greater realism in subsequent speculative fiction." Leiber discusses Lovecraft's use of space travel, hyperspace travel, hibernating races, and other concepts. The revised version first appeared in III-D-396.

368. Leiber, Fritz, Jr. "The Whisperer Re-examined." *Haunted*, 2, No. 2 (December 1964), 22-25. In *The Book of Fritz Leiber*. New York: DAW Books, 1974, pp. 143-47.

> On "The Whisperer in Darkness."

369. Leiber, Fritz, Jr. "The Works of H. P. Lovecraft: Suggestions for a Critical Appraisal." *The Acolyte*, 2, No. 4 (Fall 1944), 3-5.

> Later revised as "A Literary Copernicus" (see III-D-410).

370. Leiber, Fritz, Jr., Robert Bloch, Sam Russell, Arthur J. Cox, and Leland Sapiro. "H. P. Lovecraft: A Symposium." (Annotated by August Derleth.) *Horizons du Fantastique*, No. 21 (1972), pp. 6-11 (as "Table ronde: Une rencontre sur Lovecraft"; tr. Yves-M. Bornecque).

371. Leine, Friedrich, and Jürgen Gutsch. *Science-Fiction: Materialen und Hinweise*. Frankfurt am Main: Verlag Moritz Diesterweg, 1972, p. 5.

372. Le Lionnais, Francois. "La Beauté en mathematiques." In *Les Grands Courants de la pensée mathematique*. Ed. Francois Le Lionnais. Paris: Albert Blanchard, 1948, 1962, p. 445. New York: Dover Publications, 1971 (as *Great Currents of Mathematical Thought*; tr. Charles Pinter and Helen Kline). II, 131.

   The first mention of Lovecraft in French, in connection with a rather complex mathematical equation.

373. Lequenne, Michel. "Lovecraft, le grand ancien." *Satellite*, No. 27 (March 1960), pp. 69-73.

374. Lesko, Ed, Jr. "HPL: Politics and Fable." *Fantasy Revolution*, 1, No. 3 (20 September 1974), 13-15.

375. Lester, Colin, ed. *The International Science Fiction Yearbook*. Aylesbury, Eng.: Hazell, Watson, & Viney, 1978, pp. 348-51, passim.

376. Lévy, Maurice. "Du fantastiqe." *Études Anglaises*, No. 50 ("Du fantastique à la science-fiction américaine"), pp. 13-26.

377. Lévy, Maurice. "Fascisme et fantastique, ou le cas Lovecraft." *Caliban*, No. 7 (1970), pp. 67-78.

378. Lippi, Giuseppe. "Lovecraftiani a convegno." *Futuro Notizie* (Fanucci Editore), 2, Nos. 2/3 (1977), [13-16].

379. Lippi, Giuseppe. Review of *I miti di Cthulhu*. *Nuovo Notiziario CCSF*, No. 6 (February 1976), pp. 11-13.

380. Lippi, Giuseppe, and Fabio Pagan. "Lovecraft, una mitologia dell'orrore." *Il Piccolo*, No. 9276 (27 March 1977), p. 3.

381. Llopis, Rafael. *Esbozo de una historia natural de los cuentos de miedo*. Madrid: Ediciones Jucar, 1974, pp. 225-47.

382. Llopis, Rafael. "Introducción: En busca del paraíso perdido." In II-A-26.

383. Llopis, Rafael. "Los mitos de Cthulhu." In *Los mitos de Cthulhu*. Ed. Rafael Llopis. Madrid: Alianza Editorial, 1969, 1970, 1975, pp. 11-44.

384. Llopis, Rafael. "Precisiones sobre el libro 'Los mitos de Cthulhu.' " *Nueva Dimensión*, No. 13 (1970), pp. 151-53.

385. [Llorens Borrás, José A.?] "H. P. Lovecraft y su obra." In II-A-11.

386. [Llorens Borrás, José A.?] "Introduccion" to II-A-44.

387. Lockhart, Andrew Francis. "Little Journeys to the Homes of Prominent Amateurs." *The United Amateur*, 15, No. 2 (September 1915), 27-28, 34.

   Biographical sketch, somewhat of a panegyric; the earliest article about Lovecraft.

388. Loeb, William F., Jr. "HPL and the Construction of Character." *The HPL Supplement*, No. 3 (March 1975), pp. 17-21.

389. Long, Frank Belknap. "Introduction" to *The Early*

Long. Garden City, N.Y.: Doubleday & Co., 1975, pp. xiii-xvi. New York: Jove/HBJ (Harcourt Brace Jovanovich), Nov. 1978 (as *The Hounds of Tindalos*), pp. 16-20.

390. Long, Frank Belknap. Letter. *The HPL Supplement*, No. 3 (March 1975), pp. 8-9.

391. Long, Frank Belknap. "One Day in the Life of H. P. Lovecraft." *Whispers*, 2, Nos. 2/3 (June 1975), 20-26. *Crypt Horror Tales*, No. 8 (April 1976), pp. 33-39 (as "Aru hi no Lovecraft"; tr. Tetsuya Imamura).

392. Long, Frank Belknap. "Preface" to I-A-5.

393. Long, Frank Belknap. "Preface" to I-A-38.

394. Lovecraft, H. P. *Beyond the Wall of Sleep*. Sauk City, Wis.: Arkham House, 1943.

> Contains: August Derleth and Donald Wandrei, "By way of Introduction," pp. ix-x; Francis T. Laney, "The Cthulhu Mythology: A Glossary" (revised), pp. 415-23; W. Paul Cook, "An Appreciation of H. P. Lovecraft" (i.e., *In Memoriam: Howard Phillips Lovecraft* . . .), pp. 424-58.

395. Lovecraft, H. P. *The Californian: 1934-1938*. West Warwick, R.I.: Necronomicon Press, 1977.

> Contains: Hyman Bradofsky, "Foreword," pp. 3-4; Hyman Bradofsky, "Amateur Affairs," pp. 36-37; Rheinhart Kleiner, "Howard Phillips Lovecraft," pp. 38-41.

396. Lovecraft, H. P., and Divers Hands. *The Dark Brotherhood and Other Pieces*. Sauk City, Wis.: Arkham House, 1966.

> Contains: August Derleth, "Introduction," pp. ix-x; William Scott Home, "The Lovecraft 'Books': Some Addenda and Corrigenda," pp. 134-52; Fritz Leiber, Jr., "Through Hyperspace with Brown Jenkin: Lovecraft's Contribution to Speculative Fiction," pp. 164-78; Andrew E. Rothovius, "Lovecraft and the

New England Megaliths," pp. 179-97; Jack Laurence Chalker, "Howard Phillips Lovecraft: A Bibliograpy," pp. 198-241; C. M. Eddy, Jr., "Walks with H. P. Lovecraft," pp. 242-45; August Derleth, "The Making of a Hoax," pp. 262-67; John E. Vetter, "Lovecraft's Illustrators," pp. 268-301; August Derleth, "Final Notes," pp. 302-21.

Chalker's bibliography is updated from III-B-9; Derleth's "Final Notes" is basically a reprinting of III-C-7.

397. Lovecraft, H. P. *The Doom That Came to Sarnath*. New York: Ballantine Books, Feb. 1971, Sept. 1976.

Contains: Lin Carter, "Farewell to the Dreamlands," pp. ix-xiv; Lin Carter, "A Partial Chronology of Lovecraft's Early Work," pp. 206-08.

398. Lovecraft, H. P. *El que susurra en la oscuridad*. Barcelona: Editorial Bruguera, 1977.

Contains: Carlo Frabetti, "Presentación," pp. 5-6; August Derleth, "Introducción a H. P. Lovecraft" ("An Introduction to H. P. Lovecraft"), pp. 7-11.

399. Lovecraft, H. P. *First Writings: Pawtuxet Valley Gleaner: 1906*. West Warwick, R.I.: Necronomicon Press, 1976.

Contains: Ramsey Campbell, "Embryo Lovecraft," pp. 3-4; Marc A. Michaud, "Introduction," pp. 5-6.

400. Lovecraft, H. P. *Het gefluister in de duisternis*. Utrecht & Antwerp: A. & W. Bruna, 1968.

Contains: Aart C. Prins, "Tot ziens in de maalstrom van Azathoth," pp. 7-9; Aart C. Prins, "De verboden boeken van H. P. Lovecraft," pp. 187-89.

401. Lovecraft, H. P. *Het gefluister in de duisternis*. Utrecht & Antwerp: A. & W. Bruna, 1975.

Contains: Aart C. Prins, "De waarheid (?) omtrent Lovecraft," pp. 183-86; Aart C. Prins, "De verboden boeken van H. P. Lovecraft," pp. 187-89.

402. Lovecraft, H. P. *L'Horreur dans le musée: Les Révisions de Lovecraft*. Vol. I. Paris: Christian Bourgois, 1975. Paris: France Loisirs, 1977.

Contains: August Derleth, "Préface: Les 'Révisions' de Lovecraft" ("Lovecraft's 'Revisions' "), pp. 5-8 (1975); pp. 7-10 (1977): tr. Jacques Parsons; Francis Lacassin, "Introduction: H. P. Lovecraft 'nègre' littéraire ou accoucheur de talents?" pp. 9-30 (1975); pp. 11-32 (1977).

403. Lovecraft, H. P. *Lovecraft kessakushu: Angoku no higi*. Tokyo: Sodosha, 1972.

Contains: Katsuo Jinka, "Howard Phillips Lovecraft no shogai," pp. 399-416; Katsuo Jinka, "Sakuhin kaisetsu," pp. 417-20; Katsuo Jinka, "Howard Phillips Lovecraft sakuhin list," pp. 421-23; Hiroshi Aramata, "Kaisetsu," pp. 424-40; Katsuo Jinka, "Atogaki," pp. 441-43.

404. Lovecraft, H. P. *Lovecraft zenshu I*. Tokyo: Sodosha, 1975.

Contains: Fritz Leiber, Jr., "Kaikishosetsu no Copernicus" ("A Literary Copernicus"), pp. 441-63 (tr. Hiroshi Aramata and Mikikazu Mori); Hiroshi Aramata, "Bunkagensho toshiteno Lovecraft," pp. 481-92, 494, 497; Hiroshi Aramata, "Sakuhin kaitai," pp. 498-513.

405. Lovecraft, H. P. *Marginalia*. Sauk City, Wis.: Arkham House, 1944.

Contains: August Derleth and Donald Wandrei, "Foreword," pp. v-vii; Winfield Townley Scott, "His Own Most Fantastic Creation: Howard Phillips Lovecraft," pp. 309-31; Frank Belknap Long, "Some Random Memories of H. P. L.," pp. 332-37; T. O. Mabbott, "H. P. Lovecraft: An Appreciation," pp. 338-41; Robert H. Barlow, "The Wind That Is in the Grass: A Memoir of H. P. Lovecraft in Florida," pp. 342-50; Kenneth Sterling, "Lovecraft and Science," pp. 351-54; August Derleth, "Lovecraft as a Formative Influence," pp. 355-61; Donald Wandrei, "The Dweller in Darkness: Lovecraft, 1927," pp. 362-69.

406. Lovecraft, H. P. *Nelle spire di Medusa*. Rome: Fanucci, March 1976.

> Contains: G[ianfranco] d[e] T[urris] and S[ebastiano] F[usco], "Introduzione," pp. 5-10; Dirk W. Mosig, "Il gentiluomo di Providence," pp. 11-15 (tr. Roberta Rambelli); August Derleth, "Le 'revisioni' di Lovecraft" ("Lovecraft's 'Revisions' "), pp. 17-19 (tr. Roberta Rambelli).

407. Lovecraft, H. P. *The Occult Lovecraft*. Saddle River, N.J.: Gerry de la Ree, 1975.

> Contains: Gerry de la Ree, "Publisher's Note," pp. 3-4; Anthony Raven, "The Horned God Lives On!" pp. 13-18; Frank Belknap Long, "H. P. L. in Red Hook," pp. 21-22; Samuel Loveman, "Of Gold and Sawdust," pp. 21-22; Anthony Raven, "Lovecraft and Black Magic," pp. 31-40.

> Loveman's article declares that Lovecraft had "a hypocritical streak that few were able to recognize. . . . Howard's monomania about race was about as close to insanity as anything I can think of." Raven's second article argues that Lovecraft's knowledge of black magic was only cursory.

408. Lovecraft, H. P. *Sfida dall'infinito*. Rome: Fanucci, Sept. 1976.

> Contains: G[ianfranco] d[e] T[urris] and S[ebastiano] F[usco], "Introduzione," pp. 5-6; Sam Moskowitz, "Dall'orrore alla fantascienza" ("H. P. Lovecraft: A Study in Horror"), pp. 7-20 (tr. Roberta Rambelli).

409. Lovecraft, H. P., and Divers Hands. *The Shuttered Room and Other Pieces*. Sauk City, Wis.: Arkham House, 1959.

> Contains: August Derleth, "Foreword," pp. ix-x; Donald Wandrei, "Lovecraft in Providence," pp. 124-40; August Derleth, "Lovecraft as Mentor," pp. 141-70; Robert Bloch, "Out of the Ivory Tower," pp. 171-77; Dorothy C. Walter, "Three Hours with H. P. Lovecraft," pp. 178-90; Alfred Galpin, "Memories of a Friendship," pp. 191-201; Lin Carter, "H. P.

Lovecraft: The Books," pp. 212-49; Lin Carter, "H. P. Lovecraft: The Gods," pp. 250-67; T. G. L. Cockcroft, "Addendum: Some Observations on the Carter Glossary," pp. 268-77; George T. Wetzel, "Notes on the Cthulhu Mythos," pp. 278-86; William L. Crawford, "Lovecraft's First Book," pp. 287-90.

Wandrei recounts his 1927 visit with Lovecraft and his help in selling some Lovecraft tales. Derleth quotes many of Lovecraft's letters to him which discuss literature, affectation, Derleth's writings, and other matters. Bloch champions Lovecraft as a regional writer and clears up the matter of John Wilstach's "memoir" of Lovecraft (III-G-iv-11). Walter's article sheds light on Lovecraft's dignity and courtesy. Galpin delves deeply into Lovecraft's attitude toward music and also discusses Sonia Greene (Davis). For Carter's articles see III-D-94, 95. Cockcroft makes additions and corrections to Carter's data. Wetzel's article is a rewriting of "The Cthulhu Mythos: A Study." Crawford provides much data on Lovecraft's *The Shadow over Innsmouth* (1936).

410. Lovecraft, H. P. *Something about Cats and Other Pieces*. Sauk City, Wis.: Arkham House, 1949. Freeport, N.Y.: Books for Libraries Press, 1971.

Contains: August Derleth, "A Prefatory Note," pp. vii-ix; Rheinhart Kleiner, "A Memoir of Lovecraft," pp. 218-28; Samuel Loveman, "Howard Phillips Lovecraft," pp. 229-33; Sonia H. Davis, "Lovecraft as I Knew Him" (i.e., "Howard Phillips Lovecraft as His Wife Remembers Him"), pp. 234-46; August Derleth, "Addenda to 'H. P. L.: A Memoir,'" pp. 247-77; E. Hoffmann Price, "The Man Who Was Lovecraft," pp. 278-89; Fritz Leiber, Jr., "A Literary Copernicus," pp. 290-303.

411. Lovecraft, H. P. *A Winter Wish*. Chapel Hill, N.C.: Whispers Press, 1977.

Contains: Tom Collins, "Introduction," pp. 1-11; Rheinhart Kleiner, "A Note on Howard P. Lovecraft's Verse," p. 15.

412. Lovecraft, H. P. *Writings in The Tryout*. West Warwick, R.I.: Necronomicon Press, 1977.

Contains: S. T. Joshi, "Foreword," pp. 3-4; Marc A. Michaud, "Editor's Note," p. 4; [C. W. Smith], "Around the Circle," pp. 58-59.

413. Lovecraft, H. P. *Writings in The United Amateur: 1915-1925.* West Warwick, R.I.: Necronomicon Press, 1976.

Contains: T. E. D. Klein, "Foreword," pp. iii-xi; Marc A. Michaud, "Introduction," pp. 1-2; Andrew Francis Lockhart, "Little Journeys to the Homes of Prominent Amateurs," pp. 31-33; Rheinhart Kleiner, "A Note on Howard P. Lovecraft's Verse," p. 108.

414. Lovecraft, H. P., and Willis Conover. *Lovecraft at Last.* Arlington, Va.: Carrollton-Clark, 1975.

Contains: Harold Taylor, "Foreword," pp. xi-xii; Willis Conover, "Preface," pp. xv-xix; F. Lee Baldwin, "H. P. Lovecraft: A Biographical Sketch," pp. [60-63]; E. Hoffmann Price, "H. P. Lovecraft: Viewed by E. Hoffmann Price," pp. 158-59.

415. Loveman, Samuel. "Howard Phillips Lovecraft." *The Arkham Sampler*, 1, No. 3 (Summer 1948), 32-36.

416. Loveman, Samuel. "Lovecraft as a Conversationalist." *Fresco*, 8, No. 3 (Spring 1958), 34-36.

Lovecraft's letters are "verbal vomit," but his "conversation takes its place among the masters of that brilliant but difficult art."

417. Loveman, Samuel. "Official Criticism: Bureau of Critics." *The National Amateur*, 44, No. 2 (November 1921), 29, 33.

On "Facts concerning the Late Arthur Jermyn and His Family."

418. Lowins, Evelyne. "Celui qui inspira Lovecraft:

Arthur Machen, ou l'allusion fantastique." *Horizons du Fantastique*, No. 26 (1974), pp. 4-6.

419. Lowndes, Robert A. W. "The Editor's Page." *Magazine of Horror*, 4, No. 6 (November 1968), 4-5, 124-26. *Midnight Fantasies*, No. 1 [August 1974], pp. 2-6.

420. L[owndes], R[obert] A. W. "The Editor's Page." *Magazine of Horror*, 6, No. 6 (April 1971), 4-10.

421. Lowndes, Robert A. W. "The Editor's Page." *Weird Terror Tales*, 1, No. 3 (Fall 1970), 4-9.

422. Lowndes, Robert A. W. "Have You Read These Books?" *The Alchemist* (Summer 1940).

423. Lowndes, Robert [A.] W. Letter. *Weird Tales*, 30, No. 2 (August 1937), 253-54.

424. Lowndes, Robert A. W. "On Lovecraft's Views of Weird Fiction." *Astral Dimensions*, No. 6 (Fall 1977), pp. 23-27.

425. Lundwall, Sam J. "Inlending" to II-A-51.

426. [Lundwall, Sam J.] "Myterna om Cthulhu: H. P. Lovecrafts råttorna i muren." In II-C-58, pp. 289-91.

427. Lundwall, Sam J. *Science Fiction: An Illustrated History*. New York: Grosset & Dunlap, 1978, pp. 33-34.

428. Lundwall, Sam J. *Science Fiction: What It's All About*. New York: Ace Books, 1971, pp. 94-96.

429. Lupoff, Dick. "Cthulhu Fhtagn! Horror Lord Meets His Monsters." *Organ*, 1, No. 8 (June 1971), 20-21, 29.

430. Luten, J. Randle. "What Makes a Story Click?" *The American Author*, 4, No. 4 (July 1932), 11-13.

> Quotes Lovecraft, Clark Ashton Smith, Edmond Hamilton, and Poe as examples of narrative technique.

431. Mabbott, T. O. Letters. *The Acolyte*, 2, No. 3 (Summer 1944), 25; 3, No. 2 (Spring 1945), 32-33.

432. Mabbott, T. O. "Lovecraft as a Student of Poe." *Fresco*, 8, No. 3 (Spring 1958), 37-39. *Fresco*, 10, No. 3 (Summer 1960), 22-24.

> Mabbott points out the several keen interpretations of Poe's tales that Lovecraft made in his tales and essays.

433. Macauley, George W. "Extracts from H. P. Lovecraft's Letters to G. W. Macauley." *The O-Wash-Ta-Nong*, 3, No. 2 (Spring 1938), 1-4.

> Memoir by an amateur journalist colleague who quotes fragments of Lovecraft's letters to him.

434. Macauley, George W. "Lovecraft and the Amateur Press." *Fresco*, 8, No. 3 (Spring 1958), 40-44.

435. McDonald, P. B. "A Letter to *The Silver Clarion*." *The Silver Clarion*, 3, No. 5 (August 1919), 3.

> Reply to a comment by Lovecraft in *The Conservative*, July 1919.

436. McEwen, Marcia. "The Cult of the Horrible." *Cavalcade*, November 1950, pp. 20-23.

437. Manganelli, Giorgio. "Vorwort" to II-A-16.

438. Manguel, Alberto. *Antología de literatura fantástica Argentina: Narradores del siglo XX*. Buenos Aires: Kapelusz, 1973, pp. 8-10, passim.

439. Marshall, Herbert, and Ronald F. Marshall. Letter. *The Providence Journal-Bulletin*, 111, No. 45 (15

November 1975), 10 (as "Straight Facts on
Lovecraft").

440. Matsui, Katsuhiro. "Lovecraftiana—sono kyozo to
jitsuzo." *Crypt Horror Tales*, No. 8 (April 1976), pp.
28-31.

441. Mayrock, Gottfried, and Erhard Ringer. "H. P.
Lovecraft." *Fantasy Atlas*, No. 2 (August 1978), p. 38.

442. Merritt, Pearl K. "Amateur Journalism Is NOT
Futile." *The American Amateur*, 2, No. 1 (September
1920), 82-83. *The Vagrant*, [Spring 1927], pp. 5-8.

Admits to being terrified by Lovecraft's tales.

443. Michaud, Marc A. "Lovecraft Began Dreaming in
the Valley." *The Pawtuxet Valley Daily Times*, 84, No.
63 (31 October 1975), 1, 9.

On Lovecraft's early writings for the Providence
newspapers. Quotes the complete text of "Can the Moon Be
Reached by Man?"

444. Michaud, Paul R. "In Paris, Lovecraft Lives." *The
Providence Evening Bulletin*, 108, No. 302 (29 December
1970), 12.

"Lovecraft has been so well received by the French, says
[Jacques] Bergier, because he was crying out against the
absurdity of a scientific civilization rapidly encroaching upon
man."

445. Michel, John B. "The Last of H. P. Lovecraft." *The
Science Fiction Fan* (November 1939).

446. Michel, John B. "Some Further Notes on
Lovecraft." *The Science Fiction Fan* (September 1940).

447. Midia, Max. "Le astuzie della passione." *Alter Alter*,
No. 9 (September 1977), pp. 61-62.

448. Miller, P. Schuyler. "Let's All Jump on HPL." *Cepheid*, 1, No. 1 (Winter 1945-46), 13-14, 19.

449. Miller, Rob Hollis. "Lovecraft and Satanism." *Nyctalops*, 2, No. 3 (January-February 1975), 9-11, 43.

450. Miske, J. Chapman. "H. P. Lovecraft: Strange Weaver." *Scienti-Snaps*, 3, No. 3 (Summer 1940), 9-12.

     Remarkably accurate and perceptive general summary of Lovecraft's life and work.

451. Moe, Donald J. "From Maurice Moe's Son." *The O-Wash-Ta-Nong*, [2, No. 2] [1937], [4].

452. Moe, Maurice W. "Howard Phillips Lovecraft: The Sage of Providence." *The O-Wash-Ta-Nong*, [2, No. 2] [1937], [3].

453. [Moidel, Jacob.] "Editorial: H. P. Lovecraft." *The National Amateur*, 49, No. 3 (January 1927), 7.

454. Molesworth, Vol. "A Modern Master of the Macabre." *Arna* (1949).

455. Moorcock, Michael. "Aspects of Fantasy." *Science Fantasy*, No. 61 (1963), pp. 78-84; No. 62 (1963), pp. 102-09.

456. Mooser, Claire. "A Study of R. H. Barlow: The T. E. Lawrence of Mexico." *Mexico Quarterly Review*, 3, No. 2 (1968), 5-12.

457. Mora, Ronaldo. "Legendo Lovecraft." *Oltre*, 1978, pp. 5-7.

458. Morris, Harry O., Jr. "HPL and Surrealism." *Fantasy Revolution*, 1, No. 3 (20 September 1974), 44.

459. [Morris, Harry O., Jr.] "Lovecraft on Tape: Impressions of Six HPL Dramatizations." *Nyctalops*, 1, No. 3 (February 1971), 3, 7.

460. Morton, James F., Jr. " 'Conservatism' Run Mad." *In a Minor Key*, No. 2 [1915], pp. [15-16].

On Lovecraft's magazine, *The Conservative*.

461. Morton, James F. "A Few Memories." *The Olympian*, No. 35 (Autumn 1940), pp. 24-28.

Lovecraft was "the last of the great classical letter-writers . . . [and] was always, above all else, the perfect gentleman."

462. Mosig, Dirk W. "An Analytic Interpretation: The Outsider, Allegory of the Psyche." *Quarber Merkur*, 15, No. 1 (March 1977), 50-55 (as "Eine analytische Interpretation: 'Der aussenseiter,' eine Allegorie der Psyche"; tr. anon.; abridged).

463. Mosig, Dirk W. "The Four Faces of 'The Outsider.' " *Nyctalops*, 2, No. 2 (July 1974), 3-10. *Il Re in Giallo*, 1, No. 2 [1976], 29-47 (as "Le quattro facce dell'estraneo"; tr. Bruno Mikovilovich).

464. Mosig, Dirk W. "The Great American Throw-Away." *The Platte Valley Review*, 6, No. 1 (April 1978), 49-57.

465. Mosig, Dirk W. "Howard Phillips Lovecraft." *Evermist*, 2, No. 1 (Winter 1975), 7-12.

466. Mosig, Dirk W. "H. P. Lovecraft." In *Lovecraftian Characters and Other Things: An Illustrated Portfolio from the Works of H. P. Lovecraft*. Ed. Jim Pitts. [Burton-on-Trent, Eng.:] Spectre Press, [1976], pp. 2-3 of enclosed 4-page booklet.

467. Mosig, Dirk W. "H. P. Lovecraft: Myth-Maker."
Requiem, 2, No. 6 (October 1976), 18, 20-21 (as "H.
P. Lovecraft: Createur de mythes"; tr. Esther
Rochon). *Whispers*, 3, No. 1 (December 1976), 48-55
(as "Myth-Maker"). *Weird Fiction Times*, No. 48
(February 1977), pp. 35-44 (as "H. P. Lovecraft:
Schöpfer eines mythos"; tr. Heinz W. Kloos).

> Important article exploring Lovecraft's philosophy of
> horror and revealing the distorted image of the myth-cycle as
> expounded by August Derleth.

468. Mosig, Dirk W. "H. P. Lovecraft: Rabid Racist—or
Compassionate Gentleman?" *Xenophile*, 2, No. 6
(October 1975), 13-14. *Weird Fiction Times*, No. 48
(February 1977), pp. 45-48 (as "Lovecraft—Rassist
oder Gentleman"; tr. Winfried Eckert).

> Urges us to look at Lovecraft's racialist views in historical
> perspective.

469. Mosig, Dirk W. "Innsmouth and the Lovecraft
Oeuvre: A Holistic Approach." *Nyctalops*, 2, No. 7
(March 1978), 3, 5.

> Studies thematic unity in Lovecraft's fiction.

470. Mosig, Dirk W. Letters. *Fantasy Crossroads*, 1, Nos.
4/5 (August 1975), 9, 117; 1, No. 6 (November
1975), 20-22 (as "H. P. Lovecraft: Part 2: Mosig vs.
de Camp Debate"); 1, No. 7 (February 1976), 1.

> Comments on de Camp's biography (see III-C-5 and
> III-D-140).

471. Mosig, Dirk W. "Poet of the Unconscious." *The Platte
Valley Review*, 6, No. 1 (April 1978), 60-66. *Il Re in
Giallo*, No. 5 [1979], 50-54 (as "Lovecraft, poeta
dell'inconscio"; tr. anon.).

> Psychoanalytical interpretation of "The City."

472. Mosig, Dirk W. "The Prophet from Providence." *Whispers*, 1, No. 2 (December 1973), 28-30, 32.

> Shows how Lovecraft anticipated the concept of "future shock" in his tales.

473. Mosig, Dirk W. "Toward a Greater Appreciation of H. P. Lovecraft: The Analytical Approach." *Whispers*, 1, No. 1 (July 1973), 22-33. In *First World Fantasy Awards*. Ed. Gahan Wilson. Garden City, N.Y.: Doubleday & Co., 1977, pp. 290-301.

> Psychoanalytical interpretation (based on the theories of C. G. Jung) of many Lovecraft stories. Both appearances are abridged.

474. Mosig, Dirk W. "The White Ship: A Psychological Odyssey." *Whispers*, 2, No. 1 (November 1974), 35-37, 39-40 (as "The White Ship: A Psychic Odyssey").

475. Moskowitz, Sam. "H. P. Lovecraft: A Study in Horror." *Science Fantasy*, No. 44 (1960), pp. 96-108, 110-12. *Fantastic*, 9, No. 5 (May 1960), 35-50 (as "A Study in Horror: The Eerie Life of H. P. Lovecraft"). In Moskowitz, *Explorers of the Infinite: Shapers of Science Fiction* (as "The Lore of H. P. Lovecraft"). Cleveland: World Publishing Co., 1963; New York: Tower Books, 1964; New York: Meridian Books, 1967; Westport, Conn.: Hyperion, 1974, pp. 243-60.

> On the science-fictional element in Lovecraft.

476. Moskowitz, Sam. "H. P. Lovecraft and the Munsey Magazines." In *Under the Moons of Mars: A History and Anthology of "The Scientific Romance" in the Munsey Magazines, 1912-1920*. Ed. Sam Moskowitz. New

York: Holt, Rinehart and Winston, 1970, pp.
373-79.

Studies and quotes many of the letters and verses that
Lovecraft wrote to *The Argosy* and other pulp magazines in
1913-14 (see I-B-v-b).

477. Moskowitz, Sam. *The Immortal Storm: A History of
Science Fiction Fandom.* Atlanta: Atlanta Science Fiction
Organization Press, 1954; Westport, Conn.:
Hyperion, 1974, passim.

478. Moskowitz, Sam. "John Buchan: A Possible
Influence on Lovecraft." *Fantasy Commentator*, 2, No. 6
(Spring 1948), 187-90, 205.

479. Moskowitz, Sam, Fritz Leiber, Jr., Edward Wood,
John Brunner. "Some Notes on HPL." *Inside and
Science Fiction Advertiser*, Nos. 16/50 (September 1956),
pp. 32-35, 57.

480. Moss, Robert F. *Karloff and Company: The Horror Film:
A Pyramid Illustrated History of the Movies.* New York:
Pyramid Publications, 1973, pp. 130-32.

481. Moya, Antonio Prometeo. "Introducción" to
II-A-57.

482. Moya, Antonio Prometeo. "Introducción" to
II-A-58.

483. Munn, H. Warner. "HPL." *Whispers*, 3, No. 1
(December 1976), 24-28 (Part I only).

484. Murat, Napoléon. "Rêve et création chez
Lovecraft." *L'Herne*, No. 12 (1969), pp. 126-32.

485. Myers, Gary. "Introduction" to *The House and the
Worm.* Sauk City, Wis.: Arkham House, 1975, pp.
vii-ix.

Records Lovecraft's influence upon his own writing.

486. Myhre, Øyvind. "Etterord." In II-A-37.

487. Nakamura, Hidoyoshi. " 'Shiroi fune': Dai ni no kokai." *Crypt Horror Tales*, No. 8 (April 1976), pp. 26-28.

      On "The White Ship."

488. Nicoll, Gregory A. "The Life and Work of Howard Phillips Lovecraft." *Equinox*, No. 3 (May 1976), pp. 21-24.

489. Norton, Haywood P. "The Strange Case of Howard Phillips Lovecraft." *Castle of Frankenstein*, 5, No. 2 (1972), 8-13.

490. Onderdonk, Matthew H. "Apostle of the Outside: William Sloane and Howard Phillips Lovecraft: A Curious Affinity." *Fantasy Commentator*, 1, No. 7 (Summer 1945), 150-55.

491. Onderdonk, Matthew H. "Charon—in Reverse, or, H. P. Lovecraft Versus the 'Realists' of Fantasy." *Fantasy Commentator*, 2, No. 6 (Spring 1948), 193-97. *Fresco*, 8, No. 3 (Spring 1958), 45-51. *Fresco*, 10, No. 3 (Summer 1960), 14-21.

      Powerful article stating that the "ageless entities [of Lovecraft's myth-cycle] which rule the cosmos were, of course, not evil in the narrow human sense except as their manifestations interfered with the small purposes of man. . . . The activity of these forces is beyond good and evil, absolutely amoral."

492. Onderdonk, Matthew H. "The Lord of R'lyeh." *Fantasy Commentator*, 1, No. 6 (Spring 1945), 103-07, 109-11, 114.

      Strong article showing how Lovecraft reconciled the horror tale with modern science and with his own mechanist materialist philosophy. The entities in Lovecraft's myth-cycle are not supernatural but "supernormal"; i.e., it is scientifically possible that they exist, ruled by laws of nature which men have yet to discover.

493. O'Neail, N. J. Letter. *Weird Tales*, 30, No. 2 (August 1937), 250-52.

494. Onishi, Tadaaki. "Yakusha atogaki." In II-A-39.

495. Orton, Vrest. "A Weird Writer in Our Midst." *Brattleboro Daily Reformer*, 16 June 1928, p. 2.

   Brief biography of Lovecraft written on the occasion of Lovecraft's visit to Orton.

496. Ostrow, Alexander. Letter. *Weird Tales*, 22, No. 4 (October 1933), 517.

   Claims that Lovecraft wrote some essays on Shakespeare during his involvement in amateur journalism (see I-E-ii-3).

497. Otahi, Roger. "À propos de Lovecraft." *Horizons du Fantastique*, 9 (1969), 59.

498. Pagan, Fabio. "L'orrore fantastico di Lovecraft e dei suoi epigoni: 'I miti di Cthulhu.' " *Il Piccolo*, NS 9017 (15 May 1976), p. 3.

499. Page, Gerald W. "The Grimoire." *Witchcraft and Sorcery*, 1, No. 6 (May 1971), 46-48.

500. Paramio, Ludolfo. *Mito e ideología*. Madrid: Alberto Corazón Editor, 1971, pp. 64-72.

501. Parker, Robert Allerton. "Such Pulp as Dreams Are Made of: (H. P. Lovecraft and Clark Ashton Smith)." *VVV*, No. 2/3 (March 1943), pp. 62-66. *Radical America*, Special issue (January 1970), pp. 70-77.

502. Pauwels, Louis, and Jacques Bergier. *Le Matin des magiciens*. Paris: Editions Gallimard, 1960. London: Anthony Gibbs & Phillips, 1963; New York: Stein &

Day, 1964, pp. 104, 142. New York: Avon Books, 1968 (3rd printing 1972), pp. 160, 218.

The first English edition bore the title *The Dawn of Magic*; the last two *The Morning of the Magicians*. Translated by Rollo Myers.

503. Penzoldt, Peter. *The Supernatural in Fiction*. London: Peter Nevill, 1952; New York: Humanities Press, 1965, pp. 164-86, passim.

Important general survey, concentrating on the structure and style of Lovecraft's fiction, and on his use of adjectives. Much of Penzoldt's book is based on theories expressed in "Supernatural Horror in Literature."

504. Popkins, George. "He Wrote of the Supernatural." *The* [Providence] *Evening Bulletin*, 101, No. 275 (25 November 1963), 37.

On C. M. Eddy, Harry Houdini, and Lovecraft.

505. Potter, John Mason. "Fans of Fantastic Tales Catching Up on 'Whodunit' Devotees." *Boston Post Magazine*, No. 24 April 1949, p. 6.

506. Price, E. Hoffman [sic]. "Howard Phillips Lovecraft." *The Acolyte*, 2, No. 4 (Fall 1944), 17-19.

507. Price, E. Hoffmann. "H. P. Lovecraft the Man." *The Diversifier*, 2, No. 5 (May 1976), 7-9.

508. Price, E. Hoffmann. Letter. *The Acolyte*, 3, No. 4 (Fall 1945), 31-32, 26 (as "E. Hoffman [sic] Price Disagrees with a Too Enthusiastic Description").

509. Price, E. Hoffmann. Letter. *Nyctalops*, 2, No. 1 (April 1973), 55-57.

On the scientific accuracy of Lovecraft's tales.

510. Price, E. Hoffmann. "A Letter in Regards Lovecraft." *Nyctalops*, 2, Nos. 4/5 (April 1976), 9-12.

511. Price, E. Hoffmann. "Lovecraft and the Stars." *The Arkham Sampler*, 2, No. 2 (Spring 1949), 27-32.

Astrological predictions of Lovecraft's life.

512. Price, E. Hoffmann. "The Lovecraft Controversy— Why?" In *The Year's Best Horror Stories: Series IV*. Ed. Gerald W. Page. New York: DAW Books, 1976, pp. 202-08.

On the controversy raised by de Camp's biography (III-C-5).

513. Price, E. Hoffmann. "The Sage of College Street." *Amateur Correspondent*, 2, No. 1 (May-June 1937), 6-7. *Stellarite*, No. 3 (December 1946), pp. 13-14. In [Corwin F. Stickney, ed.] *Amateur Correspondent: May-June 1937*. [West Warwick, R. I.: Necronomicon Press,] 1977, pp. 6-7.

The last is a facsimile reprinting of the periodical.

514. Price, E. Hoffmann, Robert Bloch, and Basil Davenport. "The Cthulhu Mythos . . . Additions and Corrections." *The Acolyte*, 2, No. 2 (Spring 1944), 28-29.

Excerpts of letters commenting on III-D-352.

515. Prins, Aart C. "De droomwereld van H. P. Lovecraft." In II-A-30.

516. Pryor, Graham. "H. P. Lovecraft and the Science of Poe." *Nyctalops*, 2, No. 1 (April 1973), 16-17.

"It is from Poe that Lovecraft draws many of his scientific sources . . . particularly from 'Eureka.' " There is, however, no evidence that Lovecraft ever read *Eureka* or was influenced by it in any way.

517. Pullen, Charles. "Howard Phillips Lovecraft." *Douglas Library Notes*, 19, Nos. 1/2 (Autumn 1970), 2-3.

518. Rennenberg, Roger. "De wereld van de nacht bij Howard Phillips Lovecraft." *Diagonael*, Nos. 3/4 (1972), pp. 311-19.

519. [Renshaw, Anne Tillery.] "Our Friend, the Conservative." *Ole Miss*, No. 2 (December 1915), pp. 2-3.

520. Reston, Rodney. "The Author—Howard Phillips Lovecraft." *The Booklover's Answer*, No. 15 (September-October 1965), pp. 146, 153-54.

521. Richardson, Darrell G. "H. P. L. on Imaginative Fiction." *Fantasy Commentator*, 2, No. 6 (Spring 1948), 203, 216-18.

522. Riley, David A. "The Mythos—a Footnote." *Shadow*, No. 7 (September 1969), pp. 45-46, 48.
    On influences upon Lovecraft's myth-cycle.

523. Rivais, Yak. "The Bottom—at Last!" *L'Herne*, No. 12 (1969), pp. 163-76.

524. Rivière, Yves. "Lovecraft, un cauchemar américain." In II-A-46.

525. Rivière, Yves. "On disait . . ." *L'Herne*, No. 12 (1969), pp. 133-34.

526. Rochon, Esther. "On the Translation of Lovecraft into French." *Fantasy Specialist: Books, Magazines for Sale*, No. 5 (Summer 1975), pp. 19-21.

527. Rogers, Tom. "Those Lousy Lovecraft Films or Why Demons Leave Home." *The Monster Times*, 1, No. 43 (September 1975), 15.

528. Rogoz, Adrian. "La vest Arkham, o poartă a infernului." *Seculol 20*, No. 4 (1973), pp. 82-84.

529. Ronan, Margaret. "A Word to the Reader . . ." In I-A-58.

530. Rosemont, Franklin. "Notes on the Legacy of Cthulhu." *Arsenal*, No. 3 (Spring 1976), pp. 107-08.
A surrealist interpretation of Lovecraft.

531. Rothovius, Andrew E. "Lovecraft and the New England Megaliths." *L'Herne*, No. 12 (1969), pp. 334-45 (as "Lovecraft et les mégalithes de la Nouvelle-Angleterre"; tr. Jacques Parsons).

532. Rottensteiner, Franz. "Elder Gods and Eldritch Horror: H. P. Lovecraft." *The Science Fiction Book: An Illustrated History*. New York: The Seabury Press, 1975; New York & Scarborough, Ontario: New American Library, 1976, pp. 56-59.

533. Rottensteiner, Franz. *The Fantasy Book: An Illustrated History from Dracula to Tolkien*. New York: Collier Books, 1978, pp. 74-81, passim.

534. Rottensteiner, Franz. "H. P. Lovecrafts *The Shadow out of Time*." *Mutant*, No. 2 (1964), pp. 29-34 (as by "Johann Nepomuk").

535. Russell, Samuel D. "A Last-Minute Editorial." *The Acolyte*, 2, No. 3 (Summer 1944), 29-30.

536. Russell, Samuel D. "Open Season on Lovecraft." *Haunted*, 1, No. 1 (March 1963), 9-10, 17; 1, No. 2 (December 1964), 38-42.

537. Sadoul, Jacques. *Histoire de la science-fiction moderne (1911-1971)*. Paris: Albin Michel, 1973, passim.

538. Sadoul, Jacques. *La Passion selon Satan*. Paris: Editions de Scorpion, 1960, pp. 153-59. *L'Herne*, No. 12 (1969), pp. 117-20.

539. St. Armand, Barton L. "Facts in the Case of H. P. Lovecraft." *Rhode Island History*, 31, No. 1 (February 1972), 3-19.

    Extensive study of *The Case of Charles Dexter Ward* and Rhode Island history. "It is my contention that Lovecraft would never have been Lovecraft without Providence—its history, its atmosphere, its legends, its peculiar and individual character."

540. St. Armand, Barton L. "H. P. Lovecraft: New England Decadent." *Caliban*, No. 12 (1975), pp. 127-55.

    Profound article emphasizing the unique way in which Lovecraft's work and thought combined elements from Puritanism and from the French Decadents. "The Horror at Red Hook" and "Pickman's Model" are extensively studied.

541. St. Armand, Barton L. "The Source for Lovecraft's Knowledge of Borellus in *The Case of Charles Dexter Ward*." *Nyctalops*, 2, No. 6 (May 1977), 16-17.

542. St. Armand, Barton L., and John H. Stanley. "H. P. Lovecraft's *Waste Paper*: A Facsimile and Transcript of the Original Draft." *Books at Brown*, 26 (1978), 31-47.

    Penetrating analysis of the literary and historical significance of the poem. The facsimile of the A.Ms. appears between pp. 34-35.

543. Scher, Ken. "You Can't Tell the Players without a Program." *Nyctalops*, 1, No. 4 (June 1971), 8-10, 40.

    Superficial description of the entities in Lovecraft's myth-cycle.

544. Scholes, Robert E., and Eric S. Rabkin. *Science Fiction: History, Science, Vision*. New York: Oxford Univ. Press, 1977, pp. 36-37, 65, 167, 169.

545. Schoonmaker, Warren K. "On Supernatural Horror

in Literature." *The Dark Brotherhood Journal*, 1, No. 2
(n.d.), 71-73.

Bibliographic data on the two Ben Abramson editions of the
book (I-A-21).

546. Schweitzer, Darrell. "Character Gullibility in Weird
Fiction: or Isn't Yuggoth Somewhere in Upstate
New York?" *Nyctalops*, 2, No. 3 (January-February
1975), 19-20.

547. Schweitzer, Darrell. " 'Hastur Is a *Place*'!!" *Nyctalops*,
2, No. 1 (April 1973), 22-23.

548. Schweitzer, Darrell. "Filming 'The Outsider.' "
Etchings and Odysseys, No. 1 (1973), pp. 65-72.

Included in his book (III-C-22).

549. Schweitzer, Darrell. "An Interview with Frank
Belknap Long." *Nyctalops*, 2, Nos. 4/5 (April 1976), 5-
8. In *SF Voices*. [Baltimore:] T-K Graphics, 1976, pp.
95-103.

550. Schweitzer, Darrell. "Lovecraft on Television."
Nyctalops, 1, No. 6 (February 1972), 12-14. *Il Re in
Giallo*, 1, No. 2 [1976], 74-78 (as "Lovecraft alla TV";
tr. Francesco Faccanoni and Giuseppe Lippi).

Included in his book (III-C-22).

551. Scott, Winfield Townley. "Bookman's Gallery." *The
Providence Sunday Journal*, 60, No. 1 (2 July 1944), Sec.
VI, p. 6 (column then titled "Bookends and Odds");
60, No. 17 (22 October 1944), Sec. VI, p. 6; 60, No.
44 (29 April 1945), Sec. VI, p. 6; 61, 17 (21 October
1945), Sec. VI, p. 6; 61, 20 (11 November 1945), Sec.
VI, p. 8; 61, 23 (2 December 1945), Sec. VI, p. 6;
61, 44 (28 April 1946), Sec. VI, p. 8; 62, 17 (20
October 1946), Sec. VI, p. 8; 63, 39 (28 March

1948), Sec. VI, p. 8; 63, 43 (25 April 1948), Sec. VI,
p. 8; 64, 11 (12 September 1948), Sec. VI, p. 6; 64,
12 (19 September 1948), Sec. VI, p. 6; 64, 14 (3
October 1948), Sec. VI, p. 8; 64, 18 (31 October
1948), Sec. VI, p. 8; 64, 43 (24 April 1949), Sec. VI,
p. 10.

Covers a wide range of topics, from biographical to critical to
bibliographical notes on Lovecraft.

552. Scott, Winfield Townley. "The Case of Howard
Phillips Lovecraft of Providence, R. I." *The Providence
Sunday Journal*, 59, No. 26 (26 December 1943), Sec.
III, p. 6.

553. Scott, Winfield Townley. *Exiles and Fabrications*.
Garden City, N.Y.: Doubleday & Co., 1961.

Contains: "His Own Most Fantastic Creation: Howard
Phillips Lovecraft," pp. 50-72; "A Parenthesis on Lovecraft as
Poet" (i.e., "Lovecraft as a Poet"; revised), pp. 73-77.

554. Scott, Winfield Townley. "Foreword" to Sonia H.
Davis. "Howard Phillips Lovecraft as His Wife
Remembers Him." *Books at Brown*, 11, Nos. 1/2
(February 1949), 1-2.

555. Scott, Winfield Townley. "The Haunter of the
Dark: Some Notes on Howard Phillips Lovecraft."
Books at Brown, 6, No. 3 (March 1944), 1-4.

"Lovecraft was an escapist to an extraordinary degree . . .
he wanted to return to . . . the 18th century or, at any rate,
his conception of the 18th century."

556. Scott, Winfield Townley. Letter. *The Acolyte*, 2, No. 4
(Fall 1944), 27.

557. Seesslen, Georg, and Bert Kling. *Romantik und
Gewalt: Ein Lexikon der Unterhaltungsindustrie*. Vol. I.
Munich: Monz Verlag, 1973, pp. 221-23.

558. Servadio, Emilio. "I mostri del cosmo." *Il Tempo*, 32, No. 351 (27 December 1975), 11.

559. Shaver, Richard S. "Lovecraft and the Deros." *Vampire*, No. 6 (June 1946), pp. 14-15.

560. Shaw, Lee. Letter. *Brown Alumni Monthly*, 72, No. 7 (April 1972), 3 (as "The Day He Met Lovecraft").

> Tells of a story by Lovecraft lost in the mails and never recovered (see I-E-ii-11).

561. Shea, J. Vernon. "The Circle Manqué." *Nyctalops*, 2, Nos. 4/5 (April 1976), 14-15.

562. Shea, J. Vernon. "H. P. Lovecraft: The House and the Shadows." *The Magazine of Fantasy and Science Fiction*, 30, No. 5 (May 1966), 82-99. *L'Herne*, No. 12 (1969), pp. 289-99. *Fiction*, No. 183 (March 1969), pp. 134-46.

> In the first appearance there is an introduction by Avram Davidson on p. 81; in the second are additional remarks by Shea and Francois Truchaud. In the last two as "À la récherche d'H. P. Lovecraft"; tr. Jacques Parsons.

563. Shea, J. Vernon. "An Introduction to the Cthulhu Mythos." *Fandom Unlimited*, No. 2 (Spring 1977), pp. 18-19.

564. Shea, J. Vernon. "The Necessity for Objectivity." *Midnight Fantasies*, No. 3 (May 1976), p. 8.

565. Shenandoah, Daniel K. "What Scared Professor Peaslee?" *Nyctalops*, 1, No. 5 (October 1971), 20-21.

> On "The Shadow out of Time."

566. Shreffler, Philip A. "H. P. Lovecraft: The Dweller upon the Saga." In *The Noble Bachelor's Red-Covered Volume*. Ed. Philip A. Shreffler. St. Louis: Birchmoor Press, 1974, pp. 17-19.

567. Silvia, Steven C. Letter. *The* [Providence] *Evening Bulletin*, 104, No. 266 (15 November 1966), 26 (as "Likes the Poe of Providence").

568. Simister, Florence Parker. "Howard P. Lovecraft." *The Streets of the City*, 1 (June 2, 1952-May 29, 1953), Script No. 58, pp. 116-17.
     Transcript of a broadcast on Station WEAN, Providence.

569. Simister, Florence Parker. "H. P. L. and 66 College St." *Streets of the City*, 8 (1959-1960), 95-96.
     Transcript of a broadcast on Station WEAN, Providence.

570. Slater, Kenneth. "Too Much Lovecraftiana?" *Fantasy Review*, 2, No. 11 (October-November 1948), 4-5.

571. Slonim, Marc. "European Notebook." *New York Times Book Review*, 17 May 1970, p. 14.
     Notes Lovecraft's increasing foreign acclaim.

572. Smith, Clark Ashton. "In Memoriam: H. P. Lovecraft." *Tesseract*, 2, No. 4 (April 1937), 5.

573. Smith, Clark Ashton. Letter. *Weird Tales*, 30, No. 1 (July 1937), 122-23. *Golden Atom*, No. 9 (December 1940), p. 15.

574. Smith, Reginald. *Weird Tales in the Thirties*. [Santa Ana, Ca.: Privately printed, June 1966], pp. 4-7, 33-34.
     On the magazine *Weird Tales*, where Lovecraft's work often appeared.

575. Solon, Ben. "Lovecraft on the Doorstep." *Haunted*, 1, No. 3 (June 1968), 87-88.

576. Souto, Marcial. "Las traducciones al castellano." *La Opinión*, No. 681 (5 August 1973), Cultural Supplement, p. 12.

577. Spina, Giorgio. "Il superuomo e la speculazione sul
l'occulto sul novecento inglese e americano." *Il
Superuomo*, No. 3 (1973), pp. 229-55.

578. Squires, Roy A. "The Mystery of The Shunned
House." *Catalog 6: Modern Literature*, (n.d.), pp. 11-13.
Bibliographical notes on *The Shunned House* (1928).

579. Starrett, Vincent. "Books Alive." *Chicago Sunday
Tribune*, 103, No. 1 (2 January 1944), Sec. 6, p. 12;
118, No. 51 (18 December 1949), Sec. 6, p. 2; 119,
No. 2 (10 January 1960), Sec. 6, p. 5.
Some of these are compiled in III-D-580.

580. Starrett, Vincent. *Books and Bipeds.* New York: Argus
Books, 1947, pp. 119-22, 203-04.

581. Sterling, Kenneth. "Caverns Measureless to Man."
Science-Fantasy Correspondent, No. 1 (1975), pp. 36-43.
Strong memoir which deeply discusses Lovecraft's scientific
studies and blasts many of the myths that have arisen about his
character. "I think it would be most fitting if H. P. Lovecraft
were remembered as a scholar and thinker as well as an
author."

582. Sterling, Kenneth. Letter. *Weird Tales*, 30, No. 1
(July 1937), 122.

583. Sterling, Kenneth. [Rebuttal to David H. Keller's
"Shadows over Lovecraft."] *Fantasy Commentator*, 3,
No. 5 (Winter 1951-52), 153-54. *Fresco*, 8, No. 3
(Spring 1958), 27-29.
See III-D-322.

584. Stewart, Randall. "Rhode Island Literature." *Rhode
Island History*, 13, No. 1 (January 1954), 1-10 (esp. 4).

585. Stokes, Bram. "H. P. Lovecraft." *Gothique*, No. 4
(May 1966).

586. [Stone, Leon.] "Lovecraftiana." *Koolinda*, No. 5 (April 1948), pp. 11-13; No. 6 (December 1949), pp. 14-15; Nos. 7/8 (1950-51), pp. 15-16; No. 9 (December 1952), pp. 11-14.

   Random biographical and bibliographical notes about Lovecraft's amateur periodical publications; from an Australian amateur press periodical.

587. Strick, Philip. *Science Fiction Movies*. London: Octopus Books, Ltd., 1976, pp. 19-21.

588. Sully, Helen. "Memories of Lovecraft: II." *The Arkham Collector*, No. 4 (Winter 1969), pp. 117-19.

   Lovecraft showed Miss Sully some New England sites in 1933. "He was a fascinating companion, teacher, and guide."

589. Svehla, Gary J. "H. P. Lovecraft: The Aesthetics of Horror." *Gore Creatures*, No. 16 (September 1969), pp. 3-13.

590. Swanson, Martin J. "Sherlock Holmes and H. P. Lovecraft." *Now* (Farleigh Dickinson Univ.), 4, No. 1 (Winter 1963), 35-37. *Baker Street Journal*, 14, No. 3 (September 1964), 162-65.

591. Szczsponik, Charlene. "H. P. Lovecraft: The Man Who Could Not Die." *Rhode Island Yearbook*, 10 (1973), 45-48.

592. Talman, Wilfred B. "Lovecraft Revisited." *Fresco*, 10, No. 2 (Winter-Spring 1960), 48-51.

   Talman records the results of word-association tests taken by Lovecraft, Frank Belknap Long, and Talman in the middle or late 1920s.

593. Talman, Wilfred B. "The Normal Lovecraft." *Dunedain*, No. 3 (1975), pp. 37-54 (as "Lovecraft— sono kyozo to jitsuzo"; tr. Tetsuya Imamura).

594. Tanzi, Roberto. "Lovecraft: Una freccia verso l'infinito." *Oltre*, 1978, pp. 9-11.

595. Taylor, John. "Poe, Lovecraft, and the Monologie." *Topic*, No. 31 (Fall 1977), pp. 52-62.
    Superficial study of Lovecraft's narrative technique.

596. Taylor, John. "A Twentieth-Century Poe." *The Washington and Jefferson Literary Journal*, 1, No. 2 (1967), 23-26 (as by "Charles Dexter Ward").

597. Thomas, Dave. "Lovecraft Revisited." *Altair*, 1, No. 1 (February 1950), 7-10.

598. Thomas, James Warren. "H. P. Lovecraft: A Portrait in Words." *Fresco*, 9, No. 1 (Fall 1958), 33-40 (with subtitle: "The Providence Years"); 9, No. 2 (Winter 1958), 33-40 (with subtitle: "New York Exile"); 9, No. 3 (Spring 1959), 35-44 (with subtitle: "Exile's End"); 9, No. 4 (Summer 1959), 34-42 (with subtitle: "Paradise Regained").
    Abridgement of his master's thesis (III-E-i-15).

599. Tierney, Richard L. "Cthulhu in Southeast Alaska." *Apollo*, No. 7 (1976), pp. 78-79.

600. Tierney, Richard L. Letter. *Nyctalops*, 1, No. 5 (October 1971), 51-52.
    Original of his essay, "The Derleth Mythos" (III-C-12).

601. Tierney, Richard L. "Lovecraft and the Cosmic Quality in Fiction." *The Diversifier*, 2, No. 5 (May 1976), 16-18, 39.
    Explores Lovecraft's views on cosmicism in literature.

602. Tierney, Richard L. "Tierney on Cosmic Wonder." *The HPL Supplement*, No. 2 (July 1973), pp. 46-48.
    Original of the III-D-601.

603. Todorov, Tzvetan. *Introduction à la littérature fantastique.* Paris: Editions du Seuil, 1970, pp. 39-40, 171. Buenos Aires: Editorial Tiempo Contemporáneo, 1972, 1974, pp. 46-47, 193. Cleveland & London: The Press of Case Western Reserve University, 1973; Ithaca, N.Y.: Cornell Univ. Press, 1975, pp. 34-35, 163.

> Both English versions are titled *The Fantastic: A Structural Approach to a Literary Genre* (tr. Richard Howard). The Spanish version is titled *Introducción a la literature fantástica* (tr. Silvia Delpy).

604. Track, William T. "H. P. Lovecraft: An Appraisal." *Spearhead*, 1, No. 2 (July 1948), [3-5].

605. Truchaud, Francois. "The Dream-Quest of Howard Phillips Lovecraft." *L'Herne*, No. 12 (1969), pp. 15-25. *Secolul 20*, No. 4 (1973), pp. 73-74 (tr. Tea Preda; abridged).

606. Truchaud, Francois. "H. P. Lovecraft et la création fantastique." In II-A-21.

607. Truchaud, Francois. "H. P. Lovecraft ou: dire l'invincible." In II-A-22.

608. Turner, James. "Preface" to I-A-68.

609. Turner, James. "Preface" to I-A-69.

610. Uno, Toshiyatsu. "Yakusha atogaki." In II-A-54.

611. Van Herp, Jacques. "Le Cinéma et Lovecraft: En forme de filmographie commentée." *L'Herne*, No. 12 (1969), pp. 185-90.

612. Van Herp, Jacques. "Fantastique et mythologies modernes." *Ides . . . et Autres*, Special issue (15 April 1978), pp. 1-64 passim.

613. Van Herp, Jacques. "Lovecraft, Jean Ray, Hodgson." *L'Herne*, No. 12 (1969), pp. 157-62.

614. Van Herp, Jacques. "Une Source de Lovecraft: Le Diable au XIXe siècle." *L'Herne*, No. 12 (1969), pp. 141-46.

615. Van Herp, Jacques. "L'Univers de H. P. Lovecraft." *L'Herne*, No. 12 (1969), pp. 147-56. *La Opinión*, No. 681 (5 August 1973), Cultural Supplement, pp. 8-11 (as "A imagen y semejanza del Bosco"; tr. anon.; abridged).

616. van Maanen, Ruud. "H. P. Lovecraft, een Man en zijn Mythe." *Drab*, 1, No. 2 (n.d.), [28-29].

617. Vax, Louis. *L'Art et la littérature fantastiques*. Paris: Presses Universitaires de France, 1974, pp. 101-03. Buenos Aires: EUDEBA, 1965 (3rd printing 1973), pp. 100-02 (as *Arte y literatura fantásticas*; tr. Juan Merino).

618. Versins, Pierre. "Les Débuts de Lovecraft dans 'Weird Tales.' " *L'Herne*, No. 12 (1969), pp. 26-27.
    Quotes the entire text of a letter by Lovecraft to Edwin Baird, published in *Weird Tales*, Sept. 1923.

619. Versins, Pierre, ed. "Lovecraft et l'indicible." *L'Herne*, No. 12 (1969), pp. 39-46.
    Collection of passages from Lovecraft's tales showing his views on science, hyperspace, machines, the monsters in his tales, and future history.

620. Versins, Pierre. "Une Surhumaine Tragédie: Ou le roman d'amour manqué de Lovecraft." *L'Herne*, No. 12 (1969), pp. 28-38.

621. Vetter, John E. "Lovecraft's Illustrators." *L'Herne*,

No. 12 (1969), pp. 312-33 (as "Les Illustrateurs de Lovecraft"; tr. Jacques Parsons).

622. Vignati, A. *El triangulo mortal de las Bermudas*. Barcelona: A. T. E., 1975.

623. Vilella, Antonio. "H. P. Lovecraft y los mitos de Cthulhu." *Terror Fantastic*, No. 5 (February 1972), pp. 56-57.

624. Wade, James. Letter. *Weird Tales*, 44, No. 7 (November 1952), 8.

625. Wade, James. "Some Parallels Between Arthur Machen and H. P. Lovecraft." *The Arthur Machen Society Occasional*, No. 4 (n.d.), pp. 3-9. *Shadow*, No. 14 (September 1971), pp. 6-11.

626. Walter, Dorothy C. "Lovecraft and Benefit Street." *The Ghost*, No. 1 (Spring 1943), pp. 27-29. *Xenon*, No. 2 (July 1944), pp. 8-11.

627. Wandrei, Donald. "The Derleth Posthumous Collaborations with Lovecraft." *The British Fantasy Society Bulletin*, 3, No. 1 (March-April 1975), 9-10.

628. Warner, Harry, Jr. *All Our Yesterdays: An Informal History of Science Fiction Fandom in the Forties*. Chicago: Advent Publishers, Inc., 1969, pp. 9-14, passim.

629. Warner, Harry, Jr. "On Speed and Lovecrafty Racism." *Amra*, 2, No. 58 (January 1973), 17.

630. Weigand, J. E. "Howard Phillips Lovecraft—Meister des Unheimlichen und des Horror." *Luther's Grusel-Magazin*, No. 9 [1974], pp. 67-72.

631. Weigand, Jörg. "Konkurrenz für Poe." *Die Welt*, No. 2 (April 1977).

632. Weinberg, Robert. "H. P. Lovecraft and Pseudo-mathematics." *Nyctalops*, 1, No. 4 (October 1971), 3-4, 48.

> Tries to argue that Lovecraft's "pseudomathematics" and "pseudogeometry," in such tales as "The Dreams in the Witch House," make no scientific sense whatever.

633. Weinberg, Robert. "Lovecraft in Astounding Stories." *Nyctalops*, 2, No. 3 (January-February 1975), 3-5, 43.

> Summary of readers' reactions to *At the Mountains of Madness* and "The Shadow out of Time" as appearing in *Astounding Stories*.

634. Weinberg, Robert. "Robert E. Howard and the Cthulhu Mythos." *Nyctalops*, 1, No. 2 (October 1970), 6.

635. Weinberg, Robert. *The Weird Tales Story*. West Linn, Oregon: FAX Collector's Editions, 1977, passim.

> On the pulp magazine, *Weird Tales*.

636. [Weinberg, Robert, ed.] *WT50: A Tribute to Weird Tales*. [Oak Lawn, Ill.: Robert Weinberg, 1974.]

> Contains: Reginald Smith, "Weird Tales in the Thirties" (abridged), pp. 12-14; Frank Belknap Long, "The Long View," pp. 33-34, 134; H. Warner Munn, "Writing for Weird Tales," pp. 36-40.

637. Weiss, Henry George. Letter. *Weird Tales*, 30, No. 3 (September 1937), 378 (as by "Francis Flagg").

638. Wesson, Helen V. "The Phenomenon of HPL." *The Fossil*, No. 154 (July 1957), pp. 1, 9-17.

> Extensive though error-riddled article emphasizing Lovecraft's work in amateur journalism.

639. Wetzel, George T. "The Dream-Gate and Other Matters." *Fantasias*, No. 4 (July 1952), pp. [8-11]. *Nyctalops*, 2, Nos. 4/5 (April 1976), 15-16.

640. Wetzel, George T. "An Early Portrait of Lovecraft." *Renaissance*, 2, No. 2 (March 1953), 3-5.

641. Wetzel, George T. "Edmund Wilson—a Critic?" *Renaissance*, 1, No. 6 (n.d.), 3-5, 12.

   Rebuttal to III-D-664.

642. Wetzel, George T. "Genesis of the Cthulhu Mythos." *Fantastic Story Mag*, No. 4 (March 1954), pp. 24-32. *Kaymar Trader*, No. 91 (January 1955). *Nyctalops*, 2, No. 3 (January-February 1975), 21-25.

643. Wetzel, George T. "The Ghoul-Changeling." *Fantasy Commentator*, 3, No. 5 (Winter 1951-52), 131-32.

644. Wetzel, George T. "Introduction" to I-A-31. In Mike Garcia. *Lovecraft: Five Art Studies*. North Hollywood, Ca.: Shroud, Publishers, 1974, pp. 3-4.

645. Wetzel, George T. "A Lovecraft Profile." *Nyctalops*, 2, No. 1 (April 1973), 18-20.

   Covers aspects of Lovecraft's amateur press work and early astronomical writing.

646. Wetzel, George T. "A Lovecraft Randomonium." *Destiny*, 1, No. 6 (Winter 1951-Spring 1952), 11-13, 29.

647. Wetzel, George T. "Lovecraft's Literary Executor." *Fantasy Commentator*, 4, No. 1 (Winter 1978-79), 34-43.

   On the legal aspects of R. H. Barlow's executorship of Lovecraft's literary estate and his dealings with August Derleth.

648. Wetzel, George T. "The Mechanistic-Supernatural of Lovecraft." *Fresco*, 8, No. 3 (Spring 1958), 54-60.

   Studies Charles Fort's influence upon Lovecraft and his use of folklore in his tales.

649. Wetzel, George T. "A Memoir of Jack Grill."
     Huitloxopetl, No. 8 (1972), pp. 27-36. *The* HPL
     Supplement, No. 3 (March 1975), pp. 46-54.

650. Wetzel, George T. "The Pseudonymous Lovecraft."
     Xenophile, 3, No. 4 (November 1976), 3-5, 73.

651. Wetzel, George T. "Random Notes: On the
     Cthulhu Mythos." *The Arkham Sampler*, 1, No. 2
     (Spring 1948), 48-49.

652. Wetzel, George T. "Some Derivations of the
     Cthulhu Mythos." *Atres Artes*, No. 3 (1940s?).

653. Wetzel, George T. "Some Thoughts on the
     Lovecraft Pattern." *Fantasy Commentator*, 1, No. 12
     (Fall 1946), 316-17, 322.

   Studies Lovecraft as a regional writer, touching upon
   Hawthorne's influence upon his work.

654. Wetzel, George T. "A Watcher of Stars." *Andromeda*,
     No. 12 (July 1955), pp. 12-14.

655. Wheelock, Alan S. "Dark Mountain: H. P. Lovecraft
     and the 'Vermont Horror.' " *Vermont History*, 155,
     No. 4 (Fall 1977), 221-28.

   Superficial analysis of "The Whisperer in Darkness."

656. Wilcox, Joseph V. Letters. *Weird Tales*, 44, No. 6
     (September 1952), 6; 44, No. 8 (January 1953), 8.

657. Willis, Paul J. "H. P. Lovecraft and the Voynich
     Manuscript." *Anubis*, 1, No. 1 (Autumn 1966), 7-11.

658. Willis, Paul J. "Possible Sources for Lovecraftian
     Themes." *Anubis*, 1, No. 4 (Autumn 1968), 34-35.

   Prints two quotations from Skinner's *Myths and Legends of Our
   Own Land* (1896), which may have inspired some of Lovecraft's
   tales.

659. Wilson, Colin. *Order of Assassins*. London: Rupert Hart-Davis, 1972, pp. 113-19.

Discussion of "The Loved Dead" and its sociological significance in the contemporary world.

660. Wilson, Colin. "Preface" to *The Mind Parasites*. Sauk City, Wis.: Arkham House, July 1967, pp. vii-xxi. New York: Bantam Books, Dec. 1968, pp. 1-13. Rome: Fanucci Editore, 1977, pp. 19-31 (as *I Parassiti della mente*; tr. A. Pollini).

661. Wilson, Colin. "Prefatory Note" to *The Philosopher's Stone*. London: Arthur Barker, 1969. New York: Crown Publishers, 1971, pp. [5-7]. New York: Warner Books, March 1974, June 1977, pp. 17-20.

662. Wilson, Colin. *The Strength to Dream: Literature and the Imagination*. London: Victor Gollancz, 1961. Boston: Houghton Mifflin Co., 1962, pp. 1-10, 111-15. Barcelona: Luis de Caralt Editor, 1965 (as *El podem de soñar*).

Violent attack on Lovecraft as one who is "sick," who has "rejected 'reality,' " and who is a "bad writer." Nevertheless, Wilson finds grudging praise for "The Shadow out of Time" as a capable attempt at science fiction.

663. Wilson, Don. "H. P. Lovecraft." *Fafrd* (August 1955). *Canadian Fandom* (June 1956).

664. Wilson, Edmund. "Tales of the Marvellous and the Ridiculous." *The New Yorker*, 21, No. 41 (24 November 1945), 100, 103-04, 106. In *Classics and Commercials: A Literary Chronicle of the Forties*. New York: Farrar, Straus & Co., Nov. 1950, Feb. 1951, Mar. 1955, Apr. 1958; Toronto: Clarke, Irwin & Co., 1950, 1951; London: W. H. Allen, 1951, 1966; New York: Random House (Vintage Books), 1962; New York: [Book-of-the-Month Club, 1966]; New

York: Noonday Press, 1967; Toronto: Ambassador Books, 1967, pp. 286-90.

Celebrated though error-riddled article condemning Lovecraft's tales as "hackwork." Wilson ultimately finds some kind words for Lovecraft's letters, for "Supernatural Horror in Literature," and for "The Colour out of Space" and "The Shadow out of Time."

665. Wolfe, Charles K., ed. *Planets and Dimensions: Collected Essays of Clark Ashton Smith.* Baltimore: The Mirage Press, 1973.

Contains: Clark Ashton Smith, "In Memoriam: H. P. Lovecraft," p. 48; Clark Ashton Smith, Letter to the Editor of *Weird Tales*, p. 49 (as "On H. P. Lovecraft—I"); Clark Ashton Smith, Letter, p. 50 (as "On H. P. Lovecraft—II"); Clark Ashton Smith, Letter, p. 75 [as "(On Tales About the Cthulhu Mythos)"].

The penultimate letter is also in III-D-26, while the last, concerning Smith's contributions to Lovecraft's myth-cycle, first appeared (as a quotation) in III-B-35, pp. 36-37 and in III-C-26, pp. 77-78.

666. Wydmuch, Marek. "Amerykánskie strachy." *Literatura,* 1972, p. 9.

667. Wydmuch, Marek. "Der erschrockene Erzähler." *Quarber Merkur,* 12, No. 1 (May 1974), 28-42.

668. Wydmuch, Marek. *Gra ze strachem: Fantastyka grozy.* Warsaw: Czytelnik, 1975, pp. 123-48, 184-85.

669. Wydmuch, Marek. "Lovecraft—oder sich treiben lassen." In II-A-24.

670. Wydmuch, Marek. " 'Wielki Cthulhu' i inni." *Nadorze,* 18, Nos. 25/26 (15 December 1974-11 January 1975), 19.

671. Wydmuch, Marek. "Wspomniena o fantastyce: czyli Erich von Däniken." *Literatura,* 22 March 1973, p. 7.

672. Zorn, Ray H. "About the Collecting of Lovecraft." *The Lovecraft Collector*, No. [1] (January 1949), pp. 1, 3-4.

673. [Zorn, Ray H.] "The Asheville Series." *The Lovecraft Collector*, No. 2 (May 1949), p. 4.

> Discovery of the astronomical articles written by Lovecraft for *The Asheville Gazette-News*.

674. [Zorn, Ray H.] "Intentions . . . Honourable." *The Lovecraft Collector*, No. 2 (May 1949), p. 2.

675. Zorn, Ray H. "Lovecraftiana Market Averages." *The Lovecraft Collector*, No. 2 (May 1949), pp. 2-3.

676. Zorn, Ray H. "Market Trends in Lovecraftiana." *The Lovecraft Collector*, No. [1] (January 1949), pp. 2, 4.

677. [Zorn, Ray H.] "Pseudonyms of HPL." *The Lovecraft Collector*, No. [1] (January 1949), p. 4.

678. [Zorn, Ray H.] "Seed." *The Lovecraft Collector*, No. 3 (October 1949), p. 4.

679. [Zorn, Ray H.] "Warke Beginneth." *The Lovecraft Collector*, No. [1] (January 1949), p. 2.

680. [Zorn, Ray H.] [Untitled.] *The Lovecraft Collector*, No. 3 (October 1949), p. 4.

> Discussion of I-A-20.

681. [Unsigned.] "And from the Hills." *The O-Wash-Ta-Nong*, [2, No. 2] [1937], [5].

682. [Unsigned.] "Arthur Machen, Master of Weird Fantasy, Inspired Lovecraft." *Fantasy Review*, 2, No. 7 (February-March 1948), 16-17.

> More about Machen than about Lovecraft.

683. [Unsigned.] "Congratulations." *The Brooklynite*, 14, No. 2 (April 1924), 1-2.

On Lovecraft's marriage.

684. [Unsigned.] "It's Cold Outside." *The Month at Goodspeed's*, 21, No. 1 (October 1949), 22.

Note about *The Outsider and Others* (I-A-15).

685. [Unsigned.] "The Kleicomolo." *The United Amateur*, 18, No. 4 (March 1919), 74-76.

On the correspondence circle of which Lovecraft was a member.

686. [Unsigned.] Letter. *The Argosy*, 74, No. 4 (March 1914), 955 (as "Georgia Girl Replies").

Rebuttal to Lovecraft's comments (I-B-v-b).

687. [Unsigned.] "News Notes." *The United Amateur*, 17, No. 4 (March 1918), 73.

A "biography" of "Lewis Theobald, Jun.," one of Lovecraft's pseudonyms. It is not by Lovecraft, as some have believed.

688. [Unsigned.] "Reprints, New Editions." *The New York Herald Tribune Weekly Book Review*, 21, No. 5 (24 September 1944), 23.

Part of this article deals with "The Lovecraft Legend."

689. [Unsigned.] "Return to R'lyeh." *The Cloven Hoof*, 5, No. 4 (July-August 1973), 12-15.

690. [Unsigned.] "Some Notes on Lovecraft." *The Science Fiction Critic*, 1, No. 10 (July 1932), 2.

691. [Unsigned.] "A Walk in the Field." *The O-Wash-Ta-Nong*, [2, No. 2] [1937], [5].

692. [Unsigned.] [Untitled.] *The National Amateur*, 72, No. 2 (December 1949), 1-2.

E. Academic Theses and Unpublished Papers

i. Academic Theses

1. Cannon, Peter. "A Case for Howard Phillips Lovecraft." Honors thesis: Stanford, 1973. vi, 58 pp.

2. Cannon, Peter. "Lovecraft's New England." M.A. thesis: Brown, June 1974. vi, 42 pp.

   Cannon studies Lovecraft's use of actual New England sites, customs, and history to achieve greater realism in his fiction. Remarking on the "significant thematic ambiguity" that "his beloved New England is the site of both beauty and horror," Cannon examines many of Lovecraft's tales, calling *The Case of Charles Dexter Ward* a "masterpiece of the supernatural historical romance."

3. Eitel, Elaine Gillum. "The Sense of Place in H. P. Lovecraft." M.A. thesis: Lamar State College of Technology (Beaumont, Texas), May 1970. [v], 12[8] pp.

4. Fish, Robert Stevens. "The Oral Interpretation of the Horror Stories of H. P. Lovecraft." M.A. thesis: Oklahoma, 1965. v, 157 pp.

5. Klein, T. E. D. "Some Notes on the Fantasy Tales of H. P. Lovecraft and Lord Dunsany." Honors thesis: Brown, May 1969. ii, 189 [i.e., 179] pp.

   Extensive if rather discursive study of Dunsany's influence upon Lovecraft. Still the most comprehensive work on the subject.

6. Koki, Arthur S. "H. P. Lovecraft: An Introduction to His Life and Writings." M.A. thesis: Columbia, 1962. vi, 350 pp.

   Koki has done sound work on Lovecraft's life, especially his early years (1890-1914), having consulted "primary source

materials: letters, birth and death certificates, wills," etc. His
coverage of Lovecraft's later life is sketchy and unsatisfying,
while what literary criticism he offers is uncoordinated and
superficial. Koki dismisses Lovecraft's "racism" as
"characteristic of his social class."

7. Lévy, Maurice. "L'univers fantastique de H. P.
   Lovecraft." Diss. University of Paris (Sorbonne),
   [1969]. ca. 200 pp.

   See III-C-17.

8. Long, Jeffrey Errold. "Unities of Opposites in H. P.
   Lovecraft's Fiction." Independent studies paper:
   Brown, 12 June 1977. iv, 58 pp.

9. Lynn, Lawrence R. "The Cthulhu Mythos in the
   Writings of H. P. Lovecraft." M.A. thesis: Univ.
   of Rhode Island, 1971. [iv], 83 pp.

   Good thesis which, although imposing a somewhat invalid
   division of Lovecraft's tales into mutually exclusive categories,
   sees Lovecraft's cosmic quality and mechanistic outlook. It
   contains fine discussions of Machen's and Poe's influence on
   the myth-cycle, although Dunsany's influence is less well
   handled. The paper suffers most from brevity and a failure to
   see that the elements defined as belonging to the myth-cycle
   hold true for many of those tales which (according to Lynn) are
   not part of the cycle.

10. McInnis, John Lawson, III. "H. P. Lovecraft: The
    Maze and the Minotaur." Diss. Louisiana State,
    May 1975. xviii, 406 pp.

    Extensive philosophical and psychological study whose
    central tenet—Lovecraft's use of the symbol of the maze as
    exemplified in "In the Walls of Eryx"—is unfortunately vitiated
    due to Kenneth Sterling's admission that the idea for the maze
    in "In the Walls of Eryx" was his and not Lovecraft's.

11. Muller, George. "The Origins of H. P. Lovecraft's
    Fiction." Independent studies paper: [Brown], 27

May 1969. [iii], 38[+3] pp.

While containing some fantastic factual blunders, Muller makes good cases for the influence of Poe, Bierce, and others upon Lovecraft, although he is sometimes too brief and superficial.

12. Poses, Roy M. "The Physiology of Fear: Horror and Terror in the Works of H. P. Lovecraft." Independent studies paper: Brown, 1974. [ii], 65[+7] pp.

A purely literary study which, although with many good points, suffers in Poses' failure fully to understand Lovecraft's philosophical and literary thought. Poses defines the majority of Lovecraft's tales as "rationally inexplicable" (i.e., tales in which "the laws of being are altered, in which the processes of cause and effect that the reader is familiar with no longer apply"), and goes on to describe Lovecraft's use of atmosphere, characterization, narrative technique, etc.

13. St. Armand, Barton Levi. "H. P. Lovecraft: The Outsider in Legend and Myth." M.A. thesis: Brown, 1966. v, 272 pp.

Still valuable, although largely superseded by St. Armand's later work. Especially valuable are detailed psychological/ literary studies of "The Horror at Red Hook" and "Pickman's Model."

14. Swartz, John DeVennish. "The Genesis of Terror: A Study of H. P. Lovecraft and His Fiction." M.A. thesis: Brown, June 1972. iii, 130 pp.

15. Thomas, James Warren. "Howard Phillips Lovecraft: A Self-Portrait." M.A. thesis: Brown, 1950. iv, 181 pp.

While Thomas has done extensive research in Lovecraft's "New York Exile" (i.e., his marriage to Sonia Greene), quoting many letters, he has let his loathing of what he calls Lovecraft's "snobbishness and race hatred" color his views: Lovecraft was "narrow and prejudiced and strait-laced and lacking in ordinary human feeling . . . he was obviously incapable of feeling the emotion of love." The paper has no literary criticism. See also III-D-598.

16. Tranzocchi, Maria. "H. P. Lovecraft." Diss. Rome University, 196-.

Only a chapter has been seen.

ii. Unpublished Papers

1. Behnke, Rolf-Ingo. "Howard Phillips Lovecraft (1890-1937) und seine Stelling Innerhalb der Anglo-Amerikanischen Weird Fiction-Literatur." Unpublished paper: Hamburg, May 1971. [iii], 50[+16] pp.

2. Burleson, Donald, tr. "La Koloro el Exsterspaco," by H. P. Lovecraft. T.Ms., 46 pp.

A translation into Esperanto of "The Colour out of Space."

3. Everts, R. Alain. [List of Lovecraft's correspondents.] T.Ms. and A.Ms., 18 pp.

4. Faig, Kenneth W., Jr. *Lovecraftian Voyages.* T.Ms., [ii], 427 pp.

Still the most comprehensive collection of biographical data on Lovecraft yet compiled.

5. Faig, Kenneth W., Jr. "Photographs and Drawings of Lovecraft: A Provisional Listing." T.Ms., 9 pp.

A listing of drawings and photos of Lovecraft, published and unpublished.

6. Faig, Kenneth W., Jr. "Questions Regarding the Literary Estate of Howard P. Lovecraft." T.Ms., 15 pp.

7. Faig, Kenneth W., Jr. "R. H. Barlow." T.Ms., 83 pp.

8. Faig, Kenneth W., Jr. "Some Lovecraft Places in Providence." Unpublished paper, 31 August 1971. 25 pp.

   The paper can be found in the John Hay Library.

9. Faig, Kenneth W., Jr. "Some Thoughts on Lovecraft as a Revisionist." T.Ms., 48 pp.

10. Munroe, Harold B. [Memoir of Lovecraft.] A.Ms., 7 pp.

    In the form of a letter to R. Alain Everts.

11. Shea, J. Vernon. *"The Thing on the Doorstep*: A Screenplay." T.Ms., 38 pp.

12. Stenger, Karl-Ludwig. "Das Werk Howard Phillips Lovecrafts." Unpublished paper: Bonn, 1977. 125 pp.

F. Book Reviews

i. Books in English

At the Mountains of Madness (1964)

1. Boucher, Anthony. "Criminals at Large." *The New York Times Book Review*, 59, No. 36 (6 September 1964), 16.

2. [Unsigned.] *Library Journal*, 89, No. 19 (1 November 1964). 4390.

At the Mountains of Madness (1971)

3. Berglund, E. P. *Nyctalops*, 1, No. 4 (June 1971), 11-13.

4. Herrera, Philip. "The Dream Lurker." *Time*, 101, No. 24 (11 June 1973), 99-100. *Nueva Dimensión*, No. 55 (May 1974), pp. 141-44 (as "El que achecha in mis sueños"; tr. anon.).

Autobiography: Some Notes on a Nonentity (1963)

5. Bertin, Eddy C. *Shadow*, No. 7 (September 1969), p. 54. *Nyctalops*, 1, No. 2 (October 1970), 15.

Best Supernatural Stories of H. P. Lovecraft (1945)

6. Scott, W. T. "Lovecraft." *The Providence Sunday Journal*, 60, No. 42 (15 April 1945), Sec. VI, p. 6.

Beyond the Wall of Sleep (1943)

7. Cuppy, Will. "Mystery and Adventure." *New York Herald Tribune Weekly Book Review*, 20, No. 19 (2 January 1944), 10.

8. de Vries, Peter. "Macabre, Lyrical and Weird." *Chicago Sun Book Week*, 2, No. 9 (26 December 1943), 4.

9. L[aney], F[rancis] T. *The Acolyte*, 1, No. 4 (Summer 1943), 26.

> Actually a pre-publication review of only the novel, *The Dream-Quest of Unknown Kadath*, as appearing in *Beyond the Wall of Sleep*.

10. [Lowndes, Robert A. W.] "Notes on the Second Lovecraft Volume." *Agenbite of Inwit*, No. 4 (Spring 1944), pp. 1-3.

11. Poster, William. "Nightmare in Cthulu [sic]." *The New York Times Book Review*, 16 January 1944, p. 19.

12. Rice, Craig. "Lovecraft Collection Is One to Read in Glaring Daylight." *The Chicago Daily News*, 10 May 1944.

The Californian: 1934-1938 (1977)

13. Mosig, Dirk W. *The Fossil*, No. 220 (October 1977), pp. 7-10.

The Case of Charles Dexter Ward (1951)

14. Laws, Frederick. *News Chronicle*. 29 February 1952.

The Case of Charles Dexter Ward (1971)

15. Biggers, Cliff. "The HPL Revival." *Future Perspective*, No. 8 (September 1976), pp. 5-6.

16. Conan, Neal J. *The Science Fiction Review*, October 1976.

17. Egan, Thomas M. *Delap's Fantasy and Science Fiction Review*, 3, No. 5 (May 1977), 32-33. *Eldritch Tales*, 1, No. 3 (March 1978), 85-86.

18. Post, J. B. *Luna Monthly*, No. 20 (January 1971), 30.

19. Walker, Paul. "Orascular Mutterings." *Luna Monthly*, Nos. 24-25 (May-June 1971), 33-34.

The Cats of Ulthar (1935)

20. [Edkins, Ernest A.] *Causerie*, February 1936, p. 13.

Collected Poems (1963)

21. Boucher, Anthony. "Criminals at Large." *The New York Times Book Review*, 68, No. 22 (1 September 1963), 14.

22. Davidson, Avram. *The Magazine of Fantasy and Science Fiction*, 26, No. 5 (May 1964), 69.

The Colour out of Space (1964)

23. Post, J. B. *Luna Monthly*, No. 8 (January 1970), p. 30.

24. [Silverberg, Robert.] *Amazing*, 38, No. 11 (November 1964), 122-23.

25. [Unsigned.] *Library Journal*, 95, No. 6 (10 February 1969), 76.

The Curse of Yig (1953)

26. [Boucher, Anthony, and J. Francis McComas]. "Recommended Reading." *The Magazine of Fantasy and Science Fiction*, 6, No. 2 (February 1954), 93-96.

Dagon and Other Macabre Tales (1965-1967)

27. Grant, Mary Kent. *Library Journal*, 90, No. 18 (15 October 1965), 4362.

28. Harris, Leo. "Unlawful Assembly." *Punch*, 253, No. (12 July 1967), 73.

29. Leiber, Fritz. *The Magazine of Fantasy and Science Fiction*, 30, No. 5 (May 1966), 47.

30. Lowndes, Robert A. W. *Magazine of Horror*, 2, No. 6 (Winter 1965-66), 80-81.

31. MacNamara, Desmond. "Mystery Man." *New Statesman*, 73 (23 June 1967), 880.

The Dark Brotherhood and Other Pieces (1966)

32. Boucher, Anthony. "Criminals at Large." *The New York Times Book Review*, 71, No. 12 (20 March 1966), 41.

33. Cevasco, George A. *Library Journal*, 91, No. 9 (1 May 1966), 2340.

34. Harrington, Clyde. "An H. P. Lovecraft Miscellany." *The Providence Sunday Journal*, 81, No. 49 (5 June 1966), Sec. 1, p. 46.

35. L[owndes], R[obert] A. W. *Magazine of Horror*, 3, No. 1 (Summer 1966), 29, 55.

36. Rottensteiner, Franz. *Quarber Merkur*, 5, No. 1 (March 1967), 72.

37. [Willis, Paul J.] *Anubis*, 1, No. 1 (Autumn 1966), 47-49.

The Doom That Came to Sarnath (1971)

38. Biggers, Cliff. "The HPL Revival." *Future Perspective*, No. 8 (September 1976), pp. 5-6.

39. Winston, Alan. *Delap's Fantasy and Science Fiction Review*, 3, No. 5 (May 1977), 33-34.

The Dream Quest of Unknown Kadath (1955)

40. [Boucher, Anthony.] "Recommended Reading." *The Magazine of Fantasy and Science Fiction*, 11, No. 6 (December 1956), 108-09.

41. Carter, Lin. *Inside and Science Fiction Advertiser*, No. 14 (March 1956), pp. 23-24.

The Dream-Quest of Unknown Kadath (1970)

42. Leiber, Fritz. *Fantastic*, 20, No. 3 (February 1971), 109-11, 128.

43. Post, J. B. *Luna Monthly*, No. 19 (December 1970), p. 21.

44. Robillard, Doug. *Procrastination*, No. 7 (n.d.), p. 25.

45. Rottensteiner, Franz. *Quarber Merkur*, 9, No. 1 (January 1971), 79-80.

46. Thiel, John. *SF Booklog*, No. 10 (July-August 1976), p. 11.

47. Walker, Paul. *The Science Fiction Review*, No. 43 (March 1971), p. 39. *Luna Monthly*, Nos. 24/25 (May-June 1971), pp. 33-34.

48. Warren, Marjorie. *Evermist*, 2, No. 1 (Winter 1975), 32.

The Dunwich Horror and Others (1963) [I-A-34]

49. Boucher, Anthony. "Report on Criminals at Large." *The New York Times Book Review*, 68, No. 17 (28 July 1963), 23.

50. Leiber, Fritz. *The Magazine of Fantasy and Science Fiction*, 26, No. 1 (January 1964), 43-45.

51. Norton, Haywood P. *Fantasy-News*, No. 9 (4 August 1973), p. 2.

The Dunwich Horror and Others (1963) [I-A-37]

52. Post, J. B. *Luna Monthly*, No. 8 (January 1970), p. 30.

53. [Unsigned.] *Publishers' Weekly*, 195, No. 6 (10 February 1969), 76.

First Writings: Pawtuxet Valley Gleaner (1976)

54. Lupoff, Richard. *Algol*, 14, No. 2 (Spring 1977), 49-52.

The Haunter of the Dark (Panther) (1963)

55. Hopewell, Lee. *Comic Media*, No. 10 (September 1973).

The Horror in the Museum and Other Revisions (1970)

56. Morris, Harry O. *Nyctalops*, 1, No. 3 (February 1971), 17-19.

57. Sutton, David A. *Shadow*, No. 14 (September 1971), p. 30.

HPL (1937)

58. [Zorn, Ray H.] *Nix Nem Quarterly Review*, 7, No. 2 (September 1937), 9.

Lovecraft at Last (1975)

59. Adams, Phoebe. *The Atlantic*, 236, No. 1 (July 1975), 83.

60. Bacon, Martha. "Lovecraft's Letters to a Young Admirer." *The Providence Sunday Journal*, 91, No. 10 (7 September 1975), Sec. H, p. 32.

61. Bertin, Eddy C. *SF-Gids*, 4, No. 5 (September 1975), 14.

62. Bryant, Roger. "Rite of Passage." *Moebius Trip Library's SF Echo*, Nos. 23/24 (August-December 1975), pp. 71-75.

63. Collins, Tom. "Lovecraft: Man and Myth."
    Mythologies, No. 6 (July-August 1975), pp. 10-15.
    Moebius Trip Library's SF Echo, Nos. 23/24 (August-
    December 1975), pp. 62-70. *SF Booklog*, No. 7
    (January-February 1976), pp. 2-3 (without title).

64. de Camp, L. Sprague. *Amra*, 2, No. 64 (October
    1975), 19.

65. Delap, Richard. *Delap's Fantasy and Science Fiction Review*,
    2, No. 3 (March 1976), 17-19.

66. Geis, R. *The Science Fiction Review*, No. 14 (August
    1975), p. 29.

67. Hartman, Matthew. *Library Journal*, 100, No. 10 (15
    May 1975), 976.

68. Harvey, Jon. *The British Fantasy Society Bulletin*, 3, No. 3
    (September-October 1975), 5.

69. Leiber, Fritz. *Fantastic*, 24, No. 6 (October 1975), 115-
    18, 128.

70. Lupoff, Richard. *Algol*, 13, No. 1 (Winter 1976), 34-
    36, 38.

71. MacPherson, W. N. *The Science Fiction Review (Monthly)*,
    No. 5 (July 1975), pp. 14-15.

72. Medoff, Randy. *The Diversifier*, 2, No. 5 (May 1976),
    38-39.

73. Mosig, Dirk W. *Evermist*, 2, No. 1 (Winter 1975), 4,
    12. *Nyctalops*, 2, Nos. 4-5 (April 1976), 29.

74. Schiff, Stuart D. "Two on Lovecraft and Others."
    Whispers, 2, Nos. 2-3 (June 1975), 58-60.

75. Wilson, Gahan. *The Magazine of Fantasy and Science
    Fiction*, 50, No. 4 (April 1976), 62-66.

76. [Unsigned.] *Publishers' Weekly*, 207, No. 15 (14 April 1975), 50.

The Lurking Fear and Other Stories (1971)

77. Berglund, E. P. *Nyctalops*, 1, No. 4 (June 1971), 11-13.

78. Herrera, Philip. "The Dream Lurker." *Time*, 101, No. 24 (11 June 1973), 99-100. *Nueva Dimensión*, No. 55 (May 1974), pp. 141-44 (as "El que achecha en mis sueños"; tr. anon.).

79. J., K. *SF Booklog*, No. 10 (July-August 1976), p. 10.

Marginalia (1944)

80. Clough, Ben C. "H. P. Lovecraft's 'Marginalia': Third Posthumous Collection of Providence Writer's Work Gives 'Probably the Best Picture' of H. P. L." *The Providence Sunday Journal*, 60, No. 34 (18 February 1945), Sec. VI, p. 6.

81. Cuppy, Will. "Mystery and Adventure." *New York Herald Tribune Weekly Book Review*, 21, No. 25 (11 February 1945), 16.

82. Farber, Marjorie. "Poesque Doodles." *The New York Times Book Review*, 25 February 1945, p. 16.

83. Starrett, Vincent. *Chicago Sunday Tribune*, 104, No. 9 (4 March 1945), Sec. 6, p. 8. *The Vigilantes*, 3, No. 1 (July 1945), 31-32.

84. [Unsigned.] "The Criminal Record: The Saturday Review's Guide to Detective Fiction." *The Saturday Review of Literature*, 28, No. 6 (10 February 1945), 27.

Medusa: A Portrait (1975)

85. MacPherson, W. N. *The Science Fiction Review Monthly*, July-August 1976.

86. Mosig, Dirk W. *SF Booklog*, No. 7 (January-February 1976), p. 18.

Nine Stories from The Horror in the Museum (1971)

87. Biggers, Cliff. "The HPL Revival." *Future Perspective*, No. 8 (September 1976), pp. 5-6.

88. Chilson, Robert. *Delap's Fantasy and Science Fiction Review*, 3, No. 4 (April 1977), 36-37.

89. MacPherson, W. N. *The Science Fiction Review Monthly*, September 1976.

The Occult Lovecraft (1975)

90. Kellar, Michael. *Fantasy Crossroads*, 1, Nos. 4-5 (August 1975), 119.

91. McFerran, Dave. *The British Fantasy Society Bulletin*, 3, No. 6 (January-February 1976), 4.

92. Searles, Baird. *The Science Fiction Review Monthly*, No. 6 (August 1975), p. 13.

The Outsider and Others (1939)

93. Cuppy, Will. "Mystery and Adventure." *New York Herald Tribune Books*, 16, No. 16 (17 December 1939), 14.

94. Hart, B. K. "H. P. Lovecraft 'of Ours' Left a Heritage of Mystery: And a Friend Makes a Book More than Glamorous of His More than Ingenious Tales." *The Providence Sunday Journal*, 60, No. 28 (7 January 1940), Sec. VI, p. 6.

95. Heath, Eldon. *Thrilling Wonder Stories*, 16, No. 1 (April 1940), 126.

96. Mabbott, T. O. *American Literature*, 12, No. 1 (March 1940), 136.

97. Wollheim, D[onald] A. *Super Science Stories*, 1, No. 2 (May 1940), 4.

98. [Unsigned.] "Horror Story Author Published by Fellow Writers; Arkham House Presents *The Outsider and Others*, by H. P. Lovecraft." *Publishers' Weekly*, 137, No. 8 (24 February 1940), 890-91.

Selected Letters I-V (1965-76)

99. Lupoff, Richard. *Algol*, 14, No. 2 (Spring 1977), 49-52.

100. Post, J. B. *Luna Monthly*, No. 67 (Spring 1977), pp. 33-34.

Selected Letters I (1965)

101. de Camp, L. Sprague. *Amra*, 2, No. 54 (April 1971), 12-13.

102. Leiber, Fritz. *The Magazine of Fantasy and Science Fiction*, 30, No. 5 (May 1966), 46-47.

Selected Letters II (1968)

103. de Camp, L. Sprague. *Amra*, 2, No. 54 (April 1971), 12-13.

104. Lowndes, Robert A. W. *Magazine of Horror*, 4, No. 6 (November 1968), 112-14.

105. Wilson, Gahan. *The Magazine of Fantasy and Science Fiction*, 36, No. 2 (February 1969), 26-27.

Selected Letters III (1971)

106. Faig, Kenneth W. *Nyctalops*, 1, No. 6 (February 1972), 21-22.

107. Post, J. B. *Luna Monthly*, Nos. 41-42 (October-November 1972), p. 50.

108. Rottensteiner, Franz. *Quarber Merkur*, 10, No. 3 (July 1972), 75-76.

109. Wade, James, and Kenneth W. Faig. *Shadow*, No. 16 (May 1972), pp. 28-32.

110. [Unsigned.] *Amra*, 2, No. 56 (June 1972), 18.

Selected Letters IV (1976)

111. Leiber, Fritz. *Fantastic*, 26, No. 2 (June 1977), 116.

112. MacPherson, W. N. *The Science Fiction Review Monthly*, July-August 1976.

113. Schweitzer, Darrell. *Black Lite*, No. 2 (October 1976), 15-17.

Selected Letters V (1976)

114. Biggers, Cliff. *Future Perspective*, No. 8 (September 1976), p. 13.

115. Leiber, Fritz. *Fantastic*, 26, No. 2 (June 1977), 116-17.

116. MacPherson, W. N. *The Science Fiction Review Monthly*, October 1976.

117. Schweitzer, Darrell. *Black Lite*, No. 3 (March 1977), pp. 19-21.

The Shadow out of Time (1968)

118. Stout, Tim. "H. P. L., Shadows out of Time." *Supernatural*, No. 1 (1969), p. 23.

119. Young, B. A. "Space Time." *Punch*, 254 (12 June 1968), 865.

The Shadow over Innsmouth (1936)

120. [Brandt, C.] *Amazing*, 11, No. 4 (August 1937), 133.

121. [Zorn, Ray H.] *Nix Nem Quarterly Review*, 7, No. 3 (December 1937), 8-9.

Something about Cats and Other Pieces (1949)

122. Boucher, Anthony. " 'Space Opera' to Melodrama: Best New Books of Science Fiction." *Chicago Daily Sun Times*, 2, No. 262 (2 December 1949), 61.

123. DeAngelis, Michael. *Gargoyle*, 1, No. 1 (1950), 9-10.

124. Hillman, Arthur F. "The Sage of Providence." *Science-Fantasy Review*, 3, No. [6] (Spring 1950), 27-29.

125. Jackson, Joseph Henry. "Fragments from Lovecraft." *San Francisco Chronicle*, 6 January 1950, p. 14.

126. M[artindale], G[eorge] D. *Fantasy Advertiser*, 4, No. 1 (March 1950), 10.

127. Scott, W. T. "H. P. L." *The Providence Sunday Journal*, 65, No. 23 (4 December 1949), Sec. VI, p. 8.

128. [Unsigned.] *Talisman*, Summer 1950.

Supernatural Horror in Literature (1945, 1973)

129. Anton, Uwe. *Ganymed Horror*, Nos. 14/15 (1975), p. 67.

130. Breen, Jon L. "The World of Mysteries—Plus."
     Wilson Library Bulletin, 48, No. 4 (December 1973),
     304.

131. Delap, Richard. *Delap's Fantasy and Science Fiction
     Review*, 2, No. 3 (March 1976), 17-19.

132. L[erner], F. *SFRA Newsletter*, No. 27 (September
     1973), p. 4.

133. Pattee, Fred Lewis. *American Literature*, 18, No. 2
     (May 1946), 175-77.

134. Post, J. B. *Luna Monthly*, No. 52 (May 1974), p. 30.

135. [Unsigned.] *Publishers' Weekly*, 204, No. 1 (2 July
     1973), 81.

3 Tales of Horror (1967)

136. Wilson, Gahan. *The Magazine of Fantasy and Science
     Fiction*, 34, No. 4 (April 1968), 42-43.

To Quebec and the Stars (1976)

137. Franc, Jeff. *Delap's Fantasy and Science Fiction Review*, 4,
     No. 2 (March-April 1978), 26-27.

138. Lupoff, Richard. *Algol*, 14, No. 2 (Spring 1977),
     49-52.

The Tomb and Other Tales (1969)

139. Berglund, E. P. *Nyctalops*, 1, No. 4 (June 1971),
     11-13.

140. Herrera, Philip. "The Dream Lurker." *Time*, 101,
     No. 24 (11 June 1973), 99-100. *Nueva Dimensión*, No.
     55 (May 1974), pp. 141-44 (as "El que achecha en
     mis sueños"; tr. anon.).

141. Post, J. B. *Luna Monthly*, Nos. 38/39 (July-August 1972), 37.

142. R[ichey], C. W. *Kliatt Paperback Book Guide*, No. 5 (April 1971), p. 11.

143. Wilson, Gahan. *The Magazine of Fantasy and Science Fiction*, 41, No. 1 (July 1971), 75-76.

The Weird Shadow over Innsmouth (1944)

144. Scott, W. T. "Howard Lovecraft's Lengthening Shade." *The Providence Sunday Journal*, 109, No. 47 (21 May 1944), Sec. VI, p. 6.

A Winter Wish (1977)

145. Lupoff, Richard. *Algol*, 16, No. 1 (Winter 1978-79), 54.

146. Morris, Harry, Jr. *Nyctalops*, 2, No. 7 (March 1978), 35.

ii. Books in Languages Other than English

Berge des Wahnsinns (1970)

1. Bondy, Francois. "Der Lovecraft-Mythos." *Merkur*, 25, No. 3 (March 1971), 292-94.

2. Drews, Jörg. "Der Mensch begehre nummer zu schauen . . ." *Süddeutsche Zeitung*, No. 267 (7-8 November 1970).

3. Hans-Eberhard. "Mit dem Unabwendbaren leben." *Badische Neueste Nachrichten*, 3 February 1971.

4. Labisch, Wilhelm E. "Angst-schlicht und einfach

Angst." *Frankfurter Rundschau*, No. 123 (29-30 September 1971).

5. Rottensteiner, Franz. *Quarber Merkur*, 9, No. 1 (January 1971), 85-86.

6. Vollmann, Rolf. "Von dem Ding, des nicht sein darf." *Stuttgarter Zeitung*, No. 116 (22 May 1971).

7. W., R. "Schauer, Schock und Schrecken." *Saarbrücker Zeitung*, No. 267 (19 November 1971).

8. [Unsigned.] "Geflügelter Schrecken." *Der Speigel*, Nos. 1-2 (1971), pp. 84-85.

De bergen van de waanzin (1973)

9. Brendall, Edith. *SF-Gids*, 2, No. 2 (August 1973), 19-20.

Cthulhu: Geistergeschichten (1968)

10. Bondy, Francois. Hessischer Rundfunk, 29 August 1969, 5:30-6:00 p.m.

    Radio broadcast.

11. Buschmann, Christel. "Gallertartiger Idiotengott: Lovecrafts Horrorgeschichten." *Die Zeit*, No. 5 (31 January 1969), p. 15.

12. D., C. I. "Edgar Allan Poe hoch drei." *Darmstädter Echo*, 14 December 1968.

13. Drews, Jörg. "Monstren aus Vorzeit und Jenseits." *Süddeutsche Zeitung*, No. 28 (1-2 February 1969).

14. Golowin, Sergius. "Die Nachtseite der neuen Welt: Ein Pionier der Science-Fiction: Howard Philips [sic] Lovecraft." *National Zeitung*, No. 379 (20 August 1970).

15. Gropp, Fritz. "E—ya—yahaaah, Hilfe! Hilfe!" *Argus*, 3 December 1968.

16. H., C. "Das völlig neue Gruselgefühl." *Hannoversche Presse*, 20 December 1968.

17. Hellwig, Klaus. "Das unbeschreibliche Grauen: Die Erzählungen von H. P. Lovecraft." *Frankfurter Rundschau*, No. 9 (11 January 1969).

18. Hertl, Edwin. "Von Geistern und Entzauberern." *Salzburger Nachrichten*, 30 August 1968.

19. Hertl, Edwin. Studio Staiermark, Österreichischer Rundfunk, 24 October 1976, 2:45-3:00 p.m.
    Radio broadcast.

20. Jenny, Urs. "Erinnerungen an die Zukunft." *Die Weltwoche*, 2 January 1969, p. 22.

21. Sager, Peter. *Bücherei und Bildung*, No. 3 (1969), p. 187.

22. Schöler, Franz."Kosmisches grauen mit Cthulhu." *Die Welt der Literatur*, No. 4 (13 February 1969), p. 9.

23. Sihler, Horst Dieter. "Lovecraft—ein bestätigtes Gerücht." *Kärntner Tagezseitung*, No. 210 (13 September 1969).

24. [Unsigned.] *Neue Züricher Zeitung*, 11 February 1969.

Dagon et autres récits de terreur (1969)

25. Faschcreau, Serge. "Il n'était pas tout à fait Poe." *La Quinzaine Littéraire*, 16-24 February 1970.

26. Klein, Gérard. *Fiction*, No. 196 (April 1970), pp. 153-54.

Dans l'abime du temps (1954)

27. M[aslowski], I[gor] B. *Fiction*, No. 14 (January 1955), pp. 109-11.

Démons et merveilles (1955)

28. Bergier, Jacques. *Fiction*, No. 27 (February 1956), pp. 113-14.

Das Ding auf der Schwelle (1969)

29. Jenny, Urs. "Wie aber sieht ein Ungeheuer aus?" *Süddeutsche Zeitung*, No. 69 (21-22 March 1970).

30. Scheck, Frank Rainer. *Quarber Merkur*, 8, No. 1 (May 1970), 85-86.

31. Schneider, Johann. "Heimisch im Unheimlichen." *National Zeitung*, No. 26 (17 January 1970).

De droomwereld van Kadath (1972)

32. Van Halsen, Charles. *SF-Gids*, 2, No. 2 (August 1973), 19 (with note by Eddy C. Bertin).

Epouvante et surnaturel en littérature (1969)

33. Fauschcreau, Serge. "Il n'était pas tout à fait Poe." *La Quinzaine Littéraire*. 16-24 February 1970.

34. Walters, Bruno. *Fiction*, No. 191 (November 1969), pp. 145-46.

Der Fall Charles Dexter Ward (1971)

35. Drews, Jörg. "Die piscomorphen Monstren." *Süddeutsche Zeitung*, Nos. 86/87 (10-11 April 1971).

36. Haldimann, Eva. Österreichischer Rundfunk (Vienna), 14 August 1971, 4:15 p.m.
    Radio broadcast.

L'Horreur dans le musée, Tome I (1975)

37. O'Gallaghan, G. *Horizons du Fantastique*, No. 37 (1975).

Je suis d'ailleurs (1961)

38. Ioakimidis, Demètre. *Fiction*, No. 90 (May 1961), pp. 137-40.

Lettres d'Arkham (1975)

39. O'Gallaghan, G. *Horizons du Fantastique*, No. 37 (1975).

Nelle spire di Medusa (1976)

40. Arthos, Giorgio, and Lorenzo Tibaldi. "Verso una rivalutazione del 'profeta di Cthulhu': Lovercraft [sic] inedito." *G sera*, NS 1, No. 93 (13 October 1976), 2.

41. Cabona, Maurizio. *Diorama*, 2, No. 2 (February 1977), 12-13.

42. Lippi, Giuseppe. *Robot*, No. 5 (August 1976), pp. 122-23.

43. Servadio, Emilio. "Alla ricerca dell' 'abissale.' " *Il Tempo*, 34, No. 7 (8 June 1977), 18.

44. [Unsigned.] *Fantascienza*, 1, No. 2 (June 1976), 8.

45. [Unsigned.] "Inediti di un maestro dell'orrore." *La Bancarella* (insert to *Il Lavoro*), 2, No. 67 (4 June 1976), 8.

Par delà le mur du sommeil (1956)

46. Bergier, Jacques. *Fiction*, No. 38 (January 1957), pp. 119-21.

Sfida dall'infinito (1976)

47. Bibliotecario, Il. *Il Borghese*, 27, No. 43 (24 October 1976), 581-82.

48. Cabona, Maurizio. *Diorama*, 2, No. 2 (February 1977), 12-13.

49. Musa, Gilda. "Novità nel mondo della fantascienza." *Paese sera* (night edition), 27, No. 303 (5 November 1976), 12.

50. Servadio, Emilio. "Alla ricerca dall' 'abissale.' " *Il Tempo*, 34, No. 7 (8 June 1977), 18.

Stadt ohne Namen (1973)

51. Albers, Heinz. "Die aufgeschreckten Monstren wehren sich." *Westdeutsche Allgemeine*, 23 February 1974.

52. Anton, Uwe. *Ganymed Horror*, Nos. 7-8 (1974), pp. 59-60.

53. B., P. "Für das Ungeheuer in uns." *Spandauer Volksblatt*, 24 February 1974.

54. Hahnl, Hans Heinz. "Von Gespenstern und Dämonen." *Arbeiter Zeitung*, No. 289 (16 December 1973).

55. Rottensteiner, Franz. *Quarber Merkur*, 11, No. 4 (December 1973), 77-79.

Träume im Hexenhaus (1971)

56. Drews, Jörg. "Amerikanische Walpurgisnacht."
Süddeutsche Zeitung, Nos. 26-27 February 1972.

Viajes al otro mundo (1971)

57. Frabetti, C. *Terror Fantastic*, No. 22 (July 1973), pp.
57-58.

12 Grusel Stories (1965)

58. Kirde, Kalju. *Quarber Merkur*, 4, No. 1 (March 1966),
47-49.

Addendum:

59. Anton, Uwe. *Ganymed Horror*, Nos. 3-4 (1973), pp.
80-83.

Reviews of several German translations of Lovecraft.

G.   Special Periodicals and Unclassifiable Data

i. Periodicals Devoted Exclusively or Largely to Lovecraft

1. *The Acolyte*. Edited and published by Francis T. Laney and Samuel D. Russell. Contributing Editors: Duane W. Rimel, Franklin Lee Baldwin, Harold Wakefield. Art Director: R. A. Hoffman. 1, No. 1 (Fall 1942), 29 pp.; 1, No. 2 (Winter 1942), 28 pp.; 1, No. 3 (Spring 1943), 29 pp.; 1, No. 4 (Summer 1943), 31 pp.; 2, No. 1 (Fall 1943), 34 pp.; 2, No. 2 (Spring 1944), 30 pp.; 2, No. 3 (Summer 1944), 30 pp.; 2, No. 4 (Fall 1944), 30 pp.; 3, No. 1 (Winter 1945), 30 pp.; 3, No. 2 (Spring 1945), 34 pp.; 3, No. 2 [i.e., 3] (Summer 1945), 32 pp.; 3, No. 4 (Fall 1945), 32 pp.; 4, No. 1 (Winter 1946), 32 pp.; 4, No. 2 (Spring 1946), 33 pp.

    Vol. 2, No. 2 (Spring 1944) was reprinted in facsimile by R. Alain Everts (Madison, Wis.) and distributed through the Necronomicon and Esoteric Order of Dagon amateur press associations.

2. *The Dark Brotherhood Journal*. Edited by George S. Record. 1, No. 1 (June 1971), 14 pp.; [1, No. 2] (n.d.), 73 pp.; 2, No. 1 (July 1973), 27 pp.

3. *Journal of the H. P. Lovecraft Society*. Edited by Doug Palmer. No. 1 (1976), [27] pp.; No. 2 (1979), [34] pp.

4. *The Lovecraft Collector*. Edited by Ray H. Zorn. No. [1] (January 1949), 4 pp.; No. 2 (May 1949), 4 pp.; No. 3 (October 1949), 4 pp.

    Reprinted in facsimile in 1976 by R. Alain Everts and distributed through the Necronomicon and Esoteric Order of

Dagon amateur press associations. Another facsimile reprint in one volume was published by Necronomicon Press (West Warwick, R.I.) in 1977; 500 numbered copies were printed.

5. *The Lovecrafter*, 47, No. 1 (20 August 1936). Edited by Donald A. Wollheim and Wilson H. Shepherd. [1] p.

    Only issue published. A gift to Lovecraft on his forty-sixth birthday. See I-B-iii-71, for the only contents.

6. *The Lovecraftsman*. Edited by Redd Boggs. No. 1 (May 1963), [2] pp.; No. 2 (Winter 1963-64), [2] pp.; No. 3 (Spring 1964), [2] pp.; No. 4 (Autumn 1965), [2] pp.

7. *Nyctalops*. Edited and published by Harry O. Morris, Jr. Assistant Editor: Edward P. Berglund. 1, No. 1 (May 1970), 14 pp.; 1, No. 2 (October 1970), 28 pp.; 1, No. 3 (February 1971), 36 pp.; 1, No. 4 (June 1971), 48 pp.; 1, No. 5 (October 1971), 66 pp.; 1, No. 6 (February 1972), 52 pp.; 1, No. 7 (Clark Ashton Smith issue) (August 1972), 100 pp.; 2, No. 1 (April 1973), 50 pp.; 2, No. 2 (July 1974), 50 pp.; 2, No. 3 (January-February 1975), 54 pp.; 2, Nos. 4-5 (April 1976), 122 pp.; 2, No. 6 (May 1977), 50 pp.; 2, No. 7 (March 1978), 52 pp.

ii. Single Issues of Periodicals Devoted to Lovecraft

1. *The Arkham Collector*, No. 4 (Winter 1969), [26] pp. Edited by August Derleth.

2. *The Californian*, 5, No. 1 (Summer 1937), 75 pp. Edited by Hyman Bradofsky.

Review

a. K[leiner], R[heinhart]. "Reviews in Brief." *The National Amateur*, 40, No. 1 (September 1937), 10-11.

3. *Crypt Horror Tales*, No. 8 (April 1976), 61 pp. Edited by Toshio Akai.

4. *The Diversifier*, 2, No. 5 (May 1976), 50 pp. Edited by A. B. and C. C. Clingan.

5. *Evermist*, 2, No. 1 (Winter 1975), 32 pp. Edited by David R. Warren.

6. *The Fantasy Fan*, 2, No. 2 (October 1934), 16 pp. (pp. 17-34). Edited by Charles D. Hornig.

7. *Fresco* (the University of Detroit Quarterly), 8, No. 3 (Spring 1958), 68 pp. Edited by Steven Eisner.

Reviews

a. Boucher, Anthony. "Recommended Reading." *The Magazine of Fantasy and Science Fiction*, 15, No. 2 (August 1958), 104-08.

b. Troy, George. "Bookman's Gallery: A Symposium on Lovecraft and Other Campus Writings." *The Providence Sunday Journal*, 73, No. 44 (4 May 1958), Sec. 3, p. 20.

c. W[esson], S[heldon]. *The Fossil*, No. 158 (July 1958), p. 86.

8. *Genso to Kaiki*, No. 4 (November 1973). Edited by Junichiro Kida and Hiroshi Aramata.

9. *L'Herne*, No. 12 (1969), 379 pp. Edited by Francois Truchaud.

Review

a. Fauschcreau, Serge. "Il n'était pas tout à fait Poe." *La Quinzaine Litteraire*, 16-24 February 1970.

10. *Nueva Dimensión*. Special issue No. 6 (May 1975), 151

pp. Edited by [Sebastián Martinez, Domigo Santos, and Luis Vigil].

11. *The Olympian*, No. 35 (Autumn 1940), 38 pp. Edited by Edward H. Cole.

12. *La Opinión*, No. 681 (5 August 1973), Cultural Supplement, 12 pp. Edited by Jacobo Timerman.

13. *Il Re in Giallo*, 1, No. 2 [1976], 126 pp. Edited by Giuseppe Lippi, et al.

14. *Rigel*, No. 3 (November 1968), [32] pp. Edited by Guido Eekhaut.

15. *Shadow*, No. 7 (September 1969), 55 pp. Edited by David A. Sutton.

16. *Scienti-Snaps*, 3, No. 3 (Summer 1940), 27 pp. Edited by Walter E. Manconette. Assistant Editor: J. Chapman Miske.

17. *Tamlacht*, 2, No. 2 (n.d.), 32 pp. Edited by Victor Boruta and Alfred A. Attanasio.

18. *Urania*, No. 310 (16 June 1963), 153 pp. Edited by Carlo Fruttero.

19. *Xenophile*, 2, No. 6 (October 1975), 48 pp. Edited by Nils Hardin.

iii. Amateur Press Associations

The *Esoteric Order of Dagon* and *Necronomicon* are two amateur press associations in which each member produces a periodical containing material related to H. P. Lovecraft and cognate subjects. (The former organization permits fiction and poetry; the latter

does not.) Periodicals are then sent to the Official
Editor, who distributes a copy of each member's
contribution to all members at specified times.
Mailings for the former were on a bi-monthly
schedule through the first five mailings (June 1973
to February 1974), then reverted to a quarterly
basis. The latter has always been quarterly. Listed
below are selected critical articles of requisite
scholarly merit from the two organizations. Many
journals have included reprints of works by
Lovecraft and reviews of books by and about
Lovecraft; these have not been listed here for
reasons of space. The complete mailings for both
organizations can be found in the John Hay Library,
Brown University.

a. The Esoteric Order of Dagon

Founders: Joseph Pumilia and Roger Bryant. Official
Editors: Roger Bryant (mailings 1 to 13); Joe
Moudry (14 to date).

Mailings: I. ca. June 1973; II. August 1973; III. October 1973;
IV. December 1973; V. February 1974; VI. May 1974; VII.
August 1974; VIII. October 1974; IX. February 1975; X. May
1975; XI. August 1975; XII. November 1975; XIII. February
1976; XIV. May 1976; XV. August 1976; XVI. October 1976;
XVII. February 1977; XVIII. May 1977; XIX. August 1977; XX.
November 1977; XXI. March 1978; XXII. June 1978; XXIII.
September 1978; XXIV. December 1978.

1. Boerem, R. [Untitled.] *Litterae Dagonis*, No. 9 (October
   1975), pp. 29, 32.

   The need to unearth obscure Lovecraft works and to have
   accurate texts of them.

2. Bryant, Roger. "Source Notes toward an Annotated

Cthulhu Mythos." *Asrar Nama*, No. 1 [June 1973],
pp. 4-6; No. 2 [August 1973], pp. 5-6; No. 3
(October 1973), pp. 6-7.

3. Cannon, Peter. "Lovecraft's Old Men." *Selected
Scribblings*, No. 1 (30 April 1977), pp. 4-8.

> Studies of Lovecraft tales featuring old men—"The Terrible
> Old Man," "The Picture in the House," et al.

4. Cockcroft, T. G. L. "Notes from a Snug Room." *After
Midnight*, No. 7 (August 1976), pp. 2-4; No. 8
(November 1976), pp. 26-28; No. 9 (February 1977),
pp. 16-18; No. 12 (November 1977), pp. 3-4; No. 13
(August 1978), pp. 4-6.

> Title varies; discusses Farnsworth Wright, the de Camp biog-
> raphy (III-C-5), and other matters.

5. [Eber, Robert M.] "H. P. Lovecraft: In the Romantic
Tradition." *Letters from Leng*, No. 1 [May 1974], pp.
2-9.

> Strong essay, although with many debatable points, asserting
> that "Lovecraft offers to the reader the viewpoint of a world
> hopelessly mired in its own materialism, with the uncurious
> never to see beyond the world they live in, and those prone to
> curiosity about the universe to bring down upon their
> heads . . . destruction and death."

6. Faig, Kenneth W. [Untitled.] *The Moshassuck Review*, 19
May 1974, pp. 2-12.

> Detailed bibliographical survey of the history of Lovecraft's
> first "book," *The Shunned House* (I-A-5).

7. Faig, Kenneth W. [Untitled.] *The Moshassuck Review*, 15
September 1974, pp. 1-11.

> Deals with supposedly "lost" fictional works by Lovecraft,
> including the celebrated "Life and Death."

8. Faig, Kenneth W. [Untitled.] *The Moshassuck Review*, 5 January 1975, pp. [1-12].

    Comprehensive article on Lovecraft's appearance in Providence newspapers.

9. Faig, Kenneth W. [Untitled.] *The Moshassuck Review*, 6 September 1975, pp. 1-9; 6 December 1975, pp. 1-15.

    On fictional works destroyed by Lovecraft.

10. [Indick, Ben.] "H. P. Lovecraft and A. Merritt." *Ibid*, No. 16 [November 1976], pp. 6-8.

11. [Indick, Ben.] "HPL as Decadent: A Consideration of St. Armand's Essay." *Ibid*, No. 14 [May 1976], pp. [8-9].

    Reply to St. Armand's "H. P. Lovecraft: New England Decadent" (III-D-540), noting that the Decadent school was only one of the many influences upon Lovecraft's thought.

12. Joshi, S. T., and Michaud, Marc A. "The Recognition of H. P. Lovecraft." *Lovecraftian Ramblings*, No. 8 (5 February 1978), pp. 2-7.

    Records the growth of critical acceptance of Lovecraft's work and thought.

13. Lord, Glenn. [Untitled.] *Zarfhaana*, No. 1 (May 1974), pp. 1-6.

    On the Lovecraft-Robert E. Howard correspondence.

14. [Moudry, Joe.] "H. P. Lovecraft and Regional Colour." *The Arkham Anchorite*, No. 10 [August 1976], pp. 2-5.

15. Schultz, David E. [Untitled.] *Cthulsz*, 2, No. 2 [February 1977], 1-4.

    On "Polaris."

16. Schultz, David E. [Untitled.] *Cthulsz*, 2, No. 2
    [February 1977], 4-6.

    On "Beyond the Wall of Sleep."

17. [Shea, J. Vernon.] "Did HPL Suffer from Chorea?"
    Outré, 2, No. 1 (May 1977), 30-31.

    Makes a strong case that Lovecraft may have had chorea
    minor, which "manifests itself in uncontrollable facial tics and
    grimaces," into adult life, and that this may have affected his
    self-image.

18. Shea, J. Vernon. "The Professional Writer *vs.* the
    Gifted Amateur." *The Miskatonic*, No. 11 [August
    1975], pp. [3-4].

    Criticism of de Camp's attacks (see III-C-5) on Lovecraft's
    amateur lifestyle.

19. Wade, James. "Lovecraft and Farnese in Harmony
    and Discord." *The Miskatonic*, 5, No. 2 (1 May 1977),
    [2-4].

    Wade, a professional composer, discusses Harold S. Farnese's
    plans for setting Lovecraft's works to music; and concludes
    that, judging from what musical samples survive, Farnese's was
    "inept, unimaginative music, stale and sub-professional." His
    judgment may be unduly harsh.

20. Wetzel, George. "An Aborted Bibliography."
    Continuity, 1, No. 3 (May 1976), 15-24.

    Gives a history of his bibliographic researches, his and
    August Derleth's publishing of them, and his complaints of
    plagiarism.

21. Wetzel, George T., and Everts, R. Alain. *Winifred
    Virginia Jackson—Lovecraft's Lost Romance.* [August
    1976.] [13] pp.

    Account of the romance between the two during the late
    1910s.

b. *The Necronomicon*

Founder and Official Editor: R. Alain Everts.

Mailings: I. March 1976; II. June 1976; III. September 1976; IV. December 1976; V. March 1977; VI. June 1977; VII. January 1978.

1. [Boerem, R.] "Lovecraft's Library: A Brief Survey." *Lovecraftmanship*, No. 2 (September 1976), pp. 5-6.

   Lovecraft's tastes as determined by the books in his library.

2. [Burnham, Crispin.] "The Yog-Sothoth Cycle of Myth Tales of Howard Phillips Lovecraft." *Pnakotic Manuscript*, No. 3 [June 1977], pp. 1-8; No. 4 [January 1978], pp. 1-6.

3. [Connors, Scott.] "Lovecraft's Other Magazine." *Kappa Alpha Tau*, 2, No. 2 (15 June 1977), pp. 2-4.

   On the lost journal *Hesperia*.

4. [Eber, Robert M.] "A Literary Analysis of *The Statement of Randolph Carter*." *Hippos from Hell*, No. 1 (June 1977), pp. [1-5].

5. Eber, Robert M. "The Quest of Iranon." *Hippos from Hell*, No. 2 [January 1978], pp. [2-5].

6. [Faig, Kenneth W.] [Untitled.] *De Tenebris*, No. 3 (11 March 1977), pp. 15-24.

   On Lovecraft's imaginary town of Dunwich and its ties with New England and on Lovecraft's genealogy.

7. [Moudry, Joe.] "Dagon, Colonial America and H. P. Lovecraft." *The Mount Erebus Quarterly*, [March 1976], pp. 2-6.

8. [Moudry, Joe.] "Francis Stevens, H. P. Lovecraft, and the Munsey Influence." *The Mount Erebus Quarterly*, 1, No. 4 [December 1976], 1-4.

9. [Schultz, David E.] "Dagon." *Yaanek*, 2, No. 2 [June 1977], [3-5].

10. [Schultz, David E.] "Lovecraft's *Fungi from Yuggoth*." *Yaanek*, 1, No. 2 [June 1976], 1-13.

11. Schultz, David E. "The White Ship." *Yaanek*, 2, No. 3 [January 1978], 1-5.

12. Schultz, David E. [Untitled.] *Yaanek*, 1, No. 1 [March 1976], [1-8].

    On the proper chronology of Lovecraft's fiction.

13. [Schultz, David E.] [Untitled.] *Yaanek*, 2, No. 1 [March 1977], [1-7].

    On "The Tomb."

14. Shea, J. Vernon. "H. P. Lovecraft and Robert Aickman: Contrast and Comparison." *JVS*, [September 1976], pp. 1-12.

    Aickman is a "master of ambiguity" while Lovecraft is somewhat too explicit; Shea also points out both authors' attention to atmosphere and the dissimilarity of their lifestyles.

iv. Unclassifiable Data

1. Artmann, H. C. "how lovecraft saved the world." In Klaus Reichert, ed. *The Best of H. C. Artmann*. Frankfurt am Main: Suhrkamp, 1975, pp. 166-68.

    A play in German whose characters are "h. p. lovecraft, esq." (franchot tone), "pickman, ein kunstmaler" (bela lugosi), and "kutlyoos schatten" (charles laughton, esq.).

2. Borges, Jorge Luis. "There Are More Things." *The Atlantic*, 236, No. 1 (July 1975), 27-29. In *El Libro de Arena*. Buenos Aires: Emecé Editores, 1975, pp. 65-77. Madrid: Alianza Editorial, 1977. New York: E. P.

Dutton, 1977 (as *The Book of Sand*; tr. Norman Thomas di Giovanni), pp. 51-59.

The story is dedicated "to the memory of H. P. Lovecraft."

3. *A Catalogue of Lovecraftiana: The Grill/Binkin Collection.* Catalogued and annotated by Mark Owings and Irving Binkin. Baltimore: The Mirage Press, 1975. x, 71 pp.

4. Chappell, Fred. *Dagon.* New York: Harcourt, Brace & World, 1968. 177 pp.

A novel loosely based on ideas in Lovecraft's fiction. It does not use the framework of Lovecraft's myth-cycle.

5. Person, Carl. *Howard Phillips Lovecraft (1890-1937): A Catalogue of 187 Items.* Tacoma, Wash.: Carl Person, Spring 1970. 20 pp.

Purchased by Queen's University Library, Kingston, Ontario.

6. Schevill, James. *Lovecraft's Follies: A Play.* Chicago: The Swallow Press, 1971. 90 pp.

A surrealist play centering around Lovecraft. It was performed in Providence by the Trinity Square Repertory Co. (director: Adrian Hall) in March-April 1971.

7. Squires, Roy A. *A Bibliographic Catalog of the Largest Collection Ever Offered for Sale of the Works of Clark Ashton Smith and H. P. Lovecraft.* Glendale, Ca.: Roy A. Squires, June 1968. [12] pp. Supplement: January 1969. [12] pp.

8. Squires, Roy A. *Clark Ashton Smith/H. P. Lovecraft/R. H. Barlow: Catalog II.* Glendale, Ca.: Roy A. Squires, [1970]. [20] pp.

9. Squires, Roy A. *H. P. Lovecraft: A Basic Collection of 100 Items: Ten Notable Items Offered Separately: A Noble Group of 155 Letters . . . and a Smaller Group.* Glendale, Ca.: Roy A. Squires, [1971]. [16] pp.

10. Squires, Roy A. *H. P. Lovecraft and the Lovecraft Circle: Books & Autographs: Catalog 8*. Glendale, Ca.: Roy A. Squires, [n.d.]. 20 pp.

11. Wilstach, John. "The Ten-Cent Ivory Tower." *Esquire*, 25, No. 1 (January 1946), 83, 160, 162.

    A fictional reminiscence. See Bloch's "Out of the Ivory Tower" (III-D-409).

Supplement

I. Works by Lovecraft in English

A. Books by Lovecraft

The Cats of Ulthar (1979)
> the [in green] / Howard / cats [in green] / Phillips /
> of [in green] / Lovecraft / ulthar [in green]
> [colophon:] April & May 1979

> [1]¹⁰ [1-20]
> [1-2]: blank; [3]: title; [4-6]: blank; [7-14]: text; [15-17]: blank;
> [18]: colophon; [19-20]: blank.
> Pamphlet; 26.2 × 17.8 cm.
> *Notes.* Published by Roy A. Squires, Glendale, Ca., although
> his name appears nowhere in the pamphlet. All type (including
> title page) in American Uncial. Off-white paper covers bear
> only title (in green) on front; 200 numbered copies each
> enclosed in white envelope with title (in green) on front.

Science versus Charlatanry (1979)
> SCIENCE VERSUS CHARLATANRY / Essays on
> Astrology / by / H. P. LOVECRAFT / and / J. F.
> HARTMANN / Edited, with / an Introduction / and
> Notes, by / S. T. JOSHI and SCOTT CONNORS /
> [publisher's device] *The Strange Company* [copyright
> page:] 1979

> [Perfect-bound]: [i-iv] [a-b] v [vi] vii [viii-x] xi-xvii [xviii] 1-53
> [54-56]
> [i]: title; [ii]: copyright page; [iii]: dedication; [iv-b]: blank; v:
> contents list; [vi]: blank; vii: "Preface"; [viii]: blank; [ix]:
> photograph of Lovecraft; [x]: blank; xi-xvii: "Introduction" by
> Connors and Joshi; [xviii]: blank; 1-6: "Astrology and the
> European War" by Hartmann; 7-9: "Science versus
> Charlatanry" by Lovecraft; 10-14: [Letter to the Editor] by
> Hartmann; 15-18: "The Falsity of Astrology" by Lovecraft; 19-

22: "Astrology and the Future" by "Isaac Bickerstaffe, Jr." [i.e., Lovecraft]; 23-28: "The Science of Astrology" by Hartmann; 29-31: "Delavan's Comet and Astrology" by "Isaac Bickerstaffe, Jr." [i.e., Lovecraft]; 32-39: "A Defense of Astrology" by Hartmann; 40-43: "The Fall of Astrology" by Lovecraft; 44-46: "[Isaac Bickerstaffe's Reply]" by "Isaac Bickerstaffe, Jr." [i.e., Lovecraft]; 47-52: "Notes" [by Joshi]; 53: "Bibliography"; [54]: blank; [55]: colophon; [56]: blank.

Bound in paper; 21.2 × 13.6 cm.

Notes. Reprint of the debate between Lovecraft and Hartmann in *The* [Providence] *Evening News,* September-December 1914. Place of publication: Madison, Wis.; 200 numbered copies.

Uncollected Prose and Poetry II (1980)

H. P. Lovecraft / [rule] / Uncollected / Prose and Poetry II / [rule] / Edited by S. T. Joshi and Marc A. Michaud / [rule] / [publisher's device] / Necronomicon Press [copyright page:] W. Warwick, R.I. . . . July 1980

[1]^{32} [i-iv] v-ix [x] [1] 2-24 [25] 26-33 [34-35] 36-51 [52-54]

[i-ii]: blank; [iii]: title; [iv]: copyright page, dedication, contents list; [v]-ix: "Introduction" by Joshi; [x]: "Acknowledgements"; [1]-5: "Ibid"; 5-23: "The Trap" (with Henry S. Whitehead); 23-24: "Collapsing Cosmoses" (with R. H. Barlow); [25]-26: "Ad Criticos: Liber Secundus"; 26-27: "Brotherhood"; 27-29: "Medusa: A Portrait"; 29-32: "The Feast"; 32-33: "Ave atque Vale"; [34]: blank; [35]-36: "Poesy"; 36-37: "Life for Humanity's Sake"; 38-41: "Vermont—A First Impression"; 41-42: "Preface to *Old World Footprints*"; 42-47: "The Old Brick Row" (i.e., letter to *The Providence Journal,* 20 March 1929); 47-49: "In Memoriam: Henry St. Clair Whitehead"; 49-50: "Robert Ervin Howard: 1906-1936"; 51: "Bibliography"; [52-54]: blank.

Bound in paper; 21.2 × 17.6 cm.; cover art by Jason Eckhardt.

B.   Contributions to Periodicals

ii. Nonfiction

"Introduction" to *The Poetical Works of Jonathan E. Hoag.*
    Lovecraft Studies, 1, No. 2 (Spring 1980), 16-20.

"Preface" to *White Fire* by John Ravenor Bullen. *Lovecraft Studies*, 1, No. 1 (Fall 1979), 20-26.

v. Letters

a. Multiple Publications

[Letters to Duane W. Rimel.] *Necronomicon Notes*, 1, No. 1 [March 1980], 3-4.

> Contains letters to Duane W. Rimel: 10 March 1935, p. 3; 16 April 1935, p. 3; 12 November 1935, p. 4.
>
> From I-B-v-a-2.

C.   Material Included in Books by Others

Gunn, James, ed. *The Road to Science Fiction #2: From Wells to Heinlein*. New York: New American Library, 1979. 535 pp.

> Contains: "Dagon," pp. 137-42.

Josi, S. T., and Marc A. Michaud, eds. *H. P. Lovecraft in "The Eyrie."* West Warwick, R.I.: Necronomicon Press, July 1979. 83 pp.

> Contains: ten letters by Lovecraft to *Weird Tales*, pp. 13-23.

[Kent, Edna M., ed.] *Gloucester: The Way Up Country: A History, Guide and Directory*. Gloucester, R.I.: Heritage Division, Gloucester Bicentennial Commission, 1976. 192 pp.

> Contains: "Lovecraft on Gloucester" [i.e., untitled poem included in letter to Frank Belknap Long, 8 November 1923; with unsigned introductory note], p. 6.

Long, Frank Belknap. *Night Fear*. Edited by Roy Torgeson. New York: Zebra Books, June 1979. 318 pp.

Contains: "The Very Old Folk" (in *The Horror from the Hills*; without title), pp. 286-94.

Rabkin, Eric S., ed. *Fantastic Worlds: Myths, Tales, and Stories.* New York and Oxford: Oxford Univ. Press, 1979. xvii, 478 pp.

Contains: "The Picture in the House," pp. 257-65.

Wolf, Leonard, ed. *Wolf's Complete Book of Terror.* New York: Clarkson N. Potter, 1979. xvi, 473 pp.

Contains: "The Picture in the House," pp. 171-77.

[Anonymous, ed.] *Announcing the Publication of* Notes High and Low *by Carrie Adams Berry.* Medford, Mass.: C. A. A. Parker, 1934. [12] pp.

Contains: Letter to [Carrie Adams Berry], [1934?], p. [9]. Letter in praise of Berry's poetry; the brochure (published by an amateur journalism acquaintance of Lovecraft's) also contains a note on Berry's verse by Virginia Woolf.

II. Works by Lovecraft in Translation

B. Contributions to Periodicals

i. Fiction

"Cool Air." *Robot*, No. 39 (June 1979), pp. 153-61 (as "Aria fredda"; tr. Stefano Negrini).

"The Quest of Iranon." *Blagdaross*, No. 1 (March 1979), pp. 14-15, 17-20 (as "La busqueda de Iranon"; tr. Alberto Santos).

ii. Nonfiction

"Notes on Writing Weird Fiction." *Blagdaross*, No. 1

(March 1979), pp. 34-36 (as "Notas sobre los escritos de literatura fantastica"; tr. Alberto Santos).

iii. Poetry

"The City." *Il Re in Giallo*, No. 5 [1979], pp. 46-49 (both in English and in an Italian tr. by Mauro Marchesani). *Novae Terrae*, No. 1 (March 1979), pp. [19-20] (as "La città"; tr. Roldano Romanelli).

Fungi from Yuggoth. "VI. The Lamp." *Novae Terrae*, No. 1 (March 1979), p. [21] (as "La Lucerna"; tr. Roldano Romanelli).

C. Material Included in Books by Others

Howard, Robert E. *Skull Face*. Milan: Editrice Nord, June 1978. xix, 338 pp.

> Contains: "In Memoria di Robert Ervin Howard" ("In Memoriam: Robert Ervin Howard"), pp. v-viii (tr. Roberta Rambelli). Translation of *Skull-Face and Others* (I-C-106).

Kirde, Kalju, ed. *Das unsichbare Auge: Eine Sammlung von Phantomen und anderen unheimlichen Erscheinungen*. Berlin: Suhrkamp, 1979. 259 pp.

> Contains: "Die Aussage des Randolph Carter" ("The Statement of Randolph Carter"), pp. 159-65 (tr. Michael Walter).

Otaki, Keisuke, ed. *Akuma no yume: Tenshi no tameiki*. Osaka: Seishinsha, 1980.

> Contains: "Sarnath omimatta saiyaku" ("The Doom That Came to Sarnath"); tr. Keisuke Otaki.

Parry, Michel, ed. *Frankeinsteins Rivalen: Gruselstories aus unserer Monster-Galerie*. Rastatt/Baden: Erich Pabel Verlag, October 1978. 161 pp.

Contains: "Die Experimente des Herbert West" ("Herbert West—Reanimator"), pp. 109-43 (tr. Rudolf Mühlstrasser). Translation of *The Rivals of Frankenstein* (I-C-150).

[Anonymous; ed.] *Monster*. Falun, Sweden: B. Wahlstroms, 1974. 155 pp.

Contains: "Monstret utrifrån" ("The Outsider"), pp. 105-14 (tr. Alf Agdler).

III.   Works about Lovecraft

A.   News Items and Encyclopedias

"Books of 1954: A Symposium." *The Observer* (London), No. 8,534 (26 December 1954), p. 7.

Includes a section by Jean Cocteau speaking in praise of a French translation of Lovecraft.

B.   Bibliographies and Glossaries

Currey, L. W., and David G. Hartwell. *Science Fiction and Fantasy Authors: A Bibliography of First Printings of Their Fiction and Selected Nonfiction*. Boston: G. K. Hall & Co., 1979, pp. 320-35.

C.   Books and Pamphlets about Lovecraft

Beckwith, Henry L. P., Jr. *Lovecraft's Providence and Adjacent Parts*. West Kingston, R.I.: Donald M. Grant, 1979. 89 pp.

Interesting description of sites mentioned in Lovecraft's fiction and visited by him.

Reviews

Burleson, Donald R. *Lovecraft Studies*, 2, No. 2 (Spring 1980), 34-36.

Coale, Sam. "Tours through Lovecraft's Haunted City and State." *The Providence Sunday Journal*, 25 November 1979, Sec. H, p. 12.

de Turris, Gianfranco, and Sebastiano Fusco. *Howard Phillips Lovecraft*. Florence: La Nuova Italia, December 1979. 145 pp.

Sound general study by Italy's leading Lovecraft scholars.

Faig, Kenneth W., Jr. *H. P. Lovecraft: His Life, His Work*. West Warwick, R.I.: Necronomicon Press, July 1979. 36 pp.

Detailed chronology of Lovecraft's life with introductory essay. Includes S. T. Joshi's "A Chronology of Selected Works by H. P. Lovecraft."

Review

Shea, J. Vernon. *Lovecraft Studies*, 1, No. 1 (Fall 1979), 30-33.

Joshi, S. T. *An Index to the Selected Letters of H. P. Lovecraft*. West Warwick, R.I.: Necronomicon Press, March 1980. 78 pp.

Joshi, S. T., and Marc A. Michaud, eds. *H. P. Lovecraft in "The Eyrie."* West Warwick, R.I.: Necronomicon Press, July 1979. 83 pp.

Collection of letters by and about Lovecraft from the letter column of *Weird Tales* magazine.

Review

Fulwiler, William. *Lovecraft Studies*, 1, No. 1 (Fall 1979), 33-37.

Joshi, S. T., and Marc A. Michaud. *Lovecraft's Library: A Catalogue*. West Warwick, R.I.: Necronomicon Press, March 1980. 91 pp.

> List of nearly 1,000 books in Lovecraft's personal library.

Review

> Boerem, R. *Lovecraft Studies*. 1, No. 2 (Spring 1980), 36-39.

St. Armand, Barton Levi. *H. P. Lovecraft: New England Decadent*. Albuquerque, N.M.: Silver Scarab Press, 1979. 56 pp.

> Slightly revised version of III-D-540.

D.   Criticism in Books or Periodicals

Burleson, Donald R. "H. P. Lovecraft and Mystery Hill." *NEARA* [New England Antiquities Research Association] *Journal*, 14, No. 4 (Spring 1980), 84-86.

Burleson, Donald R. "Humour beneath Horror: Some Sources for 'The Dunwich Horror' and 'The Whisperer in Darkness.' " *Lovecraft Studies*, 1, No. 2 (Spring 1980), 5-15.

> Brilliant study of the New England topographical and historical sources behind the two tales discussed.

Calabrese, Fabio. "Lovecraft e la scienza." *Il Re in Giallo*, No. 5 [1979], pp. 9-16.

Cannon, Peter. "Parallel Passages in 'The Adventure of the Copper Beeches' and 'The Picture in the House.' " *Lovecraft Studies*, 1, No. 1 (Fall 1979), 3-6.

Catalano, Walter. "Lovecraft e la fantascienza." *Il Re in Giallo*, No. 5 [1979], pp. 17-23.

Cook, W. Paul. "Howard P. Lovecraft's Fiction." *The Vagrant*, No. 11 (November 1919), pp. 38-39.
> Quoted in his book (III-C-4).

Faig, Kenneth W., Jr. "R. H. Barlow." *Journal of the H. P. Lovecraft Society*, No. 2 (1979), pp. [7-34].
> Has much information on Barlow's relations with Lovecraft.

Fulwiler, William. "Reflections on 'The Outsider.' " *Lovecraft Studies*, 1, No. 2 (Spring 1980), 3-4.

Giorgi, Giorgio. "Lovecraft e la poesia." *Il Re in Giallo*, No. 5 [1979], 24-32.

Joshi, S. T. "Autobiography in Lovecraft." *Lovecraft Studies*, 1, No. 1 (Fall 1979), 7-19.
> Study of autobiographical details in Lovecraft's fiction and their significance.

Joshi, S. T. "In Defense of Lovecraft." *Science-Fiction Studies*, 7, No. 1 (March 1980), 111-12.
> Rebuttal to III-C-19b.

Joshi, S. T. "Sources for the Chronology of Lovecraft's Fiction." *Lovecraft Studies*, 1, No. 2 (Spring 1980), 21-29.

Joshi, S. T. "A Style Sheet for Lovecraftian Studies." *Lovecraft Studies*, 1, No. 1 (Fall 1979), 27-29.
> Methods of citation of works by Lovecraft.

Joshi, S. T., and Marc A. Michaud. "The Prose and Poetry of Clark Ashton Smith." *Books at Brown*, 27 (1979), 81-87.
> Touches upon Lovecraft's relations with Smith.

Legrand, Gérard, and Robert Benayoun. "Lovecraft and
the Black Moon." *Cultural Correspondence*, Nos. 10-11
(Fall 1979), 16.

> Reprint of two articles from *Medium/Communication Surréaliste*,
> No. 1 (November 1953).

Leveghi, Riccardo. "Il pornografo Miller, il fantastico
Lovecraft." *Il Re in Giallo*, No. 5 [1979], pp. 5-7.

Magill, Frank N., ed. *Survey of Science Fiction Literature*.
Englewood Cliffs, N.J.: Salem Press, 1979. 5 vols.

> Includes: Dirk W. Mosig and Donald R. Burleson, "At the
> Mountains of Madness," pp. 97-101 (Vol. 1); Donald R.
> Burleson, "The Lovecraft Mythos," pp. 1284-88 (Vol. 3);
> Donald R. Burleson, "The Short Fiction of H. P. Lovecraft," pp.
> 1973-77 (Vol. 4).

> General but penetrating studies of Lovecraft's work,
> discussing his aesthetic theory, sources for his tales, literary
> influences, etc.

Menegaldo, Gilles. "La ville dans l'oeuvre de H. P.
Lovecraft." *Caliban*, No. 16 (1979), pp. 99-110.

R[osemont], F[ranklin]. "Lovecraft, Surrealism &
Revolution." *Cultural Correspondence*, Nos. 10-11 (Fall
1979), p. 17.

Selley, April. "Terror and Horror in *The Case of Charles
Dexter Ward*." *Nyctalops*, 3, No. 1 (January 1980), 8,
10-14.

[Anonymous, ed.] *Ciencia-ficción, la otra respuesta al
destino del hombre*. Buenos Aires: Timerman
Editores, 1976.

> Contains: August Derleth, "Vida de alucinado," pp. 127-35;
> August Derleth, "Genesis de una mistificación" ("The
> Making of a Hoax"), pp. 136-42; Jacques Van Herp, "Cómo
> nacieron sus monstruos," pp. 143-58; tr. anon.

E. Academic Theses and Unpublished Papers

Bender, Barry L. "Howard Phillips Lovecraft (1890-1937): Xenophobia in His Life and Work." Honors thesis: University of Manchester, 1980. [ii], 72 pp.

Hazu, Hiroaki. "The Cosmic Horror of H. P. Lovecraft." Thesis: Faculty of the Department of Liberal Arts, College of General Education, University of Tokyo, 1977. 47 pp.

F. Book Reviews

Selected Letters V (1976)

Buhle, Paul. *Lovecraft Studies*, 1, No. 2 (Spring 1980), 30-34.

Uncollected Prose and Poetry (1978).

Burleson, Donald R. *Lovecraft Studies*, 1, No. 1 (Fall 1979), 40-46.

G. Special Periodicals and Unclassifiable Data

i. Periodicals Devoted Exclusively or Largely to Lovecraft

Lovecraft Studies. Edited by S. T. Joshi. 1, No. 1 (Fall 1979), 46 pp.; 1, No. 2 (Spring 1980), 40 pp.

ii. Single Issues of Periodicals Devoted to Lovecraft

Il Re in Giallo, No. 5 [1979], 75 pp. Edited by Fabio
    Calabrese, Giuseppe Lippi, et al.

IV. Indexes

A. Works by Lovecraft

Note: An asterisk preceding an entry indicates a spurious title.

Index

419

"Astrology and the Future": I-B-ii-8; see also Supplement

Astronomy articles: I-A-67, 72; B-ii-9-98, 182-200

"Astrophobos": I-A-12, 17, 35, 71; B-iii-9

At the Mountains of Madness: I-A-15, 39, 47, 53, 84; B-i-2; C-46; II-A-2, 5, 9, 11, 17, 23, 33, 35, 60; III-B-13; D-93, 633; See also Supplement

At the Mountains of Madness and Other Novels: I-A-39

At the Mountains of Madness and Other Tales of Terror: I-A-47

At the Mountains of Madness and Other Tales of Terror: I-A-53, 84

"At the Root": I-A-71; B-ii-99

"August": I-A-25, 35, 75, 77; B-iii-10

"Autobiography: Some Notes on a Nonentity": I-A-17, 36; C-11; II-C-68; III-C-3; F-i-5

"Autobiography of Howard Phillips Lovecraft": I-A-80; B-ii-100

"Autumn": I-A-28; B-iii-11

"Ave atque Vale": I-A-28; B-iii-227; see also Supplement

"Azathoth" (fragment): I-A-19, 42, 49; B-i-3; II-A-22, 45; B-i-1; C-13

"Azathoth" (*Fungi from Yuggoth* 22): I-B-iii-63

"Background" (*Fungi from Yuggoth* 30): I-B-iii-71

"Ballade of Patrick von Flynn, Ye": I-A-28; B-iii-12

"Battle That Ended the Century, The": I-A-7, 25; B-iv-a-1; C-123; II-B-iv-1

"Bay-Stater's Policy, The": I-A-82; B-iii-13

"Beast in the Cave, The": I-A-19, 42, 49; B-i-4; II-A-22, 45; B-i-2

"Beauties of Peace, The": I-B-iii-14

"Bells": I-A-28, 43, 77; B-iii-15

"Bells, The" (*Fungi from Yuggoth* 19): I-B-iii-60

Berge des Wahnsinns: II-A-23; III-F-ii-1-8

Bergen van de Waanzin, De: II-A-33; III-F-ii-9

Best Supernatural Stories: I-A-22; III-F-i-6

"Beyond the Wall of Sleep": I-A-17, 42, 48, 54-55; B-i-5; C-38-40, 81, 88, 90-91, 184; II-A-4, 35, 55; B-i-3; C-66; III-G-iii-a-16

Beyond the Wall of Sleep: I-A-17; III-F-i-7-12

"Biographical Notice": I-A-83; C-144

"Birthday Lines to Margfred Galbraham": I-A-82

"Bolshevism": I-B-ii-101

"Book, The" (fragment): I-A-19, 42, 49; B-i-6; II-A-22, 45; B-i-4; C-13

"Book, The" (*Fungi from Yuggoth* 1): I-B-iii-42

"Bookstall, The": I-A-28; B-iii-16

"Bothon": I-B-iv-a-34; C-177

"Brick Row": see "East India Brick Row, The"

"Bride of the Sea, The": see "Unda, or, The Bride of the Sea"

"Brief Autobiograhy of an Incon-

B. Works by Others

C. Names

Note: An index to Lovecraft's pseudonyms can be found at the end of this section.

Index   445

Brown, David J.: III-D-75
Brown, Gary: III-C-12
Brown, M. E.: III-D-76
Brownlow, J. H.: I-B-iii-66
Bruna, Dick: II-A-18-19
Brunner, John: III-D-77, 479
Bryant, Roger: III-C-2c, 12; D-78-79; F-i-62; G-iii-a-2
Budrys, Algis: III-C-5h
Buhle, Paul: III-C-16; D-80; see also Supplement
Bullen, John Ravenor: I-C-6; D-i-1, ii-2
Burgin, Richard: III-D-81
Burke, W. J.: III-A-3
Burleson, Donald R.: III-E-ii-2; see also Supplement
Burnham, Crispin: III-G-iii-b-2
Buschmann, Christel: III-F-ii-11
Bush, David Van: I-B-ii-126
Butman, Robert: III-D-82

Cabona, Maurizio: III-F-ii-41, 48
Cabos, Lew: III-D-83
Cabrera, Roberto: II-A-45
Caen, Michael: III-D-84
Calabrese, Fabio: III-D-84; see also Supplement
Campbell, J. Ramsey: I-A-67; III-C-2d; D-85-87, 399
Campbell, Paul J.: I-B-ii-251
Campbell, Peter W.: III-B-21
Camporeale, Sergio: II-A-32, 41
Cannon, Peter: III-C-16; D-88; E-i-1-2; G-iii-a-3; see also Supplement
Cantoni, Sarah: II-A-10, 35; B-i-7, 46; C-22
Capanna, Pablo: III-D-89
Carneiro, André: III-D-90
Carrer, Alda: II-A-35

Carson, Robert: III-D-66
Carter, Lin: I-A-32, 51, 55; B-iii-130; C-7-11, 59; II-C-4; III-B-28; C-2, 26; D-91-99, 396, 409; F-i-41
Carter, Paul: III-D-100
Cartocci, Glauco: II-A-51-52
Casey, Calvert: II-A-17
Castillo, P.: II-C-28, 91
Catalano, Walter: see Supplement
Cerqueira, Silas: II-A-6
Cevasco, George A.: III-F-i-33
Chalker, Jack L.: I-A-43; C-11; III-B-3, 9, 27-28, 30; C-3; D-101, 396
Chancellor, John: I-A-62
Chapelot, Pierre: II-C-77
Chappell, Fred: III-D-204; G-iv-4
Chiesa, Adalberto: II-B-i-31
Chilson, Robert: III-F-i-88
Chwast, Seymore: I-C-156
Circolo H. P. Lovecraft di Torino: III-D-102
Cirlot, Juan-Eduardo: III-D-103
Claridge, John: I-A-47, 53
Clark, Mrs. F. C.: I-B-v-a-4
Clements, Jack: III-D-104
Clingan, A. B.: III-G-ii-4
Clingan, C. C.: III-G-ii-4
Clough, Ben C.: III-F-i-80
Clyne, Ronald: I-A-25
Coale, Sam: III-C-19a; see also Supplement
Coates, Walter J.: I-A-4; B-v-b-34, 40; C-12; D-ii-4; III-A-4
Coblentz, Stanton A.: I-B-iv-a-18; C-13
Cochran, Donald E.: III-B-10-13
Cockcroft, T. G. L.: I-A-32; III-B-14; D-105-07, 409; G-iii-a-4

446 Index

Index

De Nardi, Claudio: III-D-156
Dench, Ernest A.: I-B-ii-251
Derleth, August: I-A-15, 17, 19-
22, 25-26, 29, 32-37, 39, 41-43,
45-49, 52, 59, 64-65, 68-69; B-i-
27, ii-204, 209, iv-a-1; C-31-54;
E-i-1, 7-22, ii-2; II-A-8, 10, 21,
35, 45, 47, 56, 59; B-i-28; C-8-
16, 18; III-C-3, 6-7, 15; D-150-
93, 206, 370, 394, 396, 398, 402,
405-06, 409-10, 467; G-ii-1
de Ryee, William: I-D-ii-2
de Torres, Esther Zemborain:
III-D-61
Dettro, Chris: III-C-51
de Turris, Gianfranco: II-A-51-52;
III-A-5-7; D-156, 194-202, 406,
408; see also Supplement
Deutsch, Michel: III-D-203
de Vries, Peter: III-F-i-8
de Vust, Roeland: II-B-iii-5, iv-2;
III-C-5m
Díaz, Melitón Bustamante: II-A-
42-43
Dickie, James: I-C-55; II-C-17
Dickinson, Susan: I-C-56-57
Diefenbach, Volker: II-B-i-9
Diehl, Digby: III-D-343
Dietz, Laurence S.: III-D-343
Di Giovanni, Norman Thomas:
III-G-iv-2
Dillard, R. H. W.: III-D-204
Dobner, Tullio: II-C-29
Doi, Ryusuke: II-C-2, 18; III-D-
205-06
Domínguez, J. M.: II-A-45
Dore, John: I-A-47, 53
Dorfles, Gillo: III-D-207
Douglas, Drake: III-D-208
Dowdell, William J.: I-B-ii-252

Dowe, Jenne E. T.: I-B-ii-253
Drake, G. E.: I-C-58
Drews, Jörg: III-F-ii-2, 13, 35, 86
Druillet, Philippe: II-A-3, 22, 35,
51
Dumont, S.: II-A-2
Dunn, John T.: I-B-ii-252; III-D-
149
Dunsany, Lord: I-C-59-60; III-D-
236
Duperray, Max: III-D-209
Dwyer, Bernard Austin: I-B-i-19;
E-iv-a-12; II-C-9

Earle, Betty: I-D-ii-2
Eber, Robert M.: III-D-210; G-iii-
a-5; b-4-5
Eckert, Winfred: III-D-468
Eckhardt, Jason: I-A-3, 13, 83; see
also Supplement
Eddy, C. M., Jr.: I-A-43; B-iv-a-14-
17; C-36, 43, 61, 128, 130; III-D-
211-12, 396, 504
Eddy, Muriel E.: III-C-8-11, 14;
D-213-17
Eddy, Ruth: III-D-218
Edelmann, Heinz: II-A-16
Edkins, E. A.: I-B-ii-118; III-C-26-
27; D-219-20; F-i-20
Edogawa, Ranpo: II-C-19; III-D-
221
Edwards, Jay: III-D-222
Eekhaut, Guido: III-D-223; G-ii-14
Egan, Thomas M.: III-C-2e; F-i-17
Eisner, Steven: III-B-16; D-224;
G-ii-7
Eitel, Elaine Gillum: III-E-i-3
Eizykman, Boris: III-D-225
Elflandsson, Galad: III-D-226
Eliot, T. S.: I-B-iii-211

Lovecraft's Pseudonyms:

D. Periodicals

Note: Names of editors of important early periodicals (e.g., amateur journals) are given in parentheses following the entry. An asterisk prececing the entry indicates an amateur journal.

E. Foreign Languages

DATE DUE
